CONTEMPORARY'S

TEST 5: MATHEMATICS

CONTEMPORARY'S

GED

TEST 5: MATHEMATICS

PREPARATION FOR THE HIGH SCHOOL EQUIVALENCY EXAMINATION

Reviewers
Rosalie Kavadlo, Instructional Facilitator
Adult and Continuing Education
Brooklyn, New York

Debbie Thompson, Adult Education Instructor
Shoals Area Tri County Adult Education Program
Muscle Shoals, Alabama

CONTEMPORARY
BOOKS

CHICAGO

Library of Congress Cataloging-in-Publication Data

GED test 5: mathematics / Jerry Howett.
      p.   cm.
  Includes index.
  ISBN 0-8092-3778-4
    1. Mathematics—Problems, exercises, etc.   2. General educational
development tests.   I. Title.
QA43.H725   1994
513'.14'076—dc20   93-33098
                                        CIP

Photo credits: p. 10 © UPI/Bettmann; p. 20 © Jeffrey M. Spielman/
The Image Bank; p. 52 © UPI/Bettmann; p. 78 © Tim Bieber/The
Image Bank; p. 116 Courtesy of Margie Korshak Associates, Inc.;
p. 130 © Frank Whitney/The Image Bank; p. 164 © Hans Neleman/
The Image Bank; p. 176 © Tony Stone Images; p. 194 © Gary S.
Chapman/The Image Bank; p. 222 Courtesy of Tennessee Tourist
Development; p. 278 *The Daily Journal*, International Falls, Minnesota

Published by Contemporary Books, Inc.
Two Prudential Plaza, Chicago, Illinois 60601-6790
Manufactured in the United States of America
International Standard Book Number: 0-8092-3778-4
10   9   8   7   6

Published simultaneously in Canada by
Fitzhenry & Whiteside
195 Allstate Parkway
Markham, Ontario L3R 4T8
Canada

Editorial Director
Mark Boone

Editorial
Katherine Willhoite
Christine Benton
Eunice Hoshizaki
Robin O'Connor
Lisa Black
Loretta Faber

Editorial Assistant
Maggie McCann

Editorial Production Manager
Norma Underwood

Production Editor
Jean Farley Brown

Interior Design
Lucy Lesiak

Cover Design
Georgene Sainati

Typography
The Wheetley Company
Wilmette, Illinois

Cover Illustration
Mark Jasin

 Printed on recycled paper including minimum of 10% post-consumer waste.

Contents

To the Student

If you're studying to pass the GED Tests, you're in good company. In 1992, the most recent year for which figures are available, over 790,000 people took the tests. Of this number, nearly 480,000 actually received their certificates. Why do so many people choose to take the GED Tests? Some do so to get a job or to get a better one than they already have. Others take the tests so that they can go on to college or vocational schools. Still others pursue their GED diplomas to feel better about themselves and to set good examples for their children.

Americans and Canadians alike, from all walks of life, have successfully completed their GED tests and obtained diplomas. Some well-known graduates are country music singers Waylon Jennings and John Michael Montgomery, comedian Bill Cosby, Olympic gold medalist Mary Lou Retton, New Jersey Governor James J. Florio, Wendy's Old-Fashioned Hamburgers founder Dave Thomas, Delaware State Senator Ruth Ann Minner, U.S. Senator Ben Nighthorse Campbell of Colorado; motion picture actor Kelly McGillis, Famous Amos chocolate chip cookies creator Wally Amos, *Parade* magazine editor Walter Anderson, NBA referee Tommy Nuñez, and Triple Crown winner jockey Ron Turcotte.

This book has been designed to help you, too, succeed, on the test. It will provide you with instruction in the skills you need to pass, background information on key social studies concepts, and plenty of practice with the kinds of test items you will find on the real test.

WHAT DOES *GED* STAND FOR?

GED stands for the Tests of General Educational Development. The GED Test is a national examination developed by the GED Testing Service of the American Council on Education. The credential received for passing the test is widely recognized by colleges, training schools, and employers as equivalent to a high school diploma.

While the GED Test measures skills and knowledge normally acquired in four years of high school, much that you have learned informally or through other types of training can help you pass the test.

The GED Test is available in English, French, and Spanish and on audiocassette, in Braille, and in large print.

WHAT SHOULD I KNOW TO PASS THE TEST?

The test consists of five examinations in the areas of writing skills, social studies, science, literature and the arts, and mathematics. The chart below outlines the main content areas, the breakdown of questions, and the time allowed per test.

THE GED TESTS			
Test	**Minutes**	**Questions**	**Percentage**
1: Writing Skills			
Part 1: Conventions of English	75	55	Sentence Structure 35%
			Usage 35%
			Mechanics 30%
Part 2: The Essay	45	1 topic	
2: Social Studies	85	64	History 25%
			Economics 20%
			Political Science 20%
			Geography 15%*
			Behavioral Sciences 20%*
3: Science	95	66	Life Sciences 50%
			Physical Sciences 50%
4: Literature and the Arts	65	45	Popular Literature 50%
			Classical Literature 25%
			Commentary 25%
5: Mathematics	90	56	Arithmetic 50%
			Algebra 30%
			Geometry 20%

*In Canada, 20% of the test is based on Geography and 15% on Behavioral Sciences.

On all five tests, you are expected to demonstrate the ability to think about many issues. You are also tested on knowledge and skills you have acquired from life experiences, television, radio, books and newspapers, consumer products, and advertising. In addition to the above information, keep these facts in mind:

1. Three of the five tests—Literature and the Arts, Science, and Social Studies—require that you answer questions based on the reading passages or interpreting cartoons, diagrams, maps, charts, and graphs in these content areas. Developing strong reading and thinking skills is the key to succeeding on these tests.

2. The Writing Skills Test requires you to be able to detect and correct errors in sentence structure, grammar, punctuation, and spelling. You also will have to write a composition of approximately 200 words on a topic familiar to most adults.

3. The Mathematics Test consists mainly of word problems to be solved. Therefore, you must be able to combine your ability to perform computations with problem-solving skills.

WHO MAY TAKE THE TESTS?

In the United States, Canada, and many territories, people who have not graduated from high school and who meet specific eligibility requirements (age, residency, etc.) may take the tests. Since eligibility requirements vary, it would be useful to contact your local GED testing center or the director of adult education in your state, province, or territory for specific information.

WHAT IS A PASSING SCORE ON THE GED?

Again, this varies from area to area. To find out what you need to pass the test, contact your local GED testing center. However, you must keep two scores in mind. One score represents the minimum score you must get on each test. For example, if your state requires minimum scores of 40, you must get at least 40 points on every test. Additionally, you must meet the requirements of a minimum average score on all five tests. For example, if your state requires a minimum average score of 45, you must get a total of 225 points to pass. The two scores together, the minimum score and the minimum average score, determine whether you pass or fail the GED.

To understand this better, look at the scores of three people who took the test in a state that requires a minimum score of 40 and a minimum average score of 45 (225 total). Ann and Willie did not pass, but Ramon did. See if you can tell why.

	Ann	Willie	Ramon
Test 1	44	42	43
Test 2	43	43	48
Test 3	38	42	47
Test 4	50	40	52
Test 5	50	40	49
	225	207	239

Ann made the total of 225 points but fell below the minimum score on Test 3. Willie passed each test but failed to get the 225 points needed; just passing the individual tests was not enough. Ramon passed all the tests and exceeded the minimum score. Generally, to receive a GED credential, you must correctly answer half or a little more than half of the questions on each test.

MAY I RETAKE THE TEST?

You are allowed to retake some or all of the tests. Again, the regulations governing the number of times that you may retake the tests and the time you must wait before retaking them are set by your state, province, or territory. Some states require you to take a review class or to study on your own for a certain amount of time before taking the test again.

HOW CAN I BEST PREPARE FOR THE TEST?

Many libraries, community colleges, adult education centers, churches, and other institutions offer GED preparation classes. Some television stations broadcast classes to prepare people for the test. If you cannot find a GED preparation class locally, contact the director of adult education in your state, province, or territory, or call the GED Hotline (800-62-MY-GED). This hotline will give you telephone numbers and addresses of adult education and testing centers in your area. The hotline is staffed 24 hours a day seven days a week.

WHAT'S ON THE MATHEMATICS TEST?

The GED Mathematics Test consists of 56 multiple-choice questions. It measures your ability to apply math concepts, not your ability to perform complicated calculations. About one-third of the questions will be based on diagrams, charts, or graphs. About one-fourth of the questions test your ability to identify the correct way to set up a problem rather than to solve it. For some problems, you will have to decide what information is necessary to solve them. For others, the answer choice *not enough information is given* will appear as one of the five possible choices, and it may be the correct answer.

Almost all of the questions will be word problems—short stories or situations that ask a question. Most are based largely on realistic situations. Each question is followed by five possible answer choices, only one of which is correct.

The math items will test not only your ability to perform arithmetic and algebraic operations but also your ability to use problem-solving skills. Some problem-solving skills that you will need to exercise are:

- selecting necessary information in a problem

- knowing when you have not been given enough information to solve a problem

- estimating an approximate answer

This book will give you lots of practice in these and other problem-solving areas.

The GED Mathematics Test is broken down into the following content areas:

Arithmetic	50%
Algebra	30%
Geometry	20%

The 11 chapters of this book will provide you with explanations, examples, and exercises in all three of these content areas.

TEST-TAKING TIPS FOR SUCCESS

1. **Prepare physically.** Get plenty of rest and eat a well-balanced meal before the test so that you will have energy and will be able to think clearly. Last-minute cramming will probably not help as much as a relaxed and rested mind.

2. **Arrive early.** Be at the testing center at least 15 to 20 minutes before the starting time. Make sure you have time to find the room and to get situated. Keep in mind that many testing centers refuse to admit latecomers.

3. **Think positively.** Tell yourself you will do well. If you have studied and prepared for the test, you should succeed.

4. **Relax during the test.** Take half a minute several times during the test to stretch and breathe deeply, especially if you are feeling anxious or confused.

5. **Read the test directions carefully.** Be sure you understand how to answer the questions. If you have any questions about the test or about filling in the answer form, ask before the test begins.

6. **Know the time limit for each test.** The Mathematics Test has a time limit of 90 minutes.

   Some testing centers allow extra time, while others do not. You may be able to find out the policy of your testing center before you take the test, but always work according to the official time limit. If you have extra time, go back and check your answers.

   For this 56-question test, you should allow a maximum of $1\frac{1}{2}$ minutes per question. However, this is not a hard and fast rule. Use it only as a guide to keep yourself within the time limit.

7. **Have a strategy for answering questions.** Read each question carefully; reread it if you are having trouble understanding what is being asked of you. You will probably want to use the five-step approach to solving word problems discussed on pages 21–39 of this book.

8. **Don't spend a lot of time on difficult questions.** If you're not sure of an answer, go on to the next question. Answer easier questions first and then go back to the harder questions. However, when you skip a question, be sure that you have skipped the same number on your answer sheet. Although skipping difficult questions is a good strategy for making the most of your time, it is very easy to get confused and throw off your whole answer key.

   Lightly mark the margin of your answer sheet next to the numbers of the questions you did not answer so that you know what to go back to. To prevent confusion when your test is graded, be sure to erase these marks completely after you answer the questions.

9. **Answer every question on the test.** If you're not sure of an answer, take an educated guess. When you leave a question unanswered, you will always lose points, but you can possibly gain points if you make a correct guess.

   If you must guess, try to eliminate one or more answers that you are sure are not correct. Then choose from the remaining answers. Remember, you greatly increase your chances if you can eliminate one or two answers before guessing. Of course, guessing should be used only when all else has failed.

10. **Clearly fill in the circle for each answer choice.** If you erase something, erase it completely. Be sure that you give only one answer per question; otherwise, no answer will count.

11. **Practice test taking.** Use the exercises, reviews, and especially the Post-Test and Practice Test in this book to better understand your test-taking habits and weaknesses. Use them to practice different strategies such as skimming questions first or skipping hard questions until the end. Knowing your own personal test-taking style is important to your success on the GED Test.

HOW TO USE THIS BOOK

If you are a student about to prepare for the GED Tests, you are to be admired. You have decided to resume an education that had been cut short. It is never easy to get back on track after you have been derailed, but, while it may not be easy, it will not be impossible. It will require determination and a lot of hard work. Contemporary's GED Mathematics book has been designed to give you the necessary skills to succeed on the test.

Before beginning this book, you should take the Pre-Tests. These tests will give you a preview of what skills will be necessary for success on the GED Mathematics Test, but, more important, they will help you identify which areas you need to concentrate on most. Use the chart at the end of the Pre-Test to pinpoint the types of questions you answered incorrectly and to determine what skills you need special work in. You may decide to concentrate on specific areas or to work through the entire book. We strongly suggest that you *do* work through the whole book to best prepare yourself for the actual test.

This book has a number of features designed to help make the task of test preparation easier and more effective. These features include:

- a Problem Solving for the GED feature. This feature focuses on problem-solving skills that are important for success on the GED Mathematics Test. It is a good idea to carefully work through the example and explanation in these sections, even if you find that the computation issues covered in the chapter are easy for you. The problem-solving strategies described can be helpful in many different situations.

- math tips throughout the book that offer some useful hints in areas that can sometimes be troublesome

- a formulas page that contains the formulas you will need for the algebra and geometry sections of the GED Mathematics Test

- answers and their solutions provided in the answer key that will help you figure out where you went wrong. If you make a mistake, you can learn from it by studying the solution provided and then reviewing the problem to analyze your error.

After you have worked through the 11 chapters of this book, you should take the Post-Test. The Post-Test is a simulated GED Test that presents questions in the format, at the level of difficulty, and in the percentages found on the actual test. The Post-Test will help you determine whether you are ready to take the GED Mathematics Test and, if not, what areas you need to review. The Post-Test evaluation chart at the end will be especially helpful for making this decision.

We realize that practice makes perfect. Therefore, as a final indicator of your readiness for the real GED Test, we've added a Practice Test. This test is just like the Post-Test in terms of its format, level of difficulty, and percentages found on the real test. After you have completed the Practice Test, you will be able to finally determine whether you are ready to take the GED Test and, if not, what areas you need to review. As with the Post-Test, an evaluation chart is included to help you judge your performance.

Contemporary Books publishes a wide range of materials to help you prepare for the tests. These books are designed for home study or classroom use. Our GED preparation books are available through schools and bookstores and directly from the publisher. Our toll-free number is (800) 621-1918. For the visually impaired, a large-print version is available. For further information, call Library Reproduction Service (LRS) at 800-255-5002.

Finally, we'd like to hear from you. If our materials have helped you to pass the test or if you feel that we can do a better job preparing you, write to us at the address on the back of the book to let us know. We hope you enjoy studying for the GED Test with our materials and wish you the greatest success.

The Editors

Mathematics Pre-Test

The three tests that follow will help you evaluate your strengths and weaknesses in mathematics. You can take all three tests at once, or you can come back to these tests before you start each major section of the book.

Read each problem carefully. If you find some problems too difficult, don't give up on the whole test. There may be problems toward the end of each section that you don't know how to do. Skip those that are too hard and come back to them if you have time later.

When you finish, check the answers and solutions that follow the tests. Then look at the charts at the end of the tests. Use these charts as a guide to tell you the areas where you need the most work.

Even if you do very well on these pre-tests, work through the entire book. Every section includes problems and hints that will help you on the GED Test.

PRE-TEST FORMULAS

Following is a list of formulas that you may need on the pre-tests. You can refer back to this list as you work through the tests.

Area of a square	$A = s^2$; where A = area, s = side.
Area of a rectangle	$A = lw$; where A = area, l = length, w = width.
Circumference of a circle	$C = \pi d$; where C = circumference, π = 3.14, d = diameter.
Volume of a rectangular solid	$V = lwh$; where V = volume, l = length, w = width, h = height.
Pythagorean theorem	$c^2 = a^2 + b^2$; where c = hypotenuse, a and b are the legs of a right triangle.
Slope of a line	$m = \frac{y_2 - y_1}{x_2 - x_1}$; where (x_1, y_1) and (x_2, y_2) represent two points in the plane.
Simple interest	$i = prt$; where i = interest, p = principal, r = rate, t = time.
Distance as function of rate and time	$d = rt$; where d = distance, r = rate, t = time.
Total cost	$c = nr$; where c = total cost, n = number of units, r = rate (cost per unit).

PRE-TEST 1: ARITHMETIC

Directions: Solve each problem. Write your answers on another sheet of paper.

1. Find the difference between 7,986 and 20,500.

2. What is the product of 709 and 68?

3. Find the sum of 16, 385, 4012, and 856.

4. What is the quotient of 27,438 divided by 34?

5. A plane flew for six hours. For two hours the average speed was 265 mph. For four hours the average speed was 490 mph. How far did the plane travel in six hours?

6. Abe worked three hours of overtime on Thursday and four hours of overtime on Friday. He makes $12.50 an hour for overtime work. Which of the following expresses the amount Abe made for overtime work on those two days?

    (1) $(12.50) \times 3 + 4$
    (2) $12.50(3 + 4)$
    (3) $3(12.50 + 4)$
    (4) $4 \times 3 \times 12.50$
    (5) $12.50(3 \times 4)$

7. Subtract 7.42 from 300.

8. Find the sum of 2.91, 46, and 1.085.

9. Simplify $\frac{35.36}{17}$.

10. Find the product of 1.84 and 2.5.

11. Divide 156 by 6.5.

12. Round off 214.0863 to the nearest hundredth.

13. Sam drove for 262 miles on 18 gallons of gasoline. To the nearest tenth, find the average number of miles he drove on one gallon of gasoline.

14. In 1970 the population of Central County was 1.75 million; in 1980 it was 2.3 million; and in 1990 it was 2.6 million. By how much did the population increase from 1970 to 1990?

15. Find the sum of $9\frac{1}{2}$, $3\frac{2}{3}$, and $6\frac{5}{6}$.

16. How much greater is $7\frac{1}{3}$ than $5\frac{7}{8}$?

17. Find the quotient of 8 divided by $2\frac{2}{3}$.

18. What is the product of $2\frac{4}{5}$ and $3\frac{3}{4}$?

19. Find the quotient of $3\frac{1}{2}$ divided by $\frac{3}{8}$.

20. Arrange the following in order from smallest to largest: $\frac{3}{4}, \frac{2}{3}, \frac{5}{9}$, and $\frac{5}{6}$.

21. From a pipe 4 meters long Nick cut a piece that was $1\frac{3}{4}$ meters long. Assuming no waste, which of the following expresses the length of the remaining piece?

    (1) $4 - 1.75$
    (2) $4 - \frac{3}{4}$
    (3) $4 - 1.25$
    (4) $\frac{3}{4} - 4$
    (5) $4 - 1.34$

22. The Chungs spend $\frac{1}{4}$ of their income on rent and $\frac{1}{3}$ on food. They take home $1200 a month. How much do the Chungs have left each month after paying for rent and food?

23. Simplify the ratio 36:48.

24. Solve for x in the proportion: $9:x = 12:20$.

25. In a GED class of 18 students, there are 10 women. What is the ratio of the number of men to the number of women?

26. Sam Stroud bought a raffle ticket at the Uptown Community Center. His wife bought three tickets, and his son bought two. Altogether there were 300 tickets. What is the probability that someone in the Stroud family will win?

Directions: Use the table below to answer problems 27 and 28.

Starting Yearly Salaries		
	Midvale	*Central County*
Police	$18,500	$22,200
Fire fighters	16,800	18,400
Teachers	11,100	13,500

27. What is the ratio of the starting salary of a fire fighter in Midvale to the starting salary of a fire fighter in Central County?

28. What is the ratio of the starting salary of a teacher in Midvale to the starting salary of a police officer in Central County?

---

29. Change $83\frac{1}{3}\%$ to a fraction.

30. Find 6.5% of 200.

31. 24 is what percent of 40?

32. 35% of what number is 91?

33. Find the interest on $1000 at 18% annual interest for 1 year and 4 months.

Directions: Use the passage below to answer problems 34–36.

Carla started a new job with a gross salary of $1650 a month. Her employer will deduct 20% of her salary for taxes and social security. After a year Carla will be eligible for a raise of 8% of her gross salary.

34. Which of the following tells the amount Carla's employer withholds each month for social security?

(1) $330
(2) $290
(3) $240
(4) $ 40
(5) Not enough information is given.

35. What will be Carla's net pay for her first year of employment?

(1) $19,800
(2) $16,500
(3) $15,840
(4) $13,200
(5) Not enough information is given.

36. What will Carla's monthly gross salary be during her second year of employment?

(1) $1815
(2) $1782
(3) $1730
(4) $1650
(5) Not enough information is given.

ANSWERS ARE ON PAGES 6–7.

PRE-TEST

PRE-TEST 2: GEOMETRY

Directions: Solve each problem. Write your answers on another sheet of paper.

1. Find the circumference of the circle shown below.

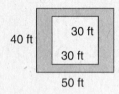

$d = 6.5$ m

2. What is the volume of a rectangular container with a length of 10 feet, a height of $3\frac{1}{2}$ feet, and a width of 4 feet?

3. Find the area of the rectangle pictured below.

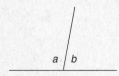

2.2 cm

6.5 cm

4. The shaded part of the diagram below shows the walkway around a swimming pool. Find the number of square feet of space on the walkway.

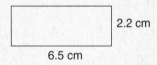

40 ft

30 ft

30 ft

50 ft

5. What is the value of 80^2?

6. Simplify $16^2 + 5^3 - 8^1$.

7. Find the value of $\sqrt{8464}$.

8. In the diagram below, $\angle a = 102.5°$. Find the measurement of $\angle b$.

a b

9. In the diagram below, $\angle a = 72°$. Find the measurement of $\angle d$.

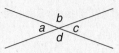

b
a   c
d

10. In $\triangle XYZ$ below, side $XY = 12$ inches and side $XZ = 10$ inches. The perimeter of the triangle is 34 inches. What kind of triangle is $\triangle XYZ$?

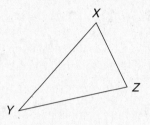

X

Z

Y

11. In $\triangle ABC$, $\angle A = 38°$ and $\angle B = 52°$. What kind of triangle is $\triangle ABC$?

12. A 5-foot-high vertical stick casts a shadow 3 feet long at the same time that a vertical pole casts a shadow 36 feet long. How tall is the pole?

13. In the picture below, $\angle C = \angle F$, and $\angle A = \angle D$. $AC = 24$, $DF = 15$, and $EF = 10$. Find BC.

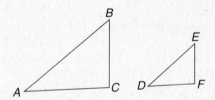

B

E

A   C   D   F

14. In $\triangle MNO$ below, $MN = 9$ and $MO = 12$. Find the length of NO.

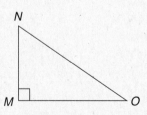

N

M   O

ANSWERS ARE ON PAGES 7–8.

PRE-TEST 3: ALGEBRA

Directions: Solve each problem. Write your answers on another sheet of paper.

1. Which point on the number line below corresponds to the value $\frac{3}{2}$?

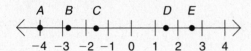

2. Simplify $+9 - (-4) + (-6) - 8$.

3. Simplify $-\frac{30}{6} + 4(-10)$.

4. Janet weighs w pounds. Which of the following expresses her weight after she loses 12 pounds?

   (1) $12w$
   (2) $12 - w$
   (3) $w - 12$
   (4) $\frac{4}{12}$
   (5) $w + 12$

5. Jack makes $6 an hour more than his wife. Which expression tells their combined income for a 40-hour week?

   (1) $40x + 6$
   (2) $40(2x + 6)$
   (3) $x(6 + 40)$
   (4) $x + x + 6$
   (5) $40 + 6x$

6. Which of the following expresses the sum of a number and three times the same number, all multiplied by five?

   (1) $5x + 3$
   (2) $x(5 + 3)$
   (3) $5(x + 3)$
   (4) $5(3x + 3)$
   (5) $5(x + 3x)$

7. Solve for x in $12x - 4 = 3x + 17$.

8. The ratio of Anton's age to his son's age is 9:2. Together their ages add up to 55. How old is Anton?

9. The area of a rectangle is 147 sq in. The length is three times the width. Find the length of the rectangle.

10. Solve for m in $6(m - 2) > 5(m + 5)$.

11. Factor the expression $n^2 - 6n$.

12. Which of the following is equal to $\sqrt{75}$?

    (1) 15
    (2) 10
    (3) 5
    (4) $3\sqrt{5}$
    (5) $5\sqrt{3}$

Directions: Use the graph below to answer problems 13 and 14.

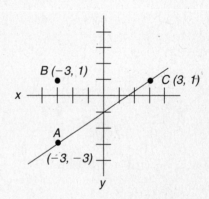

13. What is the slope of the line that passes through points A and C?

14. What is the distance from B to C on the graph?

15. Is the point $(2, 5)$ on the graph of the equation $y = 4x - 3$?

ANSWERS ARE ON PAGE 8.

Pre-Test Answer Key

PRE-TEST 1: ARITHMETIC

1. 12,514

$$\begin{array}{r} 20,500 \\ -\ 7,986 \\ \hline 12,514 \end{array}$$

2. 48,212

$$\begin{array}{r} 709 \\ \times\ 68 \\ \hline 5\ 672 \\ 42\ 54 \\ \hline 48,212 \end{array}$$

3. 5269

$$\begin{array}{r} 16 \\ 385 \\ 4012 \\ +\ 856 \\ \hline 5269 \end{array}$$

4. 807

$$\begin{array}{r} 807 \\ 34\overline{)27,438} \\ 27\ 2 \\ \hline 23 \\ 0 \\ \hline 238 \\ 238 \\ \hline 0 \end{array}$$

5. 2490 miles $(2 \times 265) + (4 \times 490) =$
$530 + 1960 = 2490$ miles

6. (2) $12.50(3 + 4)$

7. 292.58

$$\begin{array}{r} 300.00 \\ -\ 7.42 \\ \hline 292.58 \end{array}$$

8. 49.995

$$\begin{array}{r} 2.91 \\ 46. \\ +\ 1.085 \\ \hline 49.995 \end{array}$$

9. 2.08

$$\begin{array}{r} 2.08 \\ 17\overline{)35.36} \\ 34 \\ \hline 1\ 3 \\ 0 \\ \hline 1\ 36 \\ 1\ 36 \end{array}$$

10. 4.6

$$\begin{array}{r} 1.84 \\ \times\ 2.5 \\ \hline 920 \\ 368 \\ \hline 4.600 = 4.6 \end{array}$$

11. 24

$$\begin{array}{r} 24. \\ 6.5\overline{)156.0} \\ 130 \\ \hline 26\ 0 \\ 26\ 0 \\ \hline 0 \end{array}$$

12. 214.09

13. 14.6 mpg

$$\begin{array}{r} 14.55 \text{ to the nearest tenth} = \\ 18\overline{)262.00}\ \ 14.6 \text{ mpg} \\ 18 \\ \hline 82 \\ 72 \\ \hline 100 \\ 90 \\ \hline 100 \\ 90 \\ \hline 10 \end{array}$$

14. .85 million

$$\begin{array}{r} 2.60 \text{ million} \\ -1.75 \\ \hline 0.85 \text{ million} \end{array}$$

15. 20

$$\begin{array}{r} 9\frac{1}{2} = 9\frac{3}{6} \\ 3\frac{2}{3} = 3\frac{4}{6} \\ +6\frac{5}{6} = 6\frac{5}{6} \\ \hline 18\frac{12}{6} = 20 \end{array}$$

16. $1\frac{11}{24}$

$7\frac{1}{3} = 7\frac{8}{24} = 6\ \frac{8}{24} + \frac{24}{24} = 6\frac{32}{24}$

$-5\frac{7}{8} = 5\frac{21}{24} = \phantom{6\frac{32}{24}}\quad 5\frac{21}{24}$

$\overline{\phantom{-5\frac{7}{8} = 5\frac{21}{24} =}\quad\quad 1\frac{11}{24}}$

17. 3

$8 \div 2\frac{2}{3} =$

$\frac{8}{1} \div \frac{8}{3} = \frac{8}{1} \times \frac{3}{8} = \frac{3}{1} = 3$

18. $10\frac{1}{2}$

$2\frac{4}{5} \times 3\frac{3}{4} =$

$\frac{14}{5} \times \frac{15}{4} = \frac{21}{2} = 10\frac{1}{2}$

19. $9\frac{1}{3}$

$3\frac{1}{2} \div \frac{3}{8} = \frac{7}{2} \div \frac{3}{8}$

$\frac{7}{2} \times \frac{8}{3} = \frac{28}{3} = 9\frac{1}{3}$

20. In order: $\frac{5}{9}, \frac{2}{3}, \frac{3}{4}, \frac{5}{6}$

$\frac{3}{4} = \frac{27}{36}, \frac{2}{3} = \frac{24}{36}, \frac{5}{9} = \frac{20}{36}, \frac{5}{6} = \frac{30}{36}$

21. (1) $4 - 1.75$

22. $500 $\frac{1}{4} = \frac{3}{12}$ $\frac{7}{12} \times \frac{1200}{1} = 700$ $1200
$+\frac{1}{3} = \frac{4}{12}$ -700
$\frac{7}{12}$ 500

23. $36:48 =$ **3:4**

24. 15 $\frac{9}{x} = \frac{12}{20}$ 20 15 $x = 15$
$\times 9$ $12\overline{)180}$
180

25. 4:5 total 18 men:women $= 8:10 = 4:5$
women -10
men 8

26. $\frac{1}{50}$ $1 + 3 + 2 = 6$ $\frac{6}{300} = \frac{1}{50}$

27. $16,800:$18,400 =$ **21:23**

28. $11,100:$22,200 =$ **1:2**

29. $\frac{5}{6}$ $83\frac{1}{3} = \frac{83\frac{1}{3}}{100}$
$83\frac{1}{3} \div \frac{100}{1} = \frac{250}{3} \times \frac{1}{100} = \frac{5}{6}$

30. 13 $\frac{x}{200} = \frac{6.5}{100}$ 6.5 13
$\times 200$ $100\overline{)1300}$
1300.0

31. 60% $\frac{24}{40} = \frac{x}{100}$ 24 60
$\times 100$ $40\overline{)2400}$
2400

32. 260 $\frac{91}{x} = \frac{35}{100}$ 91 260
$\times 100$ $35\overline{)9100}$
9100

33. $240 1 yr. 4 mos. $= 1\frac{4}{12}$ yr.
$ = 1\frac{1}{3}$ yr.
$i = prt$
$i = \frac{1000}{1} \times \frac{18}{100} \times \frac{4}{3} = 240

34. (5) Not enough information is given. You do not know what percent is withheld for social security.

35. (3) $15,840
First find the amount of deductions.
$\frac{p}{1650} = \frac{20}{100}$ 1650 330
$\times 20$ $100\overline{)33,000}$
$33,000$
Subtract deductions from monthly salary and multiply by 12 to get yearly net pay.
1650 1320
-330 $\times12$
1320 $2\,640$
$13\,20$
15,840$

36. (2) $1782
First find the amount of her raise.
$\frac{p}{1650} = \frac{8}{100}$ 1650 132
$\times8$ $100\overline{)13,200}$
$13,200$
Add the raise to her current salary.
1650
$+132$
1782$

PRE-TEST 2: GEOMETRY

1. 20.41 m $C = \pi d$
$C = 3.14 \times 6.5$
$C = 20.41$

2. 140 cu ft $V = lwh$
$V = 10 \times 4 \times 3\frac{1}{2}$
$V = \frac{10}{1} \times \frac{4}{1} \times \frac{7}{2} = 140$ cu ft

3. 14.3 cm² $A = lw$
$A = 6.5 \times 2.2$
$A = 14.3$ cm²

4. 1100 sq ft Area of rectangle: $A = lw$
$A = 50 \times 40$
$A = 2000$ sq ft
Area of square: $A = s^2$
$A = 30^2$
$A = 900$ sq ft
Subtract the areas: $2000 - 900 = 1100$ sq ft

5. $80^2 = 80 \times 80 =$ **6400**

6. 373 $16^2 = 16 \times 16 = 256$
$5^3 = 5 \times 5 \times 5 = 125$
$8^1 = 8$
$256 + 125 - 8 = 373$

7. 92
Guess 90 because $90 \times 90 = 8100$
94 94 92 92
$90\overline{)8464}$ $+90$ $2\overline{)184}$ $\times92$
810 184 8464
364
360
4

8. 77.5° $180.0°$
$-102.5°$
$77.5°$

9. 108° $180°$
$-72°$
$108°$

10. isosceles
12 in 34 in
$+10$ -22
22 in 12 in
Since two sides are the same, $\triangle XYZ$ is isosceles.

11. right triangle

$$\begin{array}{r} 38° \\ + 52° \\ \hline 90° \end{array} \qquad \begin{array}{r} 180° \\ - 90° \\ \hline 90° \end{array}$$

Since $\angle C = 90°$, $\triangle ABC$ is a right triangle.

12. 60 ft $\quad \dfrac{\text{height}}{\text{shadow}} \quad \dfrac{5}{3} = \dfrac{x}{36}$

$$\begin{array}{r} 36 \\ \times 5 \\ \hline 180 \end{array} \qquad \begin{array}{r} 60 \text{ ft} \\ 3\overline{)180} \end{array}$$

13. 16 $\quad \dfrac{\text{base}}{\text{height}} \quad \dfrac{24}{x} = \dfrac{15}{10}$

$$\begin{array}{r} 24 \\ \times 10 \\ \hline 240 \end{array} \qquad \begin{array}{r} 16 \\ 15\overline{)240} \\ \underline{15} \\ 90 \\ \underline{90} \\ 0 \end{array}$$

14. 15
$$c^2 = a^2 + b^2$$
$$c^2 = 9^2 + 12^2$$
$$c^2 = 81 + 144$$
$$c^2 = 225$$
$$c = \sqrt{225}$$
$$c = 15$$

PRE-TEST 3: ALGEBRA

1. D

2. −1
$$+9 - (-4) + (-6) - 8$$
$$= +9 + 4 - 6 - 8$$
$$= +13 - 14 = -1$$

3. −45
$$-\dfrac{30}{6} + 4(-10)$$
$$= -5 - 40 = -45$$

4. (3) $w - 12$

5. (2) $40(2x + 6)$
$$40(x + x + 6) = 40(2x + 6)$$

6. (5) $5(x + 3x)$

7. $2\frac{1}{3}$
$$\begin{array}{r} 12x - 4 = 3x + 17 \\ -3x \qquad -3x \\ \hline 9x - 4 = \qquad 17 \\ +4 \qquad +4 \\ \hline \dfrac{9x}{9} = \qquad \dfrac{21}{9} \\ x = 2\frac{3}{9} = 2\frac{1}{3} \end{array}$$

8. 45 $\quad$ Son's age $= 2x$

Anton's age $= 9x$
$$2x + 9x = 55$$
$$\dfrac{11x}{11} = \dfrac{55}{11}$$
$$x = 5$$

9. 21 in $\quad$ width $= x \qquad A = lw$

length $= 3x \quad 147 = 3x \cdot x$
$$147 = 3x^2$$
$$\dfrac{147}{3} = \dfrac{3x^2}{3}$$
$$49 = x^2$$
$$\sqrt{49} = x$$
$$7 = x$$
$$21 = 3x$$

The length is 21 inches.

10. $m > 37$
$$\begin{array}{r} \overline{6(m - 2)} > \overline{5(m + 5)} \\ 6m - 12 > 5m + 25 \\ -5m \qquad -5m \\ \hline m - 12 > \qquad 25 \\ +12 \qquad +12 \\ \hline m > \qquad 37 \end{array}$$

11. $n(n - 6)$

12. (5) $5\sqrt{3}$
$$\sqrt{75} = \sqrt{25} \cdot \sqrt{3} = 5\sqrt{3}$$

13. $\frac{2}{3}$ $\quad m = \dfrac{y_2 - y_1}{x_2 - x_1}$

$$m = \dfrac{1 - (-3)}{3 - (-3)} = \dfrac{1 + 3}{3 + 3} = \dfrac{4}{6} = \dfrac{2}{3}$$

14. 6 $\quad$ B is 3 units to the left of the y-axis.

C is 3 units to the right of the y-axis.
The distance between them is $3 + 3 = 6$.

15. Yes $\quad$ Substitute 2 for x in $y = 4x - 3$.
$$y = 4(2) - 3 = 8 - 3 = 5$$
The point (2, 5) is on the graph.

Pre-Test Evaluation Chart

On the following chart, circle the number of any problem you got wrong. After each problem you will see the name of the section (or sections) where you can find the skills you need to solve the problem. When a problem involves more than one skill, the sections are separated by a slash (/).

This chart should help you decide which areas you need to review before you take the GED Test.

Problem	Section	Starting Page
	Pre-Test 1	
	Arithmetic	
1, 2, 3, 4, 5	The Basic Operations	15
6	Set-Up Questions	48
7, 8, 9, 10, 11, 12, 13, 14	Decimals	57
15, 16, 17, 18, 19, 20, 21, 22	Fractions	83
23, 24, 25, 26, 27, 28	Probability, Ratio & Proportion	117
29, 30, 31, 32, 33	Percents	131
34, 35, 36	Item Sets	154
	Pre-Test 2	
	Geometry	
1, 2, 3, 4	Perimeter, Circumference, Volume & Area	226
5, 6, 7	Powers & Roots	233
8, 9	Angles	252
10, 11, 12, 13, 14	Triangles	257
	Pre-Test 3	
	Algebra	
1, 2, 3,	Signed Numbers	281
4, 5, 6, 7, 8	Expressions/Equations	195
9	Using the Formulas Page	272
10	Longer Inequalities	291
11	Factoring	293
12	Square Roots	296
13, 14, 15	Rectangular Coordinate System	300

1 Whole Number Review

NUMBER VALUES AND FACTS

PLACE VALUE

Digits (0, 1, 2, 3, 4, 5, 6, 7, 8, 9) are used to write whole numbers. The number 506 is a three-digit number. The number 5600 is a four-digit number even though the last two digits (00) are the same.

Place value means that the position of each digit in a whole number determines its value. The diagram below shows the names of the first 10 whole number places.

Place Values of Whole Numbers

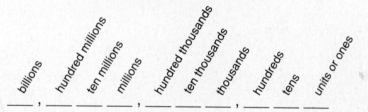

Let's compare the digit 5 as it appears in two different numbers. The 5 in the number 506 is in the hundreds place. The value of the 5 in 506 is $5 \times 100 = 500$. The digit 5 in the number 5600 is in the thousands place. The value of the 5 in 5600 is $5 \times 1000 = 5000$.

EXAMPLE What is the value of each digit in 7403? The 7 is in the thousands place. The value of 7 in 7403 is $7 \times 1000 = 7000$. The 4 is in the hundreds place. The value of the 4 in 7403 is $4 \times 100 = 400$. The digit 0 is in the tens place. The value of the 0 in 7403 is $0 \times 10 = 0$. The digit 3 is in the units (ones) place. The value of the 3 in 7403 is $3 \times 1 = 3$.

EXERCISE 1

Directions: Write the value of each underlined digit.

1. 14̲6 _____ 2̲0,019 _____ 167,28̲3 _____

2. 9,3̲60,280 _____ 480,9̲23 _____ 8̲1,240 _____

3. 2̲7 _____ 6̲7,209,488 _____ 84̲43 _____

4. 6,4̲09,255,108 _____ 34̲2,774 _____ 21,6̲40,456 _____

5. What is the value of each digit in 10,496?

value of 1 =
value of 0 =
value of 4 =
value of 9 =
value of 6 =

ANSWERS ARE ON PAGE 340.

NUMBER FACTS

To solve most problems on the GED Test, you need to know the arithmetic facts. If you cannot recall these facts quickly, you will waste time.

The Addition Facts

Exercise 2 is a review of the facts that you use to add and subtract.

EXERCISE 2

Directions: In each box, write the sum of the number on the top and the number on the side. This exercise should not take more than three minutes.

+	1	3	8	4	6	9	7	10	2	5
8	9									
1		4								
3										
6										
4			10							
9										
5										
7				17						
2										
10										

ANSWERS ARE ON PAGE 340.

The Multiplication Facts

Knowing the multiplication tables is also essential for your work in mathematics. Take the time now to make sure that you can remember them accurately and quickly.

EXERCISE 3

Directions: For each box in the table below, write the product (the answer to a multiplication problem) of the number on the top and the number on the side. A few answers have been filled in as examples.

	12	3	1	4	10	9	7	5	6	8	11	0	2
9													
7													
4		12											
5													
2							14						
1													
8													
10													

	12	3	1	4	10	9	7	5	6	8	11	0	2
12			12										
0													
11										88			
3													
6													

ANSWERS ARE ON PAGE 340.

You will also use these facts in division problems. For example,

$7 \times 3 = 21$ and $21 \div 3 = 7$.

The following exercise will give you a chance to recall the multiplication facts in both multiplication and division problems.

EXERCISE 4

Directions: Without looking at the multiplication table that you filled in, do the exercise below. Time yourself. This exercise should not take more than three minutes.

1. $5 \times 4 =$

2. $7 \times 8 =$

3. $3 \times 8 =$

4. $5 \times 9 =$

5. $6 \times 5 =$

6. $7 \times 6 =$

7. $9 \times 2 =$

8. $11 \times 11 =$

9. $12 \times 4 =$

10. $8 \times 5 =$

11. $6 \times 3 =$

12. $9 \times 6 =$

13. $8 \times 9 =$

14. $7 \times 4 =$

15. $9 \times 4 =$

16. $64 \div 8 =$

17. $42 \div 6 =$

18. $25 \div 5 =$

19. $24 \div 8 =$

20. $54 \div 9 =$

21. $36 \div 6 =$

22. $42 \div 7 =$

23. $81 \div 9 =$

24. $56 \div 8 =$

25. $49 \div 7 =$

26. $45 \div 5 =$

27. $32 \div 4 =$

28. $63 \div 9 =$

29. $48 \div 6 =$

30. $21 \div 3 =$

ANSWERS ARE ON PAGE 340.

Now is the time to review any addition or multiplication facts that you got wrong. Learn any fact that you missed before continuing to work with whole numbers.

THE BASIC OPERATIONS

This section gives you a chance to review the four basic whole number operations: addition, subtraction, multiplication, and division.

The following examples illustrate methods commonly used in the United States. You may use any method that works best for you as long as you are careful and accurate.

ADDITION

Addition is the process of combining two or more numbers to find a total. The answer to an addition problem is called a ***sum***.

EXAMPLE $2723 + 8 + 700 + 925 = ?$

```
                        2 1
 (1)    2723     (2)    2723
           8               8
         700             700
       + 925           + 925
                       4356
```

STEP 1   Line up the problem with units under units, tens under tens, and hundreds under hundreds.

STEP 2   Start with the units and add down each column. If the sum of any column is a two-digit number, put the digit on the right under the column you are adding and ***regroup*** (carry) the number on the left to the next column. The total of the units column here is 16, so you regroup the 1. The hundreds column totals 23, so you regroup the 2.

To check an addition problem, add the numbers from the bottom to the top.

```
ORIGINAL      34          CHECK      28
PROBLEM      +28                    +34
             ---                    ---
              62                     62
```

SUBTRACTION

When you subtract, you take one number away from another. The answer to a subtraction problem is called the ***difference***. When you cannot subtract one digit from another in a subtraction problem, you must ***regroup*** (borrow).

Regrouping doesn't change the value of a number. It allows you to take from a higher place value and add to a lower place value.

EXAMPLE 1   Find the difference between 1982 and 6039.

$$
\textbf{(1)} \quad \begin{array}{r} 6039 \\ -\ 1982 \\ \hline \end{array}
\qquad
\textbf{(2)} \quad \begin{array}{r} 6039 \\ -\ 1982 \\ \hline 7 \end{array}
\qquad
\textbf{(3)} \quad \begin{array}{r} ^{51} \\ \cancel{6}039 \\ -\ 1982 \\ \hline 7 \end{array}
\qquad
\textbf{(4)} \quad \begin{array}{r} ^{591} \\ \cancel{6}\cancel{0}39 \\ -\ 1982 \\ \hline \mathbf{4057} \end{array}
$$

STEP 1   Put the larger number (6039) on top. Line up the digits with units under units, tens under tens, etc.

STEP 2   Start subtracting with the units. Since you cannot take 8 from 3 in the tens column, you must regroup.

STEP 3   You cannot regroup from 0. Therefore, you must go one more place to the left. Regroup 1 from 6 to make 5 in the thousands place. Put a 1 above the 0 in the hundreds place to make 10.

STEP 4   Go back to the 3 in the tens place. Regroup again from the 10. Put a 9 in the hundreds place and put a 1 above the 3 in the tens place. Subtract each column.

To check a subtraction problem, add the answer to the number being subtracted. The result should be the top number of the original problem.

ORIGINAL PROBLEM
$$
\begin{array}{r} 49 \\ -28 \\ \hline 21 \end{array}
$$

CHECK
$$
\begin{array}{r} 28 \\ +21 \\ \hline 49 \end{array}
$$

Sometimes you will need to subtract from a number that has more than one zero in a row, and regrouping can get tricky. If you do your work neatly and carefully, you should have no problem. Look at the following example:

EXAMPLE 2   What is the difference between 10,000 and 1,450?

$$
\textbf{(1)} \quad \begin{array}{r} 10,000 \\ -\ 1,450 \\ \hline \end{array}
\qquad
\textbf{(2)} \quad \begin{array}{r} ^{01} \\ 1\!0,000 \\ -\ 1,450 \\ \hline 0 \end{array}
\qquad
\textbf{(3)} \quad \begin{array}{r} ^{09\ 1} \\ \cancel{1}0,000 \\ -\ 1,450 \\ \hline 0 \end{array}
\qquad
\textbf{(4 \& 5)} \quad \begin{array}{r} ^{09\ 91} \\ \cancel{1}0,\cancel{0}00 \\ -\ 1,450 \\ \hline \mathbf{8,550} \end{array}
$$

STEP 1   Put the larger number (10,000) on top. Line up the smaller number underneath, with units under units, tens under tens, and so on.

STEP 2   Start subtracting from the units and proceed to the tens column. Since you cannot take 5 from 0, you will need to regroup. You cannot regroup from the hundreds column or the thousands column because there are zeros in these places. You will need to regroup from a whole number. Cross out the 1 in the ten thousands column and put a 1 next to the zero in the thousands place to make 10.

STEP 3   Regroup from this 10 in the thousands place. Cross it out and write a 9 in its place. Put the borrowed 1 next to the 0 in the hundreds place.

STEP 4   Now regroup from this 10 in the hundreds place to help you subtract 5 from 0 in the tens place.

STEP 5   Subtract each column.

MULTIPLICATION

The answer to a multiplication problem is called the ***product***. When you multiply two numbers, you usually put the number with more digits on top. Start by multiplying the units.

EXAMPLE 1   Find the product of 28 and 407.

$$
\begin{array}{cccc}
 & \overset{5}{} & \overset{5}{} & \overset{5}{} \\
(1)\ \ 407 & (2)\ \ 407 & (3)\ \ 407 & (4)\ \ 407 \\
\underline{\times\ 28} & \underline{\times\ 28} & \underline{\times\ 28} & \underline{\times\ 28} \\
 & 3256 & 3256 & 3256 \\
 & & 814 & \underline{814} \\
 & & & \mathbf{11{,}396}
\end{array}
$$

STEP 1   Put 407 on top.

STEP 2   Multiply 407 by 8. Start this part of the answer under the units column. Note that $8 \times 0 = 0$, so you just bring down the regrouped digit, 5.

STEP 3   Multiply 407 by 2. Start this part of the answer under the tens column.

STEP 4   Add the results from steps 2 and 3.

To check a multiplication problem, divide the answer by one of the numbers you multiplied. The result should be the other number you multiplied.

ORIGINAL   18   **CHECK**   18
PROBLEM $\underline{\times\ 6}$ 6)108
                108

When you multiply two numbers and one number is a multiple of 10 (10, 20, 200, and so on), place the multiple of 10 at the *bottom* of the problem to make it easier to multiply.

EXAMPLE 2   Find the product of 38 and 100.

$$
\begin{array}{cc}
(1)\ \ 38 & (2)\ \ 38 \\
\underline{\times\ 100} & \underline{\times\ 100} \\
 & \mathbf{3800}
\end{array}
$$

STEP 1   Place 100 on the bottom.

STEP 2   Multiply by 100.

DIVISION

The symbols ÷ and $\overline{)}$ both mean to divide. 56 divided by 8 is written as $56 ÷ 8$ or $8\overline{)56}$. The answer to a division problem is called the **quotient**.

EXAMPLE 1 $798 ÷ 38 = ?$

$$\textbf{(1)}\quad 38\overline{)798}$$

$$\textbf{(2)}\quad \begin{array}{r} 2 \\ 38\overline{)798} \\ \underline{76} \\ 3 \end{array}$$

$$\textbf{(3)}\quad \begin{array}{r} \mathbf{21} \\ 38\overline{)798} \\ \underline{76} \\ 38 \\ \underline{38} \\ 0 \end{array}$$

STEP 1   Put the number being divided (798) inside the frame.

STEP 2   Does 38 go into 7? No. Since 38 is too big, look at the first *two* digits—79. How many times does 38 go into 79? Put a 2 above the tens place. Multiply 2 by 38; then subtract.

STEP 3   Bring down the 8. How many times does 38 go into 38? One time. Put the 1 above the units place. Multiply 1 by 38. Subtract. There is no remainder.

In problems with a **remainder**, show the remainder as part of the answer.

To check a problem, multiply the answer by the number you divided by. Then add any remainder. The result should be the number you divided into.

ORIGINAL PROBLEM
$$\begin{array}{r} 17\text{r}3 \\ 9\overline{)156} \\ \underline{9} \\ 66 \\ \underline{63} \\ 3 \end{array}$$

CHECK
$$\begin{array}{r} 17 \\ \times\ 9 \\ \hline 153 \\ +\ \ 3 \\ \hline 156 \end{array}$$

Zeros in division problems can create extra trouble. Look at the example.

EXAMPLE 2
$$\begin{array}{r} 207 \\ 13\overline{)2691} \\ \underline{26} \\ 09 \\ \underline{0} \\ 91 \\ \underline{91} \\ 0 \end{array}$$

CHECK
$$\begin{array}{r} 207 \\ \times\ 13 \\ \hline 621 \\ 207 \\ \hline 2691 \end{array}$$

The zero in the answer above holds the tens place. This zero means that 13 did not divide into 9.

The exercise below has several examples of common problems with zeros in all four of the basic operations. If you get any of the following problems wrong, study the solution carefully.

WHOLE NUMBER REVIEW

Directions: On another sheet of paper, solve and check each problem. Write your answers here.

1. 25,624 + 92,183 =

2. 60,845 − 2,926 =

3. Find the difference between 48,005 and 6,774.

4. 83 + 2096 + 194 =

5. 6 × 5708 =

6. What is the product of 349 and 74?

7. 872 × 409 =

8. Find the product of 65 and 50,000.

9. 446 ÷ 17 =

10. What is the quotient of 2464 divided by 8?

11. Find the quotient of 54,036 divided by 6.

12. 30,045 − 15,586 =

13. Find the sum of 194, 8, 2366, and 850.

14. 96 × 500 =

15. What is the difference between 3,000,000 and 816,000?

16. 7 × 29,058 =

17. 37,600 ÷ 800 =

18. What is the product of 8000 and 74?

19. What is the difference between 5,040,000 and 264,500?

20. What is the quotient of 10,710 divided by 35?

21. Find the product of 8 and 5090.

22. How much is 5076 divided by 12?

23. What is the difference between 88 and 7000?

24. Find the difference between 400,300 and 9,216.

25. Find the quotient of 2820 divided by 4.

26. What is the product of 346 and 450?

27. Find the sum of 2,900, 857, 11,630, and 405.

28. 56,423 ÷ 7 =

29. Find the difference between 807,631 and 1,300,500.

30. Find the quotient of 14,060 divided by 19.

ANSWERS ARE ON PAGES 341–342.

You should have at least 24 problems right on the last exercise. If you did not get 24 problems right, review your whole numbers skills before you go on. If you got 24 or more right, correct any problem you got wrong. Then go on to the next chapter.

2 Problem Solving and Special Topics

THE FIVE STEPS TO SOLVING WORD PROBLEMS

Most problems on the Mathematics Test of the GED will be word problems. One goal of this book is to help you master such problems.

TIP: The key to solving a word problem is to organize your thinking about it.

Take the time to do the following:

STEP 1   Find the question—what is being asked for?
STEP 2   Decide what information you need to answer the question.
STEP 3   Decide what arithmetic operation to use (addition, subtraction, multiplication, or division).
STEP 4   Do the arithmetic carefully and check your work.
STEP 5   Make sure that you answered the question asked *and* that your answer is sensible. Estimation can help you decide if your answer makes sense.

Study the following example closely.

EXAMPLE   Laura works at a part-time job 20 hours a week. She makes $5 an hour. How much money does she make a week?
STEP 1   *Question:* How much money does she make a week?
STEP 2   *Information:* 20 hours at $5 an hour.
STEP 3   *Arithmetic:* Since she makes $5 in one hour, and she works 20 hours, multiply.
STEP 4   20 hours × $5 = $100 per week.
Check: 100 ÷ 5 = 20.
STEP 5   **$100** is a *sensible* amount of money to make in one week for a part-time job. You have answered the question asked.

On the next few pages you will get a chance to practice each of these five steps.

STEP 1: UNDERSTANDING THE QUESTION

After you have read the problem, the first step in solving a word problem is to get a clear understanding of what the question is asking you to find. You will use this knowledge to select necessary information and later to see if your answer makes sense.

> **TIP:** One good strategy is to try to put the question in your own words. Sometimes this can help you visualize the problem more clearly.

Which of the answer choices below accurately restates what you are being asked to find?

Sarah bought 3 pounds of meat, 5 pounds of fruit, and 7 pounds of vegetables. What was the total weight of her purchases?

(1) Find the difference in weight between the fruit and the vegetables.

(2) Find how much Sarah's purchases weighed altogether.

(3) Find the combined weight of the meat and the vegetables Sarah bought.

Answer choice **(2)** means the same thing as "What was the total weight of her purchases?"

In the exercise below, practice deciding what you are being asked to find in each problem. Restate the problem in your own words if you think it will help.

EXERCISE 1

Directions: Which choice best expresses the question asked in each problem? *Do not solve these problems now.* You will have a chance to solve them in Exercise 4, on page 29.

1. In a recent election Mr. Sanders got 67,576 votes, and his opponent got 62,881 votes. How many more votes did Mr. Sanders get than his opponent?

   (1) Find how many people voted.
   (2) Find how many registered voters turned up at the polls.
   (3) Find the difference between the number of votes Mr. Sanders received and the number of votes his opponent received.

2. A television was on sale for $198. This was $60 less than the original price. Find the original price.

   (1) What was the sale price of the TV?
   (2) How much more did the TV cost before it was on sale?
   (3) How much did the TV cost before it was on sale?

3. Manny makes monthly payments of $190 for a new car. How much does Manny pay in one year for the car?

   (1) Find how much more Manny owes on his car.
   (2) Find Manny's total car payments for twelve months.
   (3) Find the down payment Manny made for his car.

4. Pancho drove 460 miles and used 20 gallons of gasoline. On the average, how far did he drive on one gallon of gasoline?

   (1) Find how much 20 gallons of gasoline cost.
   (2) Find out how far Pancho can drive on 20 gallons of gas.
   (3) Find out how far Pancho drove on one gallon of gasoline.

5. In September after a long diet, Gordon weighed 178 pounds. He went off his diet, and by the end of December he had gained 33 pounds. Find Gordon's weight at the end of December.

   (1) How much did Gordon weigh before his diet?
   (2) How much did Gordon weigh at the end of December?
   (3) How much did Gordon weigh in early September?

6. Together Marilyn and Calvin Howard take home $22,200 a year. Find their monthly take-home pay.

   (1) How much does Marilyn Howard take home in a month?
   (2) How much do both Marilyn and Calvin take home in a month?
   (3) How much do both Marilyn and Calvin make in a year?

7. On the open road Carmen's car gets 24 miles to the gallon. How far can she drive on the highway with 13 gallons of gas in her tank?

   (1) Find how many miles Carmen gets on one gallon of gas.
   (2) Find the number of gallons Carmen's gas tank holds.
   (3) Find the distance Carmen can drive with 13 gallons of gas.

8. Gloria is saving for a color TV listed at $385. So far she has saved $290. Find the additional amount Gloria has to save.

   (1) How much more does Gloria need to save for the TV?
   (2) How much has Gloria saved already?
   (3) What is the list price of the color TV?

ANSWERS ARE ON PAGE 342.

STEP 2: SELECTING THE NECESSARY INFORMATION

Step 2 of the five steps to solving word problems is: Decide what information you need to answer the question. Some word problems can be confusing because they contain information you do not need. Think about the following problem:

EXAMPLE The Chung family made $17,400 last year. They paid $2,580 for rent and $3,160 in taxes. After paying taxes, how much money did the Chungs have left for all their expenses?

INFORMATION
NEEDED Yearly income of $17,400 and taxes of $3,160
DO NOT NEED $2,580 rent

The problem asks: How much money did the Chungs have left after paying taxes? You do not need to know the amount of their rent to answer the question. The amount of rent they paid is *unnecessary* information. To solve this problem, simply subtract the amount the Chungs paid in taxes from the amount they made in a year.

$$\begin{array}{r} \$17{,}400 \\ -\ 3{,}160 \\ \hline \mathbf{\$14{,}240} \end{array}$$

One good strategy in working with word problems is to take a minute to decide what information you need to get an answer. Then cross out those numbers you do *not* need so that they will not confuse you.

EXERCISE 2

Directions: For each problem, state what information you need to solve each problem. Also state what information is given that you do not need. (You can lightly cross this information out if you wish.) Look back at the example above if you need help. *Do not solve these problems now.* You will solve them in Exercise 4, on page 29.

1. Of the 943 cars sold in Midvale last month, 387 were made in the United States. Of the foreign cars sold, 198 were made in Japan. How many of the cars sold in Midvale last month were made outside the United States?

   Need:

   Do not need:

2. In March 1992, 10,549 people in Center City were officially unemployed. In December 1991, 9,307 were unemployed. In March 1991, 8,248 were unemployed. By how many people did the unemployment count rise from March 1991 to March 1992?

   Need:

   Do not need:

3. Huey drove 132 miles in 3 hours. He gets 22 miles on one gallon of gas. If he drove at the same rate, how far did he drive in one hour?

   Need:

   Do not need:

4. Huey drove 132 miles in 3 hours. He gets 22 miles on one gallon of gas. How many gallons of gas did he use?

   Need:

   Do not need:

5. A child's ticket to the circus cost $6.50. An adult's ticket cost $10.50. Altogether, 1230 children attended the circus. How much money was paid for children's tickets to the circus?

   Need:

   Do not need:

6. Of the 2500 adults in Cripple Creek, 1250 are high school graduates and 750 finished college. How many adults did not finish high school?

   Need:

   Do not need:

7. California has 30,380,000 people, while New York has 18,058,000 and Texas has 17,349,000. How many more people live in the most populous state than in the second most populous?

   Need:

   Do not need:

8. Paul paid $134.40 for 64 feet of floor joists that weigh 4 pounds a foot. What was the price per foot of the joists?

   Need:

   Do not need:

9. Adrienne makes $1100 a month. She pays $285 a month for rent and $400 a month for food. How much more does she pay for food than for rent in a month?

   Need:

   Do not need:

10. Guadalupe paid $3.69 a pound for 3 pounds of boneless pork chops and $1.99 a pound for 2 pounds of bacon. How much did she pay for the pork chops?

    Need:

    Do not need:

ANSWERS ARE ON PAGE 342.

STEP 3: CHOOSING THE OPERATION

Step 3 of the five steps to solving a word problem is: Decide what arithmetic operation to use. In this section we will talk about some of the key words and the situations that give you a clue to what arithmetic operation to use in a word problem.

Addition and Subtraction

When you have to find a *total amount*, consider adding. Words such as *sum*, *total*, *altogether*, and *combined* in a question often indicate addition.

EXAMPLE 1 Mr. Swenson makes $560 a week, and Mrs. Swenson makes $540. What is their combined weekly income?
QUESTION Find combined income.
OPERATION Add their weekly incomes.

The following phrases usually mean to subtract: *How much more? How much less? How much greater? How much smaller? How much farther? Find the balance. Find the difference.*

EXAMPLE 2 Mary weighs 120 pounds. Her daughter weighs 50 pounds. How much more does Mary weigh than her daughter?
QUESTION Find how much more mother weighs than daughter.
OPERATION Subtract the daughter's weight from Mary's weight.

The words *net* and *gross* may also suggest subtraction. **Gross** refers to an amount before something has been subtracted from it. **Net** refers to the amount remaining after something has been subtracted from the gross.

EXAMPLE 3 Mark's gross monthly salary is $3000. His employer withholds $600 for taxes and social security. What is Mark's net salary for a month?
QUESTION Find net salary.
OPERATION Subtract the amount withheld from the gross amount.

Multiplication and Division

Watch for situations that suggest multiplication. A problem may give you information for one thing. Then you will be asked to find other information for several things.

EXAMPLE 1 There are 3 feet in one yard. How many feet are there in 20 yards?
QUESTION Find number of feet in 20 yards. (Here you have information for one thing and you want to find information for several things.)
OPERATION Multiply the number of feet in one yard by 20.

EXAMPLE 2   On the open road, Jack can drive 24 miles on a gallon of gasoline. How far can he drive using 10 gallons of gas?

QUESTION   Find the distance Jack can drive with 10 gallons of gas. (Here, again, you have information for one thing and you want to find information for several things.)

OPERATION   Multiply the number of miles Jack can drive on one gallon of gas by 10.

The following situations suggest division. A problem may give you information about several things. Then you will be asked to find information about one thing. Or you may be given information about a *whole* and asked to find a *part*.

EXAMPLE 3   Last year, Ruth and Gordon together paid $3000 for rent. How much rent did they pay each month?

QUESTION   Find monthly rent. [Here you have information about a *whole* (year) and you want to find information about a *part* (month).]

OPERATION   Divide the amount of rent they paid in a year by the number of months in a year.

A problem may also ask you to find how many of a certain item are contained in some bigger item. This situation also means to divide.

EXAMPLE 4   Soup is packed 24 cans to a box. How many boxes are needed to hold 1200 cans of soup?

QUESTION   Find the number of boxes needed to hold 1200 cans. (Here you want to find how many times 24 goes into 1200 or how many 24s there are in 1200.)

OPERATION   Divide the total number of cans by the number of cans one box can hold.

The ideas of sharing, cutting, and splitting also indicate division.

EXAMPLE 5   Fatima won $200 in a lottery. She decided to split the money equally among three friends and herself. How much did each one get?

QUESTION   Find what part of $200 each of the 4 people received.

OPERATION   Divide the amount Fatima won by the number of people who are going to share the money.

EXERCISE 3

Directions: First restate each question in your own words, as shown in the examples above. Then tell what arithmetic operation you need to solve each problem. *Do not solve these problems now.* You will solve them in Exercise 4, on page 29.

1. Pieter is 37 years old. His son Christopher is 8. How much older is Pieter than his son?

    Question:

    Operation:

2. Caren works 40 hours a week for $260. How much does she make in one hour?

    Question:

    Operation:

3. In November the Johnsons' utility bills were $42 for electricity, $25 for the telephone, and $53 for heat. Find the total for their November utilities.

Question:

Operation:

4. At the corner grocery all but 5 dozen of the 20 dozen eggs in the cooler are white. How many dozen eggs are white?

Question:

Operation:

5. Cheryl's gross income for the year was $18,296. Her deductions totaled $4,680. What was her net income for the year?

Question:

Operation:

6. Ezra Hollis died in 1985 at the age of 92. In what year was he born?

Question:

Operation:

7. Pat works 8 hours a day for $7.50 an hour. How much does she make in a day?

Question:

Operation:

8. Alfredo's yearly salary is $16,380. How much does he make in a month?

Question:

Operation:

9. Kim types 85 words per minute. How long does it take her to type a letter that contains 1700 words?

Question:

Operation:

10. In June the Sports Center Fund Drive had $85,000. By the end of August contributors sent another $27,000. How much was in the fund at the end of August?

Question:

Operation:

ANSWERS ARE ON PAGE 342.

STEP 4: SOLVING WORD PROBLEMS

Step 4 of the five steps to solving word problems is: Do the arithmetic carefully and check your work. This is where your skills in the basic arithmetic operations play an important part. Later, you will see how algebra and geometry can also help you solve word problems.

When you get to this point in solving a problem, be sure to do your math neatly and accurately. All the good planning in the world will not give you a correct answer if you make mistakes in your computation.

EXERCISE 4

Directions: On a separate sheet of paper, go back and solve problems 1–8 on pages 22–23; problems 1–10 on pages 24–25, and problems 1–10 on pages 27–28. Don't forget to use the steps you have learned so far. Be sure to check your answers.

ANSWERS ARE ON PAGE 342–343.

STEP 5: BEING SURE THAT YOUR ANSWER MAKES SENSE
Is the Answer Sensible?

You may have thought that once you have computed an answer to a problem, you are finished. However, on tests like the GED, you want to take one more step to avoid making unnecessary mistakes. Even if you have already checked your computation, you should always go back to make sure your answer is sensible. To show you how important this is, take a look at how Carol, a GED student, solved the following problem:

Anthony walked a total of 77 miles over the last seven days. On the average, how many miles did he walk each day?

(1) 539
(2) 84
(3) 70
(4) 11
(5)   7

Carol looked quickly at the problem and decided she would multiply 77 by 7 to find the number of miles. Doing her computation carefully, and checking her math over twice, she came up with 539 total miles. She was happy to see that answer listed as one of the choices, and she answered **(1)**.

What's wrong with Carol's work? You may have already figured out that she should have *divided* instead of multiplied. If Carol had taken an extra minute to decide *whether her answer was sensible*, she probably would have found her error. The question asks how many miles Anthony walked in *one* day. It is not sensible to think that he could walk 539 miles in a day, especially when the problem tells you he walked only 77 miles in 7 days! Even though Carol's computation was accurate, she did not use her common sense. If she had, she would have seen that she needed to rethink her solution to the problem.

Have I Answered the Question Asked?

Another part of step 5 is making sure you answered the question that was asked. Sometimes you may skip an important step. Look at this example:

A tailor needs 14 inches of blue thread, 11 inches of green, and 11 inches of white to finish his project. How many *feet* of thread does he need in all?

(1)   2
(2)   3
(3)   4
(4)   36
(5) 432

Laticia, a GED student, knew that she needed to add 14, 11, and 11 inches together to find the total length of string. She did this, checked her addition carefully, and chose answer **(4)** 36. Then she went on to the next problem.

If Laticia had taken a minute to *see if she had answered the question asked*, she would have seen that the question asks for *feet*, whereas she gave her answer in *inches*. Answer choice **(2)** is the correct response. Once Laticia got her answer in inches, she should have divided by 12 to find the number of feet.

You may want to take some time now to go over your work from Exercises 1–3. If you got a wrong answer, try to figure out why this happened. Did you choose the wrong information? Did you fail to answer the question asked? Taking time to check your answer is an important step.

ROUNDING AND ESTIMATING
Rounding Off

Look at the number 362. Is it closer to 300 or to 400?

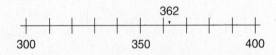

362 is closer to 400. 400 is called a **round number** because it ends with zeros. 400 is 362 *rounded off* to the nearest hundred. Rounding off numbers can sometimes help you decide whether or not your answer is sensible. Here are some steps to help you learn to round off.

RULES FOR ROUNDING OFF WHOLE NUMBERS

1. Underline the digit in the place you are rounding off to.

2. a. If the digit to the right of the underlined digit is 5 or more, add 1 to the underlined digit.
   b. If the digit to the right of the underlined digit is less than 5, leave the underlined digit as it is.

3. Change all the places to the right of the underlined digit to zeros.

EXAMPLE 1   Round off 26,489 to the nearest thousand. 2<u>6</u>,489 → 26,000

   STEP 1   Underline the digit in the thousands place, 6. Look at the digit to the right of 6. The digit is 4.
   STEP 2   Because this number is less than 5, leave the 6 and the digits to the left of 6. Change the numbers to the right of 6 to zeros.

EXAMPLE 2   Round off 196,274 to the nearest ten thousand. 1<u>9</u>6,274 → 200,000

   STEP 1   Underline the digit in the ten thousands place, 9. Look at the digit to the right of 9. The digit is 6.
   STEP 2   Because this number is more than 5, add 1 to the underlined digit. 9 + 1 = 10. (When you add 1 to 9, regroup 1 to the next column to the left.) Add 1 to the 1 already there. Then change the numbers to the right to zeros.

EXERCISE 5

Directions: Round off each number to the place indicated.

1. 63 to the nearest ten.

2. 228 to the nearest ten.

3. 439 to the nearest hundred.

4. 5620 to the nearest thousand.

5. 8098 to the nearest thousand.

6. 6982 to the nearest hundred.

7. 24,507 to the nearest thousand.

8. 38,496 to the nearest ten thousand.

9. 1063 to the nearest ten.

10. 28,092 to the nearest hundred.

11. 16,236 to the nearest hundred.

12. 1,475,290 to the nearest ten thousand.

13. 2951 to the nearest hundred.

14. 312 to the nearest ten.

15. 8059 to the nearest hundred.

ANSWERS ARE ON PAGE 343.

Estimating

As you know, the last step of the five steps to solving a word problem is: Make sure that your answer is sensible. How can rounding off numbers help you do this?

A good way to see if your answer is sensible is to estimate an answer. Round off at least one number in the problem and solve the new problem using the round number. This "rounded" problem should be easier to solve.

Now compare the answer to the "rounded" problem and the answer to the original problem. The answers should be close.

EXAMPLE A 588-acre farm can be divided up equally into 2-acre lots. How many 2-acre lots could the farm be divided into?

STEP 1 *Question:* How many 2-acre lots could the farm be divided into?
STEP 2 *Information:* 588 acres altogether and 2-acre lots.
STEP 3 *Arithmetic:* Divided up equally means to divide.
STEP 4 Divide 588 by 2. 588 ÷ 2 = 294.
STEP 5 Estimate an answer. Round off 588 to the nearest 100. Then divide 600 by the number of acres per lot. The approximate number of lots the farm can be divided into is 300. The answer, **294**, is close to 300.

Estimation is a useful tool, but it is no substitute for your own judgment. Think about every answer you get. Be sure it makes sense to you.

EXERCISE 6

Directions: Find an approximate answer for each problem below by rounding off at least one number in each problem. The problems suggest which numbers you should round off. Then compute the actual answer and compare.

1. Fred works 9 hours a day. He earns $8.25 an hour. How much does Fred earn in a day?

   Round off wage to nearest dollar:

   Approximate answer:

   Actual answer:

2. Mrs. Meida drove for 6 hours at a speed of 52 miles per hour. How far did she drive?

   Round off speed to nearest ten:

   Approximate answer:

   Actual answer:

3. On Friday 487 people attended the Central School Carnival. On Saturday 662 people attended, and on Sunday 523 people attended. Find the total attendance.

   Round off each attendance to nearest 100:

   Approximate answer:

   Actual answer:

4. Marcello makes $24,960 a year. How much does he make in a month?

   Round off salary to a number easily divided by 12:

   Approximate answer:

   Actual answer:

5. The Central County courthouse was built in 1897. How old was the courthouse in 1988?

   Round off year of construction to nearest ten:

   Round off 1988 to nearest ten:

   Approximate answer:

   Actual answer:

6. The television Magda bought was on sale for $198. She saved $58 by buying the TV on sale. What was the original price?

   Round off sale price and amount of savings to nearest ten:

   Approximate answer:

   Actual answer:

7. A half-gallon carton of orange juice costs $1.89. How much do five cartons cost?

   Round off price of one carton to nearest dollar:

   Approximate answer:

   Actual answer:

8. From a board 96 inches long, Paul cut a piece 27 inches long. How long was the leftover piece?

   Round off each length to nearest ten:

   Approximate answer:

   Actual answer:

ANSWERS ARE ON PAGE 344.

ESTIMATING WITH DIVISION

Estimation can be very useful for solving division problems. Division often takes more time to perform than the other three basic operations. With estimation you can quickly get an idea of what the answer is. Sometimes an approximate amount is all that is needed. At other times you can use your estimate to narrow down the selection in a multiple-choice setting or to check your exact answer to see if it is reasonable.

The first step in estimating the answer to a division problem is deciding how many digits the answer will have.

EXAMPLE 1 How many digits are in the answer to the problem 2241 ÷ 27?

$$27\overline{)2241} \quad \underline{\text{XX}} \quad \text{two digits}$$

SOLUTION The location of the first digit in the answer tells how many digits the answer will have. Look at the problem above. Will 27 go into 2? No, but 27 will go into 224. The first digit in the answer is in the tens place. The answer will have **two digits**.

Compatible Numbers

Numbers that divide exactly are ***compatible***. For example, 3 and 18 are compatible, but 3 and 20 are not. To estimate the answer to a division problem, find compatible numbers that are close to the numbers in the first division step. Look at the next list carefully.

Incompatible Pairs	Related Compatible Pairs
8 and 43	8 and 40 or 8 and 48
6 and 40	6 and 36 or 6 and 42
78 and 610	80 and 640
53 and 277	50 and 300

EXAMPLE 2 Use compatible numbers to choose the closest estimate to the problem 1510 ÷ 7.

(1) 20   **(2)** 200   **(3)** 350   **(4)** 700

SOLUTION The numbers 7 and 15 are not compatible, but 7 and 14 are. If you divide 1400 (a compatible number closest to 1510) by 7, the answer is 200. Choice **(2)** is closest.

EXAMPLE 3 Use compatible numbers to estimate the exact answer to the problem 4756 ÷ 82.

(1) 28   **(2)** 42   **(3)** 58   **(4)** 92

SOLUTION The numbers 8 and 47 are not compatible, but 8 and 48 are. 4800 ÷ 80 = 60. The answer closest to 60 is **(3)**.

EXERCISE 7

Directions: For problems 1–3, state the number of digits in each answer.

1. a. $9\overline{)2345}$ **b.** $4\overline{)687}$ **c.** $73\overline{)30,246}$

2. a. $29\overline{)183}$ **b.** $92\overline{)1872}$ **c.** $365\overline{)1122}$

3. a. $8\overline{)9704}$ **b.** $672\overline{)1258}$ **c.** $123\overline{)4567}$

Directions: For problems 4–8, choose the answer that seems most nearly correct. *Do not actually divide.*

4. 3)1925
   (1) 60   **(2)** 600   **(3)** 800   **(4)** 7000

5. 72)839
   (1) 800   **(2)** 100   **(3)** 10   **(4)** 5

6. 38)52,146
   (1) 1400   **(2)** 320   **(3)** 280   **(4)** 210

7. 227)6783
   (1) 30   **(2)** 40   **(3)** 50   **(4)** 60

8. 81)75,286
   (1) 90   **(2)** 700   **(3)** 900   **(4)** 9000

Directions: For problems 9–12, choose an answer by using compatible numbers. *Do not actually divide.*

9. 9)5238
   (1) 692   **(2)** 582   **(3)** 402   **(4)** 372

10. 32)23,072
   (1) 721   **(2)** 632   **(3)** 76   **(4)** 61

11. 487)30,681
   (1) 41   **(2)** 63   **(3)** 327   **(4)** 637

12. 58)12,296
   (1) 142   **(2)** 182   **(3)** 212   **(4)** 292

ANSWERS ARE ON PAGE 344.

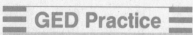

EXERCISE 8

Directions: Estimate to select the best answer to each problem.

1. Stephanie makes $34,080 in a year. How much does she make in a month?

   (1) $1290
   (2) $1530
   (3) $1960
   (4) $2840
   (5) $4010

2. Gert and Bert drove for 5 hours at a speed of 62 miles per hour. How many miles did they travel?

   (1) 248
   (2) 310
   (3) 430
   (4) 640
   (5) 860

3. A box of cereal costs $3.19. Find the cost of five boxes of the same cereal.

   (1) $ 6.38
   (2) $ 9.85
   (3) $11.45
   (4) $12.65
   (5) $15.95

4. On Friday 437 people attended the musical at the high school. On Saturday 739 people attended, and on Sunday 496 people attended. Find the total attendance.

   (1) 1482
   (2) 1512
   (3) 1672
   (4) 1852
   (5) 2092

5. In a 40-hour week Michalis makes $584. What is his hourly wage?

   (1) $ 8.60
   (2) $10.80
   (3) $12.40
   (4) $14.60
   (5) $18.20

6. To hear a jazz band 112 people paid $9.50 each. What was the total amount of the ticket sales?

   (1) $ 910
   (2) $1064
   (3) $1284
   (4) $1460
   (5) $1620

7. The yearly profit for a trucking company was $170,640. If the nine partners share the profit equally, how much will each receive?

   (1) $14,540
   (2) $16,320
   (3) $18,960
   (4) $24,380
   (5) $32,640

8. Maria paid $11.56 for 4 pounds of ham. What was the price per pound?

   (1) $1.49
   (2) $1.99
   (3) $2.29
   (4) $2.89
   (5) $3.69

ANSWERS ARE ON PAGE 344.

PROBLEMS OF TWO OR MORE PARTS

To solve many word problems on the GED Test, you will have to perform more than one operation in step 4 (the computation step) to answer the question asked. Study the following examples carefully.

EXAMPLE 1   Celia bought 2 pounds of apples that cost $.60 a pound and 5 pounds of potatoes that cost $.40 a pound. What was the total cost of her purchases?

STEP 1   *Question:* What is the total cost of the apples and the potatoes?
STEP 2   *Information:* 2 pounds of apples for $.60 a pound and 5 pounds of potatoes for $.40 a pound.
STEP 3   *Arithmetic:* Here it is useful to outline each step.
  a. Multiply the price of a pound of apples by 2.
  b. Multiply the price of a pound of potatoes by 5.
  c. Add the results of steps a and b.
STEP 4   *Solution:*
  a. $.60 × 2 = $1.20
  b. $.40 × 5 = $2.00
  c. $1.20 + $2.00 = **$3.20**
STEP 5   *Make sure the answer is sensible:* $3.20 is a reasonable amount to pay for the apples and potatoes.

EXAMPLE 2   Andrea finished cutting out 42 paper dolls in 3 hours. Her daughter cut out 12 dolls in 3 hours. Together, how many dolls did the two of them cut out per hour?

STEP 1   *Question:* How many dolls did they cut per hour?
STEP 2   *Information:* 42 dolls in 3 hours and 12 dolls in 3 hours.
STEP 3   *Arithmetic:* Outline each step.
  a. Divide 42 by 3.
  b. Divide 12 by 3.
  c. Add the results of steps a and b.
STEP 4   *Solution:*
  a. 42 ÷ 3 = 14
  b. 12 ÷ 3 = 4
  c. 14 + 4 = **18**
STEP 5   *Make sure the answer is sensible:* 18 is a sensible answer, given the information provided.

You may have chosen a different way to set up the problem above. For example, in step 3, you may have decided to add 42 and 12, then divide by 3. Whatever strategy you find most helpful is the one you should use.

EXERCISE 9

Directions: In this exercise, first make an outline for each problem as in step 3 in the preceding examples. Then solve each problem. The first one is done for you.

1. The Upperville school district spends $7800 a year to educate a child. The Central City school district spends $2100 per child. Find the difference between the costs of educating 30 children in Upperville and 30 children in Central City.
   a. Find cost for 30 children at Upperville.
   b. Find cost for 30 children at Central City.
   c. Subtract the result of step b from the result of step a.
   Solution: a.　　$7800　　　　**b.**　$ 2100　　　**c.** $234,000
   　　　　　　　X　　　30　　　　　　X　　　30　　　　　−$ 63,000
   　　　　　　　──────────　　　　　──────────　　　　　──────────
   　　　　　　$234,000　　　　　　　$63,000　　　　　　　$171,000

2. Each week Everett makes $240 and his wife makes $200. Together, how much do they make in a year?
   a.
   b.
   Solution:

3. For her store Mrs. Rivera ordered 4 cases of green beans, 6 cases of canned corn, and 10 cases of beets. If there are 20 cans to a case, what is the total number of cans in Mrs. Rivera's order?
   a.
   b.
   Solution:

4. Jermaine drove for 5 hours at a rate of 55 mph and then for 3 hours at a rate of 35 mph. How far did she drive altogether?
   a.
   b.
   c.
   Solution:

5. Alfonso works 35 hours a week for $8.50 an hour and 6 hours a week for $12.75 an hour. How much does he make in a week?
   a.
   b.
   c.
   Solution:

6. Mrs. Seltzer paid $150 down and $45 a month for 18 months for new living room furniture. What total amount did she pay for the furniture?
   a.
   b.
   Solution:

7. A charity drive raised $30,400. This was $3,000 less than last year's total. Last year's money was shared equally by five agencies. How much did each agency get last year?
   a.
   b.
   Solution:

8. Grace can type 75 words per minute. How long will it take her to type both a 1000-word letter and a 500-word memo?
   a.
   b.
   Solution:

ANSWERS ARE ON PAGE 345.

SPECIAL TOPICS WITH WHOLE NUMBERS

In the next few sections you will learn to apply your computation skills and word problem skills to special types of problems.

TOPIC 1: MEAN AND MEDIAN

A problem may ask you to find the mean or the median for a group of numbers. **Mean** is another name for *average*. To find the average of a group of numbers, add the numbers and then divide the sum by how many numbers you have added.

EXAMPLE 1 Find the average of 10, 15, 23, and 28.

$$
\begin{array}{ll}
\textbf{(1)} \quad
\begin{array}{r}
10 \\
15 \\
23 \\
+28 \\
\hline
76
\end{array}
&
\textbf{(2)} \quad
\begin{array}{r}
19 \\
4\overline{)76} \\
\underline{4} \\
36 \\
\underline{36} \\
0
\end{array}
\end{array}
$$

STEP 1 Find the sum by adding the numbers.
STEP 2 Since you have added 4 numbers, divide the sum by 4. The average of the four numbers is **19**.

Finding an average is a common application of arithmetic skills. Look at the next example.

EXAMPLE 2   Houses on Fred's block sold for $40,000, $43,000, and $52,000. What was the average selling price?

$$
\begin{array}{ll}
\textbf{(1)} & \$\ 40,000 \\
& \quad 43,000 \\
& +\ 52,000 \\
& \overline{\$135,000}
\end{array}
\qquad
\textbf{(2)}\quad
\begin{array}{r}
\$45,000 \\
3\overline{)135,000} \\
\underline{12} \\
15 \\
\underline{15} \\
0\ 000
\end{array}
$$

STEP 1   Find the sum by adding the cost of each house.

STEP 2   Divide by the number of houses, 3. The average selling price is **$45,000**.

Remember that another name for *average* is *mean*. The mean selling price for the three houses in Example 2 is $45,000.

A ***median*** is a number in the middle of a whole group of numbers. In this group, half of the numbers are above the median and half of the numbers are below the median. In Example 2, $43,000 is the median price of the three houses. $40,000 is less, and $52,000 is more.

To find a median for a group of numbers, arrange the numbers in order from smallest to largest. The number in the middle is the median.

EXAMPLE 1   Lorenzo got scores of 90, 72, 88, 85, and 93 on 5 math tests. What was his median score?

72   85   <u>88</u>   90   93

STEP 1   Arrange the scores in order from smallest to largest.

STEP 2   Underline the number in the middle, 88. The median score on the five tests was **88**.

Sometimes there are two numbers in the middle of a group of numbers. The median is the mean of these two numbers.

EXAMPLE 2   Ruby got scores of 78, 97, 72, and 84 on 4 Spanish quizzes. What was her median score?

$$
\textbf{(1)}\ \ 72\ \underline{78\ \ 84}\ 97
\qquad
\textbf{(2)}\quad
\begin{array}{r}
78 \\
+\ 84 \\
\overline{162}
\end{array}
\qquad
\textbf{(3)}\quad
\begin{array}{r}
81 \\
2\overline{)162}
\end{array}
$$

STEP 1   Arrange the scores in order from smallest to largest.

STEP 2   Underline and add the two numbers in the middle, 78 and 84.

STEP 3   Find the average (mean) of 78 and 84. **81** is the median score on the four tests.

EXERCISE 10

Directions: Solve each problem. Extra information may be given in some problems. Make sure you use only necessary information.

1. Find both the mean and the median for 353, 19, and 207.

2. Find both the mean and the median for 2046, 971, 3113, and 1850.

3. Find both the mean and the median for 240, 313, 189, and 270.

4. Ramon weighs 187 pounds. His brother Manny weighs 159 pounds. What is their average weight?

5. The noon temperature Monday was 69°F; Tuesday the noon temperature was 71°F; Wednesday it was 56°F; Thursday it was 63°F; and Friday it was 66°F. What was the mean noon temperature for those days?

6. In 1985 Fran made $24,700. In 1986 she made $23,900. In 1987 she made $25,800. What was her average salary for those years?

7. The Johnsons' phone bills were $25.66 in January, $33.27 in February, $19.28 in March, and $32.51 in April. What was their average phone bill for the first three months of the year?

8. The total weekly payroll of the Central Electric Company is $108,000. 450 people work at Central Electric, and 255 of them are women. What is the mean pay for the workers?

9. A car salesman sold three used cars for $1650 each, four used cars for $1875 each, and two used cars for $2100 each. What was the average price for the cars he sold?

10. Sylvia received the following GED scores: Writing Skills, 42; Social Studies, 47; Science, 44; Literature and the Arts, 50; and Mathematics, 45. What was her average score for social studies, science, and literature?

ANSWERS ARE ON PAGES 345–346.

TOPIC 2: NUMBER SERIES

A number series is a list of numbers in a special order or pattern. The numbers 1, 2, 3, 4, 5, 6 . . . form the most familiar series. The number 7 is the next ***term*** in the series.

To find a missing number of a number series, first find the pattern that changes the numbers from left to right.

EXAMPLE 1   Find the next term in the series 5, 8, 11, 14, . . .

STEP 1   Find how the series is changing. This series is changing by adding 3.

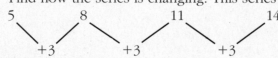

STEP 2   Add 3 to the last term.
14 + 3 = **17**

EXAMPLE 2   Find the next term in the series 2, 7, 4, 9, 6, 11, . . .

STEP 1   Find how the series is changing. This series first increases by 5 and then decreases by 3. At 11, the subtraction step is next.

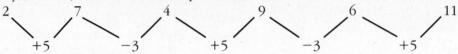

STEP 2   Subtract 3 from the last term.
11 − 3 = **8**

TIP: Pay attention to which term you are asked to find. You will not always be asked to find the "next" term.

EXAMPLE 3   Find the seventh term in the series 1, 3, 9, 27, 81, . . .

STEP 1   Find how this series is changing. This series is changing by multiplying by 3.

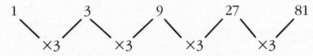

STEP 2   Find the sixth term. Multiply 81 by 3.
81 × 3 = 243

STEP 3   Find the seventh term. Multiply 243 by 3.
243 × 3 = **729**

The number series problems on the GED Test will be word problems. You will have to figure out how a series of numbers is changing and then use that knowledge to answer the question. Look at Example 4 below.

EXAMPLE 4   One day in June the 9:00 A.M. temperature was 62°F. The 10:00 A.M. temperature was 67°F. The 11:00 A.M. temperature was 72°F. If the temperature continued in the same pattern, what was the 12:00 noon temperature that day?

STEP 1   Make a diagram that shows the temperature for each hour. Then find how the series is changing. This series changes by adding 5.

STEP 2   Add 5 to the last term.
72 + 5 = **77**

EXERCISE 11

Directions: Solve each problem.

1. Find the next term in the series 6, 12, 24, 48, . . .

2. What is the sixth term in the series 81, 84, 87, 90, . . . ?

3. What is the next term in the series 32, 29, 26, 23, . . . ?

4. Find the seventh term in the series 13, 17, 21, 25, . . .

5. What is the next term in the series 10, 5, 15, 10, 20, 15, . . . ?

6. Find the eighth term in the series 100, 81, 64, 49, 36, 25, . . .

7. Find the next term in the series 5, 9, 17, 33, . . .

8. What is the eighth term in the series 2, 3, 5, 8, 12, 17, . . . ?

9. Find the next term in the series 320, 160, 80, 40, 20, . . .

10. Find the ninth term in the series 4, 8, 7, 14, 13, 26, 25, . . .

11. If the temperature in the diagram below continues in the same pattern, what will be the 7:00 P.M. temperature?

Temperature	72°F	68°F	64°F	_____
Time	4:00 P.M.	5:00 P.M.	6:00 P.M.	7:00 P.M.

12. Every month a committee is withdrawing money from a building fund at the same rate. How much will be in the account in *August*?

Balance	Month
$30,000	March
$24,000	April
$18,000	May
$12,000	June

13. This table shows the population of Bridge Creek. If the population continues in the same pattern, what will be the population of Bridge Creek in the year 2010?

Year	Pop.
1910	1,500
1930	3,000
1950	6,000
1970	12,000
1990	24,000

ANSWERS ARE ON PAGE 346.

TOPIC 3: PROPERTIES OF NUMBERS

There are three properties of numbers that you should know for the GED Test. You do not need to memorize the names of these properties, but you should be able to understand them and apply them to problems.

The Commutative Property

This property applies to both addition and multiplication. For addition it means that you can add the same two numbers in any order. The sums will be the same. For example, $6 + 3$ and $3 + 6$ both add up to 9.

We can write these properties with letters instead of numbers. You will get more practice in using letters for numbers when you work with algebra. The letters a and b stand for any two numbers.

COMMUTATIVE PROPERTY FOR ADDITION

In addition the numbers can be added in any order.

$$a + b = b + a$$

The commutative property for multiplication means that you can multiply the same two numbers in any order. The products will be the same. For example, 5×7 and 7×5 both make 35.

COMMUTATIVE PROPERTY FOR MULTIPLICATION

The commutative property for multiplication can be written in two ways:

$$a \times b = b \times a \quad \text{OR} \quad ab = ba$$

The first method uses the multiplication sign between the two letters. The second method uses no signs. When two letters stand next to each other with no signs between them, this indicates multiplication. Again, remember that a and b stand for any two numbers.

EXAMPLE   Which of the following is the same as $9 + 8$?
(1) 9×8
(2) 8×9
(3) $8 + 9$
(4) $9 - 8$

SOLUTION   Answer **(3)** is the correct choice. $9 + 8$ and $8 + 9$ both add up to 17. This is an example of the commutative property for addition.

The Associative Property

The associative property works for addition and multiplication. When you add three or more numbers, you can first add any two numbers and then add the third. The results will be the same.

ASSOCIATIVE PROPERTY FOR ADDITION
$(a + b) + c = a + (b + c)$

The parentheses group numbers together. Suppose we want to add $2 + 5 + 6$. We could first add 2 and 5 to get 7 and then add 7 and 6 to get 13. Or we could first add 5 and 6 to get 11 and then add 2 and 11 to get 13. The results are the same. If we plug in these numbers to the property above, it looks like this:

$$(2 + 5) + 6 = 2 + (5 + 6)$$
$$7 + 6 = 2 + 11$$
$$13 = 13$$

ASSOCIATIVE PROPERTY FOR MULTIPLICATION
$(ab)c = a(bc)$

In a multiplication problem, when numbers are grouped by parentheses, they can be regrouped without changing the final product. Suppose we want to solve this problem: $2 \times 3 \times 4$. We could first multiply 2×3 to get 6 and then multiply 6×4 to get 24. Or we could first multiply 3×4 to get 12 and then multiply 2×12 to get 24. For example:

$$(2 \times 3) \times 4 = 2 \times (3 \times 4)$$
$$6 \times 4 = 2 \times 12$$
$$24 = 24$$

EXAMPLE Which of the following is the same as $(10 + 12) + 15$?
(1) $10(12 + 15)$
(2) $(10 + 12)15$
(3) $10 + 15 + 12 + 15$
(4) $10 + (12 + 15)$

SOLUTION Answer **(4)** is the correct choice. We could first add 10 and 12 to get 22 and then add 22 and 15 to get 37. Or we could first add 12 and 15 to get 27 and then add 10 and 27 to get 37. This is an example of the associative property for addition.

The Distributive Property

The distributive property means that a number outside parentheses is multiplied by each number inside the parentheses. Their products are then combined according to the sign within the parentheses. You can say that the number outside parentheses is being "distributed" to both numbers on the inside.

DISTRIBUTIVE PROPERTY

The distributive property applies to both addition and subtraction.

$$a(b + c) = ab + ac$$
$$a(b - c) = ab - ac$$

Suppose we want to solve this problem: $2(6 + 3)$. The distributive property tells us that we can multiply the numbers inside the parentheses, 6 and 3, by the number outside the parentheses, 2:

$$2(6 + 3) =$$
$$(2 \times 6) + (2 \times 3) =$$
$$12 + 6 = 18$$

To check the answer, add the numbers inside the parentheses, 6 and 3, to get 9. Then multiply 9 by the number outside the parentheses. $2 \times 9 = 18$.

≡ GED Practice ≡
EXERCISE 12

Directions: Apply what you have learned about properties to choose the correct expression. Remember, a number written outside parentheses with no operation sign means multiplication.

1. Which of the following is equal to $20 + 30$?

   (1) 30×20
   (2) $30 - 20$
   (3) $30 + 30$
   (4) $30 + 20$
   (5) $20 + 20$

2. Which of the following is equal to $(5 \times 3)4$?

   (1) $(5 + 3)4$
   (2) $5(3 \times 4)$
   (3) $5(3 + 4)$
   (4) $5 + 3 \times 4$
   (5) $5 + 4 \times 3 + 4$

3. Which of the following is the same as $(9 + 7) + 4$?

   (1) $4(9 + 7)$
   (2) $9 + (7 + 4)$
   (3) $9(7 + 4)$
   (4) $7(9 + 4)$
   (5) $4(9 + 7)$

4. Which of the following is equal to $16(14 + 27)$?

   (1) $16 + 14 + 27$
   (2) $14(16 + 27)$
   (3) $27(16 + 14)$
   (4) $16 \times 14 + 27$
   (5) $(16 \times 14) + (16 \times 27)$

5. Which of the following is the same as $(3 \times 15) - (3 \times 6)$?

   (1) $3 - (15 \times 6)$
   (2) $3 \times 15 \times 6$
   (3) $3 \times 15 - 6$
   (4) $3(15 - 6)$
   (5) $15(6 - 3)$

ANSWERS ARE ON PAGE 346.

TOPIC 4: ORDER OF OPERATIONS

In many math problems you will have to perform more than one operation to get the answer. Mathematicians have agreed on a correct order to perform these operations, and it is very important that you know these rules. To see what might happen if you used an incorrect order, look at the example below:

$$10 + 4 \times 2$$

Suppose you added 10 and 4, then multiplied by 2. Your answer would be 28. However, this is an *incorrect* answer. The correct answer is found by performing the multiplication first, then adding, as shown below.

$$10 + 4 \times 2$$
$$10 + 8$$
$$18$$

Study the following **order of operations** and memorize it. Whenever you come across a problem with more than one operation, you will need to know the correct order in which to perform them.

ORDER OF OPERATIONS

When solving a problem, follow these steps in order.

1. Do operations within parentheses.

2. Do multiplication or division.

3. Do addition or subtraction.

EXAMPLE   What is the value of the expression $(4 + 8) \div 6 + 3$?

$$(4 + 8) \div 6 + 3$$
$$12 \div 6 + 3$$
$$2 + 3$$
$$5$$

STEP 1   You know from the order of operations that you need to perform the operation inside the parentheses before you do anything else. Add 4 and 8 to get 12.

STEP 2   Division should be performed before the addition. Divide 12 by 6 to get 2.

STEP 3   Add 2 to 3. The answer is **5**.

EXERCISE 13

Directions: Find the values of the following expressions.

1. $(8 \times 3) \div 4 - 6$

2. $9 + (14 - 7)$

3. $80 \div (22 - 2)$

4. $17 - (16 \div 4)$

5. $(14 \times 2) \div (5 + 2)$

ANSWERS ARE ON PAGE 346.

PROBLEM SOLVING FOR THE GED

Introducing Set-Up Questions

During a performance test a car was driven 220 miles on the highway and 88 miles on back roads. This car averaged 22 miles per gallon of gasoline. Which of the following expressions gives the number of gallons of gas the car used in this trip?

(1) $\dfrac{220 \times 88}{88}$

(2) $\dfrac{220 + 88}{22}$

(3) $220 \div 88 - 22$

(4) $20(220 + 88)$

(5) $\dfrac{88 + 22}{22}$

This problem is typical of some you will see on the GED Test. Notice that you *do not* have to do any computation in this problem. You need to know *what type* of computation is necessary, however, to get the problem right. You also need to understand and be able to use the properties of numbers you have just learned. Basically you will have to *set up* a problem without actually solving it.

Here are some hints to help you succeed with problems like this one:

1. Remember the problem-solving steps that you have learned in this chapter. Understanding the question and knowing what information you need are extremely important skills in this type of problem.

Question: How many gallons?

Information needed: 220 miles, 88 miles, 22 miles per gallon

2. Think about how you go about answering the question asked and try to put it into words.

To find the number of gallons used, you need to divide the number of miles driven by the rate of miles per gallon (mpg).

3. Once you have figured out in words how to solve the problem, plug in the appropriate numbers.

gallons used = miles driven divided by mpg

miles driven = 220 + 88

miles per gallon = 22

4. Choose the answer that expresses the correct way to set up the problem.

The horizontal fraction bar means the same as *divided by*.

(2) $\dfrac{220 + 88}{22}$

Notice the use of the division bar. The bar works like parentheses. The bar groups any numbers above it or below it. For example, in choice **(2)**, first add 220 and 88. Then divide the total by 22.

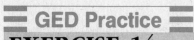

EXERCISE 14

Directions: Choose the correct solution to each problem.

1. A machine at Gaston & Company can mold 45 cylinders in one minute. A slower machine molds 30 cylinders in a minute. With both machines working at once, which of the following expressions gives the number of cylinders Gaston produces in five minutes?

   (1) $\dfrac{45 - 30}{5}$

   (2) $\dfrac{45 + 30}{5}$

   (3) $5(45 + 30)$

   (4) $(5 \times 45) - (5 \times 30)$

   (5) $(45 \div 5) + (30 \div 5)$

2. On Saturday afternoon 265 people were at the Uptown Movie Theatre. On Saturday night 304 people were there. Everyone paid $4 for a ticket. Which of the following represents the total value of the ticket sales that day?

   (1) $4 \times 265 \times 304$
   (2) $4(265 + 304)$
   (3) $265(4 + 304)$
   (4) $4 + 265 + 304$
   (5) $265 + 4(304)$

3. In February, Herb's Furniture sold 5 dining table sets at $200 each. In March, Herb sold 10 of the table sets. Which expression represents the total value of the table sets sold those two months?

   (1) $200(5 + 10)$
   (2) $5(200 + 10)$
   (3) $10(200 + 5)$
   (4) $200(5 \times 10)$
   (5) $200(10 - 5)$

4. One week Mark worked overtime for 3 hours on Wednesday and 4 hours on Thursday. For overtime Mark makes $9 an hour. Which expression tells how much Mark made in overtime for that week?

   (1) $4(3 + 9)$
   (2) $3(4 + 9)$
   (3) $9(3 + 4)$
   (4) $(4 \times 3) + 9$
   (5) $(4 \times 3) + (9 \times 3)$

5. Sharon drove for 4 hours at an average speed of 55 mph and then for 3 hours at an average speed of 40 mph. Which of the following expressions represents the total distance she drove?

   (1) $7(55 + 40)$
   (2) $55(3 + 4)$
   (3) $(3 \times 55) + (4 \times 40)$
   (4) $(4 \times 55) + (3 \times 40)$
   (5) $40(3 + 4)$

6. All but 10 dozen out of the 50 dozen eggs were sold at Marone's grocery store. Which expression represents the number of eggs that were sold?

   (1) $12(50 - 10)$
   (2) $50(12 - 10)$
   (3) $10(50 - 12)$
   (4) $(12 \times 50) - (10 \times 50)$
   (5) $12(50 + 10)$

7. Sam bought 3 shirts for $16 each and 2 pairs of pants for $24 each. Which expression represents the total price he paid for his purchases?

   (1) $(2 + 16) \times (3 + 24)$
   (2) $(3 \times 16) + (2 \times 24)$
   (3) $(2 \times 16) + (3 \times 24)$
   (4) $(22 + 24) + (2 + 3)$
   (5) $(2 \times 3) + (22 \times 24)$

8. On Monday, Marge's children collected $3.40 for charity. On Tuesday they collected $8.00, and on Wednesday and Thursday they collected $6.50 each day. Which expression represents the average amount collected on the 4 days?

   (1) $\dfrac{\$3.40 + \$8.00 + \$6.50 + \$6.50}{4}$

   (2) $\dfrac{\$3.40 + \$8.00 + \$6.50}{4}$

   (3) $\dfrac{\$3.40 + \$8.00 + \$6.50}{3}$

   (4) $\$3.40 + \$8.00 + \$6.50 + \$6.50$

   (5) $4 - (\$3.40 + \$8.00 + \$6.50 + \$6.50)$

ANSWERS ARE ON PAGE 346.

PROBLEM SOLVING REVIEW

Directions: Choose the best answer to each problem.

1. A grant of $12,500,000 is to be shared equally among 5 programs. How much will each program receive?
Which of the following best expresses the question asked in this problem?

    (1) Find the amount the five programs get altogether.
    (2) Find the amount the five programs have to share.
    (3) Find the amount each program gets in a year.
    (4) Find the amount each program gets from the grant.
    (5) Find the amount each program gets in a month.

2. Of the 420 employees of Apex, Inc., 63 regularly walk to work and 187 take public transportation. How many employees of Apex do not regularly walk to work?

    (1) 124
    (2) 233
    (3) 250
    (4) 357
    (5) 483

3. In one month the leading U.S. car manufacturer sold 259,056 cars. The second-largest manufacturer sold 120,947 cars. How many more cars did the leading manufacturer sell than the second-largest manufacturer?

    (1) 128,109
    (2) 138,009
    (3) 138,109
    (4) 139,009
    (5) 139,109

4. A year's profit of $81,480 was split evenly among the 84 employees of the Central Electric Cooperative. In addition each employee received a bonus of $200. Which operations should you use to find how much money each employee received?

    (1) Add 81,480 and 200, then divide by 84.
    (2) Multiply 81,480 by 84, then add 200.
    (3) Divide 81,480 by 84, then add 200.
    (4) Divide 81,480 by 84, then divide 200 by 84.
    (5) Add 84 and 200, then subtract it from 81,480.

5. Round off 36,498 to the nearest thousand.

    (1) 36,000
    (2) 36,500
    (3) 37,000
    (4) 37,500
    (5) 38,000

6. Craig got an oil change for $12 and bought 10 gallons of gasoline at $1.29 a gallon. To the nearest dollar, how much did Craig spend for oil and gasoline?

    (1) $12
    (2) $13
    (3) $24
    (4) $25
    (5) $26

7. Selma paid $200 down and $56 a month for 15 months for new furniture. What total amount did she pay for the furniture?

    (1) $ 256
    (2) $ 840
    (3) $ 872
    (4) $ 940
    (5) $1040

8. For the first seven months of the year Janet made $1100 a month. She got a raise and made $1300 a month for the rest of the year. Find how much she made altogether that year.

    (1) $13,200
    (2) $14,200
    (3) $14,400
    (4) $15,200
    (5) $15,600

9. Rafael drove for 6 hours at an average speed of 55 mph. Then, after he got to a big city, he drove for 2 hours at an average speed of 9 mph. How many miles did he drive altogether?

    (1) 318
    (2) 348
    (3) 385
    (4) 418
    (5) 440

10. Every day for a week Sam timed his trip home. His trips took 27, 36, 28, 39, and 40 minutes. Find the average number of minutes for these trips.

   (1) 28
   (2) 30
   (3) 32
   (4) 34
   (5) 36

11. Following are the attendance figures for each of four nights at a basketball tournament: 1024, 1263, 1137, and 1440. Find the median attendance at the games.

   (1) 1024
   (2) 1200
   (3) 1216
   (4) 1250
   (5) 1440

12. Which of the following represents the value of this expression: $30 \div 6 + (3 + 1)$?

   (1) 3
   (2) 9
   (3) 10
   (4) 13
   (5) 20

13. The chart below tells the number of homes in Central County with televisions. If the pattern continues, how many thousands of homes will have televisions in 1995?

Year	1970	1975	1980	1985	1990	1995
No. of homes with TVs (in thousands)	1	3	7	15	31	—

   (1) 63
   (2) 62
   (3) 47
   (4) 32
   (5) 31

14. Which of the following is the same as $(4 \times 9) + (4 \times 15)$?

   (1) 4 9 9 3 15
   (2) $4(9 + 15)$
   (3) $4 + 9 + 15$
   (4) $9(4 + 15)$
   (5) $15(4 + 9)$

15. Fred worked for 9 hours on Monday and 6 hours on Wednesday. He makes $12 an hour. Which expression tells how much money Fred made on those two days?

   (1) $12(9 + 6)$
   (2) $9(12 + 6)$
   (3) $6(12 + 9)$
   (4) $(12 \times 9) + (6 \times 9)$
   (5) $(12 \times 6) + 9$

ANSWERS ARE ON PAGES 346–347.

3 Decimals

WHAT ARE DECIMALS?

Decimals are parts of a whole that are expressed in tenths or multiples of tenths. Our money system is based on decimals, as is the metric system, a form of measurement that we will discuss later in the book.

In our money system dollars are represented by whole numbers. The cents, or the parts of a dollar, are written as decimals. Let's review.

dollars dimes pennies

$4 . 3 5

The 4 in $4.35 represents 4 whole dollars. The .35 represents 35 of 100 equal parts of a dollar (pennies) or 35 hundredths of a dollar. The digit 3, one place to the right of the decimal point, is in the dimes place and has a value of 30 cents. The digit 5 is in the pennies place, two places to the right of the decimal point, and has a value of 5 cents.

You already know something about decimals from handling money.

EXAMPLE 1   What is the value of the 2 in $7.82?

SOLUTION   Tell what place 2 is in. 2 is in the pennies place. The 2 has a value of **2¢**.

EXAMPLE 2   What is the value of the 8 in $7.82?

SOLUTION   Tell what place the 8 is in. 8 is in the dimes place. The 8 has a value of **80¢**.

EXERCISE 1

Directions: Find the value of each underlined digit.

1. $<u>4</u>.56 $.<u>2</u>8 $1.0<u>9</u>

2. $18.0<u>5</u> $1922.<u>4</u>3 $87.3<u>1</u>

ANSWERS ARE ON PAGE 347.

PLACE VALUE IN THE DECIMAL SYSTEM

As you saw with dollars and cents, the first place to the right of the decimal point is the dimes place. The second place to the right of the point is the pennies place. *Without* the dollar sign, the first place to the right of the point is called the **tenths place**. (A dime is one of 10 equal parts of a dollar.) The second place is called the **hundredths place**. (A penny is one of the 100 equal parts of a dollar.)

Notice that the names of the places to the right of the decimal point end with the letters *ths*. Below are the place names of the digits in 4.35 without a dollar sign.

Below is a diagram of the first six whole number places and the first six decimal places. The decimal point separates whole numbers from decimal places.

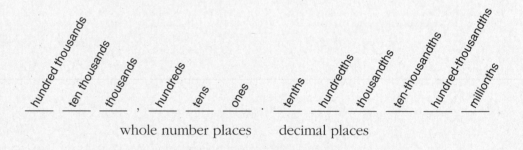

whole number places   decimal places

TIP: To learn the decimal place names, remember that 10 has one zero and tenths has one place, 100 has two zeros and hundredths has two places, 1000 has three zeros and thousandths has three places.

EXAMPLE 1   Tell how many decimal places the number 18.406 has.

SOLUTION   Count the number of digits to the right of the decimal point. 18.406 has three digits to the right of the point. 18.406 has **three** decimal places.

EXAMPLE 2   Tell what place the 6 in 18.456 is in.

SOLUTION   Count how many places to the right of the decimal point the 6 is. The 6 is three places to the right of the point. The third place to the right of the point is called **thousandths**.

EXERCISE 2

Directions: For problems 1–4, state how many decimal places each number has.

1. a. 4.907   **b.** 3806.2   **c.** 314.26

2. a. 1,976,500   **b.** 18.04   **c.** 2.87654

3. a. 59   **b.** 9.3   **c.** 4.0035

4. a. 80.538   **b.** 1264.7   **c.** 0.004502

Directions: For problems 5–8, state what place each underlined digit is in.

5. a. $8.4<u>7</u>   **b.** 1.09<u>3</u>6   **c.** $267.8<u>1</u>

6. a. 0.073<u>8</u>   **b.** $256.3<u>0</u>   **c.** 0.0004<u>5</u>

7. a. $198.1<u>3</u>   **b.** 60.<u>4</u>82   **c.** 1<u>2</u>53.4

8. a. 0.00057<u>6</u>   **b.** $93.<u>4</u>0   **c.** 7.81<u>5</u>

ANSWERS ARE ON PAGE 347.

READING DECIMALS

You have seen how place value works in the decimal system. Now you will learn how to read a decimal. As you work ahead, remember this:

> **TIP:** Remember that the place of the *last* digit of a decimal names its value.

Look at the difference between .3 and .03. In the first case the digit 3 is in the tenths place and is read as "three-tenths." In .03 the digit 3 is in the hundredths place and is read as "three-hundredths."

How is .275 read? First read the digits as though they made a whole number (275). Then look at the last decimal place. It is three places over—the thousandths. .275 is read as "two hundred seventy-five thousandths."

Finally, look at a ***mixed decimal*** such as 100.26. A mixed decimal is a number that includes both a whole number and a decimal. Read the whole number part first (100). Read the decimal point as the word *and*. Then read the decimal part (26 with the last digit in the hundredths place). 100.26 is read as "one hundred and twenty-six hundredths."

EXERCISE 3

Directions: Choose the number that is equal to the written-out number.

1. thirty-one thousandths   0.31 or .031

2. two and twelve-hundredths   2.12 or .212

3. seven hundred eighty ten-thousandths   .780 or .0780

4. one hundred and three-hundredths   0.103 or 100.03

5. seventy-one and five-tenths   71.5 or .7150

6. four and seven-thousandths   4.007 or .407

7. three and forty-nine ten-thousandths   .00349 or 3.0049

8. thirteen and thirteen-hundredths   13.13 or 0.1313

9. four hundred three and one-tenth   .4031 or 403.1

10. ten and twenty-hundredths   10.20 or 1020.0

ANSWERS ARE ON PAGE 347.

ZEROS

The digit 0 has no value, but some 0s hold other digits in their places. Look at the number below:

$$08.0060$$

The digit to the left of 8 has no use. The digit to the right of the 6 also has no use. However, the two 0s to the right of the decimal point keep the digit 6 in the thousandths place.

You can rewrite the number 08.0060 and drop two of the zeros without changing its value.

$$08.0060 = 8.006$$

The 0s in the tenths place and the hundredths place mean that there are no tenths and no hundredths. Remember, you read .6, .06, and .006 differently because they have different values.

One exception to the rule of dropping unnecessary zeros is in our money system. We write $4.50 (four dollars and fifty cents) because the system is based on hundredths of a dollar, not tenths of a dollar.

TIP: Understanding the difference between necessary and unnecessary zeros will help you throughout your work with decimals.

EXERCISE 4

Directions: Rewrite each number keeping only the necessary zeros.

1. **a.** 0.06700   **b.** 03.405   **c.** 8.0906

2. **a.** 80.0250   **b.** 0124.0090   **c.** 007.50

3. **a.** 5.0   **b.** 0.37080   **c.** 029.300

4. **a.** 06.3   **b.** 0.002300   **c.** 060.0502

ANSWERS ARE ON PAGE 347.

WRITING DECIMALS

When you begin to write a decimal, think about how many places you need:

EXAMPLE 1   Write fifty-two thousandths as a decimal.

SOLUTION   52 is a two-digit number, and the last word, *thousandths,* tells you the place value. Thousandths take three places, but 52 uses only two places. *Hold* the first place (tenths) with a zero. Fifty-two thousandths is written as **.052** or **0.052**. The zero in the units place is optional. It is often used to show that there is no whole number.

Watch for the word *and.* Remember that *and* separates whole numbers from decimals. As you recall, whole numbers with a decimal are called *mixed decimals.*

EXAMPLE 2   Write twenty-three and nine-tenths as a decimal.

SOLUTION   First write the whole number (23) and the decimal point. Then think about how many decimal places you need. Tenths are in the first decimal place to the right of the point. Twenty-three and nine-tenths is written as **23.9**.

EXERCISE 5

Directions: Write each group of words as a decimal or mixed decimal.

1. four-tenths
2. six and three-tenths
3. eighteen-hundredths
4. nine-thousandths
5. two ten-thousandths
6. thirteen-thousandths
7. ninety-six and four-tenths
8. five and sixteen-thousandths
9. seven thousand five hundred and eight-tenths
10. one hundred twenty-five thousandths
11. eighty-four and nine-thousandths
12. three hundred twelve ten-thousandths
13. two hundred four and three-hundredths
14. seventy and three hundred forty-five thousandths

ANSWERS ARE ON PAGE 347.

COMPARING DECIMALS

Which is larger, $.30 or $.04? You know that 30 cents is more than 4 cents. The decimals .30 and .04 have the same number of places. This makes them easy to compare. You know that 30 hundredths is larger than 4 hundredths because 30 is larger than 4. But how do you decide whether .031 or .31 is larger?

EXAMPLE   Which decimal is larger, 0.031 or 0.31?

STEP 1   Give the decimals the same number of places. Put a zero to the right of 0.31 to give it three places. Remember, this zero does not change the value.

┌─added zero
$$0.31 = 0.310$$

STEP 2   Compare the numbers to the right of the decimal point. Don't worry about the decimal point. 310 is greater than 31, so **0.31 is greater than 0.031**.

RULES FOR COMPARING DECIMALS

1. Give the decimals the same number of places. You can put zeros to the right of a decimal without changing its value.

2. Now that the number of places is the same, decide which decimal is larger.

EXERCISE 6

Directions: For problems 1–4, choose the larger number in each pair. Remember that your first step is to add zeros so that each number has an equal number of places.

1. a. 0.08 or 0.7   **b.** 0.62 or 0.062   **c.** 0.33 or 0.403

2. a. 0.0029 or 0.001   **b.** 0.01 or 0.101   **c.** 0.895 or 0.9

3. a. 0.8 or 0.098   **b.** 5.2 or 5.23   **c.** 0.4 or 0.0268

4. a. 0.31 or 0.295   **b.** 1.68 or 1.678   **c.** 3.004 or 3.04

5. Arrange in order from *smallest* to *largest*.

   a. 0.62, 0.062, 0.602, 0.26

   b. 0.43, 0.0034, 0.34, 0.403

   c. 0.21, 0.2, 0.305, 0.209

6. Arrange in order from *largest* to *smallest*.

   a. 0.7, 0.77, 0.67, 0.701

   b. 0.5, 0.505, 0.55, 0.511

   c. 0.112, 0.12, 0.011, 0.102

ANSWERS ARE ON PAGE 347.

PROBLEM SOLVING FOR THE GED

Comparing and Ordering

Ben has to stack cans on the shelves of the Corner Store, where he works. He wants to put the heaviest cans on the lowest shelves and increasingly lighter cans on the upper shelves. Following are the weights of the different cans Ben has to shelve: can A — 0.475 kilograms; can B — 0.5 kilograms; can C — 2 kilograms; can D — 1.75 kilograms; can E — 0.34 kilograms.

Which of the sequences lists the order in which the cans should be placed on the shelves, from lower to upper?

(1) D, A, E, B, C
(2) C, D, B, A, E
(3) D, B, E, C, A
(4) D, B, A, E, C
(5) C, E, B, D, A

This is an example of a GED-type problem where skills in comparing decimals will come in handy. Here are some hints to help you solve problems like these.

1. Make sure that the units of measurement are all the same. Sometimes you'll see problems where you'll have to convert units of measurement so that you are comparing the same things.

In this problem all weights are given in kilograms, so no conversion is necessary. Don't be concerned if you are not familiar with kilograms. Treat these units of measurement as just labels and concentrate on the numbers. You will learn more about units of measurement in Chapter 7.

2. Be sure of the *order* specified. Is it least to greatest, or greatest to least?

In this problem Ben must stack *heaviest* to *lightest*, so order the numbers from largest to smallest.

3. Follow the steps you learned for comparing decimals. In this case, give all the numbers three decimal places: A = 0.475 = .475; B = 0.5 = .500; C = 2 = 2.000; D = 1.75 = 1.750; E = 0.34 = .340.

4. Now put the numbers in order from heaviest to lightest.

C—2.000
D—1.750
B— .500
A— .475
E— .340

5. Look at the order you came up with and find the correct answer choice from the five you are given.

Answer: (2) C, D, B, A, E

EXERCISE 7

Directions: Solve each problem.

1. Following are the lengths of five pieces of galvanized pipe that Thelma needs to organize.

   piece A — 0.8 meter

   piece B — 0.95 meter

   piece C — 0.85 meter

   piece D — 0.09 meter

   piece E — 0.085 meter

   Which of the following gives these lengths in order of size from *smallest* to *largest*?

   (1) A, E, D, C, E
   (2) D, A, C, B, E
   (3) B, C, A, D, E
   (4) E, D, A, C, B
   (5) A, D, C, E, B

2. Below are the weights of 5 packages that Orville needs to sort.

   A — 0.6 lb

   B — 0.65 lb

   C — 0.5 lb

   D — 0.55 lb

   E — 0.505 lb

   Which of the following lists the packages in order from *lightest* to *heaviest*?

   (1) E, C, B, A, D
   (2) D, A, B, C, E
   (3) B, A, C, E, D
   (4) C, D, B, E, A
   (5) C, E, D, A, B

ANSWERS ARE ON PAGE 348.

ADDING AND SUBTRACTING DECIMALS

ADDITION

Think about adding money. Suppose you bought oranges for $1 and milk for 65¢. Your total bill would be $1.65. Automatically you lined up the decimal points.

$$\begin{array}{r} \$1.00 \\ +.65 \\ \hline \$1.65 \end{array}$$

Adding decimals is as easy as adding money or whole numbers.

RULES FOR ADDING DECIMALS
1. Line up the decimals with point under point.
2. Add each column and bring the decimal point straight down into each answer. Regroup to the left of the decimal point if necessary.

EXAMPLE 1   Add .8 and .4.

$$\textbf{(1)} \quad \begin{array}{r} .8 \\ +.4 \\ \hline \end{array} \qquad \textbf{(2)} \quad \begin{array}{r} .8 \\ +.4 \\ \hline 1.2 \end{array}$$

STEP 1 Line up the numbers with point under point.
STEP 2 Add the numbers and bring the decimal point straight down into the answer.

Notice in the last example that 8 tenths and 4 tenths give a sum of 12 tenths. Only one digit fits in the tenths place. Regroup the digit 1 to the units place. This is just like the regrouping you do when you add whole numbers.

EXAMPLE 2 Find the sum of 3.8, 47, .0092, and 1.83.

$$
\begin{array}{ll}
\textbf{(1)} & \begin{array}{r} 3.8 \\ 47. \\ .0092 \\ +1.83 \\ \hline \end{array}
\qquad
\textbf{(2)} & \begin{array}{r} 3.8000 \\ 47.0000 \\ .0092 \\ +1.8300 \\ \hline \mathbf{52.6392} \end{array}
\end{array}
$$

STEP 1 Line up the numbers with decimal point under decimal point. Notice that the whole number 47 is understood to have a decimal point at the right even though it is not written in the problem.
STEP 2 You may need to write zeros in the empty columns to help keep digits aligned. Add each column and bring the decimal point straight down into the answer. Regroup where necessary.

EXERCISE 8

Directions: Solve each problem. Be sure to line up the decimal points.

1. .6 + .9 =
2. .57 + .8 =
3. 16 + 9.24 + 170.3 + .369 =
4. 15.23 + 4 + 1.816 + 9.4 =
5. Add 12.3, .016, 5, and 216.
6. 4.036 + 23 + 2.19 + .084 =
7. Add 83 and 36.27.
8. $84 + $19.65 + $.23 + $1.56 =
9. Find the total of .0075, .00128, .004, and .03806.

ANSWERS ARE ON PAGE 348.

SUBTRACTION

Suppose you buy items for $1.65 at the grocery and give the cashier a five-dollar bill. How much change should you receive? As in addition, you must line up the decimal points to subtract and find the answer.

$$
\begin{array}{r}
\$5.00 \\
-1.65 \\
\hline
\$3.35
\end{array}
$$

RULES FOR SUBTRACTING

1. Use zeros to give each number the same number of decimal places. If necessary, compare the decimals to decide which is larger.

2. Line up the numbers with point under point. Be sure to put the larger number on top.

3. Subtract, regrouping if necessary. Bring the decimal point straight down into the answer.

EXAMPLE   What is the difference between .254 and .7?

(1) .254 = .254   (2)   .700
     .7   = .700   −.254
                             .446

STEP 1   Add zeros to give both numbers the same number of decimal places.
STEP 2   .700 is the larger number. Put .700 on top, regroup, and subtract.

EXERCISE 9

Directions: Solve each problem. Be sure to line up the decimal points.

1. .8 − .26 =

2. .5 − .345 =

3. 18 − .32 =

4. .09 − .075 =

5. Take .094 from .3.

6. From .008 take .0025.

7. Find the difference between .325 and .6.

8. How much more is $30 than $13.68?

9. Find the difference between 20 and 4.63.

ANSWERS ARE ON PAGE 348.

EXERCISE 10

Directions: Read each problem carefully to decide whether to add or subtract and be sure you are answering exactly what is asked for. Remember the five-step approach to problem solving you saw in Chapter 2.

1. Last season Don Johnson had a batting average of .206, which was .035 below the second baseman's average. By the end of this season Don's hitting had improved, and his average rose .095. Find his batting average at the end of the season.

2. To pay for a new sports center, the town of Troy raised $1.35 million from the state, $.85 million from the county, and $1.05 million from local businesses and individuals. The total estimated cost of the project is $4 million. How much more money does the town need?

3. A sign at a tunnel says, "height limit = 11.5 feet." When the air is low in the tires of Mark's truck, the truck is 10.65 feet tall. When the tires are full, the truck is an additional 0.2 feet high. By how much does Mark's truck clear the ceiling of the tunnel when the truck tires are full?

   (1) 0.65 ft
   (2) 0.55 ft
   (3) 0.45 ft
   (4) 0.35 ft

4. In 1980 the population of the United States was 226.8 million. In 1990 the population was 248.7 million. From 1980 to 1990 the population of the West grew by 9.6 million. By how much did the population of the rest of the country grow from 1980 to 1990?

   (1) 9.6 million
   (2) 12.3 million
   (3) 21.9 million
   (4) 31.5 million

5. The year's goal for the Central City United Fund is $5 million. By June the fund had $2.45 million, and by September it had an additional $0.95 million. Which expression tells how many millions the fund needs to reach its goal by the end of the year?

   (1) 5 + 2.45 + 0.95
   (2) (2.45 + 0.95) − 5
   (3) 5 − (2.45 + 0.95)
   (4) 2.45 − (5 − 0.95)

6. Caroline bought fourteen pints of milk for $.44 each. She also bought eight bags of chips for $1.09 each. What operations should you use to find how much she paid for everything?

   (1) Add .44 and 1.09.
   (2) Add .44 and 1.09, then multiply by the sum of 14 and 8.
   (3) Multiply 14 by the sum of 1.09 and .44.
   (4) Multiply 14 by .44, multiply 8 by 1.09, and add the two products.

ANSWERS ARE ON PAGE 349.

MULTIPLYING DECIMALS

Lou bought three pairs of socks at a cost of $1.75 a pair. To find the price of three pairs of socks, multiply the price of one pair by 3.

$$\begin{array}{r} \$1.75 \\ \times\quad 3 \\ \hline \$5.25 \end{array}$$

When you multiply a dollars-and-cents figure by a whole number, you mark off two decimal places for the cents in the answer. Now look at this example:

EXAMPLE 1   What is the product of 3.26 and .4?

(1)   3.26   **(2)**   326   **(3)**   3.26 ◄—— two places
      × .4   ×   4   × .4 ◄—— one place
                        1304   **1.304** ◄—— total of three places

STEP 1   Place the longer number on top. Put the other number beneath it, lining the numbers up at the right.

STEP 2   Multiply as you would with whole numbers.

STEP 3   Count the number of decimal places in *both* the numbers you have multiplied (3 total). Insert a decimal point so that there are 3 places to the right of it.

> **TIP:** Notice the numbers in the problem are lined up at the right. This is not the same as in addition and subtraction.

Carefully study the examples below. Look at the way each problem is written and notice where the decimal points are placed.

EXAMPLE 2   Multiply 76 by .05.

     76 ◄—— no places
× .05 ◄—— two places
3.80 ◄—— two places

Notice that in Example 2 the answer is 3.80 *or* 3.8 if you drop the unnecessary zero.

EXAMPLE 3   Find the product of 2.0413 and 0.006.

     2.0413 ◄—— four places
×   0.006 ◄—— three places
.0122478 ◄—— add a zero between the decimal point and the first number to make seven places

Notice that in Example 3 the answer had only six digits, yet the problem requires a seven-place answer. You need to add a zero between the decimal point and the first number.

> **TIP:** There are shortcuts for multiplying a decimal or mixed decimal by 10, 100, or 1000:
>
> - To multiply by 10, move the decimal point one place to the right.
>   .34 × 10 = .34 = 3.4
>
> - To multiply by 100, move the decimal point two places to the right.
>   .34 × 100 = .34 = 34
>
> - To multiply by 1000, move the decimal point three places to the right.
>   .34 × 1000 = .340 = 340

Sometimes you will see a dot (·) instead of a times sign (×) to indicate multiplication. This is just another way to show the same operation.

EXAMPLE 4   Find the product of 34.2 and 100.

$$34.2 \cdot 100 = 34.20 = \mathbf{3420}$$

Put a zero to the right of the 2 to move the decimal point two places to the right.

RULES FOR MULTIPLYING DECIMALS

1. Place the longer number on top. Put the other number underneath, lining the numbers up on the right.

2. Multiply as you would with whole numbers.

3. Count the number of decimal places in both the numbers you have just multiplied. (Decimal places are *to the right* of the decimal point.)

4. Counting from the right, insert the decimal point so that you have this total number of decimal places in your answer. Add zeros to the front of the number before placing the decimal point if you need more places.

EXERCISE 11

Directions: Solve each problem. Be careful to put the right number of decimal places in the answer.

1. .8 × .7 =

2. Multiply 20.6 by 0.3.

3. 2.09 × 0.4 =

4. 8.3 · 2.7 =

5. 0.378 × 0.6 =

6. Multiply .0004 by 30.

7. 0.8 × 0.01 =

8. Multiply 1.439 by 0.8.

9. .076 × 1.5 =

10. 4.2 · $24.80 =

11. $250 × 2.3 =

12. $1.16 × 1.25 =

13. 1.432 × 10 =

14. Multiply 0.056 by 100.

15. 0.083 × 10 =

16. Multiply 19.7 by 1000.

17. Find the product of 15 and 0.3.

18. What is the product of 143 and 2.5?

19. Find the product of 0.34 and 12.61.

20. Find the product of 1000 and 7.95.

ANSWERS ARE ON PAGE 349.

DIVIDING DECIMALS

DIVIDING DECIMALS BY WHOLE NUMBERS

The bill for three people in a restaurant came to $14.55. If they shared the bill equally, how much did each person owe? To solve this, divide the total bill by the number of people who shared it.

When you divide a decimal by a whole number, put the decimal point in the answer *directly above its position in the problem*.

$$\text{divisor} \longrightarrow 3\overline{)\$14.55} \longleftarrow \text{dividend}$$
$$\$\,4.85 \longleftarrow \text{quotient}$$

Each person owes **$4.85**.

In the rules below, the term ***dividend*** means the number being divided. The ***divisor*** is the number being divided into the dividend. The term ***quotient*** is the answer to a division problem.

RULES FOR DIVIDING A DECIMAL BY A WHOLE NUMBER

1. Put the decimal point in the quotient directly above its position in the dividend.
2. Divide as you would for whole numbers.

Study these examples carefully.

EXAMPLE 1   .168 ÷ 2 = ?

$$.084$$
$$2\overline{).168}$$

Notice the 0 in the quotient. Since 2 does not divide into 1, you must put the 8 above the 6 in the hundredths place (since you are now dividing 2 into 16). The 0 shows that there are no tenths and holds the 8 in the hundredths place.

EXAMPLE 2   Divide 29.72 by 5.

$$5.944$$
$$5\overline{)29.720}$$

Notice the extra 0 that has been added to the dividend. This zero does not change the value of the dividend. Adding a zero may allow you to carry out the answer one more decimal place and eliminate a remainder.

$$
\begin{array}{r}
5.944 \\
5\overline{)29.720} \\
\underline{25} \\
4\,7 \\
\underline{4\,5} \\
2\,2 \\
\underline{2\,0} \\
2\,0 \\
\underline{2\,0} \\
0
\end{array}
$$

TIP: There are shortcuts for dividing a number by 10, 100, or 1000. These shortcuts will be useful in your work with percents and with metric measurements.

- To divide a number by 10, move the decimal point one place to the left. $14.3 \div 10 = 1.4.3 = 1.43$

- To divide a number by 100, move the decimal point two places to the left. $14.3 \div 100 = .14.3 = .143$

- To divide a number by 1000, move the decimal point three places to the left. $14.3 \div 1000 = .014.3 = .0143$

EXERCISE 12

Directions: Solve each problem.

1. Divide 52.608 by 8.

2. Divide 9 into 758.7.

3. $14\,)\overline{10.5}$

4. .039 split 3 ways =

5. Divide 2.375 by 25.

6. $7\,)\overline{.0168}$

7. $9.6 \div 24 =$

8. $24\,)\overline{.96}$

9. $18\,)\overline{2.7}$

10. Divide 36.72 by 12.

11. $42.3 \div 100 =$

12. Divide .04 by 10.

13. Divide 1000 into 19.5.

14. $.65 \div 100 =$

ANSWERS ARE ON PAGE 350.

DIVIDING BY DECIMALS

To divide a number by a decimal, you must first change the divisor to a whole number.

EXAMPLE 1   Divide 1.842 by .06.

(1) $.06\,)\overline{1.842}$

(2) $.06.\,)\overline{1.84.2}$

(3) $\dfrac{30.7}{6\,)\overline{184.2}}$

STEP 1   Set up the problem for long division.

STEP 2   Make the divisor a whole number. Move the decimal point two places to the right. Move the decimal point in the dividend two places to the right.

STEP 3   Bring the decimal point up in the quotient directly above its new position in the dividend. Divide.

RULES FOR DIVIDING BY A DECIMAL

1. Make the divisor a whole number. Move the decimal point to the right as far as it will go.

2. Move the point in the dividend to the right *the same number of places* you moved the point in the divisor. You may need to add zeros to the dividend to move the decimal point that far.

3. Bring the decimal point up in the quotient directly above its *new* position in the dividend and divide.

Study the next examples carefully.

EXAMPLE 2   Divide .8 by .002.

$$
.002. \overline{)800.} \quad \textbf{400.}
$$

In this case we added two zeros to .8.

EXAMPLE 3   Divide 40 by .008.

(1) $.008 \overline{)40}$ **(2)** $.008. \overline{)40.000.}$ **(3)** $8 \overline{)40,000} \quad \textbf{5,000}$

STEP 1   Set up the problem for long division.
STEP 2   Make the divisor a whole number. Move the decimal point three places to the right.
STEP 3   Put a point to the right of 40. Put three zeros at the right of the point. Then move the point the same number of places to the right as you did in the divisor. Divide.

EXERCISE 13

Directions: Solve each problem.

1. 8.4 ÷ 0.2 =

2. Divide 5.25 by .5.

3. $.13 \overline{).338}$

4. .42 ÷ .028 =

5. $1.2 \overline{).324}$

6. $.04 \overline{)83.6}$

7. Divide 101.2 by 25.3.

8. 90.6 ÷ .03 =

9. 6.7 ÷ .134 =

10. Divide 64 by 1.28.

11. $.12 \overline{)96}$

12. 261 ÷ 4.35 =

ANSWERS ARE ON PAGES 350–351.

MULTIPLYING AND DIVIDING DECIMALS

The next problems let you apply your skills in multiplying and dividing decimals. These are the kinds of problems you are likely to see on the GED.

GED Practice
EXERCISE 14

Directions: Solve each problem.

1. The chart below shows the distances that three athletes are able to jump. Which operations should you use to find the average distance that the *women* are able to jump?

Cindy	5.4 feet
Paul	7.4 feet
Andrea	7.1 feet

   (1) Multiply 5.4 by 3.
   (2) Add 5.4, 7.4, and 7.1, then divide by 3.
   (3) Add 5.4 and 7.1, then divide by 3.
   (4) Add 5.4 and 7.1, then divide by 2.
   (5) Add 5.4 and 7.1.

2. On Monday, Grace worked 7 hours at her regular rate of $5.20 an hour and 2.5 hours at her overtime rate of $7.80 an hour. Choose the expression that shows how much Grace made that day.

   (1) 7($5.20 + $7.80)
   (2) 9.5($5.20 + $7.80)
   (3) $5.20(7 + 2.5)
   (4) 7($5.20) + 2.5($7.80)
   (5) $5.20 + $7.80

3. Senta drove for 2.5 hours at an average speed of 60 mph and for 1.5 hours at an average speed of 48 mph. Which expression shows the total distance she drove?

   (1) 2.5(60) + 1.5(48)
   (2) (2.5 + 1.5) + (60 + 48)
   (3) 60 × 48 × 4
   (4) 2.5(60 + 48)
   (5) 60 + 48

4. Nick cut two lengths of copper tubing each 1.45 meters long from the piece shown below. Which of the following expressions shows how long the remaining piece was?

   (1) 4 − 2 − 1.45
   (2) 2(4 − 1.45)
   (3) 4 − 2(1.45)
   (4) 4(2 − 1.45)
   (5) 4 − 1.45

   ⟵ 4 meters ⟶

ANSWERS ARE ON PAGE 351.

ROUNDING OFF DECIMALS

Suppose George works for $5.75 an hour. How much will he make in 3.5 hours? To find this amount, you would multiply $5.75 by 3.5.

$$
\begin{array}{r}
\$5.75 \\
\times \quad 3.5 \\
\hline
2\,875 \\
17\,25 \\
\hline
\$20.125
\end{array}
$$

Our money system has only two decimal places. In this problem you need to *round off* $20.125 to the nearest hundredth. In some problems you may be asked to find an answer to the nearest tenth, hundredth, thousandth, etc.

Rounding off decimals is almost the same as rounding off whole numbers.

RULES FOR ROUNDING OFF DECIMALS

1. Underline the digit in the place you are rounding off to.

2. If the digit to the right is 5 or more, add 1 to the underlined digit.

3. If the digit to the right is less than 5, leave the underlined digit as it is.

4. Drop the digits to the right of the underlined digit.

EXAMPLE   Round off 8.1942 to the nearest thousandth.

STEP 1   Underline the digit in the thousandths place. 8.194̲2
STEP 2   Look at the digit to the right of the underlined digit. Since the digit is less than 5, keep the underlined digit and drop the digit at the right. **8.194**

EXERCISE 15

Directions: Round off each of the following decimals to the place indicated.

1. Adrian pays $1.298 for a gallon of gasoline. To the nearest penny, what does he have to pay for 12 gallons of gas?

2. Lois drove for 3.5 hours at an average speed of 45 miles an hour. Find how far she drove to the nearest ten miles.

3. Frank works for 37.5 hours a week at a rate of $7.85 an hour. To the nearest dollar, how much does he make in a week?

4. An inch is equal to 2.54 centimeters. How many centimeters are there in 12 inches? Round off your answer to the nearest centimeter.

5. Find the cost of 2.4 pounds of a cheese that sells for $3.49 a pound. Round your answer to the nearest penny.

ANSWERS ARE ON PAGE 351.

REPEATING DECIMALS

Some decimal division problems don't work out evenly. For instance, if you divide .20 by 3, you get a repeating decimal, no matter how many zeros you add to the dividend.

$$\begin{array}{r} .0666 \\ 3\overline{)\,.2000} \end{array}$$

A common way to handle a repeating decimal is to round off your answer. Generally a problem will tell you what place to round off to. The answer for the example above, rounded off to the nearest thousandth, is .067.

EXAMPLE Find $1 \div .3$ to the nearest hundredth.

(1) $.3\overline{)1}$ **(2)** $\begin{array}{r} 3.333 \\ .3\overline{)1.0} \end{array}$ **(3)** $3.333 \rightarrow 3.33$

STEP 1 Set up the division problem.
STEP 2 Move the decimal point one place to the right in both divisor and dividend. Divide. Carry out the division to one more place than the answer requires so that you can round off.
STEP 3 Underline the digit in the hundredths place. Look at the digit to the right and round off. To the nearest hundredth, 3.333 is **3.33**.

EXERCISE 16

Directions: Divide and round off each problem to the decimal place indicated.

1. $.4 \div 15$ to the nearest hundredth

2. $.02 \div 3$ to the nearest hundredth

3. $.5 \div 6$ to the nearest tenth

4. $.3 \div .8$ to the nearest tenth

ANSWERS ARE ON PAGE 351.

PROBLEM SOLVING FOR THE GED

Introducing Item Sets

Some passages on the GED Math Test give enough information to produce several questions. The challenge is to pick the information you need to answer each particular question. The skills you need to solve these "item sets" are an extension of the skills you developed on page 24 when you learned to sort out necessary and unnecessary information.

Below is a sample passage followed by several typical questions. The questions are answered as examples for you. Read the passage and the questions carefully.

Examples 1–3 refer to the following situation:

Wendy and Don have seen two apartments that they like. Apartment A has monthly rent of $340.50 for the first year. The rent for the second year will be an additional $35.50 a month. The rent for apartment A includes heat. The rent for apartment B is $295 a month for two years. The rent for apartment B does not include heat. The landlord for apartment B says that the heating bills for the apartment average $55.50 a month.

EXAMPLE 1 Find the rent for apartment A for the second year.

INFORMATION
    NEEDED First year's monthly rent of $340.50, additional charge of $35.50 a month, and number of months in a year (12)
  SOLUTION **a.** $340.50 + $35.50 = $376
            b. 12 × $376 = **$4512**

EXAMPLE 2 If the landlord's estimate for the heating costs of apartment B are correct, what is the total cost of renting and heating apartment B for two years?

INFORMATION
    NEEDED Monthly rent of $295, monthly heating estimate of $55.50, and number of months in two years (24)
  SOLUTION **a.** $295 + $55.50 = $350.50
            b. 24 × $350.50 = **$8412**

Sometimes a problem introduces information that you must apply to the information in the passage you have read.

EXAMPLE 3 Don and Wendy take home $1360 a month. How much would they have left over each month after paying rent for the first year in apartment A?

INFORMATION
    NEEDED Monthly take-home pay of $1360 and monthly rent of $340.50
  SOLUTION $1360 − $340.50 = **$1019.50**

As you can see from these examples, it is very useful to think about and jot down the information you are going to need to solve a problem.

EXERCISE 17

Directions: Questions 1–5 refer to the following passage.

Store X sells a set of living room furniture for $1199.75. It offers a $100 rebate for paying cash. Store X will also sell the furniture for $150 down and installments of $45.50 a month for three years. Store Y sells the same furniture for $1279.99. Store Y offers no rebate for paying cash. Its terms for payment are $200 down and installments of $54.60 a month for two years.

1. If a buyer is considering paying cash, how much can he save by buying the furniture at store X rather than store Y?

   Information needed:

   Solution:

2. What is the total price of the furniture from store X if it is purchased in installments?

   Information needed:

   Solution:

3. What is the total price of the furniture purchased in installments from store Y?

   Information needed:

   Solution:

4. The Muellers decided to buy the furniture from the store with the lower total cost under the installment plan. How much money were they able to save?

   Information needed:

   Solution:

5. How much more does store X get for the furniture from a buyer who pays in installments than from a buyer who pays cash?

   Information needed:

   Solution:

Directions: Questions 6 and 7 refer to the following passage.

Ron is a builder. He tells the Smiths that he can build a garage for them for $15,000. He estimates that, working with an assistant, he can complete the job in 40 hours. Ron pays his assistant $8.50 an hour. Ron estimates that materials and expenses, not including his assistant, will cost $10,500.

6. If the work is done in 40 hours as planned, how much will the assistant get paid?

   Information needed:

   Solution:

7. If Ron's estimates are correct, how much profit will he make on this job?

   Information needed:

   Solution:

ANSWERS ARE ON PAGES 351–352.

DECIMALS REVIEW

Directions: For questions 1–10, answer each question.

1. Tell what place the 8 in 4026.385 is in.

2. Choose the number that is equal to seventy and sixteen-thousandths:
   .7016   70.16   70.016

3. Rewrite 060.04300 and omit unnecessary zeros.

4. Write the mixed decimal four hundred eight and fifteen ten-thousandths.

5. Arrange the following decimals in order from *smallest* to *largest*: .6, .06, .606, .066.

6. Find the sum of 36, 2.93, .065, and 4.

7. Take .0063 from .08.

8. Find the product of 3.2 and .005.

9. What is .405 divided by 15?

10. What is the quotient of 9 divided by .045?

Directions: Questions 11–20 include whole numbers as well as decimals. Choose the correct answer to each problem. Remember the problem-solving skills you have learned so far.

11. In 1980 the population of Florida was 9.75 million. By 1990 the population had increased 3.19 million. What was the population of Florida in 1990?

   (1) 14.24 million
   (2) 13.95 million
   (3) 12.94 million
   (4) 11.85 million
   (5) 3.2 million

12. Allen took a board the length of board A, below, and cut off a piece the length of board B. What was the length in yards of the remaining piece?

   (1) 1.25
   (2) 1.75
   (3) 2.25
   (4) 2.75
   (5) 4.75

   3 yards   1.75 yards

   Board A   Board B

13. David drove 223 miles on 12 gallons of gasoline. To the nearest tenth, find the average number of miles he drove on one gallon of gasoline.

(1) 20.2
(2) 19.4
(3) 18.6
(4) 18.2
(5) 16.8

14. The rate schedule below shows the hourly electricity costs for various household appliances. The Walek family has the television turned on for an average of 52 hours a week. How much do the Waleks pay each week to operate their television?

(1) $1.77
(2) $1.98
(3) $2.60
(4) $5.40
(5) $8.60

Electricity (cost per hour)	
iron	$.005
television	.034
clock	.010
radio	.022

15. All but 56.3 pounds of topsoil were sold at a sale. If the store began with 100 pounds of the topsoil and charged $.59 a pound, how much money did it make?

(1) $ 25.00
(2) $ 25.78
(3) $ 44.29
(4) $ 59.00
(5) $257.60

16. The number of hits a baseball player gets is divided by the number of times he goes to bat to give his batting average. Last season Bill was at bat 75 times, and he made 22 hits. Find his batting average. Round off your answer to the nearest thousandth.

(1) .356
(2) .333
(3) .320
(4) .299
(5) .293

17. Arrange the following lengths of pipe in order from *smallest* to *largest*:

A — 1.8 yard
B — 0.75 yard
C — 1.75 yard
D — 0.125 yard
E — 1.125 yard

(1) A, B, D, C, E
(2) A, B, C, E, D
(3) D, B, C, E, A
(4) D, B, E, C, A
(5) B, D, E, C, A

18. Charlene bought 5 yards of 36-inch-wide material for $7.80 a yard and 2.5 yards of 42-inch-wide material for $8.40 a yard. How much did she pay altogether for the material?

    (1) $81.00
    (2) $63.36
    (3) $60.00
    (4) $55.80
    (5) $50.00

19. The distance between Manny's workplace and his home is 3.6 miles. The distance between his home and his exercise class is three times that far in the same direction. How can you find out how much farther from home Manny's exercise class is than his workplace?

    (1) Multiply 3.6 by 3.
    (2) Divide 3.6 by 3.
    (3) Multiply 3.6 by 3, then subtract 3.6.
    (4) Divide 3.6 by 3, then subtract 3.6.
    (5) Add 3.6 and 3.

20. Pete is a cabinetmaker. He charges $125 for a small bookcase and $190 for a large one. One month he sold 5 small bookcases and 3 large ones. Which expression represents the gross amount Pete got for the sale of the bookcases?

    (1) (125 + 5)(190 + 3)
    (2) 125(3 + 5) + 190
    (3) 3(125) + 5(190)
    (4) 5(125) + 3(190)
    (5) 125(190) + 3(5)

Directions: Questions 21–24 refer to the following situation and mileage map.

Alfonso drove from El Paso to Dallas in 13 hours. Then he drove from Dallas to Houston in 4 hours. Finally he drove from Houston back to El Paso in 15.5 hours. Over the entire trip Alfonso bought 70 gallons of gasoline at a cost of $1.38 per gallon.

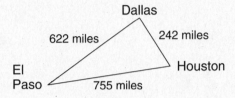

21. Find the total number of hours Alfonso spent driving on this trip.

    (1) 17
    (2) 19.5
    (3) 28.5
    (4) 30
    (5) 32.5

22. How much did Alfonso spend for gas for the entire trip?

    (1) $ 66.60
    (2) $ 70
    (3) $ 85.60
    (4) $ 96.60
    (5) $138

23. The drive from Houston back to El Paso took how many hours less than the drive from El Paso to Houston by way of Dallas?

    (1) 3
    (2) 2.5
    (3) 2
    (4) 1.5
    (5) 1

24. To the nearest unit, what was Alfonso's average speed in miles per hour for the trip from El Paso to Dallas?

    (1) 42
    (2) 48
    (3) 50
    (4) 55
    (5) 58

ANSWERS ARE ON PAGES 352–353.

4 Fractions

WRITING FORMS OF FRACTIONS

A *fraction*, like a decimal, is a way of showing a part of a whole. The picture below shows a circle divided into four equal parts. Three of these parts are shaded. We can say that three-fourths of the circle is shaded.

$\frac{3}{4}$ ← The **numerator** tells how many parts are shaded.

← The **denominator** tells how many equal parts the whole is divided into.

With fractions any number except 0 can be in the denominator. In other words, the whole can be divided into any number of equal parts. Notice how fractions are different from decimals. Decimals divide a whole into tenths, hundredths, thousandths, etc. Fractions are useful because they can divide a whole into thirds, eighths, seventeenths, or any other number.

EXAMPLE   Write a fraction that shows what part of the figure at the right is shaded.

$\frac{2}{3}$ shaded parts (the numerator)
total equal parts (the denominator)

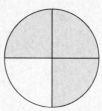

SOLUTION   Count the total number of equal parts that the figure is divided into. There are 3 equal parts. 3 is the denominator. Now count the number of shaded parts. 2 parts are shaded. 2 is the numerator. $\frac{2}{3}$ of the figure is shaded.

> **TIP:** You may see fractions written vertically, with the numerator over the denominator ($\frac{2}{3}$). You may also see fractions written horizontally, with a slash between the numerator and denominator (2/3). You should be familiar with both forms.

79

There are three uses of fractions you should know:

1. **as a part of a whole**
   $\frac{2}{3}$ of this figure is shaded

2. **as a part of a group**
   2 out of 3, or $\frac{2}{3}$ of this group, is shaded

3. **as division**
   The fraction bar also means 2 divided by 3. $\frac{2}{3}$

There are also three facts about fractions that you should know:

1. Any number over itself is equal to 1.

   $\frac{4}{4} = 1$ $\frac{1342}{1342} = 1$ $\frac{20}{20} = 1$

2. Any number with zero as a numerator equals zero.

   $\frac{0}{4} = 0$ $\frac{0}{1002} = 0$ $\frac{0}{90} = 0$

3. A fraction with a zero in the denominator has *no* meaning.

EXERCISE 1

Directions: Write a fraction that tells what part of each circle is shaded.

1.   2.   3.   4.   5.

ANSWERS ARE ON PAGE 353.

MIXED NUMBERS

A ***mixed number*** is a whole number and a fraction.

EXAMPLE   Write a mixed number that shows how many circles are shaded.

STEP 1   Count the number of completely shaded circles. 2 circles are completely shaded. 2 is the whole number.

STEP 2   Look at the partially shaded circle. The circle is divided into 4 equal parts. 4 is the denominator. 1 part of the circle is shaded. 1 is the numerator. Altogether, $\mathbf{2\frac{1}{4}}$ circles are shaded.

EXERCISE 2

Directions: Write a mixed number that tells how many wholes and parts in each set are shaded.

1.

4.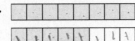

2.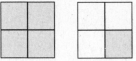

5.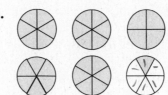

3.

6.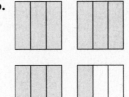

ANSWERS ARE ON PAGE 353.

PROPER AND IMPROPER FRACTIONS

A **_proper fraction_** is a fraction in which the numerator is smaller than the denominator. $\frac{2}{3}$, $\frac{99}{100}$, and $\frac{1}{5}$ are examples of proper fractions. The value of a proper fraction is always less than 1. This is because a fraction is a part of one whole.

An **_improper fraction_** is a fraction in which the numerator is as large as or larger than the denominator. $\frac{3}{3}$ and $\frac{6}{5}$ are examples of improper fractions. The value of an improper fraction is either equal to 1 or greater than 1.

EXAMPLE 1 Write an improper fraction that tells what part of the figure at the right is shaded.

$$\frac{3}{3}$$

SOLUTION The figure is divided into 3 equal parts. 3 is the denominator. 3 parts of the figure are shaded. 3 is also the numerator.

EXAMPLE 2   There are 25 students in Joe's math class. 13 of the students are women. What fraction of the class is women?

SOLUTION   In a problem like this, think of writing a fraction as putting a part over the whole. The denominator tells the total number of students in the class (the whole). 25 is the denominator. The numerator tells the number of women in the class (the part). 13 is the numerator. $\frac{13}{25}$ of the class is women.

EXAMPLE 3   Write an improper fraction that tells how many circles at the right are shaded.

$\frac{9}{4}$

SOLUTION   Remember that the denominator tells how many parts each whole is divided into. Each circle here is divided into 4 equal parts. 4 is the denominator. Altogether, 9 pieces of the circles are shaded. 9 is the numerator. $\frac{9}{4}$ of the circles are shaded.

EXERCISE 3

Directions: Write an improper fraction that tells how many parts in each set of figures are shaded.

1.

4.

1/2

2.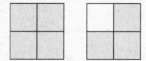

5.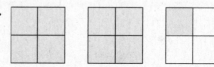

3.

6.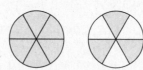

ANSWERS ARE ON PAGE 353.

EXERCISE 4

Directions: Solve each problem.

1. A yard has 3 feet. What fraction of a yard is one foot?

2. A foot has 12 inches. What fraction of a foot is 5 inches?

3. Mr. Allen makes $800 a month. His rent is $199 a month. Rent is what fraction of Mr. Allen's monthly salary?

4. Pete got 7 items wrong out of 50 on a test. What fraction of the total number of items did Pete get wrong?

5. Nina needs $200 for a new cassette deck. So far she has saved $137. What fraction of the price has she saved so far?

6. Frank ran in a 24-mile race. At the end of the first hour he had completed 11 miles. What fraction of the race did Frank complete by the end of the first hour?

7. Together Saturday and Sunday make up what fraction of a week?

ANSWERS ARE ON PAGE 353.

REDUCING FRACTIONS

Reducing means expressing a fraction in a simpler way. Look at the two circles below. The circle at the left has six out of eight parts shaded. The circle at the right has three out of four parts shaded. But as you can see, both circles have the same amount of shaded space. This means that $\frac{6}{8}$ is equal to $\frac{3}{4}$.

$\frac{6}{8}$ shaded $\frac{3}{4}$ shaded

Reducing a fraction means writing it an easier way—with smaller numbers. Reducing a fraction does not change its value. A reduced fraction is equal to the original fraction, just as $\frac{6}{8}$ is equal to $\frac{3}{4}$ above.

How do you reduce a fraction like $\frac{6}{8}$? Look at both the numerator and the denominator and decide if there is a number that will divide evenly into each. As you know, 2 will divide evenly into both 6 and 8. Divide both numerator and denominator by 2:

$$\frac{6 \div 2}{8 \div 2} = \frac{3}{4}$$

While reducing changes the numbers in a fraction, it does not change its value. Two fractions with the same value are called ***equivalent fractions***. $\frac{6}{8}$ and $\frac{3}{4}$ are equivalent fractions. The fraction $\frac{3}{4}$ is the reduced form of $\frac{6}{8}$.

RULES FOR REDUCING FRACTIONS
1. Divide both the numerator and the denominator by the same number.
2. Check the result to see whether another number will divide evenly into both the new numerator and the new denominator.

When a fraction cannot be reduced further, it is reduced to **lowest terms**. Following are some hints for reducing fractions.

> **TIP:** If both the numerator and the denominator are even numbers, you can reduce by 2.

EXAMPLE 1 Reduce $\frac{6}{10}$ to lowest terms.

STEP 1   6 and 10 are even numbers. Divide both 6 and 10 by 2.

$$\frac{6 \div 2}{10 \div 2} = \frac{3}{5}$$

STEP 2   Check $\frac{3}{5}$ to see whether another number will divide evenly into both. No other number divides evenly into both 3 and 5. $\frac{3}{5}$ is reduced to lowest terms.

EXAMPLE 2 Reduce $\frac{16}{24}$ to lowest terms.

STEP 1   16 and 24 are even numbers. Divide both by 2.

$$\frac{16 \div 2}{24 \div 2} = \frac{8}{12}$$

STEP 2 $\frac{8}{12}$ can be reduced more. Divide both 8 and 12 by 4. $\frac{2}{3}$ is reduced to lowest terms.

$$\frac{8 \div 4}{12 \div 4} = \frac{2}{3}$$

Notice that in the last example we could have divided 16 and 24 by 8.

$$\frac{16 \div 8}{24 \div 8} = \frac{2}{3}$$

Find the *largest* number to go evenly into both numerator and denominator.

> **TIP:** If one number in a fraction ends with a 5 and the other ends with a 0, or if both numbers end with 5, you can reduce by 5.

EXAMPLE 3 Reduce $\frac{25}{70}$ to lowest terms.

$$\frac{25 \div 5}{70 \div 5} = \frac{5}{14}$$

EXERCISE 5

Directions: Reduce each fraction to lowest terms.

1. $\frac{6}{10} =$ $\frac{4}{6} =$ $\frac{14}{20} =$ $\frac{4}{32} =$ $\frac{18}{36} =$ $\frac{18}{24} =$

2. $\frac{25}{35} =$ $\frac{45}{50} =$ $\frac{15}{40} =$ $\frac{45}{60} =$ $\frac{30}{45} =$ $\frac{10}{25} =$

ANSWERS ARE ON PAGE 353.

TIP: If both numbers in a fraction end with 0, you can reduce by 10 or a multiple of 10.

EXAMPLE 4   Reduce $\frac{30}{80}$ to lowest terms.

$$\frac{30 \div 10}{80 \div 10} = \frac{3}{8}$$

EXERCISE 6

Directions: Reduce each fraction to lowest terms.

$\frac{70}{100} =$ $\frac{50}{60} =$ $\frac{80}{160} =$ $\frac{40}{200} =$ $\frac{30}{200} =$ $\frac{50}{250} =$

ANSWERS ARE ON PAGE 353.

Sometimes it is hard to find a number that divides evenly into both the numerator and the denominator. In those cases you may simply have to use the "trial and error" method. Just keep trying different numbers until you find one that divides evenly into both numerator and denominator. The better you know the multiplication table, the more easily you will be able to reduce fractions.

EXAMPLE 5   Reduce $\frac{49}{56}$ to lowest terms.

STEP 1   Look at the numerator and denominator and try to find a number that goes evenly into both. You may have to try a few different numbers before you come up with one that works. Since 7 works, divide both 49 and 56 by 7.

$$\frac{49 \div 7}{56 \div 7} = \frac{7}{8}$$

STEP 2   Check to see whether another number divides evenly into both 7 and 8. No other number divides evenly into both. $\frac{7}{8}$ is reduced to lowest terms.

EXERCISE 7

Directions: Reduce each fraction to lowest terms.

$\frac{7}{28} =$ $\frac{9}{30} =$ $\frac{27}{45} =$ $\frac{22}{33} =$ $\frac{17}{34} =$ $\frac{13}{39} =$

ANSWERS ARE ON PAGE 353.

CHECKING YOUR WORK

A good way to check whether you have reduced correctly is to find the cross products. The **_cross products_** are the numerator of the first fraction multiplied by the denominator of the second and the denominator of the first fraction multiplied by the numerator of the second. When reducing is done correctly, the cross products are equal.

For example, look at $\frac{16}{20} = \frac{4}{5}$.

$\frac{16}{20} \times \frac{4}{5}$

The first cross product is $16 \times 5 = 80$.

The second cross product is $20 \times 4 = 80$.

Since the cross products are the same, $\frac{4}{5}$ is correct. Checking the cross products does not guarantee that a fraction is reduced to lowest terms, but it does guarantee that the reducing was correct.

WHY REDUCE FRACTIONS TO LOWEST TERMS?

When we use fractions in everyday life, they are most often reduced to lowest terms. You rarely see a recipe calling for $\frac{4}{8}$ of a cup of sugar; it asks for the same amount in lowest terms— $\frac{1}{2}$ cup. This is because smaller numbers are easier to work with. Likewise, on tests like the GED Math Test, the answer choices you will see are reduced to lowest terms. Sometimes, after doing your computation in a problem, you will need to reduce your answer to find the correct answer choice. This is why reducing is an important skill to practice.

WRITING FRACTIONS: WORD PROBLEMS

Remember that a fraction expresses a part of some whole. The _whole_ will be represented in the _denominator_; the _part_ of the whole is the _numerator_.

Sometimes the whole is not given in a problem. Before you can write the fraction correctly, you need to determine what the whole is.

EXAMPLE   Rose got two problems wrong and eight problems right on a quiz. What fraction of the problems did she get right?

STEP 1   The whole in this problem is the total number of problems on the quiz. You can figure out that the total is the number of problems Rose got wrong plus the number she got right.
$2 + 8 = 10$

STEP 2   Make a fraction with the total number of problems (10) as the denominator. Now put the part that she got right (8) in the numerator.

$$\frac{\text{problems right}}{\text{total problems}} \qquad \frac{8}{10}$$

STEP 3   Reduce to lowest terms. Rose got $\frac{4}{5}$ of the problems right.

$$\frac{8}{10} = \frac{4}{5}$$

> **TIP:** Your first step in writing fractions should always be to determine what the *whole* is and make that number your denominator.

EXERCISE 8

Directions: Solve each problem. Be sure each answer is reduced to lowest terms.

1. There are 6 women and 9 men in Martin's math class.
   a. What fraction of the class is women?
   b. What fraction of the class is men?
   c. One night three students were absent. What fraction of the class was absent?

2. Last season the Consolidated Electric softball team played 24 games and won 18.
   a. What fraction of the games did they win?
   b. What fraction of the games did they lose?

3. Ellen bought a coat on sale for $60. This was $30 off the original price.
   a. What was the original price?
   b. What fraction of the original price did Ellen save?
   c. What fraction of the original price did Ellen pay?

4. The Jacksons are driving from Center City to Westerville. They stop to eat after 175 miles. They still have another 125 miles to go.
   a. What is the total distance from Center City to Westerville?
   b. What fraction of the drive had they completed when they stopped to eat?
   c. What fraction of the drive did they have left to complete after they ate?

5. Carmen takes home $1200 a month. She spends $300 a month for rent, $450 a month for food, and $150 a month on car payments.
   a. What fraction of her income does Carmen spend for rent?
   b. What fraction of her income does she spend for food?
   c. What fraction of her income does she spend on car payments?
   d. Carmen saves $120 every month. What fraction of her income does she save?

ANSWERS ARE ON PAGE 353.

CHANGING IMPROPER FRACTIONS TO WHOLE OR MIXED NUMBERS

The picture at the right shows a box with four parts shaded. We can say that $\frac{4}{4}$ of the box is shaded or that 1 whole box is shaded. The number $\frac{4}{4}$ is an improper fraction. 1 is a whole number.

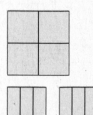

The picture at the right shows two boxes, each of which is divided into thirds. We can say that $\frac{5}{3}$ boxes are shaded or that $1\frac{2}{3}$ boxes are shaded.

To change an improper fraction to a mixed number or a whole number, divide. The fraction bar means to divide the numerator by the denominator.

EXAMPLE   Change $\frac{20}{6}$ to a mixed number.

(1) $\quad 6\overline{)20} \atop \underline{18} \atop 2 \atop 3$
(2) $\quad 6\overline{)20} \atop \underline{18} \atop 2 \atop 3\frac{2}{6}$
(3) $\quad 3\frac{2}{6} = 3\frac{1}{3}$

STEP 1   Divide the denominator (6) into the numerator (20).
STEP 2   Write the remainder over the denominator.
STEP 3   Reduce $\frac{2}{6}$ to $\frac{1}{3}$.

CHANGING IMPROPER FRACTIONS TO WHOLE OR MIXED NUMBERS

1. Divide the denominator into the numerator.

2. Write the remainder as a fraction. Put the remainder over the original denominator.

3. Reduce the remaining fraction if necessary.

EXERCISE 9

Directions: For problems 1–4, write an improper fraction and then a mixed number that express the parts of the figures that are shaded. Reduce your answer to lowest terms.

1.

2.

3.

4.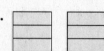

Directions: For problems 5–7, change each improper fraction to a whole or mixed number. Reduce any remaining fractions.

5. $\frac{15}{9} =$ $\frac{36}{8} =$ $\frac{13}{5} =$ $\frac{31}{6} =$

6. $\frac{6}{2} =$ $\frac{28}{16} =$ $\frac{15}{15} =$ $\frac{24}{18} =$

7. $\frac{7}{4} =$ $\frac{21}{3} =$ $\frac{50}{12} =$ $\frac{21}{6} =$

ANSWERS ARE ON PAGES 353–354.

ADDING LIKE FRACTIONS AND MIXED NUMBERS

When you add decimals, you must add tenths to tenths, hundredths to hundredths, and so on. Fractions are similar. You must add like fractions. ***Like fractions*** are fractions with the same denominators. $\frac{1}{5}$ and $\frac{2}{5}$ are like fractions. $\frac{2}{3}$ and $\frac{3}{4}$ are unlike fractions. When you add like fractions, the answer has the denominator of the fractions you added.

EXAMPLE 1   Add $\frac{1}{5} + \frac{2}{5}$.

SOLUTION   Since the denominators are the same, add the numerators: $1 + 2 = 3$. Then put this total over the denominator. $\frac{3}{5}$ is reduced to lowest terms.

$$\frac{1}{5} + \frac{2}{5} = \frac{3}{5}$$

EXAMPLE 2   Find the sum of $\frac{7}{8}$ and $\frac{3}{8}$.

STEP 1   Since the denominators are the same, add the numerators and put the total over the denominator.

$$\frac{7}{8} + \frac{3}{8} = \frac{10}{8}$$

STEP 2   Change the improper fraction to a mixed number and reduce.

$$\frac{10}{8} = 1\frac{2}{8} = \mathbf{1\frac{1}{4}}$$

RULES FOR ADDING LIKE FRACTIONS

1. Add the numerators of each fraction and put the total over the denominator used in both fractions.

2. If the answer is an improper fraction, change it to a mixed number. Reduce if you can.

When you're adding mixed numbers, add the whole numbers and fractions separately, then combine them at the end.

EXAMPLE 3   Add $7\frac{5}{12}$ and $8\frac{11}{12}$.

(1) $7\frac{5}{12}$ **(2)** $\frac{16}{12}=1\frac{4}{12}$ **(3)** $15 + 1\frac{4}{12}=16\frac{4}{12}=\mathbf{16\frac{1}{3}}$

$+8\frac{11}{12}$

$15\frac{16}{12}$

STEP 1   Since the denominators are the same, add the numerators and put the total over the denominator. Then add the whole numbers.

STEP 2   Change the improper fraction to a mixed number.

STEP 3   Add the whole number part of the answer to the mixed number and reduce.

TIP: Fraction addition problems can be written horizontally (with the numbers to the side of each other) or vertically (with one number under the other). In mixed number problems it is easier to solve the problems vertically. This makes it easy to separate the whole number parts of the problem from the fraction parts.

EXERCISE 10

Directions: Solve each problem.

1. $\frac{2}{5}+\frac{3}{5}=$ $\frac{2}{9}+\frac{4}{9}=$ $\frac{8}{15}+\frac{11}{15}=$

2. $\frac{5}{8}+\frac{5}{8}=$ $9\frac{3}{10}+4\frac{1}{10}=$ $10\frac{2}{3}+2\frac{1}{3}=$

3. $6\frac{5}{9}$ $1\frac{7}{8}$ $\frac{5}{16}$

$+7\frac{8}{9}$ $+20\frac{3}{8}$ $+\frac{7}{16}$

4. $\frac{3}{4}$ $2\frac{7}{12}$ $5\frac{4}{9}$

$\frac{1}{4}$ $4\frac{11}{12}$ $4\frac{5}{9}$

$+\frac{3}{4}$ $+9\frac{5}{12}$ $+3\frac{8}{9}$

ANSWERS ARE ON PAGE 354.

SUBTRACTING LIKE FRACTIONS

When you subtract decimals, you take tenths from tenths, hundredths from hundredths, and so on. The fractions you subtract must also have the same denominators. The difference between $\frac{4}{5}$ and $\frac{3}{5}$ is $\frac{1}{5}$.

EXAMPLE Subtract $3\frac{9}{16}$ from $10\frac{15}{16}$.

$$10\frac{15}{16}$$
$$-\ 3\frac{9}{16}$$
$$\overline{7\frac{6}{16}} = 7\frac{3}{8}$$

STEP 1 Subtract the numerators and put the difference over the denominator.
STEP 2 Subtract the whole numbers and reduce.

RULES FOR SUBTRACTING LIKE FRACTIONS AND MIXED NUMBERS

1. Subtract the numerators and put the difference over the denominator.

2. Subtract the whole numbers and reduce the fraction if you can.

EXERCISE 11

Directions: Solve each problem. Be sure every answer is reduced to lowest terms.

1. $\frac{5}{8} - \frac{1}{8} =$ $8\frac{5}{6} - 2\frac{1}{6} =$ $4\frac{7}{8} - 2\frac{3}{8} =$

2. $10\frac{4}{5} - 8\frac{1}{5} =$ $\frac{19}{20} - \frac{13}{20} =$ $6\frac{13}{15} - 2\frac{4}{15} =$

3. $\frac{25}{36} - \frac{17}{36} =$ $8\frac{5}{6} - 1\frac{1}{6} =$ $4\frac{17}{18} - 4\frac{5}{18} =$

ANSWERS ARE ON PAGE 354.

REGROUPING WITH LIKE DENOMINATORS

Sometimes when you subtract fractions, you will need to regroup from a whole number to get an answer. For example, how do you subtract $8\frac{1}{4}$ from 10?

$$10$$
$$-\ 8\frac{1}{4}$$

As you know from your work with subtracting fractions, you need to subtract fractions before you subtract whole numbers. Since there is no fraction to subtract $\frac{1}{4}$ from, you must regroup 1 from the 10. Now you will be subtracting $\frac{1}{4}$ from 1.

To make this subtraction easier, write 1 as $\frac{4}{4}$. As you recall, any number over itself is equal to 1. We write it as $\frac{4}{4}$ because we need to subtract $\frac{1}{4}$ from it, and you must always subtract *like fractions*. Now the problem looks like this:

$$9\frac{4}{4}$$
$$-\ 8\frac{1}{4}$$

Subtract as you would with any mixed numbers. Now look at the following example:

EXAMPLE 1   Take $4\frac{5}{6}$ from 8.

$$\textbf{(1)} \quad 8 \;=\; 7\frac{6}{6} \qquad \textbf{(2)} \quad 7\frac{6}{6}$$
$$\underline{-\;4\frac{5}{6} \;=\; 4\frac{5}{6}} \qquad\qquad \underline{-\;4\frac{5}{6}}$$
$$\qquad\qquad\qquad\qquad\qquad\qquad 3\frac{1}{6}$$

STEP 1   Regroup 1 from 8 and rewrite the 1 as $\frac{6}{6}$ since 6 is the denominator of the bottom fraction.

STEP 2   Subtract the numerators and put the difference over the denominator. Subtract the whole numbers. $\mathbf{3\frac{1}{6}}$ is reduced to lowest terms.

Study the next example carefully. The top number has a fraction, but this fraction is not large enough to subtract from. Notice how we add this top fraction into the problem.

EXAMPLE 2   A plumber cut a piece of pipe $6\frac{7}{8}$ inches long from a piece that was $12\frac{5}{8}$ inches long. How long was the remaining piece?

$$\textbf{(1)} \quad 12\frac{5}{8} = 11\frac{8}{8} + \frac{5}{8} = 11\frac{13}{8} \qquad \textbf{(2)} \quad 11\frac{13}{8}$$
$$\underline{-\;6\frac{7}{8} = \qquad\qquad\qquad\quad 6\frac{7}{8} \qquad\qquad -\;6\frac{7}{8}}$$
$$\qquad\qquad\qquad\qquad\qquad\qquad\qquad\qquad 5\frac{6}{8} = 5\frac{3}{4}$$

STEP 1   To find the length of the remaining piece, subtract. Notice that $\frac{5}{8}$ is too small to subtract $\frac{7}{8}$ from. Regroup 1 from 12 and rewrite the 12 as $11\frac{8}{8}$. Then add $11\frac{8}{8}$ to the $\frac{5}{8}$ we already had on top.

STEP 2   Subtract the fractions and the whole numbers and reduce. The remaining piece of pipe is $\mathbf{5\frac{3}{4}}$ inches long.

SUBTRACTING MIXED NUMBERS WITH LIKE DENOMINATORS

1. When necessary, regroup 1 from the top whole number. Rewrite the 1 with the same denominator as the fraction on the bottom. Add this rewritten 1 to the top fraction if there is one.

2. Subtract the numerators and put the difference over the denominator. Subtract the whole numbers and reduce the fraction.

EXERCISE 12

Directions: Solve each problem.

1. $9 - 1\frac{2}{3} =$ $\qquad$ $11 - 3\frac{5}{8} =$ $\qquad$ $8 - 5\frac{7}{12} =$

2. $7 - 6\frac{1}{2} =$ $\qquad$ $9 - 1\frac{1}{4} =$ $\qquad$ $12 - 2\frac{5}{16} =$

3. $5\frac{1}{8} - 2\frac{5}{8} =$ $\qquad$ $8\frac{2}{5} - 1\frac{4}{5} =$ $\qquad$ $3\frac{1}{4} - 2\frac{3}{4} =$

4.
$$24\frac{11}{16} \\ -16\frac{15}{16}$$
$$9\frac{1}{3} \\ -7\frac{2}{3}$$
$$12\frac{3}{10} \\ -4\frac{9}{10}$$

5.
$$11\frac{7}{12} \\ -8\frac{11}{12}$$
$$15\frac{7}{24} \\ -13\frac{19}{24}$$
$$20\frac{5}{36} \\ -7\frac{25}{36}$$

ANSWERS ARE ON PAGES 354–355.

UNLIKE FRACTIONS

FINDING COMMON DENOMINATORS

So far in this book you have added and subtracted like fractions—fractions that have the same denominator. Often the fractions in a problem will not have the same denominators. Suppose you want to add $\frac{1}{2}$ and $\frac{2}{3}$. The drawing below illustrates this problem.

$$\frac{1}{2} + \frac{2}{3} = ?$$

The pieces are not the same size, and you cannot add them as they are written.

To add or subtract unlike fractions, you must first find a *common denominator*. In other words you must make all fractions *like fractions* before you can add or subtract them. You must give all fractions the same, or common, denominator.

A **common denominator** is a number each denominator in a problem will divide into evenly. The lowest number that each denominator will divide into evenly is called the **lowest common denominator**.

For example, for the fractions $\frac{1}{2}$ and $\frac{2}{3}$, the lowest common denominator is 6. 6 is the lowest number both 2 and 3 will divide into evenly.

For the fractions $\frac{5}{6}$ and $\frac{3}{4}$ the lowest common denominator is 12. 12 is the lowest number both 6 and 4 will divide into evenly.

TIPS FOR FINDING A LOWEST COMMON DENOMINATOR
1. First test the largest denominator as the common denominator.
2. If that doesn't work, go through the multiplication table of the largest denominator.

EXAMPLE 1   Find the lowest common denominator for $\frac{3}{4}$ and $\frac{5}{8}$.

SOLUTION   Test the larger denominator, 8. 4 divides evenly into 8. **8** is the lowest common denominator.

EXAMPLE 2   Find the lowest common denominator for $\frac{7}{9}$, $\frac{1}{12}$, and $\frac{5}{6}$.

SOLUTION   Test the largest denominator, 12. 6 divides evenly into 12, but 9 does not. Go through the multiplication table of the largest denominator, 12, until you find the number that both 9 and 6 will divide into evenly.

$1 \times 12 = 12$, not evenly divisible by 9.
$2 \times 12 = 24$, not evenly divisible by 9.
$3 \times 12 = 36$, evenly divisible by both 9 and 6.

36 is the lowest common denominator for the three fractions because 6, 9, and 12 will all divide evenly into 36.

EXERCISE 13

Directions: Find the lowest common denominator for each set of fractions. *Do not add or subtract the fractions.*

1. $\frac{2}{5}$ and $\frac{7}{10}$ $\frac{5}{6}$ and $\frac{3}{4}$ $\frac{3}{4}$ and $\frac{5}{9}$

2. $\frac{1}{2}$ and $\frac{1}{3}$ $\frac{1}{2}$ and $\frac{5}{9}$ $\frac{5}{8}$ and $\frac{3}{20}$

3. $\frac{2}{9}$ and $\frac{5}{6}$ $\frac{7}{12}$ and $\frac{5}{8}$ $\frac{1}{4}$ and $\frac{7}{10}$

4. $\frac{1}{2}$, $\frac{3}{5}$, and $\frac{3}{4}$ $\frac{5}{6}$, $\frac{3}{4}$, and $\frac{2}{3}$ $\frac{3}{8}$, $\frac{5}{6}$, and $\frac{7}{12}$

5. $\frac{4}{9}$, $\frac{5}{6}$, and $\frac{1}{2}$ $\frac{7}{8}$, $\frac{11}{20}$, and $\frac{1}{2}$ $\frac{8}{9}$, $\frac{7}{12}$, and $\frac{2}{3}$

ANSWERS ARE ON PAGE 355.

RAISING FRACTIONS TO HIGHER TERMS

After you have found a common denominator for the fractions in an addition or subtraction problem, you must change each fraction in the problem to a new fraction with the common denominator. For $\frac{1}{2}$ and $\frac{2}{3}$ the lowest common denominator is 6. The diagram below shows each fraction changed to sixths.

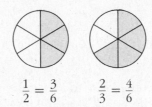

$$\frac{1}{2} = \frac{3}{6} \qquad \frac{2}{3} = \frac{4}{6}$$

The process of changing $\frac{1}{2}$ to $\frac{3}{6}$ and $\frac{2}{3}$ to $\frac{4}{6}$ is called **raising a fraction to higher terms**. It is the opposite of reducing a fraction. When you reduce a fraction, you *divide* both the numerator and the denominator by the same number. When you raise a fraction to higher terms, you *multiply* both the numerator and the denominator by the same number. You do this so that the fractions are easy to add and subtract.

To raise $\frac{1}{2}$ to sixths, ask yourself how many times the old denominator goes into the new one. 2 goes into 6 three times. Multiply both the numerator and the denominator by 3.

$$\frac{1 \times 3}{2 \times 3} = \frac{3}{6}$$

To raise $\frac{2}{3}$ to sixths, ask yourself how many times the old denominator goes into the new one. 3 goes into 6 two times. Multiply both the numerator and the denominator by 2.

$$\frac{2 \times 2}{3 \times 2} = \frac{4}{6}$$

RULES FOR RAISING A FRACTION TO HIGHER TERMS
1. Divide the old denominator into the new one to find the multiplier.
2. Multiply the old numerator by the multiplier from step 1.

EXAMPLE 1   Raise $\frac{2}{3}$ to fifteenths.

(1) $3\overline{)15}^{\,5}$ **(2)** $\frac{2 \times 5}{3 \times 5} = \frac{10}{15}$

STEP 1   Divide the old denominator, 3, into the new denominator, 15.
STEP 2   Multiply the old numerator by 5.

TIP: Raising fractions to higher terms is an important skill. You will use this skill not only in adding and subtracting fractions but also later on when you study ratio and proportion and percents. As with reducing fractions, the better you know your multiplication table, the easier you will find raising fractions to higher terms.

There are two ways to check your work when you raise a fraction to higher terms. One way is to reduce the new fraction. For the preceding example, reduce $\frac{10}{15}$ by 5. The result is $\frac{2}{3}$, which was the original fraction.

The other way to check these problems is to find the cross products. First multiply the numerator of the original fraction by the denominator of the new fraction. Then multiply the denominator of the original fraction by the numerator of the new fraction. The products should be the same.

EXAMPLE 2   Find the cross products of $\frac{2}{3} = \frac{10}{15}$.

STEP 1   Multiply the numerator of the original fraction, 2, by the denominator of the new fraction, 15.

$2 \times 15 = 30$

STEP 2   Multiply the denominator of the original fraction, 3, by the numerator of the new fraction, 10. The products are both **30**.

$3 \times 10 = 30$

EXERCISE 14

Directions: Raise each fraction to higher terms. Use the new denominator shown in each problem. Check by finding the cross products.

1. $\frac{3}{5} = \frac{?}{20}$ $\frac{5}{12} = \frac{?}{24}$ $\frac{7}{8} = \frac{?}{40}$ $\frac{3}{4} = \frac{?}{16}$

2. $\frac{5}{11} = \frac{?}{44}$ $\frac{13}{20} = \frac{?}{40}$ $\frac{7}{10} = \frac{?}{60}$ $\frac{13}{20} = \frac{?}{100}$

3. $\frac{3}{4} = \frac{?}{100}$ $\frac{5}{9} = \frac{?}{36}$ $\frac{1}{8} = \frac{?}{24}$ $\frac{1}{3} = \frac{?}{36}$

ANSWERS ARE ON PAGE 355.

ADDING AND SUBTRACTING UNLIKE FRACTIONS

The diagram below illustrates the problem $\frac{1}{2} + \frac{2}{3}$. We cannot add these fractions until they are both changed to sixths, the lowest common denominator.

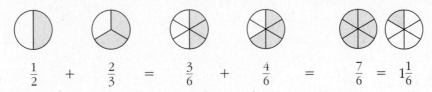

$$\frac{1}{2} \quad + \quad \frac{2}{3} \quad = \quad \frac{3}{6} \quad + \quad \frac{4}{6} \quad = \quad \frac{7}{6} \quad = \quad 1\frac{1}{6}$$

EXAMPLE 1   Add $5\frac{2}{3}$ and $3\frac{7}{9}$.

(1) $\begin{aligned} 5\frac{2}{3} &= 5\frac{6}{9} \\ +\ 3\frac{7}{9} &= 3\frac{7}{9} \end{aligned}$ **(2)** $\begin{aligned} & 5\frac{6}{9} \\ +\ & 3\frac{7}{9} \\ \hline 8\frac{13}{9} &= 8 + 1\frac{4}{9} = 9\frac{4}{9} \end{aligned}$

STEP 1   Find the lowest common denominator for 3 and 9. Since 3 divides evenly into 9, 9 is the lowest common denominator. Raise $\frac{2}{3}$ to ninths.

STEP 2   Add the numerators and put the total over the common denominator. Then add the whole numbers. Simplify the answer. **$9\frac{4}{9}$** is already reduced to lowest terms.

RULES FOR ADDING UNLIKE FRACTIONS AND MIXED NUMBERS

1. Find the lowest common denominator and raise each fraction to higher terms with the common denominator.

2. Add the numerators and put the total over the common denominator. Also add the whole numbers if there are any.

3. Simplify the answer and reduce.

When you subtract unlike fractions, you must also find a common denominator.

EXAMPLE 2   Subtract $5\frac{3}{4}$ from $8\frac{1}{3}$.

(1) $\begin{aligned} 8\frac{1}{3} &= 8\frac{4}{12} \\ -\ 5\frac{3}{4} &= 5\frac{9}{12} \end{aligned}$ **(2)** $\begin{aligned} 8\frac{4}{12} &= 7\frac{12}{12} + \frac{4}{12} = 7\frac{16}{12} \\ -\ 5\frac{9}{12} &= 5\frac{9}{12} = 5\frac{9}{12} \\ \hline & \qquad\qquad\qquad\quad 2\frac{7}{12} \end{aligned}$

STEP 1   Find the lowest common denominator, 12, and raise each fraction to twelfths.

STEP 2   Regroup 1 from 8 and rewrite the 8 as $7\frac{12}{12}$. Then add $7\frac{12}{12}$ to the $\frac{4}{12}$ you already had on top. Subtract the fractions and the whole numbers. **$2\frac{7}{12}$** is reduced to lowest terms.

RULES FOR SUBTRACTING UNLIKE FRACTIONS AND MIXED NUMBERS

1. Find the lowest common denominator and raise each fraction to higher terms with the common denominator.

2. Regroup if necessary.

3. Subtract both the fractions and the whole numbers and reduce.

EXERCISE 15

Directions: Solve each problem. Watch out for subtraction problems where you have to regroup. Be sure every answer is reduced to lowest terms.

1. $\frac{5}{6} + \frac{7}{12} =$ $\frac{2}{3} + \frac{3}{4} =$ $\frac{2}{3} + \frac{7}{12} + \frac{5}{6} =$

2. $9\frac{2}{3} + 4\frac{1}{2} =$ $10\frac{1}{8} + 3\frac{1}{3} =$ $9\frac{1}{2} + 8\frac{3}{4} + 7\frac{3}{10} =$

3. $2\frac{5}{6} + 4\frac{1}{2} =$ $\frac{1}{2} + \frac{1}{4} + \frac{3}{5} =$ $4\frac{1}{3} + 1\frac{5}{6} + 6\frac{5}{8} =$

4. $\frac{7}{10} - \frac{1}{2} =$ $2\frac{2}{3} - 1\frac{3}{4} =$ $\frac{5}{8} - \frac{3}{5} =$

5. $8\frac{1}{5} - 3\frac{3}{4} =$ $11\frac{3}{5} - 9\frac{1}{2} =$ $9\frac{1}{2} - 5\frac{2}{3} =$

6. $16\frac{1}{4} - 7\frac{5}{8} =$ $7\frac{11}{12} - 3\frac{5}{8} =$ $8\frac{7}{20} - 2\frac{3}{4} =$

ANSWERS ARE ON PAGES 355–356.

EXERCISE 16

Directions: Solve each problem. Remember to reduce every answer to lowest terms.

1. From a piece of cable 5 yards long, Ray cut a piece measuring $3\frac{2}{3}$ yards. Find the length in yards of the remaining piece.

2. Mrs. Vega bought $2\frac{1}{2}$ pounds of chicken, $2\frac{5}{8}$ pounds of ground chuck, $1\frac{3}{4}$ pounds of sausage, 10 pounds of potatoes, and $3\frac{1}{4}$ pounds of oranges.

   a. Find the weight in pounds of the meat (including chicken) Mrs. Vega bought.
   b. What was the combined weight of the potatoes and oranges?
   c. Mrs. Vega refuses to carry more than 20 pounds of groceries. She asks the store to deliver any order that is over 20 pounds. Will she have this order delivered?

3. Mr. and Mrs. Robinson are able to save $\frac{3}{16}$ of their income every month. What fraction of their income do they spend? (*Hint:* Think of their income as one whole.)

4. This problem refers to the following diagram:

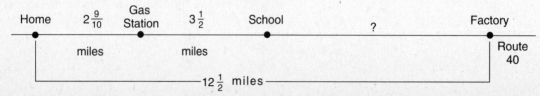

Mark's house, the nearest gas station, his daughter's school, and the factory where he works are all on Route 40. One day on his way from home to work, Mark first stopped for gas. He then drove to his daughter's school. How far did he have to drive from the school to the factory?

5. At the beginning of the week the cook at the Corner Kitchen had 100 pounds of flour and 45 pounds of sugar. Monday he used $16\frac{3}{4}$ pounds of flour. Wednesday he used $20\frac{1}{2}$ pounds, and Friday he used $24\frac{9}{16}$ pounds.

   a. How many pounds of flour did the cook use on those three days?
   b. How many pounds of flour were left when he finished on Friday?

6. By November, Paul's weight was down to $162\frac{1}{2}$ pounds. This was $43\frac{1}{2}$ pounds less than his weight had been in April. But by the end of December of the same year Paul gained 16 pounds over his November weight. Find his weight in pounds in December.

   (1) 222
   (2) $178\frac{1}{2}$
   (3) $146\frac{1}{2}$
   (4) 119
   (5) 103

7. Following are the closing prices for a share of Central Utilities stock:

Monday	Tuesday	Wednesday	Thursday	Friday
$19\frac{1}{8}$	$19\frac{5}{8}$	$20\frac{1}{8}$	$20\frac{5}{8}$	—

   If the stock followed the same pattern, what was the closing price on Friday?

   (1) $21\frac{1}{8}$
   (2) $20\frac{1}{8}$
   (3) $19\frac{5}{8}$
   (4) $19\frac{1}{8}$
   (5) $18\frac{5}{8}$

8. Fred has the following lengths of $\frac{1}{2}$-inch copper pipe: $8\frac{5}{16}$ inches, $10\frac{1}{2}$ inches, $9\frac{3}{4}$ inches, and 26 inches. If he welds together the three shortest lengths, what will be the length in inches of this new piece of pipe?

   (1) $18\frac{9}{16}$
   (2) $18\frac{13}{16}$
   (3) $20\frac{1}{4}$
   (4) $28\frac{9}{16}$
   (5) $30\frac{9}{16}$

ANSWERS ARE ON PAGES 356–357.

MULTIPLYING FRACTIONS

Multiplying fractions is less complicated than adding or subtracting fractions. To multiply fractions you do not need a common denominator, and you never need to regroup.

Think about this problem: A recipe calls for $\frac{3}{4}$ cup of sugar. If you cut the recipe in half, you will need $\frac{1}{2}$ of $\frac{3}{4}$ cup sugar. To find how much you need, multiply.

$$\frac{1}{2} \times \frac{3}{4} = \frac{3}{8}$$

TIP: To find a fraction of some quantity, you must multiply.

EXAMPLE   Find the product of $\frac{3}{8}$ and $\frac{7}{10}$.

$$\frac{3}{8} \times \frac{7}{10} = \frac{21}{80}$$

STEP 1   Multiply the numerators together.
STEP 2   Multiply the denominators together.
STEP 3   Try to reduce. $\frac{21}{80}$ is already reduced to lowest terms.

RULES FOR MULTIPLYING FRACTIONS BY FRACTIONS

1. Multiply the numerators together.

2. Multiply the denominators together.

3. Reduce the answer if possible.

EXERCISE 17

Directions: Solve each problem. Be sure every answer is reduced to lowest terms. Remember that a dot (·) indicates multiplication.

1. $\frac{3}{4} \times \frac{5}{7} =$ $\frac{2}{3} \times \frac{1}{2} =$ $\frac{1}{10} \cdot \frac{5}{8} =$ $\frac{7}{8} \times \frac{1}{5} =$

2. $\frac{1}{4} \times \frac{5}{16} =$ $\frac{3}{10} \cdot \frac{3}{5} =$ $\frac{2}{9} \times \frac{3}{5} =$ $\frac{3}{5} \times \frac{1}{6} =$

ANSWERS ARE ON PAGE 357.

CANCELLATION

There is a shortcut for multiplying fractions called **cancellation**. To cancel, find a number that divides evenly into the numerator of one fraction and the denominator of the other.

EXAMPLE 1 Find the product of $\frac{3}{4} \times \frac{8}{15}$.

STEP 1 Find a number that divides evenly into both the numerator of one fraction and the denominator of the other. Divide 3 and 15 by 3.

$$\frac{\overset{1}{\cancel{3}}}{4} \times \frac{8}{\underset{5}{\cancel{15}}}$$

STEP 2 Try the other numerator and denominator. Divide 4 and 8 by 4.

$$\frac{\overset{1}{\cancel{3}}}{\underset{1}{\cancel{4}}} \times \frac{\overset{2}{\cancel{8}}}{\underset{5}{\cancel{15}}}$$

STEP 3 Multiply the new numerators and the new denominators. Reduce if you can. $\frac{2}{5}$ is reduced to lowest terms.

$$\frac{\overset{1}{\cancel{3}}}{\underset{1}{\cancel{4}}} \times \frac{\overset{2}{\cancel{8}}}{\underset{5}{\cancel{15}}} = \frac{2}{5}$$

> **TIP:** Remember that cancellation is simply a shortcut. In some problems you will be able to cancel only once, and in other problems not at all.

Cancellation makes it easy to multiply more than two fractions together. In these problems you may be able to cancel several times. But remember to cancel only one numerator and one denominator at a time.

EXAMPLE 2 $\frac{5}{8} \times \frac{8}{9} \times \frac{7}{10} = ?$

STEP 1 Divide the 5 and the 10 by 5. Notice that you can "skip over" the middle fraction.

$$\frac{\overset{1}{\cancel{5}}}{8} \times \frac{8}{9} \times \frac{7}{\underset{2}{\cancel{10}}}$$

STEP 2 Divide 8 and 8 by 8.

STEP 3 Multiply numerators and denominators. Reduce if you can. $\frac{7}{18}$ is reduced to lowest terms.

$$\frac{\overset{1}{\cancel{5}}}{\underset{1}{\cancel{8}}} \times \frac{\overset{1}{\cancel{8}}}{9} \times \frac{7}{\underset{2}{\cancel{10}}} = \frac{7}{18}$$

EXERCISE 18

Directions: Solve each problem. Be sure every answer is reduced to lowest terms.

1. $\frac{3}{4} \times \frac{6}{7} =$ $\frac{14}{15} \times \frac{3}{7} =$ $\frac{4}{5} \cdot \frac{5}{6} =$ $\frac{4}{9} \times \frac{3}{8} =$

2. $\frac{5}{8} \times \frac{2}{15} =$ $\frac{9}{10} \times \frac{2}{3} =$ $\frac{3}{20} \times \frac{1}{3} =$ $\frac{4}{5} \times \frac{5}{24} =$

3. $\frac{2}{3} \cdot \frac{9}{20} =$ $\frac{6}{7} \times \frac{7}{8} \times \frac{4}{5} =$ $\frac{9}{10} \times \frac{1}{4} \times \frac{8}{9} =$ $\frac{3}{4} \times \frac{2}{9} \times \frac{15}{16} =$

ANSWERS ARE ON PAGE 357.

MULTIPLYING FRACTIONS AND WHOLE NUMBERS

To multiply a fraction by a whole number, rewrite the whole number as an improper fraction with a denominator of 1. The denominator 1 does not change the value of the whole number. Remember, any number divided by 1 equals itself. The 1 only pushes the whole number into the numerator position. For example, $\frac{24}{1}$ is equal to the whole number 24 because 24 divided by 1 equals 24.

EXAMPLE   There are 24 members in a club. At the last meeting $\frac{3}{4}$ of the members were present. How many people were at the meeting?

STEP 1   Rewrite the whole number 24 as an improper fraction with 1 as the denominator.

$24 = \frac{24}{1}$

$\frac{3}{4} \times \frac{24}{1}$

STEP 2   Divide the 4 and the 24 by 4.

$\frac{3}{\cancel{4}} \times \frac{\cancel{24}^{6}}{1}$
$\phantom{\frac{3}{}}_1$

STEP 3   Multiply the new numerators and denominators.

$\frac{3}{\cancel{4}} \times \frac{\cancel{24}^{6}}{1} = \frac{18}{1}$
$\phantom{\frac{3}{}}_1$

STEP 4   Change the improper fraction to a whole or mixed number. $\frac{18}{1} = \mathbf{18}$.

> **TIP:** Always check your answer to make sure it makes sense. Here are a couple of clues to help you when multiplying fractions:
>
> - When you multiply a whole number by a proper fraction, the result is smaller than the original number. For example, $12 \times \frac{1}{4} = 3$.
>
> - When you multiply two proper fractions, the product is smaller than either fraction. For example, $\frac{1}{2} \times \frac{1}{2} = \frac{1}{4}$.

EXERCISE 19

Directions: Solve each problem. Be sure every answer is reduced to lowest terms.

1. $\frac{1}{2} \times 16 =$ $10 \times \frac{2}{3} =$ $\frac{3}{8} \times 12 =$ $8 \cdot \frac{7}{10} =$

2. $\frac{2}{5} \times 10 =$ $9 \times \frac{11}{20} =$ $\frac{5}{6} \times 9 =$ $15 \times \frac{7}{100} =$

3. $18 \times \frac{2}{3} =$ $20 \cdot \frac{4}{5} =$ $\frac{4}{15} \times 36 =$ $24 \times \frac{3}{10} =$

ANSWERS ARE ON PAGE 357.

CHANGING MIXED NUMBERS TO IMPROPER FRACTIONS

To multiply with mixed numbers, you must first change the mixed numbers into improper fractions. Look at the following example to see how this is done.

EXAMPLE Change $4\frac{2}{3}$ to an improper fraction.

Multiply whole number by denominator.

$$4\frac{2}{3} = \frac{12}{3} + \frac{2}{3} = \frac{14}{3}$$

Place product over denominator.

STEP 1   Multiply the denominator (3) by the whole number (4). Put the product (12) over the denominator (3).

STEP 2   Add $\frac{12}{3}$ and $\frac{2}{3}$.

CHANGING A MIXED NUMBER TO AN IMPROPER FRACTION

1. Change the whole number to an improper fraction with the same denominator as the fraction. To do this, multiply the denominator of the fraction by the whole number. Put the product over the denominator.

2. Add the two fractions.

EXERCISE 20

Directions: Change each mixed number to an improper fraction.

1. $2\frac{2}{3} =$ $1\frac{5}{8} =$ $8\frac{2}{5} =$ $3\frac{1}{4} =$ $3\frac{5}{6} =$

2. $5\frac{4}{7} =$ $3\frac{1}{2} =$ $7\frac{1}{3} =$ $6\frac{2}{9} =$ $10\frac{1}{3} =$

3. $12\frac{3}{5} =$ $9\frac{1}{4} =$ $13\frac{2}{3} =$ $15\frac{1}{3} =$ $4\frac{3}{8} =$

ANSWERS ARE ON PAGE 358.

MULTIPLYING MIXED NUMBERS

Remember to change every mixed number to an improper fraction before you multiply. Look at how the following fraction and mixed number are multiplied:

EXAMPLE 1 $\frac{1}{3} \times 2\frac{1}{4} = ?$

STEP 1   Change $2\frac{1}{4}$ to an improper fraction.

$$2\frac{1}{4} = \frac{9}{4}$$

STEP 2   Cancel.

$$\frac{1}{\overset{}{\underset{1}{3}}} \times \frac{\overset{3}{9}}{4}$$

STEP 3   Multiply the numerators and the denominators.

$\frac{3}{4}$ is already reduced to lowest terms.

$$\frac{1}{\overset{}{\underset{1}{3}}} \times \frac{\overset{3}{9}}{4} = \frac{3}{4}$$

MULTIPLYING MIXED AND WHOLE NUMBERS AND FRACTIONS

1. Change every mixed number or whole number to an improper fraction.

2. Cancel if possible. Then multiply the numerators together and multiply the denominators together.

3. If the answer is an improper fraction, change it to a mixed number and reduce if possible.

EXAMPLE 2 $3\frac{3}{10} \times 4\frac{1}{6} = ?$

STEP 1   Change the mixed numbers to improper fractions.

$$\frac{33}{10} \times \frac{25}{6}$$

STEP 2   Cancel. Then multiply the numerators and denominators.

$$\frac{\overset{}{\underset{2}{33}}}{10} \times \frac{\overset{5}{25}}{\underset{2}{6}} = \frac{55}{4}$$

STEP 3   Change the improper fraction to a mixed number.

$$\frac{55}{4} = 13\frac{3}{4}$$

EXAMPLE 3   Find the product of $\frac{1}{3}$, 16, and $1\frac{1}{2}$.

STEP 1   Change the mixed and whole numbers to improper fractions.

$$\frac{1}{3} \times \frac{16}{1} \times \frac{3}{2}$$

STEP 2   Cancel. Then multiply the numerators and denominators.

$$\frac{1}{\cancel{3}_1} \times \frac{\cancel{16}^8}{1} \times \frac{\cancel{3}^1}{\cancel{2}_1} = \mathbf{8}$$

DIVIDING FRACTIONS

Suppose you want to divide five pies into quarters. Mathematically this problem is $5 \div \frac{1}{4}$. If you draw a picture, you can see what happens.

When you divide five pies into quarters, you get 20 pieces. Notice that the answer to $5 \div \frac{1}{4}$ gives the same answer as 5×4.

> **TIP:** It is very important to remember that in any fraction division problem the amount being divided up *must come first*.

Before you attempt to solve a fraction division problem, take a minute to make sure you have the problem set up properly. The first number (the number to the *left* of the ÷ sign) is the amount being divided up. The second number (to the *right*) is the divisor and tells what the first number is being divided *by*.

When you're dividing by a fraction, first invert (turn upside down) the fraction you are dividing by. The inverted number is called a **_reciprocal_**. Then multiply.

EXAMPLE $3\frac{1}{2} \div \frac{3}{8} = ?$

STEP 1   Change $3\frac{1}{2}$ to an improper fraction.

$$\frac{7}{2} \div \frac{3}{8}$$

STEP 2   Invert the divisor (the number you are dividing by) and change the ÷ sign to ×.

$$\frac{7}{2} \times \frac{8}{3}$$

STEP 3   Cancel and multiply the numerators and denominators.

$$\frac{7}{\cancel{2}_1} \times \frac{\cancel{8}^4}{3} = \frac{28}{3}$$

STEP 4   Change $\frac{28}{3}$ to a mixed number.

$$\frac{28}{3} = \mathbf{9\frac{1}{3}}$$

> **TIP:** When you divide by a proper fraction, the answer is always *larger* than the dividend.

RULES FOR DIVIDING BY A FRACTION

1. Change any mixed number or whole number into an improper fraction.

2. Invert the divisor (the number at the right) and change the ÷ sign to a × sign.

3. Cancel if possible. Multiply the numerators and denominators.

4. Change an improper fraction answer to a mixed number and reduce.

EXERCISE 21

Directions: Solve each problem. Be sure every answer is reduced to lowest terms.

1. $\frac{1}{3} \div \frac{1}{6} =$ $\qquad$ $5 \div \frac{5}{6} =$ $\qquad$ $4\frac{1}{2} \div \frac{3}{4} =$ $\qquad$ $2\frac{2}{3} \div \frac{2}{15} =$

2. $\frac{1}{3} \div \frac{2}{3} =$ $\qquad$ $\frac{5}{7} \div \frac{5}{14} =$ $\qquad$ $4 \div \frac{3}{8} =$ $\qquad$ $\frac{5}{9} \div \frac{3}{4} =$

3. $5\frac{5}{6} \div \frac{7}{8} =$ $\qquad$ $\frac{9}{10} \div \frac{3}{5} =$ $\qquad$ $10 \div \frac{5}{6} =$ $\qquad$ $3\frac{1}{3} \div \frac{1}{3} =$

ANSWERS ARE ON PAGE 358.

DIVIDING FRACTIONS BY WHOLE OR MIXED NUMBERS

To divide a fraction by a mixed number or a whole number, first write all whole and mixed numbers as improper fractions. Then invert the divisor (the number following the ÷ sign) and multiply.

EXAMPLE 1 $\quad 4\frac{2}{3} \div 6 = ?$

STEP 1 Change $4\frac{2}{3}$ to an improper fraction and write 6 as an improper fraction with a denominator of 1.

$$\frac{14}{3} \div \frac{6}{1} =$$

STEP 2 Invert the divisor and change the ÷ to ×.

$$\frac{14}{3} \times \frac{1}{6}$$

STEP 3 Cancel and multiply. $\frac{7}{9}$ is reduced to lowest terms.

$$\frac{\overset{7}{\cancel{14}}}{3} \times \frac{1}{\underset{3}{\cancel{6}}} = \frac{7}{9}$$

EXAMPLE 2 How many bags each holding $1\frac{1}{2}$ pounds of nails can you fill with $4\frac{1}{2}$ pounds of nails?

STEP 1 You want to find how many times $1\frac{1}{2}$ will go into $4\frac{1}{2}$. In other words, divide $4\frac{1}{2}$ by $1\frac{1}{2}$. Change both mixed numbers to improper fractions. Remember that the amount being divided up comes first.

$$4\frac{1}{2} \div 1\frac{1}{2} = \frac{9}{2} \div \frac{3}{2}$$

STEP 2 Invert the divisor and change the $\div$ to $\times$.

$$\frac{9}{2} \times \frac{2}{3}$$

STEP 3 Cancel, and multiply the numerators and denominators.

$$\overset{3}{\underset{1}{\cancel{\frac{9}{2}}}} \times \overset{1}{\underset{1}{\cancel{\frac{2}{3}}}} = \frac{3}{1}$$

STEP 4 Change the improper fraction to a whole number.

$$\frac{3}{1} = \mathbf{3}$$

EXERCISE 22

Directions: Solve each problem. Be sure every answer is reduced to lowest terms.

1. $10 \div 1\frac{1}{2} =$ $\qquad$ $1\frac{1}{3} \div 3\frac{1}{5} =$ $\qquad$ $6 \div 1\frac{1}{3} =$

2. $2\frac{1}{2} \div 3\frac{1}{4} =$ $\qquad$ $21 \div 4\frac{1}{5} =$ $\qquad$ $2\frac{2}{9} \div 2 =$

3. $\frac{9}{10} \div 3 =$ $\qquad$ $1\frac{3}{4} \div 7 =$ $\qquad$ $5\frac{5}{6} \div 7 =$

4. $\frac{3}{4} \div 3\frac{1}{5} =$ $\qquad$ $3\frac{3}{4} \div 4 =$ $\qquad$ $10 \div 1\frac{2}{3} =$

5. $12 \div \frac{2}{3} =$ $\qquad$ $\frac{3}{4} \div \frac{9}{10} =$ $\qquad$ $1\frac{2}{3} \div \frac{5}{6} =$

6. $\frac{1}{2} \div \frac{3}{4} =$ $\qquad$ $4\frac{1}{5} \div \frac{7}{10} =$ $\qquad$ $6 \div \frac{2}{9} =$

ANSWERS ARE ON PAGES 358–359.

PROBLEM SOLVING FOR THE GED

Multiplying and Dividing with Fractions

How many boards, each $\frac{1}{2}$ foot long, can be cut from a 15-foot-long board?

(1) $7\frac{1}{2}$

(2) 15

(3) $15\frac{1}{2}$

(4) 30

(5) 45

With a problem like this, it is sometimes hard to know where to start. You may not know for sure whether to divide or multiply. Remember:

- A number *multiplied* by a proper fraction gets *smaller*.

$12 \times \frac{1}{3} = 4$

- A number *divided* by a proper fraction gets *larger*.

$12 \div \frac{1}{3} = 36$

This can be confusing because it is the *opposite* of what happens when multiplying and dividing by a whole number.

If a good way to solve the problem above does not immediately pop out at you, try making some basic decisions one at a time.

1. Should my answer be more or less than 15 (the number being divided up)?

From your experiences, you can figure out that you can get *more* than 15 boards ($\frac{1}{2}$ foot long) out of a board that is 15 *whole* feet.

2. Should I multiply or divide?

Step 1 above told you that you need an answer *larger* than 15. Remember from your work in this chapter that when you *divide* by a proper fraction (like $\frac{1}{2}$), you get an answer larger than the dividend (15). Therefore, in this problem, choose division as your operation.

3. If you plan to divide, which number should come first?

As you learned in this chapter, setting up a fraction division problem is extremely important. The amount *being divided up* ALWAYS comes first. 15 boards are being divided up. Therefore, you would set up this problem this way: $15 \div \frac{1}{2} =$

4. Solve the problem.

When you divide by a fraction, invert and multiply: $15 \times \frac{2}{1} = 30$

5. Is your answer sensible?

30 is larger than 15; so yes, it is sensible.

MULTIPLYING AND DIVIDING FRACTIONS

The next problems give you a chance to apply your skills in multiplying and dividing fractions. Remember the five-step approach to solving word problems.

EXERCISE 23

Directions: Solve each problem. Be sure every answer is reduced to lowest terms.

1. One cubic foot of water weighs $62\frac{1}{2}$ pounds. How many pounds do three cubic feet of water weigh?

   Should answer be more or less than $62\frac{1}{2}$ pounds?

   Multiplication or division?

   If division, what comes first?

   Answer:

2. Jeff paid $38 for $9\frac{1}{2}$ yards of lumber. Find the price of one yard.

   Should answer be more or less than $38?

   Multiplication or division?

   If division, what comes first?

   Answer:

3. How many jars each holding $1\frac{1}{2}$ pounds of tomatoes can Margaret fill with $17\frac{1}{2}$ pounds of tomatoes?

   Should answer be more or less than 17?

   Multiplication or division?

   If division, what comes first?

   Answer:

4. Don worked for $8\frac{1}{2}$ hours at $8.20 an hour. How much did he earn?

   Should answer be more or less than $8.20?

   Multiplication or division?

   If division, what comes first?

   Answer:

5. The MacDonalds want to split up 90 acres of their farm into $1\frac{1}{2}$-acre lots. How many lots can they get from the 90 acres?

   Should answer be more or less than 90?

   Multiplication or division?

   If division, what comes first?

   Answer:

Directions: Problems 6–10 refer to the following situation. These problems include operations besides multiplication and division.

Hiro makes $21,500 a year, and his wife, Fumiko, makes $14,500. They spend $\frac{1}{5}$ of their combined income for rent, $\frac{2}{5}$ for food, and $\frac{1}{8}$ for car payments.

6. How much rent do they pay each month?
   (1) $600
   (2) $500
   (3) $450
   (4) $400
   (5) $360

7. Rent, food, and car payments use up what fraction of Hiro and Fumiko's income?
   (1) $\frac{39}{40}$
   (2) $\frac{3}{4}$
   (3) $\frac{29}{40}$
   (4) $\frac{5}{8}$
   (5) $\frac{1}{2}$

8. How much do they spend in a year on car payments?
   (1) $6000
   (2) $4500
   (3) $4000
   (4) $3600
   (5) $3000

9. Assume that a month has 30 days. How much do Hiro and Fumiko spend each day for food?
   (1) $60
   (2) $54
   (3) $48
   (4) $40
   (5) $30

10. Hiro and Fumiko save $\frac{1}{4}$ of Fumiko's salary. How much do they save in a year?
   (1) $6325
   (2) $5850
   (3) $4250
   (4) $3625
   (5) $2575

ANSWERS ARE ON PAGES 359–360.

FRACTIONS AND DECIMALS

We have mentioned decimals several times already in this chapter. Decimals and fractions are both ways of expressing parts of a whole. In this section you will learn how to change between decimals and fractions—a skill that will be very important on the GED Math Test.

CHANGING DECIMALS TO FRACTIONS

What is .321 expressed as a fraction?

To change a decimal to a fraction, first decide the number of places the decimal holds. For example, the place value of .321 is *thousandths*. Make this value the denominator of the fraction:

$$\overline{1000}$$

The numerator of the fraction will be your original number without its decimal point:

$$\frac{321}{1000}$$

EXAMPLE .25 is twenty-five hundredths. This can be written as a fraction:

$$\frac{25}{100} = \frac{1}{4}$$

If you reduce this fraction as shown above, you get the fraction $\frac{1}{4}$.

Below are several examples of decimals changed to fractions.

Decimal		Fraction
.3	three tenths	$\frac{3}{10}$
.017	seventeen thousandths	$\frac{17}{1000}$
.35	thirty-five hundredths	$\frac{35}{100} = \frac{7}{20}$

EXERCISE 24

Directions: Change each decimal to a fraction and reduce to lowest terms.

1. .6 =   .5 =   .45 =   .80 =

2. .125 =   .065 =   .15 =   .96 =

3. .024 =   .0002 =   .010 =   .34 =

ANSWERS ARE ON PAGE 360.

CHANGING FRACTIONS TO DECIMALS

Remember that the fraction bar means to divide. $\frac{1}{4}$ means 1 divided by 4. To change a fraction to a decimal, divide the denominator into the numerator.

$$4\overline{)1} \qquad \overset{.25}{4\overline{)1.00}}$$

The numerator and the denominator of a fraction are both whole numbers. When you divide the denominator into the numerator, remember to put a decimal point to the right of the numerator and to bring the point up into the answer.

Study the next examples carefully. In each example there is at least one zero to the right of the decimal point in the dividend. Sometimes one zero is enough for the division to come out evenly. Other times you'll need more than one.

Fraction	Decimal	Fraction	Decimal	Fraction	Decimal
$\frac{3}{10}$	$\overset{.3}{10\overline{)3.0}}$	$\frac{9}{20}$	$\overset{.45}{20\overline{)9.00}}$ $\underline{80}$ 100 $\underline{100}$ 0	$\frac{3}{8}$	$\overset{.375}{8\overline{)3.000}}$ $\underline{2\,4}$ 60 $\underline{56}$ 40 $\underline{40}$ 0

EXERCISE 25

Directions: Change each of these fractions to a decimal.

1. $\frac{3}{4} =$ $\qquad$ $\frac{1}{3} =$ $\qquad$ $\frac{7}{10} =$ $\qquad$ $\frac{5}{8} =$

2. $\frac{1}{2} =$ $\qquad$ $\frac{1}{20} =$ $\qquad$ $\frac{5}{6} =$ $\qquad$ $\frac{4}{9} =$

3. $\frac{1}{12} =$ $\qquad$ $\frac{2}{3} =$ $\qquad$ $\frac{3}{25} =$ $\qquad$ $\frac{1}{6} =$

ANSWERS ARE ON PAGE 360.

EXERCISE 26

Directions: Solve each problem.

1. Find the average weight in pounds of three crates that weigh $4\frac{1}{3}$ pounds, 9.5 pounds, and $5\frac{1}{6}$ pounds respectively.

    (1) $6\frac{1}{3}$

    (2) $8\frac{1}{3}$

    (3) $9\frac{1}{2}$

    (4) 18

    (5) 19

2. From a board $8\frac{1}{2}$ feet long, Al cut a piece that was 3.75 feet long. How long was the remaining piece?

    (1) $8\frac{1}{2}$

    (2) $5\frac{3}{4}$

    (3) $4\frac{3}{4}$

    (4) $4\frac{1}{4}$

    (5) $3\frac{3}{4}$

3. Find the average weight, to the nearest tenth of a pound, of three packages that weigh $2\frac{1}{2}$ pounds, $5\frac{3}{4}$ pounds, and 6.3 pounds respectively.

    (1) 2.5
    (2) 4.9
    (3) 5.8
    (4) 12.1
    (5) 14.6

4. Fran bought $\frac{3}{4}$ pound of cheese for $2.50 a pound and $1\frac{1}{2}$ pounds of coffee for $3.90 a pound. Which expression represents the amount she paid for these items?

    (1) $(\frac{3}{4} + 1\frac{1}{2}) + (2.50 + 3.90)$

    (2) $.75(2.50) + 1.5(3.90)$

    (3) $.75(2.50) + 3.90$

    (4) $2.50 + 1.5(3.90)$

    (5) $\frac{3}{4}(3.90) + \frac{3}{2}(2.50)$

5. From a ten-pound bag of flour Janina first took $3\frac{1}{2}$ pounds and then another .75 pound. Which expression represents the amount of flour (in pounds) that was left in the bag?

    (1) $(.75 + 10) - 3.5$
    (2) $3.5 - 10 - .75$
    (3) $10 + 3.5 + .75$
    (4) $10 - 3.5 - .75$
    (5) $10 \times 3.5 \times .75$

ANSWERS ARE ON PAGE 360.

COMPARING FRACTIONS

Which is larger, $\frac{3}{8}$ or $\frac{2}{5}$? If you know the decimal values of these fractions, you can compare them easily:

$$\frac{3}{8} = .375 \qquad \frac{2}{5} = .4 = .400$$

If you do not know the decimal values for the fractions, find a common denominator. Then raise each fraction to higher terms with the common denominator.

$$\frac{3}{8} = \frac{15}{40} \qquad \frac{2}{5} = \frac{16}{40}$$

$\frac{16}{40}$ is more than $\frac{15}{40}$. Therefore, $\frac{2}{5}$ is larger.

EXERCISE 27

Directions: For problems 1–3, choose the larger fraction in each pair.

1. **a.** $\frac{1}{2}$ or $\frac{4}{9}$ **b.** $\frac{2}{3}$ or $\frac{3}{5}$ **c.** $\frac{3}{4}$ or $\frac{5}{6}$

2. **a.** $\frac{13}{20}$ or $\frac{7}{10}$ **b.** $\frac{5}{8}$ or $\frac{3}{5}$ **c.** $\frac{1}{6}$ or $\frac{2}{9}$

3. **a.** $\frac{5}{6}$ or $\frac{7}{10}$ **b.** $\frac{5}{12}$ or $\frac{5}{9}$ **c.** $\frac{5}{8}$ or $\frac{11}{20}$

4. Arrange in order from *smallest* to *largest*: $\frac{5}{8}, \frac{5}{6}, \frac{7}{12}$.

5. Arrange in order from *smallest* to *largest*: $\frac{7}{10}, \frac{4}{5}, \frac{3}{4}, \frac{13}{20}$.

6. To put together her videotape, Veronica first needs to put each piece of film in order from longest to shortest. The pieces are the following lengths:

   A—$5\frac{1}{2}$ seconds

   B—5.30 seconds

   C—5.2 seconds

   D—$5\frac{2}{3}$ seconds

   E—$5\frac{7}{8}$ seconds

   In order from *longest* to *shortest*, how should Veronica line up the pieces of film?

ANSWERS ARE ON PAGE 360.

FRACTIONS REVIEW

Directions: For questions 1–16, simply solve each problem.

1. There are 20 students in Andrew's Spanish class. 11 of the students are men. Men make up what fraction of the class?

2. Reduce $\frac{48}{60}$ to lowest terms.

3. Change $\frac{52}{8}$ to a mixed number and reduce.

4. $7\frac{3}{8} + 3\frac{5}{8} + 4\frac{7}{8} =$

5. $12\frac{1}{5} - 8\frac{4}{5} =$

6. $5\frac{3}{4} + 6\frac{1}{2} + 8\frac{7}{10} =$

7. $8\frac{5}{12} - 3\frac{2}{3} =$

8. $\frac{3}{8} \times \frac{1}{6} \times \frac{4}{5} =$

9. $5 \times \frac{3}{10} =$

10. Change $7\frac{2}{3}$ to an improper fraction.

11. $3\frac{3}{4} \times 3\frac{1}{3} =$

12. $\frac{3}{4} \div \frac{1}{8} =$

13. $24\frac{1}{2} \div 3\frac{1}{2} =$

14. Change .65 to a fraction and reduce.

15. Change $\frac{6}{25}$ to a decimal.

16. Which fraction is smaller: $\frac{5}{9}$ or $\frac{2}{3}$?

Directions: Questions 17 and 18 include whole numbers and decimals as well as fractions. Choose the best answer to each. Remember what you have learned about problem solving.

17. On Friday, Paul drove 524.7 miles; on Saturday, 208.6 miles; and on Sunday, 380.9 miles. Find, to the nearest mile, the average distance Paul drove in a day.

    (1) 557
    (2) 525
    (3) 381
    (4) 371
    (5) 279

18. One day Mark swept floors for $2\frac{3}{4}$ hours, earning $7.20 per hour. He also earned a flat fee of $35.00 for yardwork. What operations should you use to find how much more Mark earned doing yardwork than he earned sweeping floors?

    (1) Add $7.20 and $35.00, then divide by $2\frac{3}{4}$.
    (2) Add $7.20 and $35.00, then multiply by $2\frac{3}{4}$.
    (3) Multiply $2\frac{3}{4}$ by $7.20, then subtract the product from $35.00.
    (4) Divide $7.20 by $2\frac{3}{4}$, then subtract the quotient from $35.00.
    (5) Subtract $7.20 from $35.00.

Directions: Questions 19–21 refer to the following.

Alfredo's employer withholds $\frac{1}{5}$ of his gross wages for federal tax, $\frac{1}{8}$ for state tax, and $\frac{1}{10}$ for social security. Alfredo's weekly gross pay is $360.

19. What fraction of his gross wages does Alfredo take home?

    (1) $\frac{23}{40}$
    (2) $\frac{17}{40}$
    (3) $\frac{9}{10}$
    (4) $\frac{7}{8}$
    (5) $\frac{4}{5}$

20. How much of Alfredo's salary is withheld each week for federal tax?

    (1) $23
    (2) $36
    (3) $40
    (4) $50
    (5) $72

21. Alfredo spends $\frac{1}{3}$ of his take-home pay for food. How much does he spend on food each week?

    (1) $ 27
    (2) $ 69
    (3) $ 80
    (4) $ 90
    (5) $120

Directions: Solve the problems.

22. If $4\frac{1}{2}$ yards of material cost $41.40, what is the cost of one yard of the material?

    (1) $ 2.30
    (2) $ 4.60
    (3) $ 8.60
    (4) $ 9.20
    (5) $10.20

23. A stock that sold for $28\frac{3}{8}$ on Monday had dropped $3\frac{1}{4}$ points by Wednesday. By Friday afternoon the stock had dropped a total of $6\frac{1}{2}$ points. Find the price of the stock on Friday afternoon.

    (1) $21\frac{7}{8}$
    (2) $22\frac{1}{8}$
    (3) $22\frac{7}{8}$
    (4) $20\frac{1}{8}$
    (5) $18\frac{5}{8}$

24. Assuming no waste, how many strips of metal each .45 inch wide can be cut from a sheet that is 90 inches wide?

    (1) 2000
    (2) 200
    (3)   20
    (4)   5
    (5)   2

25. Roger bought 3 quarts of oil for $12.50 each and got a $5 discount for paying cash. Which expression represents the amount he paid for the oil?

    (1) $(3 \times 12.50) - 5$
    (2) $5 - (3 \times 12.50)$
    (3) $5 - 3 - 12.50$
    (4) $12.50 - (3 \times 5)$
    (5) $(3 + 12.50) - 5$

ANSWERS ARE ON PAGE 361.

5 Probability, Ratio, and Proportion

PROBABILITY

Probability is the chance of something happening. Every day weather forecasters tell us what the "chances of rain" are. Gamblers use probability when they try to figure out what their chances of winning are. Probability, believe it or not, is an application of your fractions skills. We define probability as the following fraction:

$$\text{probability of an event} = \frac{\text{number of favorable outcomes}}{\text{total number of possible outcomes}}$$

What is a "favorable outcome"? This depends on what you are trying to figure out. If you are playing a slot machine in Las Vegas and want to know your chances of winning, your numerator, or ***favorable outcome***, is the number of wins. The denominator is your total number of tries. If you want to know the probability of picking a yellow marble out of a group of marbles, the *favorable outcome* is the number of yellow marbles in the group. The denominator is the total number of marbles in the group.

The next three examples refer to the picture at the right. Imagine that the arrow is free to spin. Each time it spins, it lands on one of the sections of the circle. Assume that it never lands on a line.

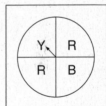

EXAMPLE 1   What is the probability that the arrow will land on yellow (Y)?

(1) $\dfrac{\text{favorable outcomes}}{\text{total outcomes}}$ $\dfrac{}{4}$ (2) $\dfrac{1}{4}$

STEP 1   Count all the possible outcomes: red, yellow, red, blue. There are four possible outcomes. 4 is the denominator.

STEP 2   Find the number of favorable outcomes, in this case the number of times yellow appears on the circle. Yellow appears only once. 1 is the numerator.
The probability that the arrow will land on yellow is $\frac{1}{4}$.

EXAMPLE 2   What is the probability that the arrow will land on red?

(1) $\dfrac{\text{favorable outcomes}}{\text{total outcomes}} \quad \dfrac{}{4}$ (2) $\dfrac{2}{4} = \dfrac{1}{2}$

STEP 1   There are four possible outcomes. 4 is the denominator.
STEP 2   Find the number of favorable outcomes, the number of times red appears in the circle. Red appears twice. 2 is the numerator. Reduce $\frac{2}{4}$ to $\frac{1}{2}$.
The probability that the arrow will land on red is $\frac{1}{2}$.

EXAMPLE 3   What is the probability that the arrow will land on green?

(1) $\dfrac{\text{favorable outcomes}}{\text{total outcomes}} \quad \dfrac{}{4}$ (2) $\dfrac{0}{4}$

STEP 1   There are four possible outcomes. 4 is the denominator.
STEP 2   Find the number of times green appears in the circle. Green never appears. 0 is the numerator.
The probability that the arrow will land on green is **0**.

> **TIP:** Remember to reduce a probability to lowest terms.

In some probability problems you may have to find the total number of possible outcomes to complete the problem.

EXAMPLE 4   A box contains 6 nickels, 4 dimes, and 2 quarters. Find the probability of picking a nickel from the box.

(1) number of nickels   6
number of dimes   4
number of quarters   + 2
total   12

(2) $\dfrac{\text{favorable outcomes}}{\text{total outcomes}} \quad \dfrac{6}{12} = \dfrac{1}{2}$

STEP 1   Find the total number of outcomes, in this case the total number of coins in the box. Add 6, 4, and 2. 12 is the denominator.
STEP 2   The number of favorable outcomes is the number of nickels in the box, 6. Reduce the fraction. The probability of picking a nickel is $\frac{1}{2}$.

EXERCISE 1

Directions: Use these cards to answer questions 1–3.

1. What is the probability of picking a jack?

2. Find the probability of picking a king.

3. What is the probability of picking a face card (king, queen, or jack)?

Directions: A die has 6 sides. Each side has a different number of dots, ranging from 1 to 6. Use this information to answer questions 4 and 5.

4. What is the probability that you will roll a 6?

5. Find the probability of rolling an odd number.

6. Ted's sock drawer contains 6 blue socks, 3 black socks, 1 white sock, and 2 plaid socks. If he chooses one at random in the dark, what is the probability that he will pick a black sock?

ANSWERS ARE ON PAGE 361.

DEPENDENT PROBABILITY

Suppose the first coin you pick from the box in Example 4 is a dime. You take that dime and set it aside from the group of coins. Now you would like to find the probability that the next coin you pick will be a nickel. Since you have removed one coin from the group, the total number of outcomes (denominator) has changed.

number of nickels	6	$\dfrac{\text{favorable outcomes}}{\text{total outcomes}}$ $\dfrac{6}{11}$
number of dimes	3	
number of quarters	+ 2	
total	11	

STEP 1   Find the total number of outcomes. This time it is the total number of coins *left* in the box. Now there are only 3 dimes. Add 6, 3, and 2. 11 is the denominator.

STEP 2   The number of favorable outcomes is the number of nickels left in the box, 6. The probability that the next coin will be a nickel is $\frac{6}{11}$.

EXERCISE 2

Directions: For questions 1–6, solve each problem.

1. A deck of cards has 52 cards. There are four aces in a deck. What is the probability of picking an ace from a deck?

2. There are 20 marbles in a bag. 16 of them are black. What is the probability of picking a black marble from the bag?

3. Bob received a shipment of shirts to sell in his store. He ordered 12 blue shirts and 6 white shirts. What is the probability that the first shirt he unwraps will be blue?

4. Mr. Robinson bought two raffle tickets. His wife bought three tickets, and his daughter bought one. Altogether 1000 tickets were sold. What was the probability that Mr. Robinson won?

5. What is the probability that someone in the Robinson family in question 4 won?

6. Out of every 200 tires that a factory produces, 15 are defective. What is the probability that a tire produced at the factory will be defective?

Directions: Questions 7–10 refer to the picture at right.

7. What is the probability that the arrow will land on 1?

8. What is the probability that the arrow will land on 2?

9. What is the probability that the arrow will land on 1 or 5?

10. What is the probability that the arrow will land on an odd number?

ANSWERS ARE ON PAGE 362.

GED Practice

EXERCISE 3

Directions: Questions 1–3 refer to the following situation.

Luba bought 1 can of white paint, 3 cans of gray paint, and 4 cans of green paint. When she got home, she realized that the cans had not been labeled.

1. What is the probability that the paint in the first can she opens will be white?

   (1) $\frac{1}{3}$

   (2) $\frac{1}{4}$

   (3) $\frac{1}{5}$

   (4) $\frac{1}{8}$

   (5) $\frac{1}{10}$

2. The first can she opened was gray. What is the probability that the paint in the second can will be white?

   (1) $\frac{1}{8}$

   (2) $\frac{1}{7}$

   (3) $\frac{2}{7}$

   (4) $\frac{5}{7}$

   (5) $\frac{6}{7}$

3. The second can turned out to be gray as well. What is the probability that the paint in the third can will be green?

   (1) $\frac{2}{3}$

   (2) $\frac{5}{6}$

   (3) $\frac{6}{7}$

   (4) $\frac{7}{8}$

   (5) $\frac{9}{10}$

ANSWERS ARE ON PAGE 362.

RATIO AND PROPORTION

RATIO

In mathematics we often compare numbers. For example, suppose 150 men and 75 women work in a factory. One way to compare these facts is to subtract. There are 75 more men working in the factory than there are women. (150 − 75 = 75.)

Another way to compare these numbers is to use a **_ratio._** The ratio of men to women working in the factory is 150 to 75 or, in reduced form, 2 to 1.

There are three ways to write ratios: with the word _to_, with a colon (:), and as a fraction. Like fractions, ratios should always be reduced. Following are the three ways to write the ratio of the number of men to the number of women working in the factory. Notice that each way is reduced.

- 150 to 75 = 2 to 1

- 150:75 = 2:1

- $\frac{150}{75} = \frac{2}{1}$

The numbers in a ratio _must_ be written in the order the problem asks for. Mixing up the order will result in an incorrect answer. Look at the following example, where we want to compare a length of wood to a length of rope.

To build a child's swing, Clay uses 5 feet of rope for every 3 feet of wood. What is the ratio of wood to rope?

The answer to this problem is $\frac{3}{5}$. Because the problem asked for wood first, the number 3 goes in the numerator. If you answered $\frac{5}{3}$, your answer would be wrong. $\frac{5}{3}$ is the ratio of _rope to wood._ Now follow this example:

EXAMPLE   Evelyn earns $1200 a month. She pays $480 in rent. What is the ratio of her income to her rent?

$$\frac{\text{income}}{\text{rent}} \quad \frac{\$1200}{\$480} = \frac{5}{2} \text{ or } 5{:}2 \text{ or } 5 \text{ to } 2$$

SOLUTION   Make a ratio with the income on top (numerator) and the rent on the bottom (denominator). Then reduce.

> **TIP:** A ratio should _always_ be reduced to lowest terms. However, a ratio written as an improper fraction should _not_ be changed to a mixed number.

TWO-STEP RATIO PROBLEMS

Ratio problems often involve more than one step. You may not be given both numbers to include in the ratio as you were in the example on page 121. Instead you may have to determine one of the numbers. Look at the example below.

EXAMPLE On a test of 20 questions Maceo got 2 questions wrong. What is the ratio of the number he got right to the number he got wrong?

(1) total questions   20
number wrong   − 2
number right   18

(2) $\dfrac{\text{right}}{\text{wrong}}$ $\dfrac{18}{2} = \dfrac{9}{1}$ or 9:1 or 9 to 1

STEP 1   One number you are asked for is the number of problems Maceo got right. You are not given this number, so you will have to figure it out. Subtract the number he got wrong from the total. This gives you the number of *correct* answers.

STEP 2   Make a ratio with the number of questions right on top and the number of questions wrong on the bottom. Then reduce.

EXERCISE 4

Directions: Solve each problem.

1. Simplify the ratio 12:15.

2. A GED class of 20 students has 12 women.

   a. What is the ratio of the number of women to the total number of students?
   b. What is the ratio of the number of men to the total number of students?
   c. What is the ratio of the number of men to the number of women?
   d. What is the ratio of the number of women to the number of men?

3. In a shop there are 105 union workers and 45 nonunion workers.

   a. What is the ratio of the number of union workers to the total number of workers?
   b. What is the ratio of the number of nonunion workers to the total number of workers?
   c. What is the ratio of the number of union workers to the number of nonunion workers?
   d. What is the ratio of the total number of workers to the number of union workers?

4. From a total yearly budget of $18,000,000, Central City spends $3,000,000 on education. What is the ratio of the amount spent on education to the amount not spent on education?

5. A test of 50 questions included 15 fraction problems and 5 decimal problems. What is the ratio of the total number of fraction and decimal problems to the number of problems on the test?

ANSWERS ARE ON PAGE 362.

PROPORTION

A **proportion** is made up of two equal ratios. For example, 2:4 = 1:2 (or $\frac{2}{4} = \frac{1}{2}$). Note that in the second form a proportion looks very much like equivalent fractions.

You learned that the cross products of equal fractions are equal to each other. In the example below, notice that both cross products are equal to 4.

$$\frac{2}{4} \times \frac{1}{2} \qquad \text{cross products: } \begin{aligned} 4 \times 1 &= 4 \\ 2 \times 2 &= 4 \end{aligned}$$

Each of the four numbers in a proportion is called an **element** or a **term**. In proportion problems one term is often missing. Your job is to find this missing term. Look at the example below. The letter n represents the missing term.

EXAMPLE 1 Find the missing term in $\frac{n}{8} = \frac{9}{12}$.

$$\textbf{(1)} \quad \begin{array}{r} 8 \\ \times 9 \\ \hline 72 \end{array} \qquad \textbf{(2)} \quad \begin{array}{r} 6 \\ 12\overline{)72} \end{array}$$

STEP 1 Find the cross product of 8 and 9.
STEP 2 Divide the cross product, 72, by 12. The value of the missing term is **6**.

RULES FOR SOLVING A PROPORTION

1. Find the cross product for the numbers that are given in the proportion.

2. Divide the cross product by the remaining number in the proportion.

EXAMPLE 2 Solve for c in $\frac{3}{7} = \frac{8}{c}$.

$$\textbf{(1)} \quad \begin{array}{r} 7 \\ \times 8 \\ \hline 56 \end{array} \qquad \textbf{(2)} \quad \begin{array}{r} 18\frac{2}{3} \\ 3\overline{)56} \end{array}$$

STEP 1 Find the cross product of 7 and 8.
STEP 2 Divide the cross product, 56, by 3. The value of c is $\mathbf{18\frac{2}{3}}$.

EXAMPLE 3 Solve for y in the proportion 5:y = 2:8.

$$\textbf{(1)} \quad \frac{5}{y} = \frac{2}{8} \qquad \textbf{(2)} \quad \begin{array}{r} 5 \\ \times 8 \\ \hline 40 \end{array} \qquad \textbf{(3)} \quad \begin{array}{r} 20 \\ 2\overline{)40} \end{array}$$

STEP 1 Rewrite the proportion in fractional form. Notice that the first term on either side of the equal sign becomes a numerator.
STEP 2 Find the cross product of 5 and 8.
STEP 3 Divide the cross product, 40, by 2. The value of y is **20**.

EXERCISE 5

Directions: Find the missing term in each proportion.

1. $\dfrac{m}{6} = \dfrac{10}{15}$ $\qquad$ $\dfrac{3}{a} = \dfrac{5}{6}$ $\qquad$ $\dfrac{4}{9} = \dfrac{y}{3}$ $\qquad$ $\dfrac{8}{7} = \dfrac{4}{x}$

2. $\dfrac{1}{3} = \dfrac{s}{5}$ $\qquad$ $\dfrac{3}{6} = \dfrac{w}{5}$ $\qquad$ $\dfrac{2}{11} = \dfrac{4}{p}$ $\qquad$ $\dfrac{2}{8} = \dfrac{9}{x}$

3. $4{:}e = 6{:}8$ $\qquad$ $3{:}7 = 4{:}y$ $\qquad$ $15{:}40 = x{:}60$ $\qquad$ $30{:}a = 12{:}16$

ANSWERS ARE ON PAGES 362–363.

PROPORTION WORD PROBLEMS

You can use proportions to solve many word problems. The key to using proportions is *setting up a problem carefully*. Like ratios, proportions are used to *compare* two numbers. It is extremely important to make sure that the numbers being compared are in the right order.

Study the next examples closely. Notice how the parts of the proportion are set up.

EXAMPLE 1 If 12 yards of lumber cost $40, how much do 30 yards cost?

(1) $\dfrac{\text{yards}}{\text{cost}} = \dfrac{12}{40} = \dfrac{30}{c}$ $\qquad$ **(2)** $\begin{array}{r} 40 \\ \times\, 30 \\ \hline 1200 \end{array}$ $\qquad$ **(3)** $\begin{array}{r} \$100 \\ 12\overline{)1200} \end{array}$

STEP 1 In this problem you are *comparing* yards to cost. Set up two ratios—yards are on the top in each ratio. Cost is on the bottom. Here *c* stands for the cost you are looking for.

STEP 2 Find the cross product of 40 and 30.

STEP 3 Divide 1200 by the other number in the proportion, 12. The cost of 30 yards of lumber is **$100**.

> **TIP:** Although *x* is often used to represent an unknown, you may want to use the first letter of the quantity you are looking for. In the example above, *c* is used to stand for *cost*. You will learn more about using letters to stand for numbers in the algebra chapter.

EXAMPLE 2 The ratio of the number of men to the number of women working in a certain hospital is 2:3. If 480 women work in the hospital, how many men work there?

(1) $\dfrac{\text{men}}{\text{women}}$ $\dfrac{2}{3} = \dfrac{m}{480}$ **(2)** $\begin{array}{r} 480 \\ \times\, 2 \\ \hline 960 \end{array}$ **(3)** $3\overline{)960}^{\,320}$ men

STEP 1   Make a proportion comparing men to women. The top number in each ratio refers to men. The bottom number refers to women. Here m stands for the unknown number of men.

STEP 2   Find the cross product of 2 and 480.

STEP 3   Divide 960 by the other number in the proportion, 3. There are **320 men** working in the hospital.

In some cases you may have to recognize how a proportion problem should be set up rather than find the solution itself. Example 3 shows this type of problem.

EXAMPLE 3 Manny drives 110 miles in 2 hours. Which expression below shows the distance he can go in 5 hours if he drives at the same speed?

(1) $\dfrac{5 \times 2}{110}$

(2) $\dfrac{110 \times 2}{5}$

(3) $\dfrac{110 \times 5}{2}$

(4) $\dfrac{110 + 5}{2}$

STEP 1   Make a proportion. The top number is miles, and the bottom number is hours. Here m stands for the unknown number of miles.

$\dfrac{\text{miles}}{\text{hours}}$ $\dfrac{110}{2} = \dfrac{m}{5}$

STEP 2   Show how you would multiply to find the first cross product.

110×5

STEP 3   Show how you would divide to find the missing number.

$\dfrac{110 \times 5}{2}$

STEP 4   Choose the solution that shows the cross product of 110 and 5 divided by the other number in the proportion, 2. This is an example of a "set-up" question that you learned about in Chapter 2. Choice **(3)** $\frac{110 \times 5}{2}$ is correct. Notice that choice **(4)** is wrong because it shows the sum instead of the product of 110 and 5.

PROBLEM SOLVING FOR THE GED

Using Proportion to Solve Word Problems

A tree 12 feet tall casts a shadow 15 feet long. The tree next to it casts a shadow 50 feet long. How many feet tall is the second tree?

(1) 27
(2) 40
(3) 47
(4) 50
(5) $62\frac{1}{2}$

At first glance you may not see that proportion will help you solve this problem. You don't see the word *ratio* or *proportion* mentioned anywhere. However, if you look closely, you will see that numbers are *being compared*. The height of a tree is being compared to the length of its shadow. This is a good clue that you may be able to use proportion to solve the problem.

The following steps should help you solve a problem like the one above.

1. Set up a ratio comparing the two quantities you are given. Remember to decide which category goes on the top of the ratio and which category goes on the bottom.

$$\frac{\text{tree}}{\text{shadow}} \quad \frac{12}{15}$$

2. Now set up a proportion using the third number you are given. Be sure to put this number in the right place, using the same order as in the ratio you have already set up.

In this problem you are given the length of another tree's shadow. Put this length in the denominator of your second ratio since this is the position of the other shadow length.

$$\frac{\text{tree}}{\text{shadow}} \quad \frac{12}{15} = \frac{x}{50}$$

3. Complete the proportion using the method you learned to find cross products.

$$12 \times 50 = 600 \qquad 15\overline{)600} \; 40$$

4. The tree is **40** feet tall. **(2)** is the correct answer.

GED Practice
EXERCISE 6

Directions: Solve each problem with a proportion.

1. The Towsons planted a 35-acre field that yielded 3150 bushels of wheat. At the same rate, how many acres would they need to produce 1890 bushels?

   (1) 17   **(4)** 30
   (2) 18   **(5)** 36
   (3) 21

2. If 6 feet of wire costs $3.40, how much do 9 feet of wire cost?

   (1) $1.70   **(4)** $4.60
   (2) $2.55   **(5)** $5.10
   (3) $3.40

3. The scale on a map says that 2 inches = 150 miles. If two cities are actually 325 miles apart, how many inches apart will they be on the map?

   (1) $3\frac{1}{4}$ **(4)** 7
   (2) $4\frac{1}{3}$ **(5)** 15
   (3) $5\frac{7}{8}$

4. How many hours will a plane take to go 1200 miles if it travels 450 miles in two hours?

   (1) $2\frac{3}{4}$ **(4)** 9
   (2) $4\frac{1}{2}$ **(5)** 12
   (3) $5\frac{1}{3}$

5. To make a certain color of paint, the ratio of blue paint to white paint is 5:2. How many gallons of blue paint are required to mix with 14 gallons of white paint?

   (1) 14   **(4)** 35
   (2) 21   **(5)** 42
   (3) 28

6. On a certain bar graph a line $2\frac{1}{2}$ inches long represents 75 degrees. How many inches of bar are required to represent 110 degrees?

   (1) $3\frac{2}{3}$ **(4)** $9\frac{2}{3}$
   (2) $4\frac{1}{2}$ **(5)** 11
   (3) $7\frac{1}{3}$

7. A snapshot that was 3 inches wide and 5 inches long was enlarged to be 12 inches long. Which expression below represents the width of the enlargement?

   (1) $\dfrac{3 + 12}{5}$ **(4)** $\dfrac{3 \cdot 5}{12}$

   (2) $\dfrac{5 \cdot 12}{3}$ **(5)** $\dfrac{5 + 12}{3}$

   (3) $\dfrac{3 \cdot 12}{5}$

8. A worker can make 16 parts in 2 hours. Which expression below represents the time the worker needs to make 100 parts?

   (1) $\dfrac{2 \times 100}{16}$ **(4)** $\dfrac{16 + 2}{100}$

   (2) $\dfrac{16 \times 100}{2}$ **(5)** $\dfrac{2}{16 \times 100}$

   (3) $\dfrac{16 \times 2}{100}$

9. A recipe calls for 2 cups of sugar for every 3 cups of flour. Which expression below shows the number of cups of sugar a cook needs with 12 cups of flour?

   (1) $\dfrac{2 \times 3}{12}$ **(4)** $\dfrac{2 \times 12}{3}$

   (2) $\dfrac{3 + 12}{2}$ **(5)** $\dfrac{2 + 12}{3}$

   (3) $\dfrac{3 \times 12}{2}$

10. Apples cost 90 cents a dozen. Which expression below represents the cost of 8 apples?

   (1) $(12 \times 8) \times 90$ **(4)** $\dfrac{90 \times 12}{8}$

   (2) $\dfrac{90 \times 8}{12}$ **(5)** $\dfrac{90 + 12}{8}$

   (3) $\dfrac{90}{12 \times 8}$

ANSWERS ARE ON PAGE 363.

TWO-PART PROPORTION WORD PROBLEMS

Your first step in solving any problem involving proportion is to decide which quantity goes on the top of each ratio and which quantity goes on the bottom. This order *must remain consistent* throughout your work in the problem.

For some proportion word problems one of the quantities to include in a ratio may not be given. You will need to find this quantity before you can continue to solve the problem. Read the next example carefully.

EXAMPLE

Carlos got 2 problems wrong for every 5 problems right on a test. How many problems did Carlos get wrong if there were 35 problems altogether on the test?

(1) $\dfrac{\text{wrong}}{\text{total}}$ $\dfrac{w}{35}$ **(2)** $\dfrac{\text{wrong}}{\text{total}}$ $\dfrac{2}{7}$ **(3)** $\dfrac{2}{7} = \dfrac{w}{35}$ $35 \times 2 = 70$ $7\overline{)70}^{\,10}$

STEP 1   The question in this problem asks you to compare the number of wrong answers to the total number of problems. First set up a ratio using a letter to stand for the number you are being asked to find.

STEP 2   You need to set up a proportion to solve the problem. Therefore, you will need another ratio that compares wrong answers to total answers. If you look at the numbers given, you find a number corresponding to *wrong* answers (2) but no number corresponding to *total* answers. You need to find a total to complete the proportion. Carlos got 2 problems wrong for every 5 problems right. This means that he got 2 wrong out of a *total* of 7 problems (wrong + right = total).

STEP 3   Now set up your proportion and solve for the missing element.

Carlos got **10 problems** wrong on the test.

> **TIP:** Before you set up a proportion, carefully read the problem over to find out whether you need to add or subtract to set up a ratio.

RATIO AND PROPORTION REVIEW

Directions: Solve each problem.

1. For every $10 Helen takes home, her employer withholds $3 for taxes and social security. Helen's gross pay each month is $1950. How much does she take home each month?

2. Pat's softball team won 5 games for every 3 games it lost. Altogether the team played 32 games. How many games did it win?

3. The ratio of the number of men to the number of women working at Apex, Inc., is 7:2. Altogether there are 360 workers at the company. How many of the workers are women?

4. The ratio of good parts to defective parts coming off the assembly line at Apex, Inc., is 20:1. Every day the factory produces 10,500 parts. How many of these parts are defective?

5. Recently 300 people in Central County took a civil service examination. For every five people who passed the examination, one person failed. How many people passed?

6. The ratio of the workers who voted to strike to the workers who voted not to strike at Apex was 3:2. 360 workers voted. How many voted to strike?

7. A ladder is placed against a building 40 feet from the ground. The bottom of the ladder is 13 feet from the side of the building. If another ladder is placed against the building at the same angle 20 feet from the ground, how far from the building will the bottom of the ladder be? *Hint:* Set up a proportion comparing the height of the ladder to the distance on the ground.

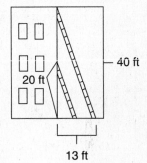

8. The picture shown at the right is to be enlarged. The short side will measure 20 inches. What will be the measurement of the long side?

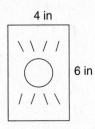

9. For every $9 that Fumiko makes she spends $7. The rest goes into her savings account. If her weekly take-home pay is $540, how much does she save each week?

10.

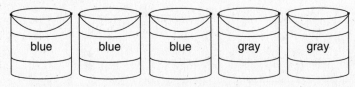

The illustration above shows the ratio of blue paint to gray paint in a special color mix. How many gallons of gray paint are needed to make a total of 30 gallons of mix?

ANSWERS ARE ON PAGES 363–364.

6 Percents

UNDERSTANDING PERCENTS

Percents are commonly used in the business world. Percents are used to measure commissions, taxes, interest, markups, and discounts. Like the decimals and fractions you have already studied, **percents** are another way of *describing the parts of a whole*.

With decimals one whole is divided into tenths, hundredths, thousandths, etc. With fractions one whole can be divided into *any* number of parts (2, 3, 4, 5, etc.). With percents one whole is always divided into 100 parts. The percent sign, %, means "per 100" or "out of 100."

Each square below is divided into 100 equal parts.

A 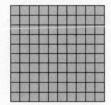   B 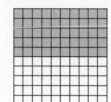   C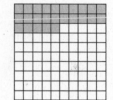

- In square A all **100** parts are shaded. We can say that **100%** of the square is shaded. 100% is the same as one whole.

- In square B **50** of the 100 parts are shaded. **50%** of the square is shaded. 50% is the same as one-half.

- In square C **25** of the 100 parts are shaded. **25%** of the square is shaded. 25% is the same as one-quarter.

- In square D **10** of the 100 parts are shaded. **10%** of the square is shaded. 10% is the same as one-tenth.

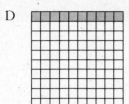 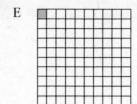 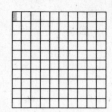

- In square E only **1** of the 100 parts is shaded. **1%** of the square is shaded. 1% is the same as $\frac{1}{100}$.

- In square F **$\frac{1}{2}$** of 1 part of the square is shaded. **$\frac{1}{2}$%** of the square is shaded. We can also say that $\frac{1}{2}$ of 1 percent of this square is shaded. You know that $\frac{1}{2}$ can be written as the decimal .5. Therefore, we can also say that .5% ($\frac{5}{10}$ of 1 percent) of the square is shaded. Any percent less than 1% has a value of less than $\frac{1}{100}$.

Mixed decimals like 2.6 and 1.05 are used to represent amounts greater than one whole. Mixed numbers like $1\frac{1}{2}$ or $10\frac{3}{4}$ also represent amounts greater than one whole. With percents one whole is represented as 100%. Percents greater than 100% represent amounts greater than one whole. For example, 150% and 1000% are greater than one whole.

> **TIP:** Remember that any percent less than 1% has a value less than $\frac{1}{100}$, and any percent greater than 100% has a value greater than 1.

EXERCISE 1

Directions: Use the following list of percents to answer the next questions.

60%	110%	99%	$\frac{1}{4}$%	6.5%	0.9%
2%	$83\frac{1}{3}$%	.65%	240%	0.1%	650%

1. From the list above, choose the percents that have a value between $\frac{1}{100}$ (1%) and one whole (100%).

2. From the list above, choose the percents that have a value greater than one whole (100%).

3. From the list above, choose the percents that have a value less than $\frac{1}{100}$ (1%).

ANSWERS ARE ON PAGE 364.

DECIMALS AND PERCENTS
Changing a Percent to a Decimal

In some problems you may need to change a percent to a decimal to make the amounts easier to work with.

When a percent contains a fraction, remember that a decimal point is understood to be to the right of the last *whole number digit*.

EXAMPLES $\quad 33\frac{1}{3}\% = .33.\frac{1}{3} = .33\frac{1}{3} \qquad 6\frac{2}{3}\% = .06.\frac{2}{3} = .06\frac{2}{3}$

In these examples $\frac{1}{3}$ and $\frac{2}{3}$ *are not place values.* The decimal point is understood to be after the 3 and after the 6 in the units place, the *last whole number digit.*

RULE FOR CHANGING A PERCENT TO A DECIMAL
Drop the percent sign (%) and move the decimal point two places to the *left*.

TIP: Remember that a whole number written without a decimal point is understood to have a decimal point to the right of the units digit.

Changing a percent to a decimal is like dividing by 100. Notice that you can drop an end zero in a decimal without changing the decimal's value.

EXAMPLES $\quad 18\% = .18. = .18 \qquad 250\% = 2.50. = 2.5$

You may have to write extra zeros to the left of the digits to move the point two places.

EXAMPLES $\quad 3.2\% = .03.2 = .032 \qquad .25\% = .00.25 = .0025$

EXERCISE 2

Directions: Change each percent to a decimal or a whole number.

1. 9% =
2. 24% =
3. 100% =
4. .3% =

5. $87\frac{1}{2}\%$ =
6. $8\frac{1}{3}\%$ =
7. .15% =
8. 275% =

9. 2.7% =
10. 3.95% =
11. 57% =
12. 1000% =

ANSWERS ARE ON PAGE 364.

Changing a Decimal to a Percent

In other problems you may need to change a decimal to a percent, again to make amounts easier to work with.

RULE FOR CHANGING A DECIMAL TO A PERCENT
Move the decimal point two places to the *right* and write the percent sign after the last digit.

EXAMPLES
.25 = .25. = 25%

.19 = .19. = 19%

3.65 = 3.65. = 365%

.625 = .62.5 = 62.5%

Notice that you do not have to write the decimal point when it moves to the end of the number.

You may have to write extra zeros to the right of the digits to move the decimal point two places.

EXAMPLES
.6 = .60. = 60%

2.7 = 2.70. = 270%

36 = 36.00. = 3600%

You do not write the decimal point when it moves between a digit and a fraction.

EXAMPLES
$.37\frac{1}{2} = .37\frac{1}{2} = 37\frac{1}{2}\%$

$.14\frac{1}{4} = .14\frac{1}{4} = 14\frac{1}{4}\%$

$.05\frac{1}{3} = .05\frac{1}{3} = 5\frac{1}{3}\%$

You can drop unnecessary zeros after you move the decimal point.

EXAMPLES
.045 = .04.5 = 4.5%

.003 = .00.3 = .3%

.0008 = .00.08 = .08%

EXERCISE 3

Directions: Change each decimal to a percent.

1. .81 =

2. .37$\frac{1}{2}$ =

3. .5 =

4. .004 =

5. .0009 =

6. .217 =

7. .03 =

8. .33$\frac{1}{3}$ =

9. 2.1 =

10. 4.85 =

11. 3.924 =

12. .015 =

ANSWERS ARE ON PAGE 364.

FRACTIONS AND PERCENTS

Changing a Fraction to a Percent

Suppose you work five days a week. Your *whole* workweek, expressed as a fraction, is $\frac{5}{5}$, or 5 out of 5 days. If you are out sick for one day, you miss one out of five days of work or $\frac{1}{5}$ of the workweek.

In percent, your *whole* workweek is 100% of the workweek. You can say that you were sick for $\frac{1}{5}$ of 100%. You know from studying fractions that to find a "fraction of" something means to multiply.

$$\frac{1}{5} \times 100\% = \frac{20}{1} = 20\%$$

In other words, you were sick for **20%** of your workweek.

CHANGING A FRACTION TO A PERCENT
Method 1　Multiply the fraction by 100%.

METHOD 1　Change $\frac{3}{4}$ to a percent.
$\frac{3}{4} \times 100\% = 75\%$

CHANGING A FRACTION TO A PERCENT

Method 2 Divide the denominator of the fraction into the numerator.
Then change the decimal point.

METHOD 2 Change $\frac{3}{4}$ to a percent.

$$4 \overline{)3.00} \quad .75 \qquad .75 = 75\%$$

When the denominator of the fraction does not divide evenly into 100, the percent will contain a fraction.

EXAMPLE 1 Change $\frac{5}{7}$ to a percent.

METHOD 1

$$\frac{5}{7} \times \frac{100\%}{1} = \frac{500}{7} = \mathbf{71\frac{3}{7}\%}$$

METHOD 2

$$.71\frac{3}{7}\% = \mathbf{71\frac{3}{7}\%}$$
$$7)5.00$$
$$\underline{4\,9}$$
$$10$$
$$\underline{7}$$
$$3$$

To change any proper or improper fraction to a percent, be sure the fraction is reduced. This makes your work easier. Look at Example 2.

EXAMPLE 2 Change $\frac{30}{25}$ to a percent.

METHOD 1 **(1)** $\frac{30}{25} = \frac{6}{5}$ **(2)** $\frac{6}{5} \times \frac{100\%}{1} = \mathbf{120\%}$

STEP 1 Reduce the improper fraction.
STEP 2 Multiply the reduced fraction by 100%.

METHOD 2 $\dfrac{1.20}{5)6.00} = \mathbf{120\%}$

Divide the numerator by the denominator and change the decimal to a percent.

EXERCISE 4

Directions: Change each fraction to a percent. Use whichever method you prefer.

1. $\frac{1}{5} =$ **5.** $\frac{14}{8} =$ **9.** $\frac{1}{6} =$

2. $\frac{5}{6} =$ **6.** $\frac{9}{10} =$ **10.** $\frac{10}{5} =$

3. $\frac{3}{8} =$ **7.** $\frac{5}{12} =$ **11.** $\frac{1}{12} =$

4. $\frac{2}{3} =$ **8.** $\frac{6}{7} =$ **12.** $\frac{2}{11} =$

ANSWERS ARE ON PAGE 364.

Changing a Percent to a Fraction

A percent can be expressed as a fraction with a denominator of 100. For example, 20% is the same as $\frac{20}{100}$.

> ### RULE FOR CHANGING A PERCENT TO A FRACTION OR A MIXED NUMBER
>
> Replace the % sign with a denominator of 100 and reduce.

EXAMPLE 1 Change 75% to a fraction.

$$75\% = \frac{75}{100} = \frac{3}{4}$$

EXAMPLE 2 Change 125% to a mixed number.

$$125\% = \frac{125}{100} = 1\frac{1}{4}$$

Some percents, like $16\frac{2}{3}\%$, are hard to reduce when you replace the percent sign with 100. To simplify these percents, divide by 100 instead of trying to reduce the fraction. You can divide by 100 because a fraction bar means "divided by."

$$\frac{16\frac{2}{3}}{100} \text{ means } 16\frac{2}{3} \text{ divided by 100.}$$

EXAMPLE 3 Change $16\frac{2}{3}\%$ to a fraction.

STEP 1 Write $16\frac{2}{3}$ over a denominator of 100.

$$\frac{16\frac{2}{3}}{100}$$

STEP 2 Rewrite the problem as a division problem.

$$16\frac{2}{3} \div 100$$

STEP 3 Change $16\frac{2}{3}$ to an improper fraction, invert 100 to $\frac{1}{100}$, and multiply.

$$\frac{50}{3} \div \frac{100}{1} \qquad \frac{\overset{1}{\cancel{50}}}{3} \times \frac{1}{\underset{2}{\cancel{100}}} = \frac{1}{6}$$

Percents containing decimals can also be changed. First change these percents to decimals. Then change the decimals to fractions and reduce.

EXAMPLE 4 Change 2.5% to a fraction.

STEP 1 Change 2.5% to a decimal by dropping the percent sign and moving the decimal point two places to the left.   2.5% = .02.5 = .025

STEP 2 Change .025 to a fraction. Three places are thousandths. 25 is the numerator, and 1000 is the denominator. Reduce the fraction to lowest terms. $.025 = \frac{25}{1000} = \frac{1}{40}$

EXERCISE 5

Directions: Change each percent to a fraction or a mixed number and reduce.

1. 45% =

2. $37\frac{1}{2}$% =

3. $6\frac{2}{3}$% =

4. 8% =

5. 2% =

6. $83\frac{1}{3}$% =

7. 24% =

8. $33\frac{1}{3}$% =

9. $28\frac{4}{7}$% =

10. 80% =

11. 150% =

12. $12\frac{1}{2}$% =

13. 1.5% =

14. .09% =

15. .6% =

16. 1% =

ANSWERS ARE ON PAGE 365.

COMMON FRACTIONS, DECIMALS, AND PERCENTS

The values on the following chart are some of the most commonly used fractions, decimals, and percents. Knowing these equivalences is useful.

EXERCISE 6

Directions: Fill in the missing numbers in the chart. The first line has been done for you.

Fraction	Decimal	Percent
$\frac{1}{4}$	.25	25%
$\frac{1}{2}$		
		75%
	.125 or .12$\frac{1}{2}$	
		20%
	.4	
$\frac{3}{5}$		
		80%
	.1	
$\frac{3}{10}$		
		70%
	.9	
	.33$\frac{1}{3}$	
$\frac{2}{3}$		

ANSWERS ARE ON PAGE 365.

PROPORTION AND PERCENTS

The most important part of working with proportions is setting them up.

Three cans are 50% of a six-pack. The statement "3 is 50% of 6" contains three facts:

6 is the whole.
3 is a part.
50 is the percent.

Each number in a percent statement fits into a proportion:

$$\frac{part}{whole} = \frac{\%}{100}$$

Whenever you use a proportion to solve a percent problem, you will use this set-up. This makes sense if you think of the right-hand ratio as comparing a *part* of a percent to the *whole* percent. The right-hand side of the proportion below is showing 50% as a part of a whole, 100%. The proportion for the six-pack problem is

$$\frac{3 \text{ cans}}{6 \text{ cans}} = \frac{50}{100}$$

Notice that the cross products of the proportion are equal.

$3 \times 100 = 300$ and $6 \times 50 = 300$

You can use proportion to solve many percent problems.

RULES FOR USING PROPORTION WITH PERCENTS

$$\frac{part}{whole} = \frac{\%}{100}$$

1. Fill in the information given in a percent problem as shown above. Use a letter to stand for the missing term.

2. Find the cross product in the proportion.

3. Divide by the remaining number in the proportion.

The first step in setting up the proportion will be determining which number is the *part*, which number is the *whole,* and which number is the *percent.* Finding the percent is usually easy because either the word *percent* or the symbol % will appear after the number. The part and the whole are a little more difficult to identify. One clue is to look for the word *of.* The *whole* usually follows this word. Once you have found the percent and the whole, the *part* will be the only number left in the problem.

Once you have identified the percent, the part, and the whole, set up a proportion. Remember that the number 100 (which stands for 100%) *always* goes in the bottom of the second ratio.

EXERCISE 7

Directions: In this exercise, practice identifying the percent, the part, and the whole. Then practice setting up proportions. The first problem is done for you.

    P   **%**   **W**

1. 18 is 50 percent of 36. $\frac{18}{36} = \frac{50}{100}$ **5.** 30% of 200 is 60.

2. 80% of 25 is 20.   **6.** 13 is equal to 20 percent of 65.

3. 45 is 10% of 450.   **7.** 107 is 100% of 107.

4. 16% of 25 equals 4.   **8.** 50 is 50 percent of one hundred.

ANSWERS ARE ON PAGE 365.

PERCENT PROBLEMS

In the next examples you will learn how to use proportion to solve percent problems. In percent problems one of the three elements needed to set up a proportion will be missing. In other words you will be trying to find a percent, a whole, or a part. As with any proportion, be sure you put each number in the correct position when solving the problem.

Finding the Percent

EXAMPLE   27 is what percent of 45?

(1) $\dfrac{\text{part}}{\text{whole}}$ $\dfrac{27}{45} = \dfrac{x}{100}$ **(2)**   **(3)** $\begin{array}{r} 60\% \\ 45)\overline{2700} \\ \underline{270} \\ 00 \end{array}$

where (2) is:
$$\begin{array}{r} 27 \\ \times 100 \\ \hline 2700 \end{array}$$

STEP 1   Fill in the terms of the proportion. Always put 100 in the lower right. 45 follows the word *of.* 45 is the whole. Put 45 in the lower left. 27 is the part. Put 27 in the upper left. You are looking for the percent. Let *x* stand for the percent.

STEP 2   Find the cross product of 27 and 100.

STEP 3   Divide 2700 by the remaining number in the proportion, 45. 27 is **60%** of 45.

EXERCISE 8

Directions: Solve each problem. Be sure to set up a proportion first.

1. 9 is what percent of 36?

2. 14 is what percent of 35?

3. 50 is what percent of 75?

4. 40 is what percent of 16?

5. 120 is what percent of 160?

ANSWERS ARE ON PAGES 365–366.

Finding the Part

EXAMPLE 1   What is 15% of 60?

(1) $\dfrac{\text{part}}{\text{whole}}$ $\dfrac{p}{60} = \dfrac{15}{100}$ **(2)** $\begin{array}{r} 15 \\ \times 60 \\ \hline 900 \end{array}$ **(3)** $100\overline{)900}\,^{9}$

STEP 1   Fill in the terms of the proportion. Always put 100 in the lower right. Put 15 in the upper right. 60 follows the word *of*. 60 is the whole. Put 60 in the lower left. You are looking for the part. Let *p* stand for the part.

STEP 2   Find the cross product of 60 and 15.

STEP 3   Divide 900 by the remaining number in the proportion, 100. 15% of 60 is **9**.

EXAMPLE 2   Find $62\frac{1}{2}$% of 56.

(1) $\dfrac{\text{part}}{\text{whole}}$ $\dfrac{p}{56} = \dfrac{62\frac{1}{2}}{100}$ **(2)** $56 \times 62\frac{1}{2} =$ **(3)** $100\overline{)3500}\,^{35}$

$\dfrac{\overset{28}{\cancel{56}}}{1} \times \dfrac{125}{\underset{1}{\cancel{2}}} = 3500$

STEP 1   Fill in the terms of the proportion. Put 100 in the lower right. Put $62\frac{1}{2}$ in the upper right. 56 follows the word *of*. 56 is the whole. Put 56 in the lower left. You are looking for the part. Let *p* stand for the part.

STEP 2   Find the cross product of 56 and $62\frac{1}{2}$.

STEP 3   Divide 3500 by the remaining number in the proportion, 100. $62\frac{1}{2}$% of 56 is **35**.

In some problems the number we call the *part* is larger than the whole. This happens when you are finding more than 100% of a number.

EXAMPLE 3 What is 180% of 250?

(1) $\dfrac{\text{part}}{\text{whole}}$ $\dfrac{p}{250} = \dfrac{180}{100}$ **(2)** $\begin{array}{r} 250 \\ \times 180 \\ \hline 20\,000 \\ 25\,0 \\ \hline 45,000 \end{array}$ **(3)** $\begin{array}{r} 450 \\ 100\overline{)45,000} \end{array}$

STEP 1 Fill in the terms of the proportion. 180 goes in the upper right, and 100 goes in the lower right. 250 follows the word *of*. 250 is the whole. Put 250 in the lower left. You are looking for the part. Let p stand for the part.

STEP 2 Find the cross product of 250 and 180.

STEP 3 Divide 45,000 by the remaining number in the proportion, 100. 180% of 250 = **450**.

EXERCISE 9

Directions: Solve each problem using proportions.

1. Find 30% of 90.

2. Find 65% of 140.

3. What is $16\frac{2}{3}\%$ of 72?

4. Find 8.5% of 500.

5. What is 300% of 60?

ANSWERS ARE ON PAGE 366.

Finding the Whole

You will often know that you need to find the whole because there is no number following the word *of*. Following the word *of*, there will be a phrase such as *what number*.

EXAMPLE 8 is 50% of what number?

(1) $\dfrac{\text{part}}{\text{whole}}$ $\dfrac{8}{w} = \dfrac{50}{100}$ **(2)** $\begin{array}{r} 100 \\ \times 8 \\ \hline 800 \end{array}$ **(3)** $\begin{array}{r} 16 \\ 50\overline{)800} \end{array}$

STEP 1 Fill in the terms of the proportion. 50 goes in the upper right, and 100 goes in the lower right. The words *what number* follow the word *of*. The *whole* is missing. Let w stand for the whole. 8 is the part. Put 8 in the upper left.

STEP 2 Find the cross product of 8 and 100.

STEP 3 Divide 800 by the remaining number in the proportion, 50.
8 is 50% of **16**.

EXERCISE 10

Directions: Solve each problem using proportions.

1. 18 is 50% of what number?　　**3.** 2 is $12\frac{1}{2}$% of what number?

2. 24 is 15% of what number?　　**4.** 86 is 200% of what number?

ANSWERS ARE ON PAGE 366.

TYPES OF PERCENT PROBLEMS

You now know how to use proportion to solve three kinds of percent problems: (1) finding the part, (2) finding the percent, and (3) finding the whole. Remember that the whole usually follows the word *of*, and when the percent is given, it has the percent sign (%).

Your first step in any percent problem is *to find what element is missing*.

EXAMPLE 1　What are you looking for (the *part*, the *percent*, or the *whole*) in this problem: What is 60% of 45?

SOLUTION　60 is the percent because it has the percent sign. 45 is the whole because it follows the word *of*. You are looking for the **part**.

EXAMPLE 2　What are you looking for (the *part*, the *percent*, or the *whole*) in this problem: 12 is 50% of what number?

SOLUTION　The words *what number* follow the word *of*. You are looking for the **whole**. 50 is the percent, and 12 is the part.

EXAMPLE 3　What are you looking for (the *part*, the *percent*, or the *whole*) in this problem: 16 is what percent of 64?

SOLUTION　The problem does not contain a percent. You are looking for the **percent**. 16 is the part, and 64 is the whole.

EXERCISE 11

Directions: First state what is being asked for (the part, the percent, or the whole) in each problem. Then go back and solve each problem.

1. 16 is what percent of 32?　　**6.** 15 is what percent of 45?

2. Find 80% of 90.　　**7.** What is 3.6% of 900?

3. 30 is 60% of what number?　　**8.** 120 is what percent of 80?

4. What is $4\frac{1}{2}$% of 800?　　**9.** $33\frac{1}{3}$% of what number is 45?

5. What percent of 50 is 14?　　**10.** What is 8.6% of 200?

ANSWERS ARE ON PAGES 366–367.

PERCENT WORD PROBLEMS

To solve percent word problems, first decide whether you are looking for the part, the percent, or the whole. Study the next examples carefully.

EXAMPLE 1   Mr. Gomez pays $80 for a suit. He puts a 30% markup on each suit that he sells in his store. Find the amount of the markup.

(1) $\dfrac{\text{part}}{\text{whole}} \quad \dfrac{m}{80} = \dfrac{30}{100}$
(2) $\begin{array}{r} 80 \\ \times\ 30 \\ \hline 2400 \end{array}$
(3) $100\overline{)2400}^{\ \$24}$

STEP 1   Decide whether you are looking for the part, the percent, or the whole. 30 is the percent, and $80, the cost of the suit, is the whole. You are looking for the part, the amount of the markup. Fill in the terms of the proportion. Let m stand for the markup.

STEP 2   Find the cross product of 80 and 30.

STEP 3   Divide 2400 by the remaining number in the proportion, 100. The amount of the markup is **$24**.

EXAMPLE 2   Mrs. Jackson makes $200 a week. She spends $60 a week for food. Food represents what percent of Mrs. Jackson's income?

(1) $\dfrac{\text{part}}{\text{whole}} \quad \dfrac{60}{200} = \dfrac{x}{100}$
(2) $\begin{array}{r} 60 \\ \times\ 100 \\ \hline 6000 \end{array}$
(3) $200\overline{)6000}^{\ 30\%}$

STEP 1   Decide whether you are looking for the part, the percent, or the whole. $60 is the *part* Mrs. Jackson spends on food. $200 is her *whole* income. You are looking for the percent of her income she spends for food. Fill in the terms of the proportion. Let x stand for the percent.

STEP 2   Find the cross product of 60 and 100.

STEP 3   Divide 6000 by the remaining number in the proportion, 200. Mrs. Jackson pays **30%** of her weekly income for food.

EXAMPLE 3   Lois got a 6% commission for selling a house. Her commission was $3000. Find the selling price of the house.

(1) $\dfrac{\text{part}}{\text{whole}} \quad \dfrac{3000}{w} = \dfrac{6}{100}$
(2) $\begin{array}{r} 3000 \\ \times\ 100 \\ \hline 300{,}000 \end{array}$
(3) $6\overline{)300{,}000}^{\ \$50{,}000}$

STEP 1   Decide whether you are looking for the part, the percent, or the whole. 6 is the percent. $3000 is the part Lois received as a commission. You are looking for the whole, the selling price of the house. Fill in the terms of the proportion. Let w stand for the whole price of the house.

STEP 2   Find the cross product of 3000 and 100.

STEP 3   Divide 300,000 by the remaining number in the proportion, 6. The selling price of the house was **$50,000**.

EXERCISE 12

Directions: First write down what is being asked for in each problem—the *part*, the *percent*, or the *whole*. Then set up a proportion and solve each problem.

1. A jacket originally selling for $40 was on sale for 15% off the original price. How much is saved by buying the jacket on sale?

2. Mr. and Mrs. Shin need $8000 for a down payment on a house. So far they have saved $6000. What percent of the total amount have they saved?

3. Alfredo earns $250 a week. His employer deducts 12% of his earnings for taxes and social security. How much is deducted from Alfredo's weekly pay?

4. John now weighs 172 pounds. This is 80% of what John weighed a year ago. How much did John weigh a year ago?

5. Fiona makes $600 a month and pays $150 a month for rent. Rent is what percent of her income?

6. The sales tax in Muhammed's state is 6%. How much tax does Muhammed have to pay for a television that costs $240?

7. Eighteen people showed up for David's evening math class. This represents 75% of the number registered for the class. How many people are registered for the class?

8. Mr. Kee pays $20 for a pair of shoes. He puts a $6 markup on every pair of shoes in his store. The markup is what percent of the price Mr. Kee pays?

    (1) 6%
    (2) 10%
    (3) 20%
    (4) 30%
    (5) 40%

9. Eva sells cosmetics for a 9% commission. In November her sales were $3840. How much did she make in commissions in November?

    (1) $384.00
    (2) $345.60
    (3) $307.20
    (4) $268.80
    (5) $230.40

ANSWERS ARE ON PAGE 367.

MULTI-STEP PERCENT PROBLEMS

In many percent problems you must do more than simply find the missing element. Once you have set up a proportion and found the part, the whole, and the percent, you may have to use this information to find yet another number. With this kind of problem, remember that you will need to perform a series of steps to get your answer. The first step *always* is setting up a proportion.

Finding the Part

In the following example, first you need to find the part, then you must add this amount to the whole to get a total amount.

EXAMPLE 1   The owner of the Victoria Clothing Store pays $75 each for men's suits. He puts a 40% markup on each suit. How much does he charge for each suit?

(1) $\dfrac{\text{part}}{\text{whole}}$ $\dfrac{p}{75} = \dfrac{40}{100}$ **(2)** $\begin{array}{r} 75 \\ \times\ 40 \\ \hline 3000 \end{array}$ **(3)** $100\overline{)3000}\ ^{30}$ **(4)** $\begin{array}{r} 75 \\ +\ 30 \\ \hline \$105 \end{array}$

STEP 1   You want to find the selling price of the suit, but first you need to find the part, the amount of the markup. Fill in the terms of the proportion. 40 is the percent, and 75 is the whole. Let p stand for the part.

STEP 2   Find the cross product of 75 and 40.

STEP 3   Divide 3000 by the remaining number in the proportion, 100. The part, or markup, is $30.

STEP 4   Although you have found the missing element in the proportion, you are not finished. The question asks how much the owner charges for a suit. This is his cost plus the markup. Add $30 to the original price. The selling price of the suit is **$105**.

In other problems you may have to subtract the part from the original amount.

EXAMPLE 2   A chair originally sold for $130. It was on sale at a 20% discount. Find the sale price of the chair.

(1) $\dfrac{\text{part}}{\text{whole}}$ $\dfrac{p}{130} = \dfrac{20}{100}$ **(2)** $\begin{array}{r} 130 \\ \times\ 20 \\ \hline 2600 \end{array}$ **(3)** $100\overline{)2600}\ ^{26}$ **(4)** $\begin{array}{r} \$130 \\ -\ 26 \\ \hline \$104 \end{array}$

STEP 1   You want to find the sale price of the chair, but first you need to find the part, the amount of the discount. Fill in the terms of the proportion. 20 is the percent, and 130 is the whole. Let p stand for the part.

STEP 2   Find the cross product of 130 and 20.

STEP 3   Divide 2600 by the remaining number in the proportion, 100. The part, or discount, is $26.

STEP 4   The question asks you for the sale price. To get this, subtract the discount from the original price. Subtract $26 from $130. The sale price of the chair is **$104**.

> **TIP:** One key to solving a percent problem is to read the question carefully and *understand what you are being asked to find*.

EXERCISE 13

Directions: For questions 1–7, solve each problem.

1. The owner of Gordon's Shoe Store pays $12 for a pair of children's shoes. He puts a 45% markup on each pair. Find the selling price of a pair of children's shoes at Gordon's.

2. A farm with a market value of $120,000 was assessed for 60% of its market value. The farm is taxed at 2% of the assessed value. Find the yearly tax on the farm.

3. Floria makes $15,600 a year. She spends 25% of her salary on rent. How much rent does Floria spend each month?

4. Fran bought new furniture for $1800. She paid 15% down and $50 a month for 36 months. Find the total amount she paid for the furniture.

5. The 100th Street Block Association wants to raise $500 to plant trees on its street. By the end of two weeks the association raised 65% of the amount it wanted. How much more did it need to raise?

   (1) $565
   (2) $500
   (3) $325
   (4) $250
   (5) $175

6. Arthur's gross salary is $3000 a month. His employer withholds 10% for federal tax, 5% for social security, and 5% for state tax. Find Arthur's net salary for the month.

   (1) $2000
   (2) $2400
   (3) $2550
   (4) $2800
   (5) $3000

7. The population of Pleasant Hill was 2200 in 1983. By 1993 the population was 125% more than the 1983 population. How many people lived in Pleasant Hill in 1993?

   (1) 2375
   (2) 2750
   (3) 3275
   (4) 3450
   (5) 4950

ANSWERS ARE ON PAGES 367–368.

Rate of Increase and Rate of Decrease

In some percent problems you will have to find the rate, in percent, that an amount changes over a period of time. You must compare the change (or difference) to the original amount. In the proportions for these problems *the part is always the change, and the whole is always the original amount*. When an amount goes up, the percent of change is called the ***rate of increase***. When an amount goes down, the percent of change is called the ***rate of decrease***.

EXAMPLE 1   Nina bought some living room furniture for $2500. Only a month later, she found that she had to sell it. Because it was not brand-new, she received only $2100 from the sale. What was the rate of decrease on the furniture?

STEP 1   Subtract to find the difference between the two amounts.

$$\begin{array}{r} \$2500 \\ -2100 \\ \hline \$\ \ 400 \end{array}$$

STEP 2   Fill in the terms of the proportion. $2500, the *original* amount, is the whole. $400, the difference, is the part. Let x stand for the percent.

$$\frac{\text{part}}{\text{whole}} \quad \frac{400}{2500} = \frac{x}{100}$$

STEP 3   Find the cross product of 400 and 100.

$$\begin{array}{r} 400 \\ \times\ 100 \\ \hline 40{,}000 \end{array}$$

STEP 4   Divide 40,000 by the remaining number in the proportion, 2500. The rate of decrease was **16%**.

$$\begin{array}{r} 16 \\ 2500\overline{)40{,}000} \end{array}$$

> **TIP:** Whenever you are finding percent of increase or decrease, you are comparing an amount of change to the *original* number. Therefore, the bottom number in the proportion is always the *original* number.

EXAMPLE 2   Over the past 10 years the population of Little Lake, Minnesota, has increased from 1200 to 1500 people. What was the rate of increase in the population?

STEP 1   Subtract to find the amount of the increase (or difference).

$$\begin{array}{r} 1500 \\ -\ 1200 \\ \hline 300 \end{array}$$

STEP 2　Fill in the terms of the proportion. The part, or change (or difference), is 300. The whole, or original, is 1200. Let x stand for the percent.

$$\frac{\text{part}}{\text{whole}}\quad\frac{300}{1200} = \frac{x}{100}$$

STEP 3　Find the cross product of 300 and 100.

$$\begin{array}{r} 300 \\ \times\ 100 \\ \hline 30,000 \end{array}$$

STEP 4　Divide 30,000 by the remaining number in the proportion, 1200. The rate of increase is **25%**.

$$\begin{array}{r} 25 \\ 1,200\overline{)30,000} \\ 24\ 00 \\ \hline 6\ 000 \\ 6\ 000 \\ \hline \end{array}$$

EXERCISE 14

Directions: Solve each problem.

1. The price of a dozen eggs increased from $.84 to $.90. What was the percent of increase in the price of the eggs?

2. Sal wants to know the rate of decrease in the value of his motorcycle. He bought it for $1200 and can get only $900 if he sells it now. What is the rate of decrease?

3. The unemployment rate rose from 10% to 12%. By what percent did the unemployment rate rise?

4. A company's workers have been asked to take a pay cut. An assembly line worker's weekly wages would decrease from $300 to $275. What is the percent of decrease?

5. The Porter family bought their house in 1960 for $25,000. They sold it in 1993 for $85,000. Find the rate of increase in the market value of the house.

   (1) 30%
   (2) 40%
   (3) 100%
   (4) 200%
   (5) 240%

6. The Vernon Tool and Die Company bought a new lathe for $3600. One year later the lathe was worth $3312. By what percent did the value of the lathe depreciate?

   (1) 5%
   (2) 8%
   (3) 10%
   (4) 12%
   (5) 15%

ANSWERS ARE ON PAGE 368.

Finding the Whole

In some percent problems finding the whole is only the first step to solving the problem. Then you must use that whole to find an amount of change. Study the next example carefully.

EXAMPLE Max wants to buy a used car. He has saved $1200, which is 40% of the amount he needs. How much more does Max have to save?

STEP 1 Set up the proportion. 40 is the percent, and 1200 is the part he has saved. Let w stand for the whole.

$$\frac{part}{whole} \quad \frac{1200}{w} = \frac{40}{100}$$

STEP 2 Find the cross product of 1200 and 100.

$$\begin{array}{r} 1200 \\ \times \quad 100 \\ \hline 120{,}000 \end{array}$$

STEP 3 Divide 120,000 by the remaining number in the proportion, 40. The total price of the car is $3000.

$$\begin{array}{r} 3\,000 \\ 40\overline{)120{,}000} \end{array}$$

STEP 4 Subtract what Max has saved from the price of the car. He still needs **$1800**.

$$\begin{array}{ll} total & \$3000 \\ saved & -1200 \\ \hline needs & \$1800 \end{array}$$

EXERCISE 15

Directions: Solve each problem.

1. Fred has a car worth $6000. This is 80% of the amount he paid for the car last year. Find how much the value of the car depreciated.

2. During the last election in Central County, 4800 voters went to the polls. This represents 60% of the registered voters. How many registered voters in Central County did not go to the polls?

3. Joe bought a stereo on sale for $342. This was 90% of the original price. How much did Joe save by buying the stereo on sale?

4. The Acevedos have saved $6900, which is 75% of the amount they need for a down payment on a house. How much more do they need?

5. Membership in the Uptown Tenants Association is 120% of what it was one year ago. There are currently 1800 members in the association. How many people joined since this time last year?

ANSWERS ARE ON PAGE 368.

SUCCESSIVE PERCENTS

In some problems you will need to find a percent of a number, then find a percent of this *new* number. This is called finding **successive percents**.

EXAMPLE 1   A total of 25% of the 1500 employees of Grant Machine Tool Company belong to the union. Of these union members 20% voted in favor of a strike. How many union members voted to strike?

STEP 1   Figure out how many employees are in the union by setting up a proportion as you learned earlier. Find the cross product of 1500 and 25, then divide by the remaining term. 375 is the number of union members at Grant.

$$\frac{x}{1500} = \frac{25}{100} \qquad \begin{array}{r} 1500 \\ \times\ 25 \\ \hline 37{,}500 \end{array} \qquad 100 \overline{)37{,}500}^{\ 375}$$

STEP 2   Now find 20% of 375 to figure out how many union members voted to strike. Set up a proportion and solve for the missing number. **75** union members voted to strike.

$$\frac{x}{375} = \frac{20}{100} \qquad \begin{array}{r} 375 \\ \times\ 20 \\ \hline 7500 \end{array} \qquad 100 \overline{)7500}^{\ 75}$$

Notice that you *cannot* solve this problem by adding 25% to 15% and taking 40% of 1500. This type of problem requires you to figure out each percent separately. How is this different from Example 2?

EXAMPLE 2   The manager at Hank's Appliances gives a 15% discount off the list price for refrigerators. He gives an additional 5% discount off the list price if the customer pays in cash. If a refrigerator's list price is $800, and it is paid for in cash, what is the total discount on the refrigerator?

(1) $\begin{array}{r} 15\% \\ +\ 5\% \\ \hline 20\% \end{array}$ **(2)** $\dfrac{x}{800} = \dfrac{20}{100}$ $\begin{array}{r} 800 \\ \times\ 20 \\ \hline 16{,}000 \end{array}$ $100 \overline{)16{,}000}^{\ 160}$

STEP 1   A total discount of 20% is given if the customer pays in cash. Notice that the additional 5% is taken off the *original list price*, not the discounted price.

STEP 2   Find 20% of $800 by using the proportion method. The total discount is **$160**.

In Example 2 both discounts (15% and 5%) are taken off the list price. Therefore you add them together, then find the total percent discount. However, in Example 1 the first percent you had to find was of *all employees*. The second percent you had to find was of *union members*. Therefore it would be incorrect to add the two percents together.

TIP: When two or more percents are given in a problem, read it carefully to determine whether you should add the percents together or use successive percents.

EXERCISE 16

Directions: First decide whether you must add percents together or find successive percents. Then solve the problems.

1. A cut-rate toy store gives a discount of 18 percent off all marked prices. During a clearance sale, it gave an additional 10% off the discounted price. What would the clearance price be of a rocking horse marked $50?

2. Ms. Vitale, a piano teacher, reduces her regular lesson rate by 12% for senior citizens. She also takes 5% off her regular rate for students who pay before the 15th of the month. If her regular rate is $15 per hour, how much would an hour of piano lessons cost a senior citizen who pays before the 15th?

3. Out of a class of 40 students, 30 percent are black, 25 percent are white, and the rest are Hispanic. How many students in this class are not Hispanic?

4. Out of the 1400 people scheduled to tour an automobile factory one day, 14% did not show up. 75% of these "no-shows" were from the Toronto Tour Group. How many people who did not make it to the auto factory tour were from this tour group?

5. Twenty-five percent of all household accidents are caused by carelessness. Of these, 35% involve children. Out of an estimated 240,000 household accidents per year, how many are caused by carelessness and also involve children?

ANSWERS ARE ON PAGE 369.

SHORTCUTS WITH PERCENTS

You can save time with some percent problems. Remember that 50% is the same as one-half. Finding one-half of a number is the same as dividing by 2.

EXAMPLE 1   In a recent village election 248 people voted. Women represented exactly 50% of the voters. How many women voted?

50% of 248 = 248 ÷ 2 = 124

SOLUTION   Divide the total number of voters by 2. **124** women voted.

You can find 10% of a number by dividing by 10. The fastest way to divide by 10 is to move the decimal point one place to the left.

EXAMPLE 2   Beatrice saves 10% of her take-home pay. She makes $598.50 a week. How much does she save each week?

10% of $598.50 = $59.8.50 = $59.85

SOLUTION   Move the decimal point one place to the left. She saves **$59.85** each week.

To find a multiple of 10%, such as 20% or 30% or 40%, first find 10% of the number. Then multiply by 2 or 3 or 4.

EXAMPLE 3   In a regional school 30% of the children live on farms. There are 1400 children in the school. How many of the children live on farms?

     (1) 10% of 1400 = 140   **(2)** 30% of 1400 = 3 × 140 = 420

STEP 1   Find 10% of 1400.
STEP 2   Multiply 140 by 3. **420** children live on farms.

EXERCISE 17

Directions: Solve each problem.

1. Find 50% of 138.

2. What is 10% of 60?

3. What is 20% of 360?

4. Find 10% of 21.489.

5. Find 40% of 360.

6. Find 30% of $8.50.

7. Find 50% of $18,500.

8. What is 60% of 700?

9. What is 10% of 2.6?

10. Find 50% of 79.

11. Fumio paid a 10% deposit on a car that cost $13,680. What was the amount of the deposit?

     (1) $ 684
     (2) $1368
     (3) $1710
     (4) $2736
     (5) $3680

12. Memorial Auditorium has 1280 seats. At a recent concert 50% of the seats were empty. How many seats were empty?

     (1) 640
     (2) 576
     (3) 482
     (4) 256
     (5) 128

13. Phil and his brother went on a 900-mile automobile trip. Phil drove 30% of the way. How many miles did he drive?

     (1) 90
     (2) 180
     (3) 210
     (4) 270
     (5) 300

14. The Garcias have paid off 50% of their $68,000 mortgage. How much have they paid?

     (1) $ 6,800
     (2) $17,000
     (3) $34,000
     (4) $42,500
     (5) $51,000

ANSWERS ARE ON PAGE 369.

PROBLEM SOLVING FOR THE GED

Working with Item Sets

Miriam lives near the border between two states. She is planning to purchase a lawn mower that is priced at $149 in both states. State A charges a sales tax of 7%; state B charges no sales tax. If she buys the lawn mower in the state with no sales tax, she will need to have the mower delivered. The store's delivery charge is either $21 or 6% of the purchase price, whichever amount is higher. Miriam wants to spend as little money as possible to get the lawn mower.

1. How much will the mower cost in state A, including tax?

    (1) $ 10.43
    (2) $ 149.00
    (3) $ 159.43
    (4) $ 180.83
    (5) $1043.00

2. How much will the mower cost in state B, including delivery?

    (1) $21.00
    (2) $157.94
    (3) $170.00
    (4) $180.43
    (5) $204.08

As you know, there will be some "item sets" on the GED Math Test. An item set consists of a passage, graph, or chart that is followed by several questions. To answer the questions, you must be able to sort through all of the information given and choose the specific information you need. One good way to organize information is to jot down a rough chart.

As you read through the passage above, you can see that Miriam is comparing two purchases—one made in one state and another made in a different state. Notice how this simple chart can help you keep track of the facts. Jot down the information where it belongs; the work has been started for you.

	State A	State B
Cost of Mower	$149	
Tax		
Delivery Charge		

Now that you have sorted the information, go back and answer the questions above. From which store can Miriam get the mower for less money?

Since the mower costs $159.43 in state A and $170 in state B, it will cost her less money in state A.

GED Practice
EXERCISE 18

Directions: Solve each problem. To help you, create a chart for the information.

Vicki and Brad Bachman are deciding which of two homes to buy. They can purchase a home in Lincoln for $47,700 with a 12% down payment. They can also purchase a home in Milwaukee for $58,900 with an 8% down payment. The Bachmans figured out that they would need to spend an additional $6200 for home improvements in the Lincoln home and $2945 in the Milwaukee home.

1. How much more of a down payment would the Bachmans have to pay for the Lincoln home than the Milwaukee home?

(1) $ 912
(2) $ 1012
(3) $ 4712
(4) $ 5724
(5) $11,200

2. What percent of the price of the Milwaukee home would the Bachmans have to pay for home improvements?

(1) 2
(2) 3
(3) 5
(4) 40
(5) 90

3. How much would the Bachmans pay for the Lincoln home, including the home improvements?

(1) $ 8669
(2) $11,924
(3) $50,645
(4) $53,900
(5) $54,912

ANSWERS ARE ON PAGE 369.

SIMPLE INTEREST
Interest for Whole Years

Interest is money that money makes. You *are paid* interest when your money is in a savings account because the bank is using your money to make other investments. You *pay* interest when you borrow money. You not only pay your loan back, but you give an additional amount of money (interest) in payment for the bank's help. Interest is one of the most common applications of percents.

RULES FOR FINDING INTEREST

To find interest, you need three things:

1. the principal—the amount of money borrowed or saved

2. the rate—the percent used to find the interest

3. the time—the number of years (or part of a year) that the money is borrowed or saved.

Multiply the principal by the rate by the time.

This rule is often written as the formula $i = prt$ where i is the interest, p is the principal, r is the rate, and t is the time. When letters are written side by side with no arithmetic sign between them, they should be multiplied. To use this formula, set up a fraction multiplication problem. $i = p \times r \times t$

EXAMPLE 1   Find the interest on $800 at 6% annual interest for one year.

(1) $800 \times \dfrac{6}{100} \times 1 = ?$ **(2)** $\dfrac{\overset{8}{\cancel{800}}}{1} \times \dfrac{6}{\underset{1}{\cancel{100}}} \times \dfrac{1}{1} = \$48$

STEP 1   Set up the problem like a fraction problem. $800 is the principal. 6% is the rate. Write 6% as the fraction $\frac{6}{100}$. One year is the time.

STEP 2   Cancel and multiply. The interest is **$48**.

> **TIP:** If the time in an interest problem is exactly one year, you do not have to put 1 in the problem. The answer will be exactly the same.

EXAMPLE 2   Find the interest on $500 at $8\frac{1}{2}$% annual interest for one year.

STEP 1   Set up the problem like a fraction problem. $500 is the principal. $8\frac{1}{2}$% is the rate. Write $8\frac{1}{2}$% as a fraction with a denominator of 100.

$$500 \times \dfrac{8\frac{1}{2}}{100} = ?$$

STEP 2   Cancel 500 and 100 by 100. You now have the simplified problem $5 \times 8\frac{1}{2}$.

$$\dfrac{\overset{5}{\cancel{500}}}{1} \times \dfrac{8\frac{1}{2}}{\underset{1}{\cancel{100}}}$$

STEP 3   Change $8\frac{1}{2}$ to an improper fraction and multiply by 5. The interest is $42.50.

$$\dfrac{5}{1} \times \dfrac{17}{2} = \dfrac{85}{2} = \textbf{\$42.50}$$

Multi-Step Interest Problems

In some problems you will have to find a new amount. The new amount is the interest plus the original principal.

EXAMPLE 3   Roger borrowed $6000 at a rate of 12% for one year to make home improvements. How much did he have to repay at the end of the year?

STEP 1 $6000 is the principal, and 12% is the rate. Write 12% as a fraction.

$$6000 \times \frac{12}{100} =$$

STEP 2   Cancel 6000 and 100 by 100 and multiply. The interest for one year is $720.

$$\frac{\overset{60}{\cancel{6000}}}{1} \times \frac{12}{\underset{1}{\cancel{100}}} = \$720$$

STEP 3   Add the interest to the principal. Roger must repay **$6720**.

$$\begin{array}{r} \$6000 \\ + \ 720 \\ \hline \$6720 \end{array}$$

TIP: Read interest problems carefully to see whether you are being asked for just the interest or the interest plus the principal.

Interest for Parts of a Year

The time in an interest problem is measured in years. If the time in a problem is not one whole year, make a fraction that expresses the time as a part of a year. For example, six months is $\frac{6}{12}$ or $\frac{1}{2}$ year. Two years and four months is $2\frac{4}{12}$ or $2\frac{1}{3}$ years.

EXAMPLE   Find the interest on $500 at 9% annual interest for eight months.

(1) 8 months $= \dfrac{8}{12} = \dfrac{2}{3}$ year   **(2)** $\dfrac{\overset{5}{\cancel{500}}}{1} \times \dfrac{\overset{3}{\cancel{9}}}{\underset{1}{\cancel{100}}} \times \dfrac{2}{\underset{1}{\cancel{3}}} = \$30$

STEP 1   Change 8 months to a fraction of a year.

STEP 2 $500 is the principal. 9%, or $\frac{9}{100}$, is the rate, and $\frac{2}{3}$ year is the time. Cancel and multiply. The interest is **$30**.

EXERCISE 19

Directions: Solve each problem.

1. Find the interest on $3000 at 12.5% annual interest for one year.

2. How much money will Sara have at the end of one year on $800 deposited in a savings account earning $5\frac{1}{4}$% interest?

3. What is the interest on $5000 at 9% annual interest for two years?

4. Find the interest on $800 at 6% annual interest for nine months.

5. How much interest did Emilita pay on $900 at 11.5% annual interest for six months?

6. The Millers paid interest on $500 borrowed at 14% annual interest for one year and six months. How much interest did they pay?

7. Sally had $2000 deposited in her savings account for two years and six months. If she earned 6% interest, how much was in the account at the end of that time?

8. The Lewis family borrowed $900 at 13% annual interest for one year and eight months. How much did they repay at the end of that time?

9. To the nearest penny, find the interest on $4000 at 10% annual interest for two years and four months.

10. If you borrow $1200 at 14.75% annual interest for nine months, how much do you have to repay at the end of that period?

ANSWERS ARE ON PAGE 370.

PROBLEM SOLVING FOR THE GED

When Not Enough Information Is Given

Greg wants to buy a coat that costs $89.50 plus clothing tax. He has $106.00 in his wallet, but he wants some of this cash to pay for lunch, which will cost $5.80 plus a 4% meal tax. How much money will Greg have left over after he buys the coat but before he buys lunch?

(1) $ 6.09
(2) $12.92
(3) $16.50
(4) $21.50
(5) Not enough information is given.

The last answer choice in this item is one that will appear in some problems on the GED Math Test. It means that you are unable to answer the question because the passage has left out some information that you need to solve the problem.

In the example above, you cannot tell how much money Greg would have left over because you do not know the *total* cost of the coat. The situation states that the coat costs $89.50 *plus clothing tax.* Is the clothing tax 5%? 6%? You are not given this information. You cannot assume that the tax is the same rate that you have in your state. Also, do not be fooled by the *meal tax* of 4% given in the problem. This will help you figure out tax on food, but not on clothing.

Here are some hints to help you with problems in which "Not enough information is given" is listed as a possible answer choice:

1. Carefully read the situation through once, then read the question. As you learned in Chapter 2, this is always the first step in problem solving. Your second step is to decide what information you need to answer the question.

In the problem above, you need to know the cost of the coat plus the tax.

2. If you find that you may be missing some necessary information, skim your answer choices to see if "Not enough information is given" is listed. If it is, *do not* immediately choose this as your answer! Instead, jot down the fact that you are missing.

In this problem you are not given the amount of the clothing tax. Though this is a clue that (5) may be the right answer, you shouldn't choose it too quickly. Jot down *amount of tax on coat* as the information you are missing.

3. Look at the problem again to see if there is another way to get the missing information. If this is a multi-step problem, you may have to take another step to find the information you need. Also see if some numbers appear as words or appear in a chart with the problem. Sometimes information expressed this way is harder to find.

In the problem above, there is no other way to find the clothing tax.

4. Once you feel that you understand the problem and are definitely missing some necessary information, choose answer **(5)**.

GED Practice
EXERCISE 20

Directions: Questions 1–4 refer to the following situation.

For the first three months, Fred will make $1250 a month. Then he will get a 10% raise for the remainder of the year. At the end of a year he will receive an additional 8% raise if he does well on his performance review. Fred's employer withholds 15% of his gross salary for federal tax, state tax, and social security.

1. How much will Fred make the first year?

    (1) $15,000
    (2) $15,275
    (3) $15,750
    (4) $16,125
    (5) Not enough information is given.

2. How much is withheld each month, for the first three months, from Fred's salary?

    (1) $ 87.50
    (2) $127.50
    (3) $187.50
    (4) $206.25
    (5) Not enough information is given.

3. How much is withheld for the first year from Fred's gross salary for social security?

    (1) $1875
    (2) $1250
    (3) $ 875
    (4) $ 750
    (5) Not enough information is given.

4. What will be Fred's monthly gross salary for the second year if he does well on his performance review?

    (1) $1485
    (2) $1450
    (3) $1385
    (4) $1350
    (5) Not enough information is given.

Directions: Questions 5–7 refer to the following situation.

Paul and Ruth plan to renew the lease for their apartment. Their current rent is $250 a month. They have a choice of a two-year renewal at an 8% increase or a three-year renewal at an increase of 10%. If they take the two-year renewal and stay on for a third year, the rent will go up an additional 10%.

5. If they choose the two-year renewal, what will the monthly rent be for the second year?

    (1) $258
    (2) $266
    (3) $270
    (4) $278
    (5) Not enough information is given.

6. If they choose the three-year renewal, what will the monthly rent be for the second year?

    (1) $275
    (2) $270
    (3) $265
    (4) $260
    (5) Not enough information is given.

7. If they choose the two-year renewal, but stay on for a third year at an additional 10% rent, what will the monthly rent be for the third year?

    (1) $307
    (2) $297
    (3) $277
    (4) $270
    (5) Not enough information is given.

ANSWERS ARE ON PAGE 370.

PERCENTS REVIEW

Directions: For questions 1–13, solve each problem.

1. Write the ratio 18:24 in simplest form.

2. Simplify the ratio $\frac{20}{36}$.

3. Find *s* in $\frac{s}{15} = \frac{6}{20}$.

4. What is the value of *x* in 5:12 = *x*:84?

5. Change the decimal .95 to a percent.

6. Write 3.2% as a decimal.

7. Write $\frac{5}{8}$ as a percent.

8. Change $37\frac{1}{2}$% to a fraction.

9. Find 2.7% of 360.

10. What percent of 35 is 21?

11. 75 is 20% of what number?

12. 150% of what number is 48?

13. Find the interest on $450 at 8% annual interest for nine months.

Directions: For questions 14–22, choose the best answer.

14. Pete's socks are not stored together in pairs. In his drawer there are 2 blue socks, 5 brown socks, 4 black socks, and 1 white sock. What is the probability that the first sock Pete grabs from the drawer will be black?

    (1) $\frac{1}{12}$

    (2) $\frac{1}{4}$

    (3) $\frac{1}{8}$

    (4) $\frac{1}{3}$

    (5) $\frac{2}{3}$

15. Consolidated Utilities' softball team won 12 games and lost 8 last season. What was the ratio of the number of games the team won to the number of games it played?

    (1) 3:2
    (2) 2:5
    (3) 3:5
    (4) 5:3
    (5) 5:2

16. Kate worked for 40 hours at $4.50 per hour. She also worked for 6 extra hours and earned $38.40 in overtime. At the same rate, how much can she make for 10 hours of overtime work?

    (1) $32
    (2) $51.20
    (3) $64
    (4) $76.80
    (5) $96

17. For every $5 in her budget Mrs. Murphy spends $2 on food. Her weekly budget is $215. Which expression below represents the amount she spends each week on food?

    (1) $\frac{5 \times 215}{2}$

    (2) $\frac{5 + 2}{215}$

    (3) $\frac{5 \times 2}{215}$

    (4) $5 \times 2 \times 215$

    (5) $\frac{2 \times 215}{5}$

18. The ratio of the number of people who voted to the number of voters who stayed home was 3:5 in the last election in Midvale. Out of 38,000 registered voters, how many actually voted in the last election?

(1) 10,133
(2) 14,250
(3) 23,750
(4) 28,500
(5) 47,500

19. Mr. Santiago sells shoes for a 5% commission. He earned $115 in commissions one week. Find the total value of the shoes he sold that week.

(1) $ 5.75
(2) $ 57.50
(3) $ 575.00
(4) $ 580.75
(5) $2300.00

20. Adrian wants to buy a used car that costs $1200. He has already saved $1000. What percent of the total price has he already saved?

(1) $16\frac{2}{3}$%
(2) 20%
(3) 80%
(4) $83\frac{1}{3}$%
(5) $86\frac{2}{3}$%

21. The price of a gallon of gasoline went from $1.20 down to $1.05. By what percent did the price of a gallon drop?

(1) $12\frac{1}{2}$%
(2) 15%
(3) 20%
(4) 85%
(5) $87\frac{1}{2}$%

22. A stereo listed for $350 is on sale for 20% off the list price. The sales tax is 6%. What total price does a customer pay for the stereo if he buys it on sale?

(1) $324.00
(2) $259.00
(3) $262.20
(4) $296.80
(5) $301.00

Directions: Questions 23–25 refer to the following situation.

Mr. Allen wants to buy a new band saw. The saw is on sale in his town for $695. In his town he must pay 6% sales tax and a $50 shipping charge. The saw is for sale in another town across the state line. In that town the price of the saw is $749, but there is no sales tax in that state. The out-of-state dealer charges a 10% shipping charge. Mr. Allen estimates that if he borrows a friend's truck and picks up the saw himself, gas will cost $12 each way.

23. Find the total cost of the band saw including tax and shipping in Mr. Allen's hometown.

(1) $816.70
(2) $786.70
(3) $745
(4) $736.70
(5) Not enough information is given.

24. What is the total cost of the band saw in the other state including gas and tolls if Mr. Allen picks up the saw himself?

(1) $761
(2) $773
(3) $827.90
(4) $847.90
(5) Not enough information is given.

25. To the nearest dollar, what is the shipping cost on the band saw if it is purchased from the out-of-state dealer?

(1) $80
(2) $75
(3) $70
(4) $42
(5) Not enough information is given.

ANSWERS ARE ON PAGES 371–372.

7 ✛ Measurement

STANDARD OR IMPERIAL MEASUREMENTS

Below are some standard units of measurement for length, time, liquid measure, and weight. These are the units commonly used in the United States. This system is also called the ***imperial system*** because it was the standard in the British Empire.

In the chart below, the larger unit of measurement is on the left. Next to it on the right is an equivalent in smaller units. Abbreviations are in parentheses.

Take the time to memorize any of the units and equivalents that you do not know. You will need to know these units for problems later in this chapter and on the GED Test. They are also helpful to know for everyday life!

UNITS OF MEASURE

Measures of Length
1 foot (ft) = 12 inches (in)
1 yard (yd) = 36 inches
1 yard = 3 feet
1 mile (mi) = 5280 feet
1 mile = 1760 yards

Measures of Time
1 minute (min) = 60 seconds (sec)
1 hour (hr) = 60 minutes
1 day = 24 hours
1 week (wk) = 7 days
1 year (yr) = 365 days

Liquid Measures
1 pint (pt) = 16 ounces (oz)
1 cup = 8 ounces
1 pint = 2 cups
1 quart (qt) = 2 pints
1 gallon (gal) = 4 quarts

Measures of Weight
1 pound (lb) = 16 ounces (oz)
1 ton (T) = 2000 pounds

CONVERTING MEASUREMENTS

In some word problems on the GED Test, and in many situations you encounter in everyday life, you need to be able to change one unit of measurement into another. For instance, if you needed a certain number of ounces of liquid, and the liquid is being sold by the quart, you would have to **convert** (change) the number of ounces needed into the number of quarts needed to figure out how much to buy.

Method 1: Using Proportion to Convert Measurements

In other chapters you have seen how useful proportion is. You can also use proportion to change (or convert) from one unit of measurement to another.

> **TIP:** Remember from your work with proportions that each ratio must have the same label on top and the same label on the bottom.

EXAMPLE 1   Change 5 pounds to ounces.

(1) $\dfrac{\text{pounds}}{\text{ounces}}$ $\dfrac{1 \text{ lb}}{16 \text{ oz}} = \dfrac{5 \text{ lb}}{x}$ **(2)** $\begin{array}{r} 16 \\ \times\, 5 \\ \hline 80 \end{array}$ **(3)** $\begin{array}{r} 80\,\text{oz} \\ 1\overline{)80} \end{array}$

STEP 1   To start, you must know how many ounces are in one pound. Show this relationship in the ratio of pounds to ounces. On the left is the ratio of 1 lb to 16 oz. On the right put 5 lb in the pounds' position. Let x stand for the number of ounces you need to find.

STEP 2   Find the cross product of 16 and 5.

STEP 3   Divide 80 by the remaining number in the proportion, 1.
5 pounds is equal to **80 ounces**.

> **RULES FOR CHANGING UNITS OF MEASUREMENT**
>
> **1.** Figure out the equivalent between the two units. Show this relationship in a ratio on the left. On the right side of the proportion, make a ratio using the unit of measurement you do know. Use the letter x to represent the missing unit.
>
> **2.** Find the cross product.
>
> **3.** Divide by the remaining number in the proportion.

EXAMPLE 2   Dahlia is making soup that calls for 10 quarts of liquid. She needs to know how many gallons this is so that she can choose a large enough pot. How many gallons is 10 quarts?

(1) $\dfrac{\text{gallons}}{\text{quarts}}$ $\dfrac{1 \text{ gal}}{4 \text{ qt}} = \dfrac{x}{10 \text{ qt}}$ **(2)** $\begin{array}{r} 10 \\ \times\, 1 \\ \hline 10 \end{array}$ **(3)** $\begin{array}{r} 2\frac{2}{4} = 2\frac{1}{2} \text{ gal} \\ 4\overline{)10} \end{array}$

STEP 1 Make a proportion. On the left is the ratio of 1 gallon to 4 quarts. On the right, put *x* in the gallons' place and 10 in the quarts' place.

STEP 2 Find the cross product of 1 and 10.

STEP 3 Divide 10 by the other number in the proportion, 4.
10 quarts is equal to **$2\frac{1}{2}$ gallons**.

As you can see, you cannot set up the correct proportion if you do not know equivalent measurements. Make sure you know the equivalent units on page 165 before you go any further in this chapter.

> **TIP:** When you are converting a larger unit into smaller units (feet into inches, for example), the number of units obtained will be greater than the number of units you started with. When you are converting smaller units into larger units (inches into feet, for example), you will get a smaller number of units than you started with.

Method 2: Multiplying and Dividing to Convert Measurements

The proportion method of converting measurement is very useful in most cases. However, there are some times when you just "know" to multiply or divide based on your everyday use of measurement.

EXAMPLE 1 Michelle bought 3 feet of tape. How many inches of tape is this?

SOLUTION You know that there are 12 inches in 1 foot. To find the number of inches in 3 feet, you can simply multiply 3 by 12.
$12 \times 3 = $ **36 inches**

> **TIP:** *Multiply* when changing from a larger to a smaller unit (e.g., from feet to inches). This is true because you will be getting *more* of the smaller unit.

EXAMPLE 2 Ralph worked on an assignment for 150 minutes. How many hours was this?

SOLUTION You know that there are 60 minutes in an hour. To find the number of hours in 150 minutes, divide 150 by 60.
$150 \div 60 = $ **$2\frac{1}{2}$ hours**

> **TIP:** *Divide* when changing from a smaller unit to a larger unit (e.g., minutes to hours). This is true because you will be getting *fewer* of the larger unit.

EXERCISE 1

Directions: Change each measurement to the new unit indicated.

1. 40 ounces = _____ pounds

2. 3 tons = _____ pounds

3. 6 feet = _____ yards

4. 23 days = _____ weeks

5. 14 ounces = _____ pound

6. 6 gallons = _____ quarts

7. 2640 feet = _____ mile

8. 100 inches = _____ yards

9. 20 ounces = _____ cups

10. 30 quarts = _____ pints

11. 3 miles = _____ feet

12. 2 yards = _____ feet

Directions: Solve each problem.

13. A group of neighbors cooked 130 quarts of tomatoes. They wanted to can them in gallon jars. How many gallon jars did they need for canning?

14. Pieter and his son went camping for three whole days. Altogether how many hours did they camp?

15. Deborah's car was double-parked for 45 minutes. For what fraction of an hour was her car double-parked?

16. Paul climbed a mountain that is 10,560 feet high. Find the mountain's height in miles.

17. On Thursday, Pat typed steadily for 200 minutes, and she is paid by the hour. For how many hours should Pat be paid for this typing job?

18. Frank has to carry 3 tons of cement. If his truck carries a maximum of 500 pounds at a time, how many trips will Frank have to make?

ANSWERS ARE ON PAGE 372.

METRIC MEASUREMENTS

The ***metric system*** is used in most countries outside the United States. In many ways the metric system is much easier to use than the standard system. Metric units are based on tens, hundreds, thousands, and so on.

- The basic unit of weight in the metric system is the ***gram***. A gram is about $\frac{1}{450}$ of a pound. A raisin weighs about one gram.

- The basic unit of length in the metric system is the ***meter***. A meter is just a little longer than a yard.

- The basic unit of liquid measure in the metric system is the ***liter***. A liter is a little greater than a quart.

Following are four prefixes used in metric measurements. Learn their meanings before you go on.

Prefix	Meaning
milli-	$\frac{1}{1000}$ or .001
centi-	$\frac{1}{100}$ or .01
deci-	$\frac{1}{10}$ or .1
kilo-	1000

EXAMPLE 1 One kilometer = _____ meters.

SOLUTION *Kilo* means 1000. One kilometer = 1000 meters.

EXAMPLE 2 One millimeter = _____ meter.

SOLUTION *Milli* means $\frac{1}{1000}$. One millimeter = $\frac{1}{1000}$ meter.

Below are the most common metric measurements. Take the time now to learn these units before you go on.

METRIC UNITS OF MEASURE

Measures of Length
meter (m) = 1000 millimeters (mm)
1 meter = 100 centimeters (cm)
1 kilometer (km) = 1000 meters

Measures of Weight
1 gram (g) = 1000 milligrams (mg)
1 gram = 100 centigrams (cg)
kilogram (kg) = 1000 grams

Liquid Measures
1 liter (l) = 1000 milliliters (ml)
1 liter = 100 centiliters (cl)
1 liter = 10 deciliters (dl)

SIMPLIFYING MEASUREMENTS

Answers to measurement problems can often be simplified.

Suppose the answer to a problem is 15 inches. Since 15 inches is more than one foot, you can change the answer to feet and inches. This is called *simplifying*.

EXAMPLE 1 Change 15 inches to feet and inches.

STEP 1 The next unit of measurement larger than inches is feet. Divide 15 inches by 12, the number of inches in one foot.

$$\begin{array}{r} 1 \text{ ft } 3 \text{ in} \\ 12\overline{)15} \\ \underline{12} \\ 3 \end{array}$$

STEP 2 Write the remainder in inches. 15 inches = **1 ft 3 in**. The answer could also be expressed as $1\frac{3}{12} = 1\frac{1}{4}$ **ft**.

RULES FOR SIMPLIFYING MEASUREMENT
1. Divide the number of units in your answer by the number of these units contained in the *next larger* unit of measurement.
2. Write the remainder in terms of the smaller unit.

EXAMPLE 2   Simplify 150 minutes.

$$
\begin{array}{r}
2\ \text{hr } 30\ \text{min} \\
60\overline{)150} \\
\underline{120} \\
30
\end{array}
$$

STEP 1   The next unit of measurement larger than minutes is hours. Divide 150 minutes by 60, the number of minutes in an hour.

STEP 2   Write the remainder in minutes. 150 minutes = **2 hr 30 min**. The answer could also be expressed as $2\frac{30}{60} = \mathbf{2\frac{1}{2}}$ **hr**.

In some problems you will find the remainder written in terms of the smaller unit. In other problems you will find the remainder changed to a fraction or a decimal.

EXERCISE 2

Directions: Solve each problem. Read carefully to find out how each answer should be expressed.

1. Change 19 inches to feet and inches.

2. Change 75 seconds to minutes and seconds.

3. Change 36 ounces to pounds and ounces.

4. Change 25 feet to yards and a fraction of a yard.

5. Change 200 minutes to hours and minutes.

6. Change 4500 pounds to tons and pounds.

7. Change 15 quarts to gallons and a fraction of a gallon.

8. Change 75 inches to yards and inches.

9. Change 15,840 feet to miles.

10. Change 100 ounces to pounds and a fraction of a pound.

11. Maria made 9 pints of jam. Express the amount in quarts and pints.

12. Sam hiked for 40 days. Express the time in weeks and days.

ANSWERS ARE ON PAGE 373.

WHOLE NUMBER ANSWERS IN MEASUREMENT

Sometimes you will see by the way a problem is worded that *only a whole number* answer is correct. However, when you work out the problem, you may come up with an answer that includes a fraction or a remainder. Look at the following example:

EXAMPLE How many class sessions, each 1 hr 45 min long, fit into an 8-hour day?

(1) 3
(2) 4
(3) 5
(4) 7
(5) 8

(1) 1 hr 45 min = $1\frac{3}{4}$ hr   **(2)** $8 \div 1\frac{3}{4} =$

$$8 \div \frac{7}{4} =$$

$$8 \times \frac{4}{7} =$$

$$\frac{32}{7} = 4\frac{4}{7}$$

STEP 1 Convert 1 hr 45 min to hours.
STEP 2 Divide the 8-hour day by $1\frac{3}{4}$ hours.
STEP 3 In this case the question asks for the number of class sessions, so the fraction of a class section ($\frac{4}{7}$) is not necessary. Only 4 class sessions will fit into this amount of time. Therefore choice **(2)** is correct.

EXERCISE 3

Directions: Solve each problem.

1. Ben needs $2\frac{2}{3}$ yards of lumber to make a wall cabinet. How many cabinets can he make from 10 yards of lumber?

    (1) 10
    (2) 5
    (3) 4
    (4) 3
    (5) 2

2. Altagracia needs $1\frac{3}{4}$ cups of flour to make a cake. How many cakes can she make from 8 cups of flour?

    (1) 6
    (2) 5
    (3) 4
    (4) 3
    (5) 2

ANSWERS ARE ON PAGE 373.

SCALES AND METERS

READING RULERS

Being able to read and use inch or centimeter rulers is an important skill. Figure 1 below shows a six-inch ruler.

Figure 1

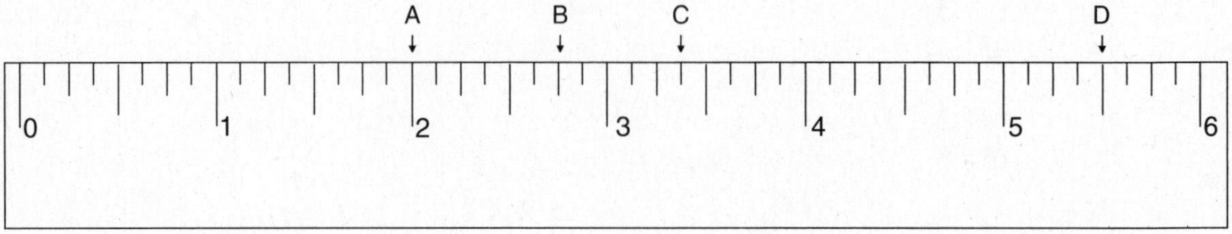

The longest lines on the ruler are inch lines. They are numbered 1, 2, 3, etc. The second-longest lines are $\frac{1}{2}$-inch lines. The next-longest lines are $\frac{1}{4}$-inch lines. The shortest lines are $\frac{1}{8}$-inch lines. To read a length on the ruler, decide how far to the right of zero a point is.

EXAMPLE 1   Tell how far to the right of zero the points marked A, B, C, and D on Figure 1 are.

SOLUTION   Point A—**2 inches**
Point A is at the line labeled 2.

Point B—**$2\frac{3}{4}$ inches**
Point B is between 2 and 3 inches. The point is at the third $\frac{1}{4}$-inch line between 2 and 3.

Point C—**$3\frac{3}{8}$ inches**
Point C is between 3 and 4 inches. The point is at the third $\frac{1}{8}$-inch line between 3 and 4.

Point D—**$5\frac{1}{2}$ inches**
Point D is between 5 and 6 inches. The point is at the longest line between 5 and 6, which is the $\frac{1}{2}$-inch line.

Figure 2

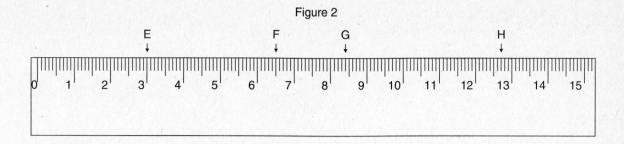

The longest lines on this scale are the centimeter lines, labeled 1, 2, 3, etc. The next-longest lines are the $\frac{1}{2}$-centimeter or .5-centimeter lines. The shortest lines are millimeter lines or .1-centimeter lines. Notice in the next example that the distances on the centimeter scale are all given in decimals.

EXAMPLE 2 Tell how far to the right of zero the points marked E, F, G, and H on Figure 2 are.

SOLUTION   Point E—**3 centimeters**
Point E is at the third-longest line to the right of zero.

Point F— **6.5 centimeters**
Point F is between 6 and 7 centimeters. The point is at the middle line, which is .5 centimeter.

Point G—**8.4 centimeters**
Point G is between 8 and 9 centimeters. The point is at the fourth millimeter or the .4-centimeter line.

Point H—**12.7 centimeters**
Point H is between 12 and 13 centimeters. The point is at the seventh millimeter or the .7-centimeter line.

READING METERS

A **_meter_** is a device used to measure time, distance, speed, or amount of energy. For example, a thermo_meter_ measures temperature, and a speedo_meter_ measures speed. Figure 3 below is a meter that measures amperes. **Amperes** are a measure of an amount of electrical current.

Figure 3

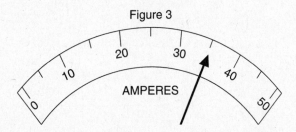

AMPERES

EXAMPLE   What is the reading in amperes of the meter in Figure 3?

SOLUTION   **35 amperes**. The arrow in Figure 3 is exactly halfway between 30 and 40 amperes. The halfway point is 35.

EXERCISE 4

Directions: Solve each problem.

1. Tell how far to the right of zero the points marked J, K, L, M, and N on Figure 4 are.

Figure 4

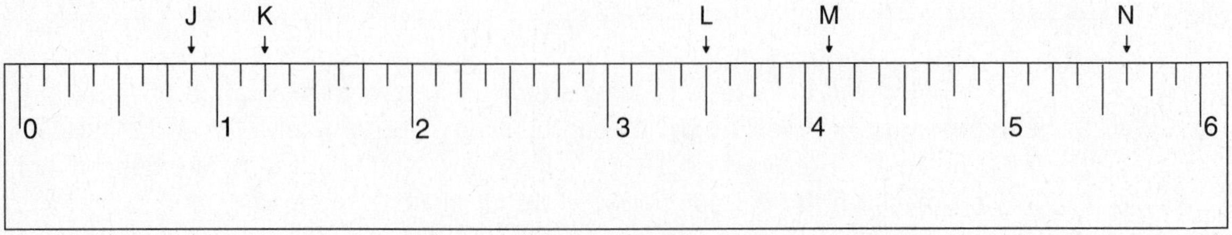

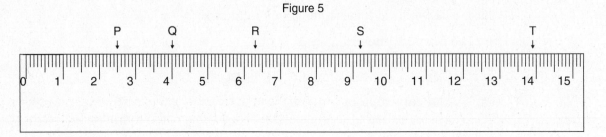

2. Tell how far to the right of zero the points marked P, Q, R, S, and T on Figure 5 are.

Figure 5

3. Approximately what is the reading in amperes of the meter in Figure 6?

Figure 6

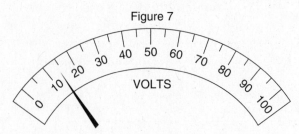

4. Figure 7 shows a voltmeter. Volts are a measure of electromotive force. Approximately what is the reading in volts of the meter in Figure 7?

Figure 7

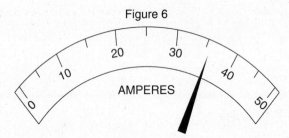

5. In Figure 8 it takes the meter $\frac{1}{10}$ of a second to rise one volt. Approximately how many seconds has it taken to rise to the amount shown?

Figure 8

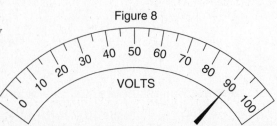

ANSWERS ARE ON PAGE 373.

≡ GED Practice ≡
MEASUREMENT REVIEW

Directions: Choose the best answer to each problem.

1. At a price of $4.80 a pound, what is the cost of 2 lb 4 oz of cheese?

   (1) $ 9.60
   (2) $10.80
   (3) $12.60
   (4) $14.40
   (5) $19.20

2. Which of the following represents the average weight of three boxes that weigh 2.5 kg, 0.96 kg, and 1.2 kg respectively?

   (1) 2.5 + 0.96 + 1.2
   (2) 2(2.5 + 0.96 + 1.2)
   (3) 2.5 × 0.96 × 1.2
   (4) $\dfrac{2.5 + 0.96 + 1.2}{3}$
   (5) 2.5 + 0.96 + 1.2

3. Fred bought 5 cans of tomato paste. Each weighed 14 ounces. Find the total cost of the cans.

   (1) $ .07
   (2) $ .17
   (3) $ .70
   (4) $7.00
   (5) Not enough information is given.

4. From a cable 4 meters long, Italo cut a piece 1.15 meters long. Find the length in meters of the remaining piece.

   (1) 3.85
   (2) 3.15
   (3) 2.85
   (4) 2.15
   (5) 1.85

5. Gianni needs 3 yd 18 in of material to make a suit. How many suits can he make from 15 yards of material?

   (1) 5
   (2) 4
   (3) 3
   (4) 2
   (5) 1

6. For a blood drive at Carmen's office the workers donated 36.5 liters on Wednesday, 42.2 liters on Thursday, and 50.1 liters on Friday. To the nearest tenth of a liter, what was the average amount donated each day?

   (1)   42.9
   (2)   50.1
   (3)   58.8
   (4)   64.4
   (5) 128.8

Use the 3-inch ruler pictured below to answer questions 7 and 8.

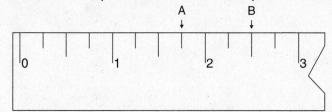

7. How many inches is point A from the point marked 0?

   (1) $\frac{3}{4}$
   (2) 1
   (3) $1\frac{1}{4}$
   (4) $1\frac{3}{4}$
   (5) 2

8. What is the distance in inches between points A and B?

   (1) $\frac{1}{4}$
   (2) $\frac{1}{2}$
   (3) $\frac{3}{4}$
   (4) 1
   (5) $1\frac{1}{4}$

ANSWERS ARE ON PAGES 373–374.

8 Graphs and Tables

WHAT IS A GRAPH?

A **graph** is a way of organizing numbers visually. You have seen and probably used a variety of graphs in newspapers, on television, and in magazines. Basically a graph takes a lot of numerical information (often called **data**) and shows it in "picture" form.

A **circle graph** is one way to show data visually. A circle represents the whole, and the "pie-shaped" pieces show the different sizes of the parts. Often the parts of a circle graph are expressed in percents. When the parts of a circle graph are percents, the parts must add up to 100% or one whole.

Think about this information: The Johnson family uses a budget to organize their expenses. They spend 30% of their income for food, 25% for rent, 20% for clothes, and 15% for other expenses. They save 10%. Notice that the percents add up to a total of 100%, or the Johnsons' entire income.

The graph at the right shows the budget for the Johnson family.

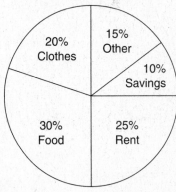

JOHNSON FAMILY BUDGET

Graph Organization

Notice that the circle graph has a title (Johnson Family Budget) and labels for each category (savings, rent, food, clothes, and other).

TIP: It is important that you look at the title and all labels on a graph before you attempt to examine any numerical information.

FINDING SPECIFIC INFORMATION

Once you are familiar with the way a graph is organized and the type of information it provides, you should be able to find specific information.

EXAMPLE 1 What percent of the Johnson family budget goes for food?

SOLUTION Find the category labeled "food" on the graph. The percent in this category is **30%**.

JOHNSON FAMILY BUDGET

To answer the question in Example 1, you simply read the data presented on the graph.

USING INFORMATION FROM A GRAPH

To answer some questions on the GED, you must perform mathematical operations using information provided on the graph.

EXAMPLE 2 Rent represents what fraction of the Johnsons' budget?

(1) rent = 25%   (2) $25\% = \frac{25}{100} = \frac{1}{4}$

STEP 1 Find the category labeled "rent" on the graph. Rent is 25% of the budget.

STEP 2 Change 25% to a fraction. Make a fraction with 25 as the numerator and 100 as the denominator. Reduce the fraction. Rent is $\frac{1}{4}$ of the budget.

Look at the circle graph below. The categories are the same, but each percent has been converted to a fraction. Notice that the fractions add up to one whole.

Clothes $\frac{1}{5} = \frac{20}{100} = 20\%$

Food $\frac{3}{10} = \frac{30}{100} = 30\%$

Rent $\frac{1}{4} = \frac{25}{100} = 25\%$

Savings $\frac{1}{10} = \frac{10}{100} = 10\%$

Other $\frac{3}{20} = \frac{15}{100} = 15\%$

Total $\frac{100}{100} = 100\% = 1$ whole

Sometimes you have to apply information on a graph to information you are given in a problem.

EXAMPLE 3 The Johnsons take home $1200 a month. According to the circle graph, how much do they pay each month for rent?

(1) $\frac{r}{1200} = \frac{25}{100}$ (2) $\begin{array}{r} 1200 \\ \times\ \ 25 \\ \hline 30{,}000 \end{array}$ (3) $\begin{array}{r} \$300 \\ 100\overline{)30{,}000} \end{array}$

STEP 1 This is a simple percent problem. Fill in the proportion. 25 is the percent, and $1200 is the whole monthly budget. Let r stand for the part, or rent, which is missing.

STEP 2 Find the cross product of 1200 and 25.

STEP 3 Divide by the other number in the proportion, 100. The Johnsons pay **$300 a month** for rent.

EXERCISE 1

Directions: Use the graph below to answer the following questions.

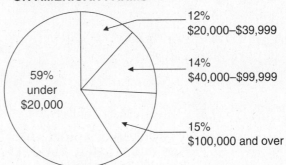

**VALUE OF YEARLY SALES
ON AMERICAN FARMS**

Source: Statistical Abstract of the U.S.

1. What percent of American farms had yearly sales between $20,000 and $39,999?

2. What percent of farms had yearly sales under $20,000?

3. There are 200 farms in Central County. If they follow the national pattern, how many of the farms in the county had yearly sales of $100,000 and over?

   (1) 15
   (2) 30
   (3) 90
   (4) 150
   (5) 185

4. What percent of farms have yearly sales of $40,000 and over?

   (1) 14%
   (2) 15%
   (3) 20%
   (4) 29%
   (5) 59%

5. Which of the following expresses the fraction of farms with yearly sales of $100,000 and over?

   (1) $\frac{3}{20}$

   (2) $\frac{1}{5}$

   (3) $\frac{1}{4}$

   (4) $\frac{2}{5}$

   (5) $\frac{17}{20}$

ANSWERS ARE ON PAGE 374.

OTHER CIRCLE GRAPHS

Not all circle graphs are divided into percents or fractions. For example, the parts of a circle graph may also be measured in cents as parts of a whole dollar. The following graph shows the source of a dollar of the U.S. federal budget Notice that the sections add up to 100 cents or $1.

EXERCISE 2

Directions: Use the circle graph below to answer questions 1–6.

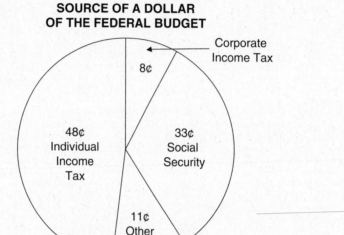

**SOURCE OF A DOLLAR
OF THE FEDERAL BUDGET**

Total Federal Budget: $900 billion
Source: Statistical Abstract of the U.S.

1. What percent of the federal budget comes from individual income tax?

2. Corporate income tax is what fraction of individual income tax?

3. Social security tax is about what fraction of the source of the federal budget?

4. The amount of the federal budget that comes from social security tax is how many times the amount that comes from the source labeled "other"?

5. How many dollars of the federal budget come from corporate income tax?

6. According to the graph, which of the following statements is true?

   (1) Individual income tax and social security tax make up over 80% of the budget.
   (2) Corporate income tax represents the greatest source of the budget.
   (3) Social security tax payments make up over half of the budget.
   (4) Together social security tax and corporate income tax make up 25% of the budget.
   (5) Individual income taxes were higher than ever before.

ANSWERS ARE ON PAGE 374.

≡ GED Practice ≡
EXERCISE 3

Directions: Use the circle graphs below to answer questions 1–4.

SOURCES OF ENERGY FOR ELECTRIC UTILITY INDUSTRY

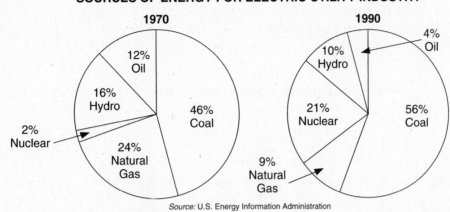

Source: U.S. Energy Information Administration

1. In 1970 natural gas was about what fraction of the energy source for electric utilities?

   (1) $\frac{1}{4}$

   (2) $\frac{1}{3}$

   (3) $\frac{1}{2}$

   (4) $\frac{3}{4}$

   (5) Not enough information is given.

2. For the years shown on the graphs, which two sources increased as a percent of the total energy source for electric utilities?

   (1) hydro and oil
   (2) natural gas and oil
   (3) coal and nuclear
   (4) nuclear and hydro
   (5) natural gas and hydro

3. The percent of energy coming from nuclear power in 1990 was how many times greater than the percent coming from nuclear power in 1970?

   (1) twice
   (2) $5\frac{1}{2}$
   (3) $10\frac{1}{2}$
   (4) 15
   (5) 19

4. Together nuclear and natural gas made up what fraction of the energy source for electric utilities in 1990?

   (1) $\frac{9}{10}$

   (2) $\frac{3}{5}$

   (3) $\frac{1}{2}$

   (4) $\frac{2}{5}$

   (5) $\frac{3}{10}$

ANSWERS ARE ON PAGE 374.

BAR GRAPHS

A **bar graph** is more complicated than a circle graph. To find the values represented on a bar graph, you must read two sets of information. One set of information goes up and down along the **vertical axis** (side). The other set of information goes across along the **horizontal axis** (bottom).

Below is a bar graph that shows noon temperatures for five days. The vertical axis, running up and down along the left side, measures temperature in degrees. The horizontal axis, across the bottom of the graph, lists the days of the week.

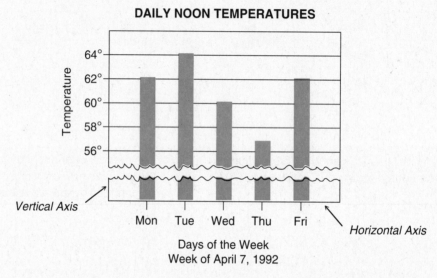

DAILY NOON TEMPERATURES

Days of the Week
Week of April 7, 1992

EXAMPLE 1 According to the graph what was the noon temperature on Wednesday?

SOLUTION Find Wednesday on the horizontal axis. Follow the bar above "Wed" to the top. Read the temperature straight across on the axis to the left. The bar stops at the line labeled "60°." The temperature at noon on Wednesday was **60°**.
　　　　　Notice also that the specific dates mentioned can be found by looking at the note below the graph itself. Important information can be found in places other than the title and the axes, so be sure to read *all* information contained on a graph.

EXAMPLE 2 On what day was the temperature 57°?

SOLUTION Look halfway between 56° and 58° to estimate 57° on the vertical axis. Look across until you find a bar that rises to this point. The bar labeled "Thu" ends halfway between 56° and 58°. The noon temperature was 57° on **Thursday**.

EXERCISE 4

Directions: Use the bar graph below to answer the following questions.

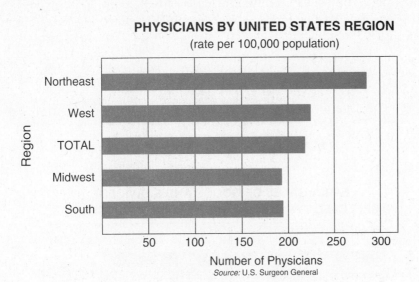

PHYSICIANS BY UNITED STATES REGION
(rate per 100,000 population)

Region

Number of Physicians
Source: U.S. Surgeon General

1. Which region has approximately 225 physicians per 100,000 population?

2. Which region has the most physicians per population?

3. Which two regions have fewer physicians per 100,000 people than the total nation?

4. The population of Central County is 300,000. Central County is in the West. If Central County is typical of the region, approximately how many physicians are there in the county?

  (1) 200
  (2) 225
  (3) 450
  (4) 675
  (5) 900

5. The total population of the United States is about 250,000,000. According to the graph, approximately how many physicians are there in the United States?

  (1)   210
  (2)   5,400
  (3)   35,000
  (4) 270,000
  (5) 540,000

6. A typical city of 50,000 people in the Midwest has about how many doctors?

  (1) 190
  (2) 95
  (3) 75
  (4) 50
  (5) 25

ANSWERS ARE ON PAGE 374.

MORE BAR GRAPHS

Bar graphs sometimes use different kinds of bars to compare information. The following graph uses two different kinds of bars to compare dollar amounts for different years. Practice working with graphs like this one containing more information.

EXERCISE 5

Directions: Use the graph below to answer the following questions.

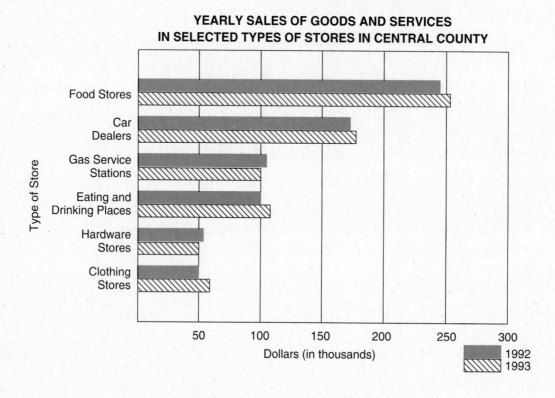

YEARLY SALES OF GOODS AND SERVICES IN SELECTED TYPES OF STORES IN CENTRAL COUNTY

1. What was the approximate yearly total for sales of goods and services for
   a. food stores in 1993?
   b. car dealers in 1992?
   c. eating and drinking places in 1992?

2. Which establishments had lower sales in 1993 than in 1992?

3. By approximately how much did sales at eating and drinking places increase from 1992 to 1993?

   (1) $ 10
   (2) $ 100
   (3) $ 1000
   (4) $ 10,000
   (5) $100,000

4. In 1993 hardware stores did approximately what fraction of the business of gas service stations?

   (1) $\frac{3}{4}$

   (2) $\frac{1}{2}$

   (3) $\frac{1}{3}$

   (4) $\frac{1}{4}$

   (5) $\frac{1}{5}$

5. Which of the following is closest to the combined 1992 income for the car dealers and clothing stores?

   (1) $ 200
   (2) $ 20,000
   (3) $125,000
   (4) $175,000
   (5) $225,000

6. Which of the following is closest to the combined 1992 and 1993 income for food stores?

   (1) $1,000,000
   (2) $ 500,000
   (3) $ 250,000
   (4) $ 100,000
   (5) $ 50,000

ANSWERS ARE ON PAGE 375.

LINE GRAPHS

A *line graph*, like a bar graph, has information on both a vertical axis and a horizontal axis. Line graphs are useful for displaying trends or patterns over time.

The figure below is a line graph that shows the net income from a farm.

NET INCOME FROM GIORGIO'S BERRY FARM

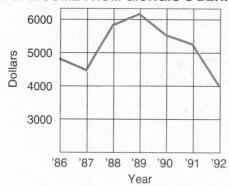

EXAMPLE 1   What was the net income in 1987?

SOLUTION   Find '87 on the horizontal axis. Follow the line labeled "'87" up until it meets the continuous heavy line. Read the dollar income on the vertical axis directly to the left. The point on the vertical axis is halfway between $4000 and $5000. The net income in 1987 was **$4500**.

EXAMPLE 2   In what year shown on the graph was net income above $6000?

SOLUTION   Find $6000 on the vertical axis. Read across to the point on the line that is above $6000. Read the year on the horizontal axis directly below the point. The net income was above $6000 in **1989**.

PREDICTING RESULTS

A trend in numbers can help you make a projection. A *projection* is a prediction based on past and current patterns.

Look again at the graph above.

EXAMPLE 3   If the trend for Giorgio's farm continues as it did from 1989 to 1992, which of the following best expresses the projection for 1993 income?

(1) 1993 income will be above $4000.
(2) 1993 income will be $4000.
(3) 1993 income will be below $4000.

SOLUTION   According to the graph, income from the farm has been dropping each year since 1989. The 1992 income was about $4000. The trend suggests that 1993 income will be less than $4000. Choice **(3)** is correct.

EXERCISE 6

Directions: Use the graph below to answer questions 1–6.

UNEMPLOYMENT RATES IN THE UNITED STATES AND JAPAN

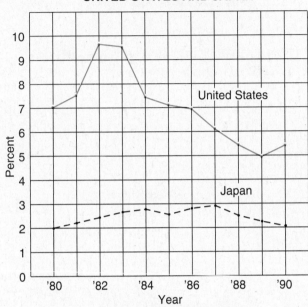

Source: U.S. Bureau of Labor Statistics

1. What is the label on the vertical axis?

   (1) unemployment
   (2) United States
   (3) Japan
   (4) Percent
   (5) Bureau of Labor Statistics

2. In which year was the unemployment rate in the United States the lowest?

   (1) 1980
   (2) 1982
   (3) 1987
   (4) 1988
   (5) 1989

3. For the years shown on the graph, approximately what was the highest unemployment rate in Japan?

   (1) 1%
   (2) 1.5%
   (3) 2.2%
   (4) 3%
   (5) 5%

4. In what year was the difference between the unemployment rates of Japan and the United States greatest?

   (1) 1981
   (2) 1982
   (3) 1983
   (4) 1985
   (5) 1989

5. Which of the following best describes the information on the graph?

   (1) While the unemployment rates for both countries fluctuated, the change was greater in the United States.
   (2) The unemployment rates rose the same amounts for both countries.
   (3) The unemployment rates for both countries dropped rapidly.
   (4) While the unemployment rates for both countries fluctuated, the change was greater in Japan.
   (5) Both countries had almost no unemployment.

6. If the trend shown for the last three years on the graph continues, which of the following best describes the unemployment rate in Japan for 1991?

   (1) more than in 1990
   (2) less than in 1990
   (3) the same as in 1990
   (4) about 3%
   (5) about 1%

ANSWERS ARE ON PAGE 375.

TABLES

Another graphic representation of data that is often found in newspapers and books is a table. A ***table*** is a list of exact numbers displayed in columns and rows. Although graphs make quick comparisons of numbers easy, tables allow for greater accuracy because they provide actual values. The table below compares the populations of fifteen large metropolitan areas in the United States.

POPULATION* OF THE FIFTEEN LARGEST METROPOLITAN AREAS IN THE U.S.

	1980	1990
New York City	17,540,000	18,087,000
Los Angeles	11,498,000	14,532,000
Chicago	7,937,000	8,066,000
San Francisco	5,368,000	6,253,000
Philadelphia	5,681,000	5,899,000
Detroit	4,753,000	4,665,000
Boston	3,972,000	4,172,000
Washington, D.C.	3,251,000	3,924,000
Dallas	2,931,000	3,885,000
Houston	3,100,000	3,711,000
Miami	2,644,000	3,193,000
Atlanta	2,138,000	2,834,000
Cleveland	2,834,000	2,760,000
Seattle	2,093,000	2,559,000
San Diego	1,862,000	2,498,000

*to the nearest thousand

Source: Bureau of the Census, U.S. Dept. of Commerce

EXAMPLE 1 What was the population of metropolitan Miami in 1980?

SOLUTION Find Miami in the list of cities. Look to the right in the column labeled "1980." The population of metropolitan Miami in 1980 was **2,644,000**.

EXAMPLE 2 By how much did the population of metropolitan Philadelphia increase from 1980 to 1990?

1990 population	5,899,000
1980 population	− 5,681,000
	218,000

SOLUTION Subtract the 1980 population of Philadelphia from the 1990 population. The increase was **218,000** people.

EXERCISE 7

Directions: Use the table below to answer questions 1–4.

Union Membership (in thousands)				
	1985	**1987**	**1989**	**1991**
Steelworkers	572	494	481	459
Garment Workers	210	173	153	143
Communication Workers	524	515	492	492
United Automobile Workers	974	998	917	840
Service Employees	688	762	762	881
State, County, and Municipal Employees	997	1032	1090	1191

Source: A.F.L.–C.I.O.

1. By what amount did the membership decrease in the United Automobile Workers union from 1989 to 1991?

2. What was the 1990 membership in the Service Employees union?

   (1) 762
   (2) 881
   (3) 762,000
   (4) 821,000
   (5) Not enough information is given.

3. Which of the following expresses the average number of members in the Garment Workers union for the years 1989 and 1991?

   (1) $2(210 + 173)$

   (2) $\dfrac{2}{173 + 153}$

   (3) $\dfrac{2}{153 + 143}$

   (4) $\dfrac{153 + 143}{2}$

   (5) $\dfrac{153,000 + 143,000}{2}$

4. If the trend for membership in the Steelworkers union continues, which of the following best expresses the projected membership for 1993?

   (1) the same as the 1991 membership
   (2) about the same as the 1985 membership
   (3) less than the 1991 membership
   (4) more than the 1991 membership
   (5) about half of the 1989 membership

Directions: Use the table below to answer questions 5–8.

Characteristics of College Freshmen (in percent)				
	1970	**1980**	**1985**	**1990**
Sex: Male	55	49	48	46
Female	45	51	52	54
Political orientation:				
Liberal	34	20	21	23
Middle of the road	45	60	57	55
Conservative	17	17	19	20

Source: Statistical Abstract of the United States

5. What was the first year shown on the table in which females represented more than half of college freshmen?

6. In 1980, what fraction of college freshmen said that their political orientation was liberal?

(1) $\frac{1}{10}$

(2) $\frac{1}{5}$

(3) $\frac{1}{2}$

(4) $\frac{3}{4}$

(5) $\frac{4}{5}$

7. In 1970, what was the ratio of college freshmen who said that they were conservative to those who said that they were liberal?

(1) $\frac{3}{4}$

(2) $\frac{2}{3}$

(3) $\frac{1}{2}$

(4) $\frac{1}{4}$

(5) $\frac{1}{5}$

8. If the trend shown on the table continues, which of the following best expresses the percent of students who will describe themselves as conservative in 1995?

(1) 15%

(2) 20%

(3) 25%

(4) more than 20%

(5) a little less than in 1990

ANSWERS ARE ON PAGE 375.

☰ GED Practice ☰
GRAPHS AND TABLES REVIEW

Directions: Use the following line graph and circle graph to answer questions 1–6.

**MAYNARD FAMILY
AVERAGE MONTHLY INCOME**

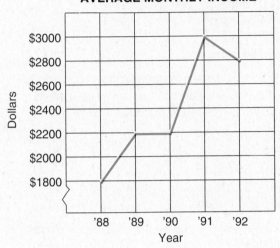

**MAYNARD FAMILY
FEBRUARY EXPENDITURES**
(percent of total take-home pay)

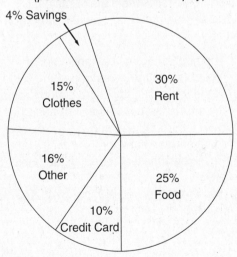

1. What was the Maynard family's average monthly income in 1991?

2. In what year did the Maynards' income first read $2200 per month?

3. Together the categories of credit card, savings, and other are equal to what single category in the Maynards' budget?

4. How much did the Maynards save each month in 1992?

   (1) $ 72
   (2) $ 88
   (3) $112
   (4) $120
   (5) $280

5. How much did the Maynards spend each month for rent in 1989?

   (1) $900
   (2) $840
   (3) $780
   (4) $660
   (5) $540

6. If the trend from 1991 to 1992 continues, which of the following best predicts the approximate monthly expenditures for credit card bills for 1993?

   (1) about $500
   (2) about $400
   (3) about $350
   (4) about $260
   (5) less than $200

Directions: Use the following bar graph and table to answer questions 7–12.

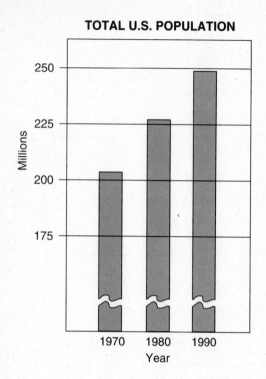

TOTAL U.S. POPULATION

U.S. Population by Race			
	1970	**1980**	**1990**
Race			
White	87.6%	83.1%	80.3%
African-American	11.1	11.7	12.1
American Indian, Eskimo	NA*	0.6	0.8
Asian, Pacific Islander	NA	1.6	2.9
Other	1.3	3.0	3.9
Total	100.0	100.0	100.0

*NA means not available.

Source: U.S. Census

7. What was the approximate population of the United States in 1990?

8. In 1990 what percentage of the United States population was Asian or Pacific Islander?

9. In 1990 about how many African-Americans were in the United States?

   (1) 12 million
   (2) 15 million
   (3) 30 million
   (4) 50 million
   (5) 80 million

10. For each decade (from 1970 to 1980 and from 1980 to 1990), the population of the United States increased approximately how much?

   (1) 10 million
   (2) 25 million
   (3) 50 million
   (4) 100 million
   (5) 200 million

11. Which racial group on the table came closest to doubling in population from 1980 to 1990?

   (1) white
   (2) African-American
   (3) American Indian, Eskimo
   (4) Asian, Pacific Islander
   (5) other

12. Which of the following statements best expresses the patterns shown in the graph and table?

   (1) The population rose steadily, and the racial mix of the country changed.
   (2) While the racial mix of the country remained the same, the population decreased.
   (3) Both the population and the racial mix remained the same.
   (4) Race relations worsened as the population grew.
   (5) Race relations steadily improved from 1970 to 1990.

MEDIAN HOUSEHOLD INCOME BY RACE AND ETHNICITY
1979 AND 1989

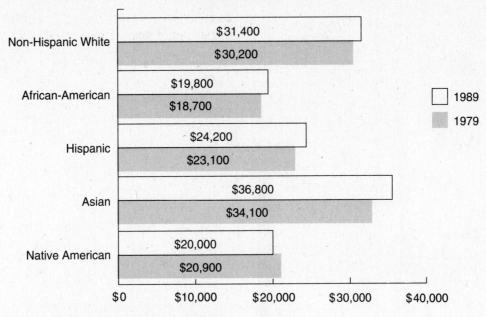

Note: 1979 income expressed in 1989 dollars.
Source: 1980 and 1990 Censuses of Population and Housing

13. The median household income for African-Americans represented what percentage of median household income for non-Hispanic whites?

    (1) 50%
    (2) 63%
    (3) 75%
    (4) 80%
    (5) 67%

14. Which group posted a net loss of $900 in median household income between 1979 and 1989?

    (1) non-Hispanic whites
    (2) African-Americans
    (3) Hispanics
    (4) Asians
    (5) Native Americans

15. By about what percentage did Asians' median household income increase between 1979 and 1989?

    (1) 8%
    (2) 10%
    (3) 5%
    (4) 6%
    (5) 15%

ANSWERS ARE ON PAGES 375–376.

9 The Basics of Algebra

Algebra, like all the math you have studied so far, is a tool you can use to solve many problems. In this chapter you will become familiar with some of algebra's most important and powerful features:

- First, you will learn to use letters to represent unknown numbers, sometimes called *variables*. An algebraic expression always contains a variable, or an unknown. Any letter can be used to represent an unknown, but x and n are most commonly used.

- Second, you will learn about *equations*. An equation is a statement that two amounts are equal. You can write an equation with words or with symbols. Here is an equation written with symbols:

$$9 + 6 = 15$$

In words this equation says, "Nine plus six is equal to fifteen."

You will learn to solve equations using the basic arithmetic operations of addition, subtraction, multiplication, and division.

Following are examples of equations with the four basic operations.

$$\text{Addition equation:} \quad m + 43 = 74$$
$$\text{Subtraction equation:} \quad 39 = y - 15$$
$$\text{Multiplication equation:} \quad 6x = 132$$
$$\text{Division equation:} \quad \frac{w}{7} = 10$$

- Third, you will work with specific types of equations called *formulas*. Formulas will be extremely helpful in your work with algebra and geometry. A formula is a rule expressed in math symbols. Formulas point to solutions for problems. For example, $A = lw$ (area equals length times width) is the formula for finding the area of a square or rectangle.

Once you have mastered these basic algebra concepts, you're on your way to solving many different kinds of word problems found on the GED.

WRITING ALGEBRAIC EXPRESSIONS

In algebra, letters are often used to stand for numbers that we want to find. We call these letters **variables** or **unknowns**. To use algebra, you must learn to translate words into algebraic expressions.

On the next page there are several examples of algebraic expressions using the four basic arithmetic operations of addition, subtraction, multiplication, and division. Read each example carefully. The letters you see represent unknown numbers, or variables. Watch for the words that suggest which mathematical operations to write. Any letter can be used to represent an unknown number.

BASIC ALGEBRAIC EXPRESSIONS

Example	Expression	Notes
A number increased by four	$x + 4$ or $4 + x$	*Increased by* means add.
Nine more than a number	$r + 9$ or $9 + r$	*More than* means to add.
Eight less than a number	$y - 8$	*Less than* means subtract.
Eight decreased by a number	$8 - y$	*Decreased by* means to subtract. (Compare the order of this example to that of the last one.)
Four times a number	$4e$	*Times* means to multiply. (Notice that there is no sign between the number and the unknown in multiplication expressions.)
The product of ten and a number	$10b$	A *product* is the answer to multiplication.
A number divided by 5	$m/5$ or $\frac{m}{5}$	Notice that the divisor goes on the bottom.
Five divided by a number	$5/m$ or $\frac{5}{m}$	The unknown is the divisor here.
One-fourth of a number	$\frac{1}{4}m$ or $\frac{m}{4}$	Remember that $\frac{1}{4}$ of a number is equal to that number over four.
The quotient of a number divided by 5	$\frac{n}{5}$	A *quotient* is the answer to division.

Notice that with subtraction and division of unknowns, the order of the letters and numbers is very important. For example, the expression $y - 8$ is *not* equal to the expression $8 - y$. The first means "take 8 away from a number." The second means "take a number away from 8." Similarly the expression $\frac{m}{5}$ is *not* the same as the expression $\frac{5}{m}$.

EXERCISE 1

Directions: Write an algebraic expression for each of the following. Use the letter x to represent each unknown.

1. A number increased by nine

2. The product of seven and a number

3. Fives times a number

4. The sum of a number and eight

5. A number minus ten

6. One less than a number

7. Three divided by a number

8. A number decreased by twenty

9. A number divided by fifteen

10. A number plus one-half

11. The quotient of a number divided by two

12. Four more than a number

ANSWERS ARE ON PAGE 376.

USING VARIABLES IN WORD PROBLEMS

As a first step in solving some word problems it is helpful to express number relationships with variables. In the next examples, watch again for the words that suggest which mathematical operations to write.

EXAMPLE 1   Let r represent the amount of rent that Max pays in a month. Next year Max will have to pay $20 more each month for rent. Write an expression that tells his monthly rent next year.

$r + 20$

SOLUTION   The expression "$20 more" means to add. Max's monthly rent this year is r. His monthly rent next year will be $r + 20$.

EXAMPLE 2   Four friends jointly won w dollars in a raffle. They decided to share the money equally. Write an expression for the amount each person received.

$\frac{w}{4}$

SOLUTION   To share equally means to divide. The total amount they won was w. The amount each received was w divided by 4, or $\frac{w}{4}$.

EXERCISE 2

Directions: Write an expression for the situation described in each problem.

1. Jack makes w dollars an hour. He will get a $2-an-hour raise. Write an expression for his new hourly wage.

2. Normally there are s students in John's GED class. Because of bad weather, five students were absent one night. Write an expression for the number of students who came to class that night.

3. Meat costs c per pound. Write an expression for the cost of three pounds of meat.

4. Let i stand for Ellen's gross income. Of her income $\frac{1}{5}$ goes for taxes and social security. Write an expression for the amount of Ellen's income that is withheld for taxes and social security.

5. The total town budget for summer programs is x. Four programs share the money equally. Write an expression for the amount each program gets.

6. The Smiths take home *t* dollars every month. They spend $\frac{5}{6}$ of their take-home pay for basic expenses. Write an expression for the amount of their basic expenses each month.

7. The length of a rectangle is *l*. The width is two inches less than the length. Write an expression for the width of the rectangle.

   (1) $2l$

   (2) $2 - l$

   (3) $l + 2$

   (4) $l - 2$

   (5) $\frac{l}{2}$

8. The sales tax in Bill's state is 6% (.06). Write an expression for the amount of tax Bill has to pay on an item that costs *m* dollars.

   (1) $m - 6$

   (2) $m + 6$

   (3) $\frac{m}{6}$

   (4) $6m$

   (5) $.06m$

9. Frank is *y* years old. Write an expression for his age in 10 years.

   (1) $y + 10$

   (2) $y - 10$

   (3) $10y$

   (4) $\frac{y}{10}$

   (5) $\frac{2y}{10}$

10. Beverly weighs *p* pounds. Write an expression for her weight after she loses 15 pounds.

   (1) $p + 15$

   (2) $p - 15$

   (3) $15p$

   (4) $\frac{p}{15}$

   (5) $2(p + 15)$

ANSWERS ARE ON PAGE 376.

SOLVING ONE-STEP EQUATIONS

Look at this equation: $m + 43 = 74$. This equation is asking you "What number plus 43 will give me a sum of 74?" You may be able to figure out the answer just by trying different values for m. Your knowledge of mathematics may be enough to solve a problem like this. However, if you have trouble seeing a solution right away, algebra can help you handle this type of problem easily. Also, as problems with unknowns become more complex, you will find algebra more and more useful.

The equal sign ($=$) makes an equation like an old-fashioned balance scale. Imagine a scale with weights on one side and apples on the other side. If you remove an apple from one side, you must remove a corresponding weight from the other side to keep the scale balanced.

You can "balance" an equation like the one above by performing the *same* operation on both sides of the equal sign.

When you solve an equation, your goal is to get the unknown to stand alone. In other words, to solve the equation $m + 43 = 74$, you want to get the *m alone* on one side of the equation. As you can see, m is not alone in the equation $m + 43 = 74$; it has $+ 43$ right next to it.

How can you get the unknown (m in this case) to stand alone? In an equation with one operation (such as addition), you can get the unknown to stand alone by performing the **inverse** (opposite) operation on both sides of the equation.

- The inverse of addition is subtraction.

- The inverse of subtraction is addition.

- The inverse of multiplication is division.

- The inverse of division is multiplication.

RULE FOR SOLVING EQUATIONS WITH ONE OPERATION

Identify the operation in the equation. Then perform the inverse operation on *both* sides of the equation to get a statement that means "Unknown = value" or "Value = unknown."

Remember: Whatever you do to one side of an equation you *must* do to the other side.

EXAMPLE 1   Solve for the unknown in $m + 43 = 74$.

$$
\begin{array}{rcr}
m + 43 & = & 74 \\
\underline{-\ 43} & & \underline{-\ 43} \\
m & = & 31
\end{array}
$$

SOLUTION   On the left side, 43 is added to the unknown. Since the inverse of addition is subtraction, subtract 43 from both sides. The solution for m is 31. **$m = 31$.**

To check the solution for an equation, substitute the value of the unknown into the equation. For Example 1, replace m with 31.

$$
\begin{array}{r}
\text{Check}\quad m + 43 = 74 \\
31 + 43 = 74 \\
74 = 74
\end{array}
$$

The correct solution to an equation makes both sides of the equation equal. When you substitute 31 for m in the equation in Example 1, both sides of the equation equal 74. This means that 31 is the correct solution.

EXAMPLE 2   Solve and check the equation $39 = y - 15$.

$$
\textbf{(1)}\quad
\begin{array}{rcr}
39 & = & y - 15 \\
\underline{+\ 15} & & \underline{+\ 15} \\
54 & = & y
\end{array}
\qquad
\textbf{(2)}\quad
\begin{array}{rcl}
39 & = & 54 - 15 \\
39 & = & 39
\end{array}
$$

STEP 1   On the right side of the equation 15 is subtracted from the unknown. The inverse of subtraction is addition, so add 15 to both sides. The solution for y is 54. **$y = 54$.**

STEP 2   To check, substitute 54 for y in the original equation.

EXERCISE 3

Directions: Solve and check each equation.

1. $f + 20 = 57$	**5.** $n + 36 = 60$	**9.** $20 = a + 19$
2. $b - 19 = 28$	**6.** $18 = d - 6$	**10.** $g - 1 = 80$
3. $33 = k - 8$	**7.** $c - 4 = 27$	**11.** $m + 16 = 200$
4. $42 = t + 7$	**8.** $41 = e + 18$	**12.** $43 = r - 7$

ANSWERS ARE ON PAGE 376.

SOLVING EQUATIONS WITH MULTIPLICATION AND DIVISION

In the next examples you will see equations with multiplication and division. Remember that the inverse of multiplication is division. The inverse of division is multiplication.

EXAMPLE 1   Solve and check the equation $6x = 132$.

(1) $6x = 132$ **(2)** $6x = 132$

$\dfrac{6x}{6} = \dfrac{132}{6}$ $6(22) = 132$

$\boldsymbol{x = 22}$ $132 = 132$

STEP 1   On the left side the unknown is being multiplied by 6. Since the inverse of multiplication is division, divide both sides of the equation by 6. On the left side you get $1x$. Write this simply as x. On the right side you get the solution, 22.

STEP 2   To check, substitute 22 for x in the original equation.

> **TIP:** When the number 1 appears before the unknown, as in $1x$, the unknown is written by itself. This is because any value multiplied by 1 is the same value.

EXAMPLE 2   Solve and check the equation $10 = \dfrac{w}{7}$.

(1) $10 = \dfrac{w}{7}$ **(2)** $10 = \dfrac{w}{7}$

$10 \times 7 = \dfrac{w}{7} \times \dfrac{7}{1}$ $10 = \dfrac{70}{7}$

$\boldsymbol{70 = w}$ $10 = 10$

STEP 1   On the right side of the equal sign the unknown is being divided by 7. Since multiplication is the inverse of division, multiply both sides of the equation by 7. The solution for w is 70.

STEP 2   To check, substitute 70 for w.

EXERCISE 4

Directions: Solve and check each equation.

1. $8y = 96$

2. $11 = 2d$

3. $15p = 75$

4. $25z = 100$

5. $\dfrac{x}{3} = 9$

6. $9 = \dfrac{m}{4}$

7. $\dfrac{a}{5} = 8$

8. $\dfrac{c}{9} = 2$

ANSWERS ARE ON PAGE 376.

WRITING ONE-STEP EQUATIONS TO SOLVE WORD PROBLEMS

In the previous section you learned to solve one-step equations. On the GED Test you may have to read a word problem and *write an equation* based on it before you can solve the problem.

At the beginning of this chapter you learned to write algebraic expressions from words. To write equations from words, watch for verbs such as *is* or *equals*. These verbs tell you where to put the equal sign.

EXAMPLE 1 A number increased by twelve is twenty. Find the number.

$$\textbf{(1)}\ x + 12 = 20 \qquad \textbf{(2)}\ \begin{array}{r} x + 12 = 20 \\ -12 \quad -12 \\ \hline x = 8 \end{array} \qquad \textbf{(3)}\ \begin{array}{r} x + 12 = 20 \\ 8 + 12 = 20 \\ 20 = 20 \end{array}$$

STEP 1   Use a letter to represent the unknown in the expression "a number increased by twelve." The verb *is* tells you to put the equal sign before 20.

STEP 2   Solve the equation by subtracting 12 from both sides. The solution is **8**.

STEP 3   Check by substituting 8 for x in the original equation.

EXAMPLE 2 Andy's gross pay minus the $45 his employer withholds each week is his net pay. Andy's net pay is $325 a week. What is Andy's gross pay?

$$\textbf{(1)}\ x - 45 = 325 \qquad \textbf{(2)}\ \begin{array}{r} x - 45 = 325 \\ +45 \quad +45 \\ \hline x = 370 \end{array}$$

STEP 1   Use a letter to represent Andy's gross pay. Then write an equation that expresses the gross pay minus the amount withheld. The verb *is* in the first sentence tells you where to put the equal sign.

STEP 2   Solve the equation by adding 45 to both sides. The solution is 370. Andy's gross pay is **$370** a week.

You may have found the two problems above easy to solve without writing an equation. This is OK. You should use whatever method is successful for you. However, as word problems get more challenging, you will find that equations can make your work a lot easier. Therefore it's a good idea to practice writing and solving them.

EXERCISE 5

Directions: For questions 1–6, match the verbal equation on the left with the algebraic equation on the right by writing the correct letter in the space provided.

_____ **1.** A number increased by nine is fifteen.

_____ **2.** Two-thirds of a number equals twelve.

_____ **3.** A number divided by three is twenty.

_____ **4.** When you subtract a number from sixteen, the result is ten.

_____ **5.** The product of a number and three is twenty.

_____ **6.** When a number is divided by seven, the result is four.

a. $\frac{3}{n} = 20$

b. $3s = 20$

c. $t + 15 = 9$

d. $7a = 4$

e. $c + 9 = 15$

f. $\frac{2}{3}x = 12$

g. $16 - y = 10$

h. $\frac{a}{7} = 4$

i. $\frac{d}{3} = 20$

j. $\frac{2}{3}(12) = x$

Directions: For questions 7–12, write an equation for each statement. Then solve for the unknown number.

7. Nine less than a number is fifteen.

8. The product of six and a number is 27.

9. A number divided by five equals fifty.

10. Three is equal to a number decreased by five.

11. Sixty is equal to three-fourths of a number.

12. The product of seven and a number is 84.

Directions: For questions 13–16, write and solve an equation for each problem.

13. The original price minus a $40 discount is the price Max paid for a new color TV. He paid $290 for the TV. Find the original price.

14. The total payroll at Acme, Inc., divided by 15 is the amount each employee takes home every week. Every worker takes home $195 a week. Find the total weekly payroll.

15. Sandy pays one-fourth of her monthly income for rent. Her monthly rent is $520. How much is her income each month?

16. Of the members of a block association 75% (.75) came to the last meeting. Altogether, 90 people attended the meeting. How many people belong to the association?

ANSWERS ARE ON PAGES 376–377.

SOLVING LONGER EQUATIONS
WRITING LONGER ALGEBRAIC EXPRESSIONS

At the beginning of this chapter you learned to write algebraic expressions with the four basic operations of addition, subtraction, multiplication, and division.

Algebra is a useful way to write mathematical relationships that contain more than one of these basic operations. Read the next examples carefully. Watch for the words that suggest which mathematical operations to write.

ALGEBRAIC EXPRESSIONS WITH MULTIPLE OPERATIONS

Example	Expression	Notes
The sum of a number and one-third of the same number	$c + \frac{1}{3}c$	*Sum* means to add, and *one-third of* means to multiply.
Twice a number decreased by seven	$2k - 7$	*Twice* means to multiply, and *decreased by* means to subtract.
Twice the quantity of a number decreased by seven	$2(k - 7)$	*Twice* means to multiply, and *decreased by* means to subtract. *Quantity* groups the expression *a number decreased by seven.* (Compare this example to the last one to see how parentheses are used.)
Three more than half a number	$\frac{1}{2}r + 3$ or $\frac{r}{2} + 3$	*More than* means to add, and *half* can mean to multiply by $\frac{1}{2}$ or to divide by 2.
The sum of six and a number, all multiplied by three	$3(p + 6)$	The parentheses group the sum together.
Five divided into the sum of three and a number	$\frac{x + 3}{5}$ or $(x + 3)/5$	The fraction bar groups the $x + 3$ together. First find the sum. Then divide by 5.

EXERCISE 6

Directions: For questions 1–8, match the verbal expression on the left with the algebraic expression on the right by writing the correct letter in the space provided.

_____ **1.** Two less than seven times a number.

_____ **2.** The quantity m minus five, divided by four.

_____ **3.** A number increased by eight times itself.

_____ **4.** Twice the quantity of a number increased by six.

_____ **5.** Three more than one-half of a number.

_____ **6.** Twice a number subtracted from seven times the same number.

_____ **7.** Six more than twice a number.

_____ **8.** Three times a number subtracted from sixteen.

a. $7c - 2c$

b. $16 - 3p$

c. $2a + 6$

d. $y + 8y$

e. $7c - 2$

f. $2(g + 6)$

g. $\dfrac{m - 5}{4}$

h. $\frac{1}{2}s + 3$

i. $3p - 16$

Directions: For questions 9–17, write an algebraic expression for each verbal expression. Use x to represent the unknown number.

9. Twice a number increased by six.

10. Five less than the product of eight and a number.

11. The sum of two times a number and four times the same number.

12. Eight more than half a number.

13. Subtract one from one-third of a number.

14. Take three times a number from fifteen.

15. Four divided into the quantity of a number increased by seven.

16. The sum of twelve and a number, all multiplied by ten.

17. The quantity of four less than a number, all multiplied by nine.

ANSWERS ARE ON PAGE 377.

SOLVING EQUATIONS WITH MORE THAN ONE OPERATION

Earlier in this chapter you learned to solve one-step equations. But look at this equation:

$$4m + 2 = 26$$

As you can see, both multiplication and addition are involved. To solve equations with more than one operation, you still want to get the unknown value *by itself* on one side. To do this, use the inverse operation for every operation in the equation.

> **TIP:** In equations with both multiplication or division and addition or subtraction, remember that you *must* take care of addition and subtraction first. Then multiply and divide.

EXAMPLE 1   Solve for m in $4m + 2 = 26$.

$$
\begin{array}{ll}
\textbf{(1)} & 4m + 2 = 26 \\
& \underline{ - 2 \quad - 2} \\
& 4m = 24
\end{array}
\qquad
\begin{array}{ll}
\textbf{(2)} & \frac{4m}{4} = \frac{24}{4} \\
\\
& m = 6
\end{array}
$$

STEP 1   Since 2 is being added on the left side of the equal sign, use the inverse operation of addition. Subtract 2 from both sides of the equation. You are now left with the equation $4m = 24$.

STEP 2   Since m is being multiplied by 4, use the inverse operation, division. Divide both sides of the equation by 4. The solution is 6. ***m* = 6**.

EXAMPLE 2   Solve for s in $5 = \frac{s}{3} - 7$.

$$
\begin{array}{ll}
\textbf{(1)} & 5 = \frac{s}{3} - 7 \\
& \underline{+ 7 \qquad + 7} \\
& 12 = \frac{s}{3}
\end{array}
\qquad
\begin{array}{ll}
\textbf{(2)} & 3 \cdot 12 = \frac{s}{3} \cdot 3 \\
\\
& 36 = s
\end{array}
$$

STEP 1   Add 7 to both sides.

STEP 2   Multiply both sides by 3. The solution is 36. **36 = *s***.

EXAMPLE 3   Find the value of r in $\frac{2}{3}r + 5 = 23$.

$$
\begin{array}{ll}
\textbf{(1)} & \frac{2}{3}r + 5 = 23 \\
& \underline{\phantom{\frac{2}{3}r} - 5 \quad - 5} \\
& \frac{2}{3}r = 18
\end{array}
\qquad
\begin{array}{ll}
\textbf{(2)} & \frac{3}{2} \cdot \frac{2}{3}r = \frac{18}{1} \cdot \frac{3}{2} \\
\\
& r = 27
\end{array}
$$

STEP 1   Because 5 is being added and subtraction is the inverse of addition, subtract 5 from both sides.

STEP 2   Since r is multiplied by $\frac{2}{3}$, divide both sides of the equation by $\frac{2}{3}$. Remember that to divide by a fraction means to multiply by the reciprocal of the fraction. Multiply both sides of the equation by $\frac{3}{2}$. The solution is 27. ***r* = 27**.

EXERCISE 7

Directions: Solve and check each equation.

1. $7m - 2 = 54$

2. $\frac{a}{3} + 5 = 9$

3. $7 = \frac{c}{2} + 3$

4. $82 = 9d + 10$

5. $25c - 17 = 183$

6. $\frac{w}{2} - 7 = 3$

7. $2 = 6x - 10$

8. $\frac{1}{3}p + 8 = 11$

9. $40 = 13z + 14$

10. $\frac{n}{2} + 3 = 7$

11. $\frac{3}{4}y - 3 = 12$

12. $39 = 16k - 9$

13. $10 = 6a + 7$

14. $9r + 15 = 18$

ANSWERS ARE ON PAGES 377–378.

SOLVING EQUATIONS WITH PARENTHESES

Part of the information in some equations may be contained in parentheses. A set of parentheses groups together the numbers and letters that are to be multiplied or divided by some other amount. In the expression $5(m + 6)$, both m and 6 are to be multiplied by 5.

Before you can solve an equation that has parentheses, you must get rid of the parentheses. To do this, multiply each number and letter inside the parentheses by the number on the outside. This is an application of the distributive law, which you learned in Chapter 2. See pages 45–46 if you need a review of this law.

EXAMPLE 1
$5(m + 6)$
$5 \cdot m + 5 \cdot 6$
$5m + 30$

EXAMPLE 2
$3(2m - 1)$
$3 \cdot 2m - 3 \cdot 1$
$6m - 3$

To solve an equation that contains parentheses, first multiply the terms inside the parentheses by the number on the outside. Then follow the rules for solving equations. Remember that a dot $(\cdot)$ between two numbers or letters means multiplication.

EXAMPLE 3 Solve for c in $4(c - 6) = 12$.

STEP 1 Multiply both c and 6 by 4.

$$4(c - 6) = 12$$
$$4c - 24 = 12$$

STEP 2 Add 24 to both sides.

$$4c - 24 = 12$$
$$\underline{+ 24 \quad + 24}$$
$$4c = 36$$

STEP 3 Divide both sides by 4. The solution is 9. **$c = 9$**.

$$\frac{4c}{4} = \frac{36}{4}$$
$$c = 9$$

EXERCISE 8

Directions: Solve each equation.

1. $3(x + 4) = 27$

2. $10 = 5(a - 3)$

3. $36 = 4(c + 4)$

4. $28 = 7m - 32$

5. $3(y - 2) = 3$

6. $80 = 8(s + 7)$

7. $3(t + 10) = 90$

8. $7(m - 2) = 28$

ANSWERS ARE ON PAGE 378.

SUBSTITUTING TO SOLVE EQUATIONS

On the GED Test you can use answer choices to solve equations. Remember that an equation is a statement that two amounts are equal. When you substitute the correct solution into an equation, you will get two equal amounts.

EXAMPLE 1 Choose the correct solution to $5m - 1 = 49$.

(1) 8   **(2)** 9   **(3)** 10   **(4)** 12

STEP 1 Substitute each answer choice.
(1) $5(8) - 1 = 40 - 1 = 39$, which does not equal 49.
(2) $5(9) - 1 = 45 - 1 = 44$, which does not equal 49.
(3) $5(10) - 1 = 50 - 1 = 49$, which equals 49.
STEP 2 Choose answer choice **(3)**. The solution is $m = 10$.

EXAMPLE 2 Choose the correct solution to $2(x + 3) = 24$.

(1) 8   **(2)** (9)   **(3)** 10   **(4)** 11

STEP 1 Substitute each answer choice.
(1) $2(8 + 3) = 2(11) = 22$, which does not equal 24.
(2) $2(9 + 3) = 2(12) = 24$, which equals 24.
STEP 2 Choose answer choice **(2)**. The solution is $x = 9$.

EXERCISE 9

Directions: Substitute answer choices to solve each equation.

1. $6x - 3 = 45$
   (1) 6   **(2)** 7   **(3)** 8   **(4)** 9

2. $2y + 1 = 27$
   (1) 12   **(2)** 13   **(3)** 14   **(4)** 15

3. $\frac{w}{5} + 6 = 10$
   (1) 4   **(2)** 5   **(3)** 10   **(4)** 20

4. $25 = 3z - 2$

    (1) 7   **(2)** 9   **(3)** 11   **(4)** 13

5. $18 = m + 11$

    (1) 7   **(2)** 9   **(3)** 10   **(4)** 14

6. $50 = 4n + 2$

    (1) 12   **(2)** 20   **(3)** 36   **(4)** 48

7. $2(r - 3) = 10$

    (1) 4   **(2)** 5   **(3)** 8   **(4)** 9

8. $6(p + 1) = 60$

    (1) 15   **(2)** 12   **(3)** 10   **(4)** 9

9. $72 = 8(c + 4)$

    (1) 12   **(2)** 10   **(3)** 9   **(4)** 5

10. $30 = 3(f - 2)$

    (1) 10   **(2)** 12   **(3)** 14   **(4)** 20

ANSWERS ARE ON PAGE 378.

EXERCISE 10

Directions: For questions 1–6, match the verbal expression on the left with the algebraic equation on the right by writing the correct letter in the space provided.

_____ **1.** Half a number decreased by five is six.

_____ **2.** Three times a number plus four equals nineteen.

_____ **3.** Four times a number increased by one is twenty-one.

_____ **4.** Twice a number decreased by nine is equal to seven.

_____ **5.** The product of six and a number increased by three is twelve.

_____ **6.** Five times a number decreased by two equals nine.

a. $6m + 3 = 12$

b. $2x - 9 = 7$

c. $4d + 1 = 21$

d. $5n - 2 = 9$

e. $\frac{a}{2} - 5 = 6$

f. $3x + 4 = 19$

Directions: For questions 7–12, write and solve an equation for each statement. Use x to represent the unknown number.

7. One less than three times a number is five.

8. Four times a number decreased by two equals eighteen.

9. When twice a number is increased by one, the result is thirteen.

10. Ten more than six times a number equals thirty-four.

11. Eight less than half a number is twelve.

12. When the quotient of a number divided by eight is decreased by three, the result equals six.

ANSWERS ARE ON PAGES 378–379.

WRITING AND SOLVING LONGER EQUATIONS

You learned earlier in this chapter to write one-step equations from words. To write longer equations, follow the same procedure. Watch for verbs such as *is* and *equals*. These verbs tell you where to put the equal sign.

EXAMPLE 1   Eight more than three times a number is twenty. Find the number.

STEP 1   Use a letter to represent the unknown in the expression "eight more than three times a number." The verb *is* tells you to put the equal sign before 20.

$$3x + 8 = 20$$

STEP 2   Solve the equation. Your first step is to subtract 8 from both sides.

$$\begin{array}{rcr} 3x + 8 &=& 20 \\ -8 & & -8 \\ \hline 3x &=& 12 \end{array}$$

STEP 3   To get the unknown alone, divide both sides by 3. $x = 4$.

$$\frac{3x}{3} = \frac{12}{3}$$
$$x = 4$$

EXAMPLE 2   One-third of a number decreased by seven equals four. Find the number.

STEP 1   Use a letter to represent the unknown and write the equation. The verb *equals* tells you where to put the equal sign.

$$\frac{1}{3}x - 7 = 4$$

STEP 2   Solve the equation. Your first step is to add 7 to both sides.

$$\begin{array}{rcr} \frac{1}{3}x - 7 &=& 4 \\ +7 & & +7 \\ \hline \frac{1}{3}x &=& 11 \end{array}$$

STEP 3   To get the unknown alone, multiply both sides by 3. $x = 33$.

$$3 \cdot \frac{1}{3}x = 11 \times 3$$
$$x = 33$$

SOLVING EQUATIONS WITH SEPARATED UNKNOWNS

Sometimes the unknowns are separated in an equation. You must combine the unknowns before you can solve the equation. The numbers next to letters can be added *only* if the letters are the same. Look at these examples carefully.

$$
\begin{array}{ccc}
5x & 4a & 6c \\
+\,2x & +\,a & -\,5c \\
\hline
7x & 5a & c
\end{array}
$$

Notice that in the second example a is understood to be $1a$. In the third example the answer c is the same as $1c$.

Consider the following examples:

EXAMPLE 1   Solve for x in $5x - 2x + 8 = 26$.

STEP 1   Combine the unknowns (x's): $5x - 2x = 3x$.

$$5x - 2x + 8 = 26$$
$$3x + 8 = 26$$

STEP 2   To get the unknowns alone on one side, first perform the inverse of addition. Subtract 8 from both sides.

$$
\begin{array}{rcl}
3x + 8 & = & 26 \\
-\,8 & & -\,8 \\
\hline
3x & = & 18
\end{array}
$$

STEP 3   Divide both sides by 3. The solution is 6.
$x = 6$.

$$\frac{3x}{3} = \frac{18}{3}$$
$$x = 6$$

EXAMPLE 2   Solve for a in $9a - 3 = 2a + 11$.

STEP 1   To combine the a's on one side of the equal sign, use the inverse of addition. Subtract $2a$ from both sides.

$$
\begin{array}{rcl}
9a - 3 & = & 2a + 11 \\
-\,2a & & -\,2a \\
\hline
7a - 3 & = & 11
\end{array}
$$

STEP 2   Use inverse operations again to isolate the $7a$ on the left side. Add 3 to both sides.

$$
\begin{array}{rcl}
7a - 3 & = & 11 \\
+\,3 & & +\,3 \\
\hline
7a & = & 14
\end{array}
$$

STEP 3   Divide both sides by 7. The solution is 2.
$a = 2$.

$$\frac{7a}{7} = \frac{14}{7}$$
$$a = 2$$

Notice that in Example 2 the unknowns are combined on the side with the greater value ($9a$ is more than $2a$). Later on, when you learn about positive and negative numbers, you will be able to subtract $9a$ from $2a$. For now, however, always combine unknowns on the side that has the greatest unknown value.

EXAMPLE 3   Solve for y in $20 - 2y = 3y$.

STEP 1   The unknowns are on different sides of the equal sign. Combine them on the side with the greater unknown value by adding $2y$ to both sides.

$$
\begin{array}{rcl}
20 - 2y & = & 3y \\
+\,2y & & +\,2y \\
\hline
20 & = & 5y
\end{array}
$$

STEP 2   Divide both sides by 5. The solution is 4. **$y = 4$**.

$$\frac{20}{5} = \frac{5y}{5}$$
$$4 = y$$

RULES FOR SOLVING EQUATIONS WITH SEPARATED UNKNOWNS

1. Combine the unknowns.
   a. If the unknowns are on the *same* side of the equal sign, combine them according to the rules for adding or subtracting numbers.
   b. If the unknowns are on *different* sides of the equal sign, combine them by using inverse operations.
2. Use inverse operations to solve the equation.

EXERCISE 11

Directions: Solve and check each equation.

1. $5y - y = 19 + 9$

2. $6t + 8 + 4t = 58$

3. $9c = 44 - 2c$

4. $8m = 2m + 30$

5. $4a + 55 = 9a$

6. $4p = p + 18$

7. $6f = 14 - f$

8. $3 = y + 8y$

9. $8r + 17 = 5r + 32$

10. $7n - 9 = 3n + 7$

11. $6z + 11 = 5z + 20$

12. $5y - 4 = 2y + 77$

ANSWERS ARE ON PAGE 379.

PROBLEM SOLVING FOR THE GED

Using Algebra to Solve Word Problems

The Millers, the Rigbys, and the Smiths went on a camping trip. The Millers spent $100 more than the Rigbys, and the Smiths spent twice as much as the Millers. If the cost of the trip was $580 altogether, how much did the Smith family spend?

    (1) $ 70
    (2) $100
    (3) $170
    (4) $195
    (5) $340

When you use algebra to solve a word problem, your goal is to *write and solve an equation* based on the problem. There are several steps that will help you do this.

1. Use x to represent the amount of money the Rigbys spent.

x = $ spent by Rigbys

2. Put the other facts from the problem into an algebraic expression.

The Millers spent $100 more than the Rigbys, which we have represented with x.
$x + 100$ = $ spent by Millers

The Smiths spent twice as much as the Millers. Write an algebraic expression for this amount.
$2(x + 100)$ = $ spent by Smiths

3. Once you have written algebraic expressions for the information in the problem, write an equation.

In this problem you are told that the amount spent by all three families was $580. Your equation should look like this:
$x + (x + 100) + 2(x + 100) = 580$

4. Solve the equation.

$$
\begin{aligned}
x + (x + 100) + 2(x + 100) &= 580 \\
2x + 100 + 2x + 200 &= 580 \\
4x + 300 &= 580 \\
-300 \qquad\quad &\;\; -300 \\
\hline
4x &= 280 \\
\frac{4x}{4} &= \frac{280}{4} \\
x &= \$70
\end{aligned}
$$

5. Now that you know the value of x, you can solve the problem.

This problem asks for the amount the Smiths spent. Substitute $70 for x in the expression $2(x + 100)$.

$2(70 + 100) = 340$

Answer: **(5) $340**

EXERCISE 12

Directions: Solve each problem. Your first step should be to use a variable to stand for a value you do not know. Follow the steps described on page 213 if you need help.

1. The sum of two consecutive whole numbers is 27. Find the numbers. (The word *consecutive* means one following another.)

2. The sum of three numbers is 60. The second number is two more than the first. The third number is two more than the second. Find the three numbers.

3. There are six times as many union workers as there are nonunion workers at the Acme Dye Plant. Eight fewer than the number of union workers is equal to four times the number of nonunion workers. How many union workers are there at the plant?

4. There are three times as many women in a GED class as there are men. When the number of women is decreased by two, the result is the same as when the number of men is increased by ten. Find the number of men and women in the class.

5. Juan and his boss Felipe are housepainters. For every dollar that Juan gets, Felipe gets $3. They made $360 for painting a house. How much did Felipe make on the job?

6. Mr. Migliaccio makes twice as much money as his wife does. Together the Migliaccios make $294 a week. Which of the following expressions gives the amount of money Mrs. Migliaccio makes per week?

    (1) $(294 \times 2) - 294$

    (2) $\frac{294}{3}$

    (3) $\frac{294}{2}$

    (4) $294 \div \frac{1}{2}$

    (5) $294 \div \frac{1}{3}$

7. Paul, Jeff, and Jerry worked together fixing Paul's car. Jeff worked twice as many hours as Jerry, and Paul worked six hours more than Jeff. Altogether they worked 51 hours. How many hours did Paul work?

8. In the last local election in Centerville three voters failed to vote for every voter who went to the polls. There are 22,000 registered voters in Centerville. How many of them failed to vote during the last election?

9. David is four times as old as Laila. Nancy is two years older than David. If Laila is eighteen years old, which of the following expressions gives Nancy's age?

(1) $\frac{18}{4} + 2$

(2) $18 + 4 + 2$

(3) $18 + 2$

(4) $(4 \times 18) + 2$

(5) $4(18 + 2)$

10. Unextended, the ladder Audrey uses to reach the roof of her house is one-half the height of the house. The ladder can then extend 5 more feet. If Audrey's house is forty feet tall, which of the following expressions gives the length of the ladder, fully extended?

(1) $(\frac{1}{2} \times 40) + 5$

(2) $(\frac{1}{2} \times 40) - 5$

(3) $\frac{1}{2}(40 + 5)$

(4) $(2 \times 40) + 5$

(5) $(2 \times 40) - 5$

ANSWERS ARE ON PAGES 379–380.

FORMULAS

WHAT IS A FORMULA?

A ***formula*** is an algebraic equation much like those you have been working with. A formula is different from an equation in one way: It is a rule that is always true. For example, when you learned that interest = principal × rate × time in Chapter 6, you were really using a formula: $i = prt$. The equations you have been working with so far have only *one* letter. Formulas have more than one letter. In this chapter and in Chapter 10, on geometry, you will learn to use many different formulas to help you solve problems.

To use any formula, you substitute values you *do* know for certain letters in the formula. When you ***substitute***, you replace a letter with a number. For example, how can you solve the problem below?

Sam put $2,000 in a savings account that pays 5% interest per year. He left the money in for one year. How much interest did he earn?

As you probably remember from your work in **Chapter** 6, you need to use the formula $i = prt$. You are looking for i (interest), so you substitute the values given in the problem for the other letters of the formula. The principal (p) is $2000, the rate ($r$) is 5% (.05), and the time (t) is 1.

$$i = p \times r \times t$$
$$i = \$2000 \times 5\% \times 1$$
$$i = \$100$$

In the example below, notice how your work with equations in this chapter can help you with formulas.

EXAMPLE   Margaret received $360 in interest payments from the $3000 she put in her savings account. Her rate of interest was 6%. How long did her money have to stay in the account to earn this interest?

(1) $\quad i = prt$
(2) $\$360 = \$3000 \times 6\% \times t$
(3) $\$360 = \$180 \times t$
(4) $\dfrac{\$360}{\$180} = \dfrac{\$180 \times t}{\$180}$
$\qquad\quad 2 = t$

STEP 1   Since this is an interest problem, write down the formula for simple interest.
STEP 2   Substitute values you do know for the letters in the formula. You know that the interest is $360, the principal is $3000, and the rate is 6%. Time (t) is the value you are trying to find.
STEP 3   As a first step in solving the equation, multiply $3000 by 6%. Then substitute the result in the equation.
STEP 4   As with any equation, your goal is to get the unknown value *alone* on one side. Since t is being multiplied by 180, use the inverse operation, division. Divide *both sides* of the equation by 180. **t = 2 years**.

RULES FOR USING FORMULAS TO SOLVE WORD PROBLEMS

1. Choose the formula you need and *write it down*.

2. Substitute values you *do* know for the letters in the formula.

3. Solve the equation using inverse operations where necessary.

In the next chapter you will learn more about different formulas and when they can be used. You will not need to memorize any formulas because you will be provided with a "formulas page" with the GED Math Test. On this page you will find all the formulas you will need to solve problems on the GED. You will, however, need to be able to choose and use the correct formula. This section and the following chapter will help you learn to do this effectively.

THE DISTANCE FORMULA

One formula that will appear on the GED formulas page is the ***distance formula***.

$$d = rt$$

In this formula d = distance, r = rate, and t = time. In other words you must multiply the rate by the time to find distance. Remember that when two numbers or letters appear next to each other with no operation symbol between them, you multiply them. Let's take a look at a word problem in which this formula would be helpful:

Linda drove 180 miles at a consistent speed of sixty miles per hour. How many hours did she drive?

Follow the rules for using formulas to solve word problems:

1. Choose a formula and write it down.
$$d = rt$$

2. Substitute the values you know for the letters.
$$180 = 60t$$

3. Solve the equation by using inverse operations. You want to get the unknown (t) alone on a side.
$$\frac{180}{60} = \frac{60t}{60}$$
$$3 = t$$

Linda drove for **3 hours**.

TOTAL COST FORMULA

Another formula on the GED formulas page tells you how total cost relates to unit cost and number of units:

$$c = nr$$

In this formula c = total cost, n = number of units, and r = rate, or cost per unit. Use this formula to solve the following problem.

Kate bought some towels for $7.90 each. Her total bill came to $31.60. How many towels did she buy?

1. Choose a formula and write it down.

$$c = nr$$

2. Substitute the values you know for the letters.

$$\$31.60 = n(\$7.90)$$

3. Solve the equation using inverse operations.

$$\frac{\$31.60}{\$7.90} = \frac{n(\$7.90)}{\$7.90}$$

$$4 = n$$

Kate bought 4 towels.

You may have found that you did not need a formula to solve either the distance problem or the total cost problem. This is fine—you should use whatever method you find successful. But formulas can be useful as problems get more difficult, so you should become familiar with working with them.

EXERCISE 13

Directions: Try using formulas to solve the following problems.

1. A plane travels 1676 miles in 4 hours. What is the plane's rate of travel?

2. A manufacturer sold $111.25 worth of hammers to a hardware store. The cost per unit of the hammers was $1.25. How many hammers did the hardware store buy?

3. Temperature can be read in two different ways—Celsius and Fahrenheit. To change from one system to another, you use the following formula:

$F = (\frac{9}{5})C + 32$, where F = degrees in Fahrenheit and C = degrees in Celsius.

If the temperature was 20 degrees Celsius on Tuesday, what was the temperature in Fahrenheit?

4. Anne's savings account earned $32.50 interest in $\frac{1}{2}$ year. If the bank's interest rate was 5%, how much money did Anne have in the bank to begin with?

ANSWERS ARE ON PAGE 380.

THE BASICS OF ALGEBRA REVIEW

Directions: For questions 1–4, write out the following expressions.

1. Write an algebraic expression for a number increased by eleven.

2. Write an expression for the sum of three times a number and one-third of the same number.

3. Cheese costs *c* per pound. Write an expression for the cost of four pounds of cheese.

4. Andrew's gross salary is *s*. He takes home $\frac{4}{5}$ of his gross salary. Write an expression for Andrew's take-home salary.

Directions: For questions 5–12, solve each equation.

5. $9x = 108$

6. $\frac{c}{4} = 8$

7. $14 + x = 3x - 8$

8. $\frac{21}{p} + 1 = 8$

9. $\frac{1}{8}y = 24$

10. $12.5 = a + 1.5$

11. $96 + 2x = x + 101$

12. $20 - 4z = 5z - 35$

Directions: For questions 13–19, choose the correct solution.

13. Write an equation for "a number decreased by eighteen is one."

    (1) $18x = 1$

    (2) $x + 18 = 1$

    (3) $\frac{x}{18} = 1$

    (4) $x - 18 = 1$

    (5) $x = 18$

14. Write an equation for "four-fifths of a number is forty."

    (1) $4x - 5 = 40$

    (2) $x = 40$

    (3) $5x - 4 = 40$

    (4) $5x = 40$

    (5) $\frac{4}{5}x = 40$

15. Write an equation for "nine times a number decreased by five is the same as six times the same number increased by seven."

    (1) $9x + 5 = 6x$
    (2) $9x - 5 = 7$
    (3) $9x - 6x = 7$
    (4) $9x - 6x = 5$
    (5) $9x - 5 = 6x + 7$

16. When Ron's truck was full, it weighed 7.5 tons. The weight he carried at that time was 3.25 tons. How many tons does Ron's truck weigh when it is empty?

    (1) 3.25
    (2) 4.25
    (3) 10.75
    (4) 21.75
    (5) 42.50

17. 10% (.10) of Sal's take-home pay goes for car payments each month. His car payments are $84 a month, and his rent is $260 per month. How much is Sal's take-home pay each month?

    (1) $ 8.40
    (2) $ 34.40
    (3) $ 344
    (4) $ 840
    (5) $3440

18. There are 25 more women than men in the night school Louise attends. Altogether there are 115 students in the school. How many women attend the night school?

(1) 25
(2) 45
(3) 70
(4) 90
(5) 140

19. Sam and Joe are painters. Sam makes $2 an hour less than Joe. On a job that took them both 40 hours to complete they made $440. How much does Sam make an hour?

(1) $ 3.50
(2) $ 4.50
(3) $ 6.50
(4) $45
(5) $65

Directions: Questions 20–23 refer to the following situation.

During the annual Walk for Peace, Nina walked a total of six miles more than her husband Ed. Their combined mileage was 46. Ed's company pledged to donate $1.00 for each mile that Ed and Nina walked.

20. How many miles did Nina walk?

(1) 6
(2) 14
(3) 20
(4) 26
(5) 40

21. What is the total amount that Ed's company must donate for Ed's and Nina's participation in the walk?

(1) $ 6
(2) $20
(3) $40
(4) $46
(5) Not enough information is given.

22. What more do you need to know to find out the total number of hours that Ed walked?

(1) the hours that Nina walked
(2) Ed's rate of walking
(3) the distance traveled by Ed
(4) the time that Ed stopped walking
(5) the time that Ed started walking

23. Three of Nina's friends each donated $.50 per mile that Nina and her husband walked. Which of the following expressions gives the total amount of money donated by Nina's three friends?

(1) $3 \times \$.50$
(2) $46 \times \$.50$
(3) $3(46 \times \$.50)$
(4) $\dfrac{46 \times \$.50}{3}$
(5) $(3 + \$.50)46$

Directions: For questions 24 and 25, choose the best answer.

24. Kathleen Webster makes $280 a month more than her husband, Mel. Together they make $1760 per month. How much money does Kathleen make in one month?

    (1) $ 360
    (2) $ 740
    (3) $ 840
    (4) $1020
    (5) $1480

25. Ten times a number decreased by seven equals 101 plus that number. Find the number.

    (1) 12
    (2) 13
    (3) 18
    (4) 20
    (5) 23

ANSWERS ARE ON PAGE 381.

10 Geometry

COMMON GEOMETRIC FIGURES

Geometry is the study of lines, angles, flat figures, and three-dimensional shapes. Geometry is useful in many practical situations you may encounter in everyday life. For example, when you need to figure out how much fencing you should buy to surround a garden or how much liquid you'll need to fill a water tank, knowledge of geometry can help. Many problems in this chapter will show examples of these uses. Geometry also makes up 20 percent of the GED Math Test, and the problems in this chapter will help you prepare for this as well.

To solve geometry problems, you must know some special terms. Take the time now to memorize the terms you do not already know.

An **angle** is a figure made of two lines extending from the same point, called a **vertex**. Figures 1, 2, and 3 are examples of angles. The angle in Figure 2 is larger than the other two angles because its opening is larger.

A **right angle** looks like a square corner. Figure 3 is a right angle. A small square inside the angle is often used to indicate a right angle. Many everyday objects contain examples of right angles. The top and side of a door form a right angle. The corners of this page are right angles. You will learn the names of other types of angles later in this chapter.

Parallel lines are lines that run in the same direction. Parallel lines never cross no matter how far they are extended. Train tracks are examples of parallel lines. Figures 4, 5, and 6 each show pairs of parallel lines. In Figure 4 the two parallel lines are vertical. **Vertical** means running straight up and down. The parallel lines in Figure 5 are horizontal. **Horizontal** means running straight across. The parallel lines in Figure 6 are neither vertical nor horizontal.

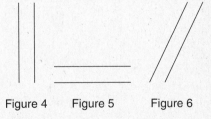

Figure 4   Figure 5   Figure 6

Perpendicular lines are lines that cross or meet to form right angles. Figure 7 is an example of perpendicular lines. The wood or metal supports of a window are usually perpendicular lines.

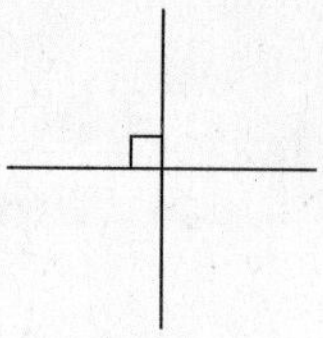

Figure 7

Three common flat shapes are the rectangle, the square, and the triangle. These three shapes are examples of plane figures. A **plane figure** is completely flat.

A **rectangle** is a four-sided figure with four right angles. The sides across from each other are parallel and equal in length. Figure 8 is a rectangle. A short side and a long side of a rectangle are perpendicular to each other. Rectangles are very common figures. Most walls, floors, windows, and doors are rectangles.

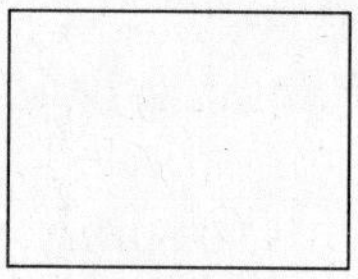

Figure 8

A **square** is a four-sided figure with four right angles and four equal sides. The sides across from each other are parallel. The only difference between a square and a rectangle is that the sides of a square all have the same measurement. Figure 9 is a square.

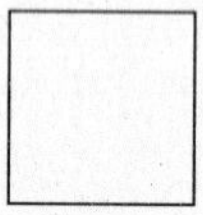

Figure 9

A **triangle** is a three-sided figure. Figures 10, 11, and 12 are all triangles. In Figure 10 each side has a different measurement. In Figure 11 each side has the same measurement. In Figure 12 two of the sides are the same and the third side is longer. You will learn the names of different types of triangles later.

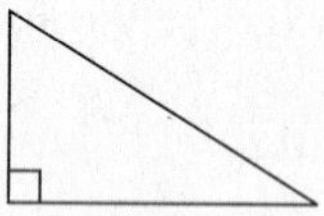

Figure 10 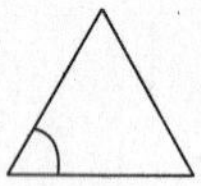   Figure 11

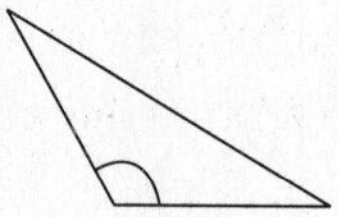

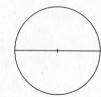

Figure 12

Another common plane figure is the **circle**. A circle is a flat figure made up of a curve. Every point of the curve is the same distance from the center. Figure 13 shows a circle. The **diameter** of a circle is a line that crosses the circle through its center from one side to the other. It also measures the distance across the circle. The **radius** of a circle is a line from the center of the circle to any point on the curve of the circle. A radius is half the distance across a circle. In other words, a radius is half of the diameter of a circle.

Figure 13

Three-dimensional figures are sometimes called **solids**. Figures 14, 15, 16, and 17 show four common solids. Figure 14 shows a **rectangular solid**. The corners of a rectangular solid are all right angles. A cardboard carton is the shape of a rectangular solid.

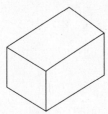

Figure 14

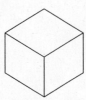

Figure 15

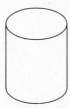

Figure 16

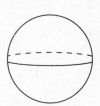

Figure 17

Figure 15 shows a **cube**. A cube is a special type of rectangular solid in which each side has the same measurement. A child's letter blocks are usually in the shape of cubes.

Figure 16 shows a **cylinder**. The top and bottom of a cylinder are circles. The sides of a cylinder are at right angles to the top and bottom. A tin can is in the shape of a cylinder.

Figure 17 shows a **sphere**. *Sphere* is the geometrical term for the shape of a ball.

The next exercise gives you a chance to test your knowledge of the geometrical terms you have learned so far. Be sure you know the terms above before you try this exercise.

EXERCISE 1

Directions: For questions 1–9, fill in the blank.

1. Lines that run in the same direction and do not cross each other are called

_____ lines.

2. A four-sided figure with four right angles and four equal sides is called a

_____.

3. Lines that cross or meet each other to form right angles are called

_____ lines.

4. Two lines extending from the same point form an _____.

5. Lines running straight up and down are called _____ lines.

6. Lines running straight across are called _____ lines.

7. A measure of the distance across a circle is called the _____.

8. A line from the center of a circle to the curve that forms the circle is called

the _____.

9. The geometrical term for the shape of a basketball is a _____.

Directions: Identify the following figures.

10.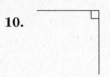

11.

12.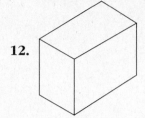

13.

14.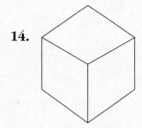

15.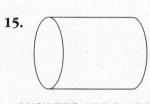

ANSWERS ARE ON PAGE 381.

PERIMETER AND CIRCUMFERENCE

Perimeter is the measurement of the distance around a flat figure. The following are the formulas for finding the perimeter of a rectangle, a square, and a triangle. As you know, these formulas will be provided for you on the GED Test, but it is useful to memorize them.

PERIMETER FORMULAS

Perimeter of a rectangle: $P = 2l + 2w$, where P = perimeter, l = length, w = width

Perimeter of a square: $P = 4s$, where P = perimeter, s = side

Perimeter of a triangle: $P = a + b + c$, where P = perimeter and a, b, c are the sides of a triangle

---

As you recall, to use a formula, start by substituting letters with any values that you know.

EXAMPLE 1 Find the perimeter of the rectangle pictured at the right.

$P = 2l + 2w$
$P = 2(6.5 \text{ m}) + 2(3.2 \text{ m})$
$P = 13 \text{ m} + 6.4 \text{ m}$
$P = 19.4 \text{ m}$

SOLUTION Replace l with 6.5 m and w with 3.2 m in the formula $P = 2l + 2w$. The perimeter of the rectangle is **19.4 meters**.

6.5 m

3.2 m

EXAMPLE 2 Find the perimeter of the square shown at the right.

$P = 4s$
$P = 4(3 \text{ ft})$
$P = 12 \text{ ft}$

3 ft

SOLUTION Replace s with 3 ft in the formula $P = 4s$. The perimeter of the square is **12 feet**.

EXAMPLE 3 Find the perimeter of the triangle shown at the right.

$P = a + b + c$
$P = 2.5 \text{ in} + 2.5 \text{ in} + 4 \text{ in}$
$P = 9 \text{ in}$

2.5 in   2.5 in
4 in

SOLUTION Replace *a* with 2.5 inches, *b* with 2.5 inches, and *c* with 4 inches in the formula $P = a + b + c$. The perimeter of the triangle is **9 inches**.

> **TIP:** In problems like these examples you may find it just as easy to add up the length of the sides instead of using a formula. In more challenging problems, however, you may find that using a formula is a big help.

The distance around a circle is called the ***circumference***, not the perimeter. The formula for the circumference of a circle includes the Greek letter π (pi). The letter π stands for the ratio of the circumference of a circle to the diameter.

The value of π is approximately 3.14 or $\frac{22}{7}$. The symbol that means "approximately equal to" is ≈. We write $\pi \approx 3.14$, or $\pi \approx \frac{22}{7}$.

> **TIP:** It is useful to be familiar with *both* values of π, because in some problems a fraction is easier to use, while in others a decimal will make the computation easier.

CIRCUMFERENCE FORMULA

The formula for the circumference of a circle is

$C = \pi d$, where C = circumference, $\pi \approx 3.14$ or $\frac{22}{7}$, and d = diameter

EXAMPLE 4 Find the circumference of the circle shown at the right.

$C = \pi d$
$C = 3.14 \times 5 \text{ ft}$
$C = 15.70 = 15.7 \text{ ft}$

5 ft

SOLUTION Replace π with 3.14 and *d* with 5 ft in the formula $C = \pi d$. The circumference of the circle is **15.7 feet**.

EXAMPLE 5 Find the circumference of the circle shown at the right. Use $\frac{22}{7}$ for π.

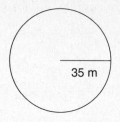

(1) $d = 2 \times 35 = 70$ m

(2) $C = \pi d$
$C = \frac{22}{7} \times 70$
$C = 220$ m

STEP 1   Notice that the picture shows the radius of the circle. To find the diameter, multiply the radius by 2.

STEP 2   Replace π with $\frac{22}{7}$ and d with 70 m in the formula $C = \pi d$. The circumference of the circle is **220 m**.

EXERCISE 2

Directions: For questions 1–9, solve each problem.

1. What is the perimeter of the rectangle shown at the right?

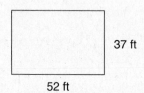

37 ft

52 ft

2. Find the perimeter of the triangle shown at the right.

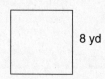

19 cm   19 cm

19 cm

3. Find the perimeter of the square shown at the right.

8 yd

4. Find the perimeter of a rectangle with a length of $2\frac{3}{4}$ inches and a width of $1\frac{1}{2}$ inches.

5. Find the perimeter of a square with a side that measures $\frac{1}{2}$ inch.

6. Find the perimeter of a triangle whose sides measure $7\frac{3}{4}$ inches, $9\frac{1}{4}$ inches, and $10\frac{1}{2}$ inches, respectively.

7. What is the perimeter of a rectangle that is 6.3 miles long and 5.2 miles wide?

8. Each side of a square measures 1.75 meters. Find the perimeter of the square.

9. What is the perimeter of the triangle shown at the right?

Directions: For questions 10–13, use $\pi \approx 3.14$ unless told to do otherwise.

10. What is the circumference of a circle with a diameter of 10 yards?

11. Find the circumference of the circle pictured at the right. In this problem, use $\pi \approx \frac{22}{7}$.

12. Find the circumference of a circle (to the nearest tenth) with a diameter of 1.5 cm.

13. Find the circumference of a circle with a diameter of 14 yards. In this problem, use $\pi \approx \frac{22}{7}$.

ANSWERS ARE ON PAGES 381–382.

ESTIMATING PI

You learned that the most common approximations for the value of π are 3.14 and $\frac{22}{7}$. A quick way to estimate an answer to a circumference problem is to use the whole number 3 for π.

EXAMPLE Which of the following is closest to the circumference of a circle with a diameter of 15 feet?

(1) 30 ft   **(2)** 35.3 ft   **(3)** 47.1 ft   **(4)** 52.9 ft

$$C = \pi d$$

$$C = 3 \times 15$$

$$C = 45 \text{ ft}$$

STEP 1 Replace π with 3 and d with 15 ft in the formula $C = \pi d$.
STEP 2 Choose the answer that is closest to 45 ft.
        Choice **(3) 47.1 ft** is closest.

EXERCISE 3

Directions: Choose the best answer to each problem. To estimate the answers, give π the approximate value of 3.

1. Find the circumference of the circle shown at the right.

   (1) 13 ft   **(2)** 15.7 ft   **(3)** 23.6 ft   **(4)** 31.4 ft

2. What is the circumference of a circle with a diameter of four yards?

   (1) 20.2 yd   **(2)** 16.4 yd   **(3)** 12.6 yd   **(4)** 10.8 yd

3. Find the circumference of the circle pictured at the right.

   (1) 4.8 m   **(2)** 6.9 m   **(3)** 9.8 m   **(4)** 13.2 m

4. What is the circumference of a circle with a *radius* of 6 inches?

   (1) 6.7 in   **(2)** 18.9 in   **(3)** 37.7 in   **(4)** 49.4 in

5. Find the circumference of the circle shown at the right.

   (1) 314 in   **(2)** 157 in   **(3)** 78.5 in   **(4)** 39.3 in

6. Find the circumference of a circle with a *radius* of $\frac{1}{2}$ foot.

   (1) 3.1 ft   **(2)** 6.2 ft   **(3)** 9.3 ft   **(4)** 12.4 ft

7. Which of the following is closest to the circumference of a circle with a diameter of 96 inches?

   (1) 300 in   **(2)** 600 in   **(3)** 3,000 in   **(4)** 10,000 in

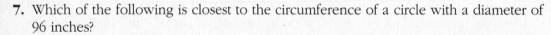

ANSWERS ARE ON PAGE 382.

PERIMETER AND CIRCUMFERENCE WORD PROBLEMS

Remember that perimeter is a measure of the distance around a flat figure. The phrase "find the distance around" means to find the perimeter. Fencing, weatherstripping, and framing are some practical applications of perimeter.

Problems with Different Units of Measurement

Watch out for problems where the units of measurement change. It is important to include labels with any numbers you are using—for example, feet or inches, pounds or ounces.

EXAMPLE How many feet of picture framing are required to go around a square picture with a side of 30 inches?

(1) $P = 4s$ **(2)** $P = 120$ in   **(3)** $\quad \dfrac{10}{12\overline{)120}}$ ft

$\quad\quad P = 4 \times 30$ in

STEP 1 Write the formula for the perimeter of a square. Substitute the length of one side.

STEP 2 Find P, the total number of inches in the perimeter.

STEP 3 Notice that the question asks for the number of *feet*, and you have found the number of *inches*. To find the number of feet in 120 inches, either set up a proportion or divide as shown above. **10 feet** of framing are required to go around the picture.

"Backward" Perimeter Problems

So far you have been working on problems where you need to find perimeter. In some problems you may be *given* the perimeter and one other dimension of a figure. You will then be asked to find the other dimension. Your work with equations will help you a great deal with this type of problem.

EXAMPLE Sam has a rectangular garden surrounded by 50 feet of fencing. The fencing is 10 feet wide. How long is the fencing?

(1) $\quad P = 2l + 2w$

(2) $\quad 50 = 2l + (2 \times 10)$

(3) $\quad 50 = 2l + 20$

(4) $\quad \begin{array}{r} 50 = 2l + 20 \\ -20 \quad\quad -20 \\ \hline 30 = 2l \end{array}$

(5) $\quad \dfrac{30}{2} = \dfrac{2l}{2}$

$\quad\quad 15 = l$

STEP 1 Write down the formula for perimeter.

STEP 2 Substitute the values you *do* know: $P = 50$ and $w = 10$.

STEP 3 Do the computation on the right side of the equation.

STEP 4 To get the unknown value alone, use inverse operations and first subtract 20 from each side.

STEP 5 Using inverse operations again, divide both sides by 2. $l = $ **15 feet**.

EXERCISE 4

Directions: For questions 1–3, solve each problem. Draw a figure if it will help you visualize a problem.

1. Mark wants to put a frame around an 8-inch by 10-inch photograph. How many inches of framing does he need?

2. The garden in Sylvia's yard is 26 meters long and half as wide. How many meters of fencing does she need to enclose the garden?

3. Find the measurement of the side of the largest square frame that can be made from 100 inches of framing. Express your answer in feet and inches.

Directions: Problems 4–6 refer to the following situation. You may want to try drawing a rough picture of the figure being described.

There are six windows on the second floor of Mrs. Jackson's house. Each window has a base of 36 inches and a height of 42 inches. Around each window Mrs. Jackson wants to put weatherstripping that costs $.60 a foot.

4. What is the distance in inches around one window on the second floor of Mrs. Jackson's house?

5. Find the measurement in feet around all the windows on the second floor.

6. What is the total cost of weatherstripping for the six windows?

7. Workers are putting brick trim around the edge of a circular pool in the park in Central City. The diameter of the pool is 50 feet. How many 9-inch-long bricks are needed to go around the edge of the pool? Your answer must be a whole number.

8. Paul has 19 feet of oak trim to put around a rectangular countertop that he is building in his kitchen. The width of the counter is 30 inches. How many feet long can the countertop be if Paul uses all of the oak trim?

9. Which of the following represents the perimeter of the figure at the right?

    (1) 2.3×1.4
    (2) $2 \times 2.3 \times 1.4$
    (3) $(2 \times 2.3) + (2 \times 1.4)$
    (4) $\dfrac{2.3 + 1.4}{2}$

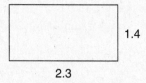

10. Which of the following represents the perimeter of the figure at the right?

    (1) $2(1.6) + 2.4$
    (2) $1.6 + 2.4$
    (3) $1.6 + 2(2.4)$
    (4) $2(1.6) + 2(2.4)$

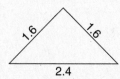

ANSWERS ARE ON PAGES 382–383.

POWERS AND ROOTS

POWERS

Before you go on to study area, you need to learn two skills that you will use in both algebra and geometry. These skills—finding powers and roots—are an extension of the arithmetic skills you have already developed.

The figure 5^2 is read as "five to the second power." The 5 is called the **base**. The 2 is called the **exponent**. The exponent tells how many times to write the base in a multiplication problem.

RULE FOR FINDING POWERS
1. Write the base as many times as the exponent indicates.
2. Multiply.

EXAMPLE 1 What is the value of 5^2?

SOLUTION Write 5 two times and multiply.

$5^2 = 5 \times 5 = 25$

A number to the second power is called the **square** of a number. We can say that 5 squared is 25.

EXAMPLE 2 Evaluate 4^3.

SOLUTION Write 4 three times and multiply. The first product is $4 \times 4 = 16$. The next product is $16 \times 4 = 64$.
$4^3 = 4 \times 4 \times 4 = 64$

A number to the third power is called the **cube** of a number. We can say that 4 cubed is 64.

EXAMPLE 3 Find the value of $.03^2$.

SOLUTION Write .03 two times and multiply. Notice that the answer has four decimal places.
$.03^2 = .03 \times .03 = .0009$

EXAMPLE 4 Evaluate $(\frac{2}{3})^3$.

SOLUTION Write $\frac{2}{3}$ three times and multiply.

$(\frac{2}{3})^3 = \frac{2}{3} \times \frac{2}{3} \times \frac{2}{3} = \frac{8}{27}$

A BASE OF 1
The number 1 is a special case with powers. 1 to any power equals 1.

EXAMPLE 5   What is 1^6?

SOLUTION   Write 1 six times and multiply. Notice that no matter how many times you multiply 1 by 1, you will get 1 as the answer.

$$1^6 = \mathbf{1 \times 1 \times 1 \times 1 \times 1 \times 1}$$

AN EXPONENT OF 1
Any number to the first power is that number.

EXAMPLE 6   What is 7^1?

SOLUTION   There is no multiplication in this problem. 7 to the first power means simply to write 7 one time.

$$7^1 = \mathbf{7}$$

AN EXPONENT OF 0
Any number to the 0 power is 1.

EXAMPLE 7   What is 8^0?

SOLUTION   The zero power actually means a number divided by itself.

$$8^0 = \tfrac{8}{8} = \mathbf{1}$$

REVIEWING THE ORDER OF OPERATIONS

You can use powers in combination with other operations. As you learned in Chapter 2, there is a specific order in which to perform operations. The list below shows you where powers fit into this order:

1. Do operations that are grouped in parentheses.

2. Find powers (and roots, which you will learn about in this chapter).

3. Do multiplication or division.

4. Do addition or subtraction.

EXAMPLE 1   Simplify $3^2 + 2^4$.

    (1) $3^2 = 3 \times 3 = 9$ **(2)** $9 + 16 = \mathbf{25}$

         $2^4 = 2 \times 2 \times 2 \times 2 = 16$

STEP 1   Find the value of each power.
STEP 2   Add the results.

EXAMPLE 2　Find the value of xy^2 when $x = 9$ and $y = 3$.

$$xy^2 = 9 \cdot 3^2$$
$$= 9 \cdot 9$$
$$= \mathbf{81}$$

STEP 1　Substitute 9 for x and 3 for y.
STEP 2　Find 3 to the second power.
STEP 3　Multiply 9 by 9.

EXERCISE 5

Directions: Find the value of each of the following.

1. 6^2

2. 1^3

3. 5^3

4. $(\frac{3}{5})^2$

5. 3^5

6. $5^2 + 3^2$

7. $5^3 - 10^2$

8. $(.06)^2$

9. 12^0

10. 25^2

11. $11^2 - 4^2$

12. $(.005)^2$

13. $10^0 + 10^1 + 10^2$

14. 20^3

15. 13^1

16. $(\frac{1}{4})^3$

17. 10^4

18. $8^2 - 2^4$

19. $3^3 + 7^2$

20. $(0.1)^3$

ANSWERS ARE ON PAGE 383.

SQUARE ROOTS

In addition to finding powers, another important operation is finding **square roots**. This operation is indicated by the symbol $\sqrt{}$. The square root of a number is found by asking, "What number multiplied by itself will give me this number?"

EXAMPLE 1　Find $\sqrt{25}$.

SOLUTION　5 multiplied by itself gives 25.

$$\sqrt{25} = \mathbf{5}$$

EXAMPLE 2　Find $\sqrt{144}$.

SOLUTION　12 multiplied by itself gives 144.

$$\sqrt{144} = \mathbf{12}$$

Following is a list of common perfect square roots. Take the time now to memorize this list.

$\sqrt{1} = 1$	$\sqrt{64} = 8$	$\sqrt{225} = 15$
$\sqrt{4} = 2$	$\sqrt{81} = 9$	$\sqrt{400} = 20$
$\sqrt{9} = 3$	$\sqrt{100} = 10$	$\sqrt{900} = 30$
$\sqrt{16} = 4$	$\sqrt{121} = 11$	$\sqrt{1600} = 40$
$\sqrt{25} = 5$	$\sqrt{144} = 12$	$\sqrt{2500} = 50$
$\sqrt{36} = 6$	$\sqrt{169} = 13$	$\sqrt{3600} = 60$
$\sqrt{49} = 7$	$\sqrt{196} = 14$	

There are several methods for finding the square roots of larger numbers. One method is to estimate the square root by using knowledge of common square roots.

EXAMPLE 3 Find $\sqrt{700}$.

STEP 1 Look at the square roots chart. Notice that the $\sqrt{700}$ falls between the $\sqrt{400}$ and the $\sqrt{900}$.

STEP 2 Next decide which known square root the problem comes closest to. In this case $\sqrt{700}$ falls about halfway in between the other two roots. Therefore your answer will fall about halfway between 20 and 30. $\sqrt{700} \approx$ **25**. (To the nearest hundredth the square root is 26.46.)

Another method is to average. The averaging method for finding a square root is a good way to improve your estimating skills. Study the next examples carefully. Think about the first "guess" in each solution.

EXAMPLE 4 Find $\sqrt{484}$.

STEP 1 Guess a round number that you think may be fairly close to the correct answer. For example, 50 is a bad guess because $50 \times 50 = 2500$. But 20 is a good guess because $20 \times 20 = 400$, which is much closer to 484.

STEP 2 Divide 20 into 484. Ignore the remainder.

STEP 3 Average the division answer, 24, with the guess, 20.

STEP 4 Check by multiplying 22 by itself. Since $22 \times 22 = 484$, **22** is the square root of 484.

Another way to find a square root is to use the answers provided in a multiple-choice question. Substitute each answer until you find the correct square root.

EXAMPLE 5 Find $\sqrt{841}$.

(1) 21   **(2)** 29   **(3)** 31   **(4)** 39   **(5)** 41

SOLUTION Multiply each answer choice by itself.

$$
\begin{array}{ll}
\textbf{(1)} \quad
\begin{array}{r}
21 \\
\times\ 21 \\
\hline
21 \\
42 \\
\hline
441
\end{array}
&
\textbf{(2)} \quad
\begin{array}{r}
29 \\
\times\ 29 \\
\hline
261 \\
58 \\
\hline
841
\end{array}
\end{array}
$$

Choice **(2) 29** is correct. $29 \times 29 = 841$

You could combine this method with the method shown in Example 3 to narrow down the answer choices you need to substitute. Look at the list of common square roots. The $\sqrt{841}$ will fall somewhere between the $\sqrt{400}$ and the $\sqrt{900}$. Since the $\sqrt{400} = 20$ and the $\sqrt{900} = 30$, your answer should be between 20 and 30.

Now look at the multiple-choice answers listed in Example 5. Right away you should see that answer choices (3), (4), and (5) are too large. That narrows your choices to (1) and (2).

EXERCISE 6

Directions: Find the following square roots. Use any of the methods shown in the previous examples.

1. $\sqrt{196}$

    (1) 12
    (2) 14
    (3) 18

2. $\sqrt{441}$

    (1) 21
    (2) 23
    (3) 29

3. $\sqrt{1024}$

    (1) 38
    (2) 34
    (3) 32

4. $\sqrt{1521}$

    (1) 31
    (2) 33
    (3) 39

5. $\sqrt{361}$

    (1) 19
    (2) 21
    (3) 29

6. $\sqrt{676}$

    (1) 22
    (2) 26
    (3) 32

7. $\sqrt{1849}$

    (1) 43
    (2) 47
    (3) 51

8. $\sqrt{3364}$

    (1) 52
    (2) 56
    (3) 58

ANSWERS ARE ON PAGES 383–384.

AREA

Area is a measure of the amount of surface within the perimeter of a flat figure. Area is measured in square units—for example, square inches, square feet, or square meters.

The figure at the right represents a rectangle that has a length of 5 inches and a width of 3 inches. The surface of the rectangle is covered with 15 small squares. Each square is one square inch. The surface, or area, of the rectangle is 15 square inches.

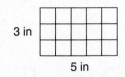

Following are the formulas for area that you will use in this section. The formulas will be given on the GED, but it is also useful to memorize them.

AREA FORMULAS

Area of a rectangle: $A = lw$, where A = area, l = length, and w = width
Area of a square: $A = s^2$, where A = area and s = side
Area of a triangle: $A = \frac{1}{2}bh$, where A = area, b = base, and h = height
Area of a circle: $A = \pi r^2$, where A = area, $\pi \approx 3.14$ or $\frac{22}{7}$, and
r = radius

EXAMPLE 1 Find the area of the rectangle pictured at the right.

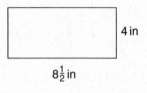

$A = lw$

$A = 8\frac{1}{2} \times 4$

$A = \frac{17}{2} \times \frac{4}{1} = 34$ square inches

SOLUTION Replace l with $8\frac{1}{2}$ and w with 4 in the formula $A = lw$ and multiply. The area is **34 square inches**.

Notice that the answer is labeled *square inches*. This label is often abbreviated *sq in*.

EXAMPLE 2 Find the area of a square whose side measures 7 feet.
$A = s^2$
$A = 7^2$
$A = 7 \times 7 = 49$ sq ft

SOLUTION Replace s with 7 in the formula $A = s^2$. The area is **49 sq ft**.

The length and width of a rectangle are perpendicular to each other. The base and height of a triangle are also at right angles to each other. Look at the location of the base and height for each triangle below.

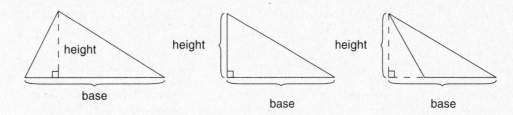

In the triangle at the left the height is inside the triangle. In the middle triangle the height is the left-hand side. For the triangle at the right the height is an imaginary line from the top of the triangle to an extension of the base.

You can think of the area of a triangle as half the area of some four-sided figure. The figure at the right is a rectangle with a length (base) of 9 meters and a width (height) of 6 meters. The shaded part of the rectangle is a triangle with a base of 9 meters and a height of 6 meters. You can use this idea to remember that the area of a triangle ($\frac{1}{2}bh$) is half the area of a rectangle.

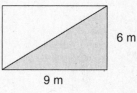

EXAMPLE 3 Find the area of a triangle with a base of 9 meters and a height of 6 meters.

$A = \frac{1}{2}bh$

$A = \frac{9 \times 6}{2} = 27$ square meters

SOLUTION Replace b with 9 and h with 6 in the formula $A = \frac{1}{2}bh$. The area of the triangle is **27 sq in**, which is exactly half the area of the rectangle.

Notice that the answer is labeled square meters. The label is often abbreviated m^2.

TIP: Sometimes the area of a triangle may be represented as $\frac{bh}{2}$, which, as you know from your study of fractions, is the same as $\frac{1}{2}bh$. You should be familiar with both forms.

EXAMPLE 4 Find the area of a circle with a radius of 3 inches.
$A = \pi r^2$
$A = 3.14 \times 3^2$
$A = 3.14 \times 9 = 28.26$ sq in

SOLUTION Replace π with 3.14 and r with 3 in the formula $A = \pi r^2$. The area of the circle is **28.26 sq in**.

EXERCISE 7

Directions: Solve each problem.

1. Find the area of each figure.

a. What is the area of the rectangle pictured at the right?

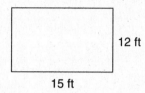

b. What is the area of the square shown at the right?

c. Find the area of the triangle shown at the right.

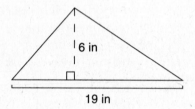

2. Find the area of a rectangle with a length of 8 inches and a width of $3\frac{1}{2}$ inches.

3. What is the area of a square whose side measures 6.5 meters?

4. Find the area of the triangle pictured at the right.

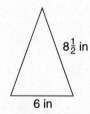

5. To the nearest square centimeter, find the area of a rectangle whose length is 12.6 cm and whose width is 5.4 cm.

6. Which of the following expressions represents the area (in square

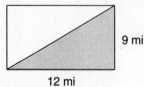

miles) of the shaded portion of the picture at the right?

(1) 9×12

(2) $12 + 9$

(3) $\frac{1}{2}(12 + 9)$

(4) $\frac{1}{2}(12 \times 9)$

(5) $\frac{1}{2}(12 + 12 + 9 + 9)$

7. What is the area of a square if the side measures $\frac{3}{8}$ inch?

    (1) $1\frac{1}{2}$ sq in

    (2) $1\frac{1}{8}$ sq in

    (3) $\frac{9}{16}$ sq in

    (4) $\frac{9}{64}$ sq in

    (5) $\frac{1}{8}$ sq in

8. Find the area of the triangle pictured at the right.

    (1) 26 cm^2
    (2) 52 cm^2
    (3) 76.5 cm^2
    (4) 81 cm^2
    (5) 153 cm^2

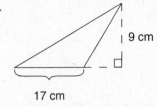

9 cm

17 cm

9. Find the area of the circle pictured at the right.

    (1) 3140 sq yd
    (2) 314 sq yd
    (3) 125.6 sq yd
    (4) 62.8 sq yd
    (5) 31.4 sq yd

10 yd

ANSWERS ARE ON PAGE 384.

AREA WORD PROBLEMS

This section gives you a chance to apply your knowledge of area to practical situations. The word *area* will not always appear where you need to use this skill. Instead you will need to recognize when to use the formulas for area you have learned in this section.

Sometimes you may wonder whether you should be finding perimeter or area. Remember that area is a measurement of the amount of surface on a flat figure. Finding how much carpet to put on a floor, how much paint to put on walls, and how much material to buy for sewing all involve finding area. Perimeter measures *distance around* something—fencing and framing are two common situations where the perimeter formula is useful.

EXAMPLE 1   Luba wants to put carpet on her bedroom floor. Her bedroom measures 9 feet by 10 feet. How many square feet of carpet does she need?

$A = lw$
$A = 9 \times 10 = 90$ sq ft

SOLUTION   There are two clues that tell you to find the area in this problem. One is the word *carpet*. Carpet covers a surface. The other clue is *square feet*. Only area is measured in square feet. Replace w with 9 and l with 10 in the formula $A = lw$. The answer is **90 square feet**.

Problems with Different Units of Measurement

Watch out for area problems where you need to change units of measurement. When finding area, you cannot multiply feet by inches or yards by feet. First you must convert, or change, one unit to another. Before you go on, learn the following equivalents:

FINDING SQUARE INCHES AND FEET

1 square foot = 12 inches × 12 inches = 144 square inches
1 square yard = 3 feet × 3 feet = 9 square feet

Add these to the list of measurement equivalents you saw on page 165 of Chapter 7.

EXAMPLE   How many square *yards* of fabric does Ernie need to cover the figure below?

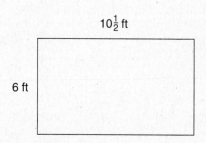

$10\frac{1}{2}$ ft

6 ft

STEP 1   Figure out how many square feet Ernie
needs by using the formula $A = lw$.

$A = lw$
$A = 10\frac{1}{2} \times 6$
$A = 63$ sq ft

STEP 2   Since the problem asks for square yards, convert
the square feet into square yards by setting up a
proportion. On the left is the ratio of 1 square yard to
9 square feet. On the right, put the area of the figure in
square feet on the bottom. Put x in the place of square yards.

$$\frac{1 \text{ sq yd}}{9 \text{ sq ft}} = \frac{x}{63}$$

STEP 3   Find the cross product of 1 and 63.

$$\begin{array}{r} 63 \\ \times\ 1 \\ \hline 63 \end{array}$$

STEP 4   Divide 63 by the remaining number in the proportion.
Ernie needs **7 square yards** of fabric.

$$\begin{array}{r} 7 \text{ sq yd} \\ 9\overline{)63} \end{array}$$

"Backward" Area Problems

In some area problems you will be given the area and one dimension for a rectangle. Then you will have to find the other dimension. In the example below, notice how your work with equations helps you solve "backward" problems easily.

EXAMPLE A gallon of paint covers 300 square feet of walls. The walls in Carla's house are 8 feet high. What is the total length of wall that a gallon of paint will cover in Carla's house?

(1) $A = lw$ **(2)** $300 = l \times 8$ **(3)** $\frac{300}{8} = \frac{l \times 8}{8}$

$$8\overline{)\,300.0}^{\,37.5\text{ ft}}$$

STEP 1 Decide what formula to use and write it down. You are given area in this problem, so use the area formula for a rectangle.

STEP 2 Substitute values you know for letters in the formula.

STEP 3 Use inverse operations to get the unknown, l, alone on one side. Division is the inverse of multiplication, so divide both sides by 8. The length of the wall is **37.5 feet**.

EXERCISE 8

Directions: Solve each problem.

1. Colin is putting new wood flooring in the spare room of his house. The room is 9 feet wide and 12 feet long. How much flooring will Colin need for the house?

2. The two figures at right have the same area. How long is one side of the square?

3 ft

27 ft

3. How many square inches of glass does Mark need to cover a photograph that measures 8 inches by 10 inches?

4. Bill wants to put 2-foot by 2-foot carpet tiles on the floor of his living room, which is shown at the right. Find the fewest number of carpet tiles Bill needs to completely cover the floor.

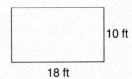

10 ft

18 ft

5. A gallon of floor paint will cover about 200 square feet of concrete. The floor of Harold's basement is 25 feet wide and 40 feet long. How many gallons of paint does Harold need to put one coat of paint on the basement floor?

6. The picture at the right shows the garden in Robert's yard. He wants to cover the garden with plastic because of a sudden drop in temperature. How many square yards of plastic does he need?

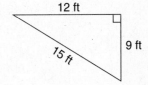

12 ft

15 ft

9 ft

7. Mary wants to make curtains for the three windows in her living room. For each pair of curtains she needs material measuring 6 feet by 8 feet. Altogether how many square yards of material does she need?

8. Roman wants to repave a circular patio. The radius of the patio is 20 feet. How large is the surface that he wants to repave?

9. One package of grass seed contains enough to grow 400 square feet of lawn. Find the measurement of the side of the largest square that can be covered in grass from the seed in the package.

   (1) 400
   (2) 200
   (3) 80
   (4) 40
   (5) 20

10. Phil used the package of grass seed in problem 9 to cover a side yard that is only 10 feet wide. Find the length in feet of the section of yard that he can cover with the seed from one package.

    (1) 40
    (2) 80
    (3) 100
    (4) 160
    (5) 200

11. Which of the following represents the area of the figure at the right?

    (1) $(2 \times 8) + (2 \times 12.5)$
    (2) 8×12.5
    (3) $2 \times 8 \times 12.5$
    (4) $8 + 12.5$
    (5) Not enough information is given.

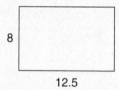

12. Which of the following represents the area of the figure at the right?

    (1) $2(5.8) + 6$
    (2) 5.8×6
    (3) $5.8 \times 6 \times 2$
    (4) $\dfrac{5.8 \times 6}{2}$
    (5) Not enough information is given.

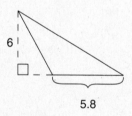

ANSWERS ARE ON PAGES 384–385.

VOLUME

Volume is a measure of the amount of space inside a three-dimensional or solid figure. You have already learned the names *rectangular solid, cube*, and *cylinder*. Volume is measured in cubic units such as cubic inches, cubic feet, and cubic meters.

Following are the formulas for finding the volume of three common three-dimensional figures. These formulas will be given on the GED, but it may be useful to memorize them.

VOLUME FORMULAS

Volume of a rectangular solid or container: $V = lwh$, where $V = volume$, $l =$ length, $w =$ width, and $h =$ height

Volume of a cube: $V = s^3$, where $V =$ volume and $s =$ side
Volume of a cylinder: $V = \pi r^2h$, where $V =$ volume, $\pi \approx 3.14$, $r =$ radius, and $h =$ height

EXAMPLE 1   Find the volume of the rectangular solid.

$V = lwh$
$V = 11 \times 8 \times 6 =$ **528 cu in**

SOLUTION   Replace l with 11, w with 8, and h with 6 in the formula $V = lwh$.

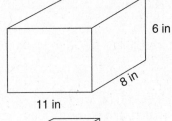

6 in

8 in

11 in

EXAMPLE 2   Find the volume of the cube.

$V = s^3$
$V = 6^3$
$V = 6 \times 6 \times 6 =$ **216 cu in**

SOLUTION   Replace s with 6 in the formula $V = s^3$.

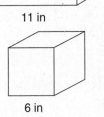

6 in

EXAMPLE 3   Find the volume of the cylinder.

$V = \pi r^2h$
$V = 3.14 \times 3^2 \times 10$
$V = 3.14 \times 9 \times 10 =$ **282.6 cu in**

SOLUTION   Replace π with 3.14, r with 3, and h with 10 in the formula $V = \pi r^2h$. First find 3^2. Then multiply across.

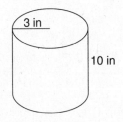

3 in

10 in

A *sphere* is a three-dimensional shape like a basketball. The radius of a sphere is the distance from the center to the outside. The formula for a sphere is not given on the formulas page on the GED, but it *will* be given to you in any problem for which it is needed.

EXERCISE 9

Directions: For questions 1–10, solve each problem. Give each answer the correct label.

1. Find the volume of the figure shown at the right.

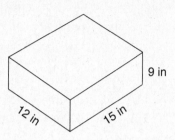

9 in

12 in   15 in

2. Find the volume of the cube shown at the right.

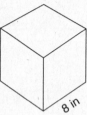

8 in

3. What is the volume of a rectangular box that has a base of $5\frac{1}{4}$ inches, a height of $2\frac{2}{3}$ inches, and a width of $3\frac{1}{2}$ inches?

4. The base of a cube measures 1.2 centimeters. Find the volume.

5. Find the volume of a rectangular solid with a base of 30 feet, a height of $\frac{1}{2}$ foot, and a width of 5 feet.

6. What is the volume of a cylinder with a radius of 10 feet and a height of 35 feet?

7. What is the volume in cubic meters of soil that the truck at the right can carry if it is filled to the top?

   (1) 14 cm³

   (2) 24 cm³

   (3) 48 cm³

   (4) 64 cm³

   (5) 4 cm³

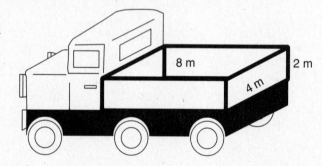

8 m   2 m

4 m

8. Find the volume of the cylinder pictured at the right. Round your answer to the nearest tenth of a cubic meter.

   (1) 0.5
   (2) 0.9
   (3) 1.3
   (4) 3.5
   (5) 7.0

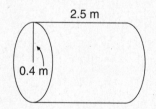

2.5 m

0.4 m

9. Which represents the volume of a cube with a base that measures $1\frac{1}{4}$ inches?

    (1) $4 \times 1\frac{1}{4}$

    (2) $\frac{1}{2} \times 1\frac{1}{4} \times 1\frac{1}{4}$

    (3) $2(1\frac{1}{4}) + 2(1\frac{1}{4})$

    (4) $1\frac{1}{4} \times 1\frac{1}{4} \times 1\frac{1}{4}$

    (5) $(1\frac{1}{4})^2$

10. The formula for the volume of a sphere is $V = \frac{4}{3}\pi r^3$, where V is the volume and r^3 is the radius. Find, to the nearest cubic inch, the volume of a sphere with a radius of 3 inches. Approximate π with 3.14.

    (1) 226

    (2) 113

    (3) 85

    (4) 38

    (5) 13

Questions 11 and 12 refer to the carton below.

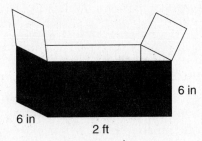

6 in

6 in

2 ft

11. What is the volume in cubic inches of the carton?

    (1) 36

    (2) 72

    (3) 216

    (4) 432

    (5) 864

12. How many boxes that measure 1 foot by 6 inches by 1 inch can you fit into the carton?

    (1) 6

    (2) 12

    (3) 15

    (4) 20

    (5) 24

ANSWERS ARE ON PAGE 385.

MORE PERIMETER, AREA, AND VOLUME WORD PROBLEMS

On the GED Test you may have to find the area of figures other than rectangles, squares, triangles, and circles. For these figures formulas will be provided for you.

EXAMPLE 1 The figure at the right is a trapezoid. In this figure the top and the bottom are parallel. The left and right sides are not. The formula for the area of a trapezoid is $A = \frac{h(b_1 + b_2)}{2}$, where A is the area, h is the height, and b_1 and b_2 are the parallel sides. Find the area of the trapezoid pictured at the right.

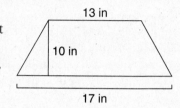

$$A = \frac{h(b_1 + b_2)}{2}$$

$$A = \frac{10(13 + 17)}{2}$$

$$A = \frac{10 \times 30}{2} = \mathbf{150\ in}$$

SOLUTION Replace h with 10, b_1 with 13, and b_2 with 17 in the formula given in the problem. Remember to do the operation in the parentheses first.

Note: In some problems like the one above, you will find small numbers written below and to the right of a variable (b_1). These numbers are used for identification only. Do not confuse them with numbers involved in computation.

In some problems you may be asked to find the area of complicated figures. These figures are often made up of two or more simple figures.

EXAMPLE 2 Find the area of the figure shown at the right.

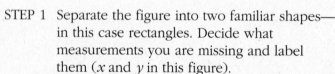
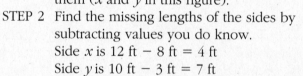

STEP 1 Separate the figure into two familiar shapes—in this case rectangles. Decide what measurements you are missing and label them (x and y in this figure).

STEP 2 Find the missing lengths of the sides by subtracting values you do know.
Side x is 12 ft − 8 ft = 4 ft
Side y is 10 ft − 3 ft = 7 ft

STEP 3 Find the area of each rectangle by using the correct formula. First replace l with 4 and w with 3 in the formula $A = lw$. Then replace l with 12 and w with 7 in the formula $A = lw$.
Area I = lw
     = 4 × 3
     = 12 sq ft
Area II = lw
     = 12 × 7
     = 84 sq ft

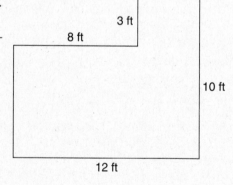
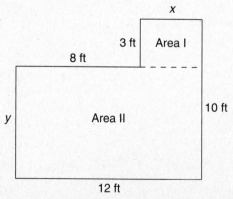
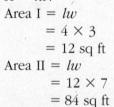

STEP 4 Add the areas of the two rectangles. The total area of the figure is **96 sq ft**.
Area I + Area II = 12 + 84 = 96 sq ft
  As you saw in Example 2, you can often figure out missing measurements by looking at the figures and subtracting measurements that you do know. However, watch out for problems where not enough information is given to allow you to do this.

EXAMPLE 3 How many square feet are in the figure at the right?
  (1) 60
  (2) 84
  (3) 100
  (4) 140
  (5) Not enough information is given.

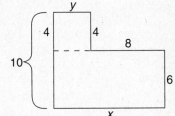

STEP 1 Divide the figure into two familiar shapes and decide what measurements you are missing. Label them with letters.
STEP 2 Figure out the missing lengths by subtracting values you know. As you can see, without knowing the length of side *x*, you cannot figure out the length of side *y* either. There is not enough information to solve this problem. Answer choice **(5)** is correct.

EXERCISE 10

Directions: Solve each problem.

1. A parallelogram is a four-sided figure with two pairs of parallel sides. The sides across from each other are equal in length. The formula for the area of a parallelogram is $A = bh$ where A is the area, b is the base, and h is the height. Find the area of the parallelogram pictured at the right.

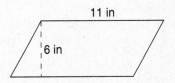

2. The formula for the surface area of a sphere is $A = 4\pi r^2$, where A is the area, π is approximately 3.14, and r is the radius. Find the surface area of a sphere with a radius of 10 inches.

3. The formula for the area of a trapezoid is $A = \frac{h(b_1 + b_2)}{2}$, where A is the area, h is the height, and b_1 and b_2 are the parallel sides. Find the area of the trapezoid pictured at the right.

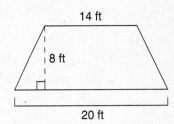

4. Find the total number of inches around the figure shown at the right.

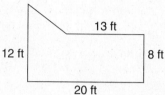

5. Find the number of square inches on the surface of the figure in problem 4.

6. Find the area of the figure shown at the right.

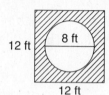

7. Which of the following expressions gives the number of square feet in the shaded part of the figure shown at the right?

(1) $12^2 + \pi(8^2)$
(2) $(12 + 1) + 8$
(3) $12^2 - 8^2$
(4) $12^2 - \pi(8^2)$
(5) $12^2 - \pi(4^2)$

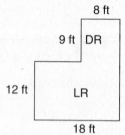

8. The diagram at the right shows the measurements of the floor of the Porters' living room and dining room. How many square yards of carpet do they need to cover the floors of both rooms?

(1) 24
(2) 32
(3) 40
(4) 48
(5) 54

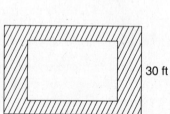

9. The shaded part of the figure at the right shows the walkway around the pool at the local community center. The pool is a rectangle that measures 34 feet by 18 feet. Find the number of square feet on the surface of the walk.

(1) 388
(2) 444
(3) 612
(4) 888
(5) 1500

10. For the construction of a new building a hole was dug 4 yards deep, 20 yards wide, and 30 yards long. Which of the following do you need to know to find out how many truckloads were needed to carry all the dirt away from the hole?

(1) the diameter of the hole
(2) the amount of dirt in each truckload
(3) the number of hours it took
(4) the length of the truck
(5) the amount of dirt left over at the site

11. Find the measurement in inches of the side of a square that will have the same area as the rectangle pictured at the right.

(1) 2
(2) 4
(3) 8
(4) 16
(5) 32

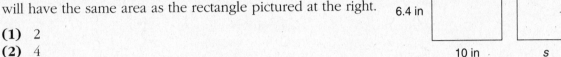

6.4 in

10 in   s

12. Each figure at the right has the same area. Find the base of the rectangle at the right.

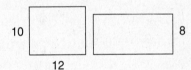

10

12

8

13. Which of the following represents the area of the figure shown at the right?

(1) 19
(2) 38
(3) 73
(4) 130
(5) Not enough information is given.

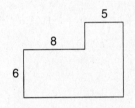

5

8

6

14. Which of the following represents the area of the figure at the right?

(1) 120
(2) 124
(3) 140
(4) 160
(5) Not enough information is given.

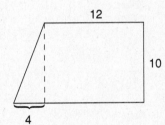

12

10

4

ANSWERS ARE ON PAGES 385–386.

ANGLES

You learned on page 223 that an angle is formed by two lines extending from the same point. The point is called the *vertex* of an angle. The symbol ∠ stands for the word *angle*. Sometimes a small letter follows the symbol, identifying, or naming, the angle: ∠*a*, ∠*b*, ∠*c*.

The size or opening of an angle is measured in degrees (°). The category of an angle depends on the number of degrees, or the size of the opening. Following is a list of angle categories. In the illustrations a small curve indicates the angle opening.

An **acute angle** has less than 90°. Examples:

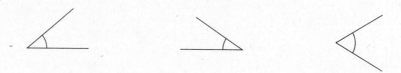

A **right angle** has exactly 90°. A right angle is often shown with a small square at the vertex. Examples:

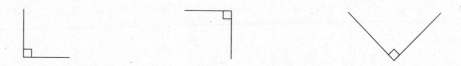

An **obtuse angle** has more than 90° but less than 180°. Examples:

A **straight angle** has exactly 180°. Examples:

A **reflex angle** has more than 180° but less than 360°. Examples:

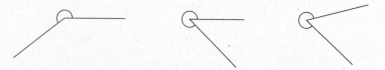

Notice that both the right angle and the straight angle always contain an exact number of degrees, 90° and 180°. For the other angles a range of degrees is possible. For example, an acute angle could be 2° or 89°, since both of these measurements are more than 0° and less than 90°.

Notice also that it is important to have some indication of the opening of an angle. For the two angles shown at the right the lines that form the angles look the same. However, the angle at the left is an acute angle, and the angle at the right is reflex.

Memorize the names of the angles before you try the next exercise.

EXERCISE 11

Directions: For problems 1–12, identify each angle by name (acute, right, obtuse, straight, or reflex).

1.

2.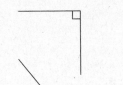

3.

4.

5.

6.

7.

8.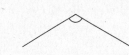

9.

10.

11.

12.

Directions: For problems 13–20, tell what kind of angle contains each of the following numbers of degrees.

13. 40°

14. 100°

15. 180°

16. 220°

17. 90°

18. 83°

19. 175°

20. 300°

ANSWERS ARE ON PAGE 386.

ANGLE RELATIONSHIPS

Angles are sometimes referred to with letters. For example, ∠AOB refers to the straight angle shown at the right. The angle can also be called ∠BOA. In both cases the vertex O is in the middle.

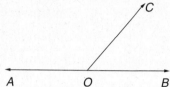

Another line extending from point O forms two new angles. ∠BOC is acute, and ∠AOC is obtuse.

Suppose ∠BOC measures 50°. To find the measurement of ∠AOC, take 50° from 180°, since the straight angle ∠AOB measures 180°.

$$\angle AOC = 180° - 50° = 130°$$

∠AOC and ∠BOC are called *supplementary angles*.

SUPPLEMENTARY ANGLES

Supplementary angles are two or more angles whose sum is 180°.

$$\angle A + \angle B = 180°$$

In the picture at the right ∠DEF is a right angle. Suppose ∠GEF = 35°. To find ∠DEG, take 35° from 90°.

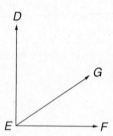

∠DEG and ∠GEF are called *complementary angles*.

$$\angle DEG = 90° - 35° = 55°$$

COMPLEMENTARY ANGLES

Complementary angles are two or more angles whose sum is 90°.

$$\angle A + \angle B = 90°$$

In the picture at the right two lines intersect (cross) at point O. Suppose ∠WOZ measures 70°. ∠WOY must measure 180° − 70° = 110° because ∠WOY and ∠WOZ are supplementary.

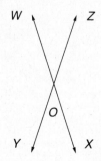

In the picture at the right ∠WOY and ∠ZOX, which both measure 110°, are called *vertical angles*; ∠WOZ and ∠YOX, which both measure 70°, are also called vertical angles.

VERTICAL ANGLES

> **Vertical angles** are two angles opposite each other when two straight lines intersect. Vertical angles are equal.

EXAMPLE 1   Find the supplement of an angle measuring 65°.

SOLUTION   Supplementary angles add up to 180°. Take 65° from 180°. The supplement of a 65° angle is **115°**.
180° − 65° = 115°

EXAMPLE 2   ∠AOB in the figure at the right measures 90°. Find the measurement of angle x.

SOLUTION   Take 30° from 90°. ∠x measures **60°**.
90° − 30° = 60°

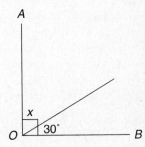

EXAMPLE 3   Which angle is vertical to ∠u in the picture at the right?

SOLUTION   ∠**s** is vertical to ∠u, because ∠s is opposite ∠u.

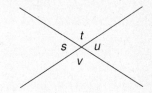

You learned earlier that parallel lines are lines that run side by side and never cross. When two parallel lines are intersected by a third line, called a **transversal**, a set of four angles is created at each point of intersection. In the figure at the right, lines m and n are parallel. Line t is the transversal. For this situation the following statements are true:

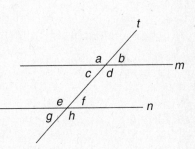

• The four acute angles (b, c, f, and g) are equal.

• The four obtuse angles (a, d, e, and h) are equal.

• Each acute angle is supplementary to each obtuse angle.

EXAMPLE 4   In the picture below lines a and b are parallel. How many degrees are in ∠x?

SOLUTION   Each acute angle is equal to 50°. ∠x is a supplementary obtuse angle. Subtract 50° from 180°.
∠x = 180° − 50° = **130°**

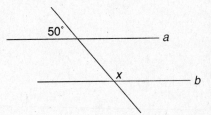

EXERCISE 12

Directions: For questions 1–4, solve each problem.

1. How many degrees are in the complement of a 48° angle?

2. How many degrees are in the supplement of a 48° angle?

3. Find the complement of an angle measuring 25°.

4. Find the supplement of an angle measuring 63°.

Directions: Problems 5–8 refer to the illustration at the right.

5. Which angle is vertical to ∠*y*?

6. What is the sum of ∠*w*, ∠*x*, ∠*y*, and ∠*z*?

7. If ∠*w* measures 75°, how many degrees are in ∠*x*?

8. If ∠*x* measures 119°, how many degrees are in ∠*w*?

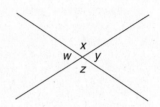

9. To hang her mother's painting safely, Wendy stretched wires in the angles shown at right. If ∠*b* is 80° and ∠*a* and ∠*c* are equal, how many degrees is ∠*a*?

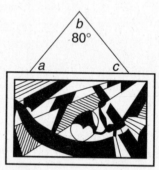

10. The supplement of an acute angle is always what kind of angle?

11. How many degrees are in ∠*m* in the picture at the right?

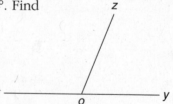

12. If an angle measures 37°, an angle vertical to it must measure how many degrees?

13. ∠*XOZ* in the picture at the right measures 110.5°. Find the number of degrees in ∠*YOZ*.

14. A surveyor stretched a wire line across a street as shown at right. If ∠*a* is 30°, how many degrees is ∠*z*?

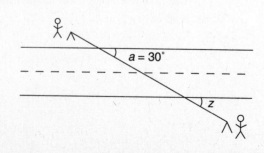

15. How many degrees are in ∠*b* at the right?

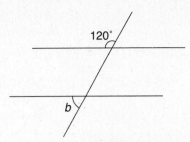

ANSWERS ARE ON PAGES 386–387.

TRIANGLES

A triangle is a three-sided figure. Each of the three points where the sides meet is called a *vertex* of the triangle. The three angles inside a triangle add up to 180°.

Listed below are four of the most important types of triangles.

An **equilateral triangle** has three equal sides. The word *equilateral* means "equal sides." This triangle also has three equal angles. Each angle is $\frac{1}{3}$ of 180°, or 60°. An equilateral triangle can also be called *equiangular*, which means "equal angles." Examples of equilateral triangles:

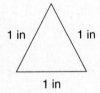

An **isosceles triangle** has two equal sides. The third side may be longer or shorter than the other two sides. An isosceles triangle also has two equal angles. The two equal angles are called the *base angles*. The angle with a different measurement is called the *vertex angle*. Examples of isosceles triangles:

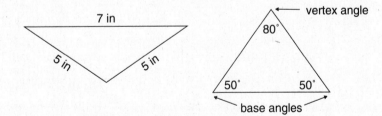

A **scalene triangle** has three sides with different measurements. It also has three angles of different sizes. Examples of scalene triangles:

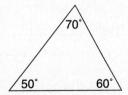
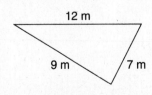

A ***right triangle*** has one right angle. The long side across from the right angle is called the ***hypotenuse***. The other two sides are called the ***legs***. A right triangle can be either scalene or isosceles. When a scalene or an isosceles triangle contains one right angle, the triangle is called a *right triangle*. Examples of right triangles:

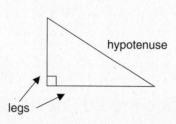

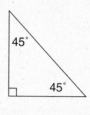

The symbol △ stands for the word *triangle*. A side of a triangle is sometimes referred to by the two letters that form the end points of each side. For △*ABC*, side *BC* is the hypotenuse and sides *AB* and *AC* are the legs of this right triangle.

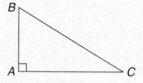

An angle of a triangle can be referred to by the letter that forms the vertex of the angle. For △*ABC*, ∠*A* is the right angle. Sometimes three letters are used to refer to an angle of a triangle. The letter of the vertex must be in the middle. For the triangle above, ∠*A* is the same as ∠*BAC* or ∠*CAB*.

Some questions on the GED Test will require you to find the measurement of a given angle. In some problems you will be given a drawing of the angle. In other problems you will simply use your knowledge of triangle facts to find an angle's measurement. It may be helpful to draw your own diagram if one is not provided.

EXAMPLE 1 In triangle *PQR*, ∠*P* = 35° and ∠*Q* = 45°. Find the measurement of ∠*R*.

(1) ∠*P* + ∠*Q* + ∠*R* = 180°
(2) 35° + 45° + ∠*R* = 180°
$$80° + ∠R = 180°$$
(3) $$∠R = 180° − 80°$$
$$∠R = 100°$$

STEP 1 You know that all three angles of a triangle add up to 180°, so set up an equation.
STEP 2 Substitute the values you know.
STEP 3 Subtract 80° from each side to find your answer: **100°**.

EXAMPLE 2 In △*STU* ∠*S* = 60° and ∠*T* = 30°. What kind of triangle is *STU*?

(1)   60°   **(2)**   180°
$$+ \ 30°$$ $$− \ \ 90°$$
$$\overline{90°}$$ $$\overline{90°}$$

STEP 1 Add the measurements of ∠*S* and ∠*T*.
STEP 2 Subtract the sum from 180°. The measurement of ∠*U* is 90°. A triangle with one right angle is a **right triangle**.

EXAMPLE 3 What is the measurement of ∠x in
the drawing at the right?

(1) 35°   180°   (2) 180°
    + 70°   − 105°   − 75°
    ─────   ──────   ──────
    105°   75°   105°

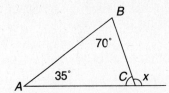

STEP 1 You know that ∠A, ∠B, and ∠C must add up to 180°. Add the measurement of
∠A and ∠B and subtract from 180° to find the measurement of ∠C. ∠C is 75°.

STEP 2 You know from your work with angles that ∠C and ∠x make a straight angle and
that straight angles measure 180°. To find the measurement of ∠x, subtract the
measurement of ∠C from 180°. The measurement of ∠x is **105°**.

Memorize the triangle definitions in this section before you try the next
exercise.

EXERCISE 13

Directions: Solve each problem.

1. Identify each of the following triangles as right, isosceles, scalene, or equilateral.

a.

f.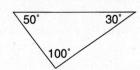

b.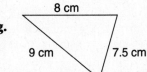

g.

c.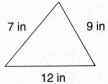

h.

d.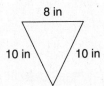

i.

e.
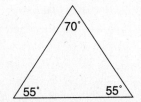
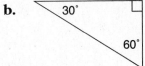

Directions: Questions 2–4 refer to the picture at the right.

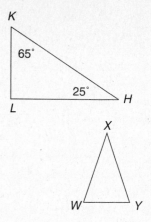

2. Find the measurement of ∠*L*.

3. What kind of triangle is △*KLH*?

4. Side *KH* is called the _____.

Directions: Questions 5–6 refer to the picture at the right.

5. In the triangle at the right, ∠*W* = 65° and ∠*X* = 50°. Find the number of degrees in ∠*Y*.

6. What kind of triangle is △*WXY*?

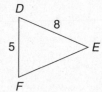

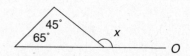

7. In △*ABC*, ∠*A* = 30° and ∠*B* = 60°. How many degrees are there in ∠*C*?

8. What kind of triangle is △*ABC* in problem 7?

9. The vertex angle of an isosceles triangle measures 82°. How many degrees are there in each base angle?

10. Each base angle of an isosceles triangle measures 63°. How many degrees are there in the vertex angle?

11. In the triangle at the right, side *DE* measures 8 inches and side *DF* measures 5 inches. The perimeter of the triangle is 21 inches. What kind of triangle is △*DEF*?

12. In triangle *PQR*, ∠*P* = 25° and ∠*Q* = 35°. What kind of triangle is △*PQR*?

13. In triangle *XYZ*, side *XY* is 4 inches long, and side *YZ* is 5 inches long. The perimeter of the triangle is 16 inches. What kind of triangle is △*XYZ*?

14. What is the sum of the two acute angles in a right triangle?

15. Find how many degrees are in angle *x* in the picture at the right.

ANSWERS ARE ON PAGE 387.

SIMILARITY

When you say that two things are *similar*, you mean that they are alike in some ways but they are not identical. In geometry similar figures have the same shape but different sizes. For example, the two triangles below are considered similar even though they are different sizes. The reason is that the angles are the same size.

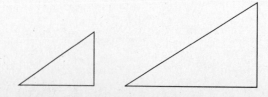

The ***corresponding*** (matching) sides of similar figures can be written as a proportion. The drawing below shows two similar rectangles.

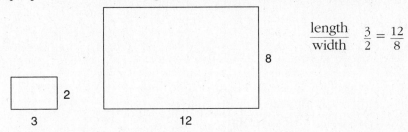

$$\frac{\text{length}}{\text{width}} \quad \frac{3}{2} = \frac{12}{8}$$

For the small rectangle above, the ratio of the length to the width is 3:2. The ratio of the length to the width (the corresponding sides) of the larger rectangle is 12:8, which can be reduced to 3:2. These two rectangles are similar because the corresponding sides are proportional. In other words the ratio of the length to the width of each rectangle is 3:2.

SIMILAR TRIANGLES

Learning about similar triangles will help you solve some of the problems on the GED Test. Two triangles are similar if one of the following two statements is true:

RULES FOR DETERMINING SIMILAR TRIANGLES

1. If any two angles of one triangle are equal to two angles of another triangle, the two triangles are similar.

2. If the sides of one triangle are proportional to the sides of another triangle, the two triangles are similar.

EXAMPLE 1 In triangle *DEF*, $\angle D = 50°$ and $\angle E = 75°$. In triangle *GHI*, $\angle G = 55°$ and $\angle I = 50°$. Are these triangles similar? If they are not similar, tell why.

(1) $\begin{array}{r} 50° \\ + 75° \\ \hline 125° \end{array}$ $\begin{array}{r} 180° \\ - 125° \\ \hline 55° \end{array} = \angle F$ **(2)** $\begin{array}{r} 55° \\ + 50° \\ \hline 105° \end{array}$ $\begin{array}{r} 180° \\ - 105° \\ \hline 75° \end{array} = \angle H$

STEP 1 Find $\angle F$. Subtract the sum of $\angle D$ and $\angle E$ from 180°.

STEP 2 Find $\angle H$. Subtract the sum of $\angle G$ and $\angle I$ from 180°. Each triangle has angles measuring 50°, 55°, and 75°. Since the triangles have equal angles, they are **similar**.

EXAMPLE 2 Are the two triangles pictured below similar? If they are not similar, state why.

 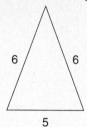

STEP 1 Set up a proportion with the corresponding sides.

$\frac{3}{2} \overset{?}{=} \frac{6}{5}$

STEP 2 Cross multiply.

$3 \times 5 = 15$

$6 \times 2 = 12$

STEP 3 Since the cross products are not equal, the two triangles are **not similar**.

USING SIMILAR TRIANGLES TO SOLVE WORD PROBLEMS

Once you know that two triangles are similar, you can use the following fact to solve many problems:

> ### CORRESPONDING SIDES
>
> Corresponding sides of similar triangles are proportional.

To be able to use this fact, you must be able to pick out which sides of two different triangles are *corresponding* sides. To do this easily, just remember that *corresponding sides are always opposite equal angles*. What are the corresponding sides in the figures below?

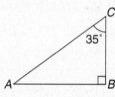 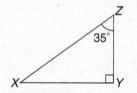

Side *AB* "corresponds" to side *XY* because both sides are across from angles measuring 35°. Sides *BC* and *YZ* are corresponding sides because they are opposite equal angles measuring 55°. (You know that these angles measure 55° because the third angle is a right angle, measuring 90°.) Finally, you know that sides *AC* and *XZ* are corresponding because the angles opposite them measure 90°.

EXAMPLE 3 In triangle *ABC* at the right, *AB* = 9 ft and *BC* = 18 ft. In triangle *GHI*, *GH* = 5 ft. Find the length of *HI*.

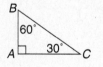

(1) $\dfrac{\text{short leg}}{\text{hypotenuse}} \quad \dfrac{9}{18} = \dfrac{5}{x}$ (2) $\begin{array}{r} 18 \\ \times\ 5 \\ \hline 90 \end{array}$ (3) $9\overline{)90}^{\,10\text{ ft}}$

STEP 1 First notice that these triangles are similar. Each has angles of 30°, 60°, and 90°. Set up a proportion with the corresponding sides of each triangle. Let *x* stand for the hypotenuse of triangle *GHI*.

STEP 2 Find the cross product of 18 and 5.
STEP 3 Divide by the remaining number in the proportion, 9. The length of side *HI* is **10 feet**.

EXAMPLE 4 A vertical yardstick casts a two-foot shadow. At the same time a building casts a 48-foot shadow. How tall is the building?

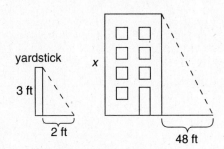

STEP 1 Draw a picture that shows the height and shadow of each figure.
STEP 2 Notice that you have two similar right triangles. The long leg of each triangle is the height of the object. The short leg is the length of the shadow. Make a proportion with the height and shadow of each object. Since the other measurements are given in feet, write the height of the yardstick as 3 feet. Let *x* stand for the height of the building.

$$\frac{\text{height}}{\text{shadow}} \quad \frac{3}{2} = \frac{x}{48}$$

STEP 3 Find the cross product of 3 and 48.

$$\begin{array}{r} 48 \\ \times\ 3 \\ \hline 144 \end{array}$$

STEP 4 Divide by the remaining number in the proportion, 2. The building is **72 feet** tall.

$$2\overline{)144}\ \ ^{72\ \text{ft}}$$

EXERCISE 14

Directions: Solve each problem.

1. Are the rectangles pictured at the right similar? If they are not, state why.

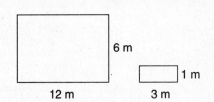

2. Are the rectangles pictured at the right similar? If they are not, state why.

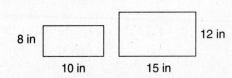

3. In triangle *MNO* ∠*M* = 45° and ∠*N* = 85°. In triangle *PQR* ∠*P* = 50° and ∠*Q* = 45°. Are these two triangles similar? If they are not, state why.

4. In triangle *ABC* ∠*A* = 60° and ∠*B* = 50°. In triangle *DEF* ∠*D* = 50° and ∠*E* = 80°. Are these two triangles similar? If they are not, state why.

5. Are the triangles pictured at the right similar? If they are not, state why.

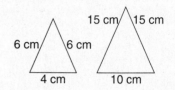

6. In the triangles pictured at the right, ∠*J* and ∠*M* are right angles. Are these triangles similar? If they are not, state why.

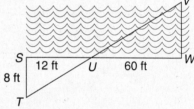

7. In triangle *JKL* above, *JK* = 8 inches and *JL* = 12 inches. In triangle *MNO*, *MN* = 14 inches. Find the length of side *MO*.

8. A six-foot-tall vertical post casts a five-foot shadow. At the same time a tree casts a 65-foot shadow. How tall is the tree?

9. In the picture at the right ∠*S* and ∠*W* are both right angles. Are the two triangles similar?

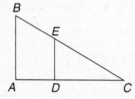

10. In the picture with problem 9, *VW* is the distance across a river. Find the measurement of *VW*.

11. In triangle *ABC*, ∠*CDE* and ∠*CAB* are both right angles. Are triangles *CAB* and *CDE* similar?

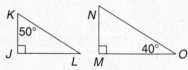

12. In problem 11 *CD* = 15 in, *AD* = 10 in, and *DE* = 6 in. Find *AB*.

ANSWERS ARE ON PAGES 387–388.

CONGRUENCE

Congruent figures have the same shape and the same size. The corresponding angles of congruent figures are equal, as are the corresponding sides. Congruent figures are identical. Corresponding sides are opposite equal angles. In addition, corresponding angles are opposite equal sides.

Following are the conditions that make two triangles congruent.

CONGRUENCY CONDITION 1

If two angles and a corresponding side of one triangle are the same measurements as two angles and corresponding side of another triangle, the triangles are congruent. This is called the **angle**, **side**, **angle** requirement (ASA).

EXAMPLE 1 The two triangles at the right are congruent because two angles and a corresponding side are equal in each triangle.

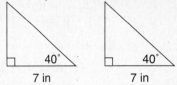

EXAMPLE 2 The two triangles at the right are *not* congruent because the equal sides are not corresponding. One side measuring 5 feet is opposite an angle measuring 45°. The other side measuring 5 feet is opposite an angle of 90°.

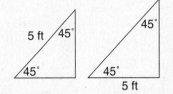

CONGRUENCY CONDITION 2

If two sides and a corresponding angle of one triangle are the same measurements as two sides and corresponding angle of another triangle, the triangles are congruent. This is called the **side, angle, side** requirement (SAS).

EXAMPLE 3 The two triangles at the right are congruent because two sides and a corresponding angle are the same in both triangles.

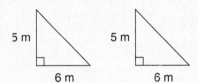

EXAMPLE 4 The two triangles at the right are *not* congruent because the equal sides are not corresponding.

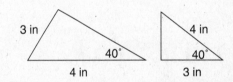

CONGRUENCY CONDITION 3

If the three sides of one triangle are the same measurements as the three sides of another triangle, the two triangles are congruent. This is called the **side, side, side** requirement (SSS).

EXAMPLE 5 The two triangles at the right are congruent because the three sides are the same in both triangles.

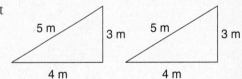

EXAMPLE 6 Are the triangles at the right congruent? If they are not, state why.

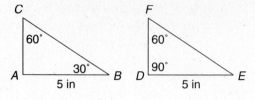

SOLUTION Find the missing angles: ∠A is 90°, and ∠E is 30°. Since the angles and corresponding sides are equal, the triangles are congruent.

EXAMPLE 7 For the triangles at the right, *GH = JK* and *GI = JL*. Of the following conditions, which together with the given information is enough to guarantee that △*GHI* is congruent to △*JKL*?

A. *HI = KL*
B. ∠*G* = ∠*K*
C. ∠*G* = ∠*J*

(1) A only
(2) B only
(3) C only
(4) A or B
(5) A or C

SOLUTION Condition A is enough to fulfill the *side, side, side* requirement. Condition C is enough to fulfill the *side, angle, side* requirement. The best choice is answer **(5)**. Notice that condition B involves angles that are not corresponding.

EXERCISE 15

Directions: For problems 1–6, decide whether each pair of triangles is congruent. If they are congruent, state which requirement the triangles fulfill (ASA, SAS, or SSS). If they are not congruent, state why.

1.

4.

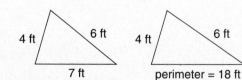

2.

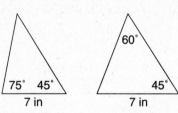

5.

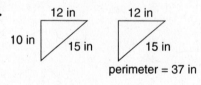

3.

6.

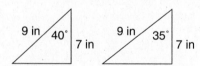

7. Which of the following conditions, along with the information given on the triangles at the right, is enough to guarantee that the triangles are congruent?

(1) $AC = DF$
(2) $\angle B = \angle E$
(3) $AB = EF$

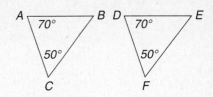

8. Which of the following conditions, along with the information given on the triangles at the right, is enough to guarantee that the triangles are congruent?

(1) $\angle Y = \angle U$
(2) $\angle X = \angle S$
(3) $\angle Z = \angle T$

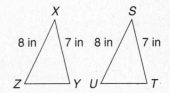

9. Which of the following conditions, along with the information given on the triangles at the right, is enough to guarantee that the triangles are congruent?

(1) $GI = JL$
(2) $GI = KL$
(3) $HI = JL$

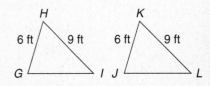

10. For the two triangles at the right $MO = PR$ and $NO = QR$. Which of the following conditions, along with the information you already have, is enough to guarantee that $\triangle MNO$ is congruent to $\triangle PQR$?

A. $\angle N = \angle R$
B. $\angle MN = \angle PQ$
C. $\angle O = \angle R$

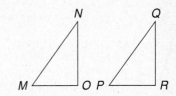

(1) A only
(2) B only
(3) C only
(4) A or B
(5) B or C

ANSWERS ARE ON PAGE 388.

PYTHAGOREAN THEOREM

A Greek mathematician named Pythagoras discovered a special relationship among the sides of a right triangle. We call his discovery the **Pythagorean theorem** or the Pythagorean relationship.

With this theorem you can find the length of any side of a right triangle if you know the lengths of the other two sides.

PYTHAGOREAN THEOREM

The square of the **hypotenuse** (the side opposite the right angle) is equal to the sum of the squares of the other two sides.

$c^2 = a^2 + b^2$, where c = hypotenuse and a and b are the legs of a right triangle.

$$c^2 = a^2 + b^2$$

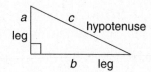

EXAMPLE 1   Some groups of whole numbers are easy to use in the Pythagorean theorem. The combination of 3, 4, and 5 is one of the most common groups known as a *Pythagorean triple*. If 3 and 4 represent the lengths of the legs of a right triangle, does 5 represent the length of the hypotenuse? Substitute the values in the Pythagorean theorem to find out.

$$a^2 + b^2 = c^2$$
$$3^2 + 4^2 = 5^2$$
$$9 + 16 = 25$$

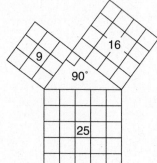

Since both sides are equal, the set of numbers can be the sides of a right triangle. Note that the longest side of a right triangle is always the hypotenuse.

EXAMPLE 2   Find the length of the hypotenuse in the triangle at the right.

(1) $c^2 = a^2 + b^2$ **(2)** $c = \sqrt{100}$
    $c^2 = 6^2 + 8^2$ $c = \textbf{10 in}$
    $c^2 = 36 + 64$
    $c^2 = 100$

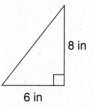

STEP 1   Replace a with 6 and b with 8 in the formula $c^2 = a^2 + b^2$.
STEP 2   The formula gives the value of the hypotenuse squared. To find the length of the hypotenuse, find the square root of 100.

To work with the Pythagorean theorem, you may need to review the section on squares and square roots starting on page 233.

In some problems you may be given the length of the hypotenuse and the length of one of the legs. To find the length of the other leg, you can still use the Pythagorean theorem.

EXAMPLE 3 Find the length of the missing leg in the triangle below.

(1)　　$c^2 = a^2 + b^2$
　　　　　$15^2 = a^2 + 9^2$
(2)　　$225 = a^2 + 81$
(3)　　$225 = a^2 + 81$
　　　　　$\underline{-81 \qquad -81}$
　　　　　$144 = a^2$
(4)　　$\sqrt{144} = a$
　　　　　$\mathbf{12 = a}$

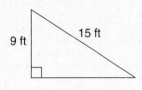

STEP 1　Write down the Pythagorean theorem and substitute in the values you know.
STEP 2　Find the values of the squares.
STEP 3　To get the unknown, a, alone on one side, subtract 81 from both sides.
STEP 4　To find a, find the square root of both sides of the equation.

> **TIP:** In some problems you will have to recognize that a figure is a right triangle. The picture or problem may say nothing about a right triangle, the hypotenuse, or legs. Drawing a picture may help you see that the problem involves a right-triangle relationship.

EXAMPLE 4 A boat sails 20 miles east of port and then 15 miles south to an island. How far is the boat from the port if you measure in a straight line?

(1)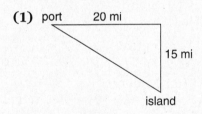

(2) $c^2 = a^2 + b^2$　　**(3)** $c = \sqrt{625}$
$c^2 = 20^2 + 15^2$　　　　　$c = 25$ mi
$c^2 = 400 + 225$
$c^2 = 625$

STEP 1　Make a drawing to see how to solve the problem. East is normally to the right on a map, and south is toward the bottom. Notice that the actual distance from the port is the hypotenuse of a right triangle.
STEP 2　Replace a with 20 and b with 15 in the formula $c^2 = a^2 + b^2$.
STEP 3　Find the square root of 625. The boat is **25 miles** from the port.

EXERCISE 16

Directions: Solve each problem. Use the formulas page when necessary.

1. Find the hypotenuse of the triangle at the right.

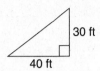

2. One leg of a right triangle measures 10 inches. The other measures 24 inches. Find the length of the hypotenuse.

3. In triangle *XYZ* at the right, side *XY* = 12 inches and side *YZ* = 5 inches. Find the length of *XZ*.

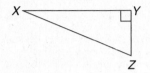

4. What is the length of the hypotenuse of a right triangle whose legs measure 12 yards and 16 yards?

5. Joanna drove 60 miles west from Bonesville to Mactown and then 45 miles south to Steven City. She returned to Bonesville on Route 3. How far is it from Steven City to Bonesville on Route 3?

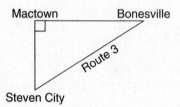

6. One leg of a triangle measures 18 yards. The hypotenuse measures 30 yards. Find the length of the other leg.

ANSWERS ARE ON PAGE 388.

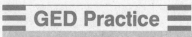
EXERCISE 17

Directions: Choose the correct answer for each of the following problems.

1. In triangle *ABC* below *AB* = 16 feet and *AC* = 34 feet. Find the length in feet of *BC*.

(1) 20
(2) 25
(3) 30
(4) 32
(5) 40

2. A 17-foot ladder just touches the bottom of a window. The bottom of the ladder is 8 feet from the bottom of the building. Find the distance *d* in feet from the ground to the bottom of the window.

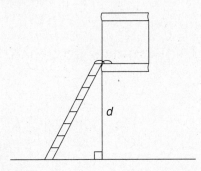

(1) 12
(2) 15
(3) 18
(4) 20
(5) 25

3. Louie drove 48 miles directly north and then 36 miles directly west. Find the shortest distance in miles from the point where he ended up to his starting point.

(1) 24
(2) 36
(3) 48
(4) 60
(5) 360

4. On a bike trip Manuel rode 15 miles directly west and then 36 miles directly south. Which expresses the distance from the point where he started to the point where he ended his trip?

(1) $2(15) + 2(36)$
(2) 15×36
(3) $\sqrt{15^2 + 36^2}$
(4) $\sqrt{15 + 36}$
(5) $\dfrac{15 + 36}{2}$

ANSWERS ARE ON PAGE 388.

PROBLEM SOLVING FOR THE GED

Using the Formulas Page

To make a flower vase, Tina chose a 20-cubic-inch ceramic mold. If the mold stood five inches tall and was 2 inches long, how many inches was the width?
- **(1)** 1
- **(2)** 2
- **(3)** 5
- **(4)** 10
- **(5)** 20

In problems on the GED Math Test you will not be told when to use the formulas page provided with your test booklet. Instead you will need to infer from the problem that a formula would help you solve the problem. Then you will need to choose the right formula from the list and use it correctly.

Here are some hints to help you do this.

1. Read the problem carefully. If a geometric shape is being described, this is a clue that a formula may come in handy.

> In the problem above, you can tell by words such as *tall* and *long* and *width* that a shape is being described.

2. Decide what shape you are dealing with and what formula may apply. Remember that *perimeter* measures distance around, *area* measures a flat surface, and *volume* measures solid figures.

Here is an additional clue:

> perimeter = plain units (inches)
> area = squared units (square inches)
> volume = cubed units (cubic inches)

In this problem you are given the clue *20 cubic inches.* This tells you that you will need a formula for *volume.* The shape being described is a *rectangular container.*

3. Find the correct formula and apply it. In this problem we find that the formula for the volume of a rectangular container is $V = lwh$.

$$V = lwh$$
$$20 = 2 \times w \times 5$$
$$20 = 10 \times w$$
$$2 = w$$

Answer: **(2) 2**

Most of the information on the formulas page deals with geometric shapes. You have learned other formulas (such as the interest formula) that are also given on the formulas page. Remember to consult the formulas page when you need help with these problems as well.

Let's apply information from the formulas page (page 274) to the following two examples.

EXAMPLE 1 The figure at the right represents the surface that Molly needs to cover with plywood. How many square inches of wood does she need?

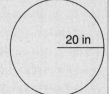

20 in

(1)   31.4
(2)   62.8
(3) 125.6
(4) 314
(5) 1256

In the example it is clear that the surface to be covered is circular. Since you know what shape is being discussed, your next step should be to decide what you are trying to find and which formula to use.

The example asks you to cover a surface. This means that you would want to find the area of the shape. You would then find the formula for area of a circle on the formulas page.

$A = \pi r^2$
$A = 3.14(20^2)$
$A = 3.14(400)$
$A = 1256$

You would choose **(5) 1256** as the number of square inches of plywood that Molly needs.

EXAMPLE 2 Geraldo wants to mark off the center circle on the new basketball court constructed for the neighborhood kids. If the circumference of the circle is supposed to be about 37.7 feet, what is the diameter of the center circle he needs to mark (to the nearest foot)?

In this example you've been given the circumference. What you need to find is the diameter. Find the formula for circumference of a circle on the formulas page and substitute the known values into the formula.

$C = \pi d$
$37.7 = 3.14(d)$
$\frac{37.7}{3.14} = d$
$12.006 = d$

The diameter of the center circle on the basketball court should be **12 feet**.

FORMULAS

AREA *(A)* of a:

square	$A = s^2$; where s = side
rectangle	$A = lw$; where l = length, w = width
parallelogram	$A = bh$; where b = base, h = height
triangle	$A = \frac{1}{2}bh$; where b = base, h = height
circle	$A = \pi r^2$; where $\pi \approx 3.14$, r = radius

PERIMETER *(P)* of a:

square	$P = 4s$; where s = side
rectangle	$P = 2l + 2w$; where l = length, w = width
triangle	$P = a + b + c$; where a, b, and c are the sides
circumference *(C)* of a circle	$C = \pi d$; where $\pi \approx 3.14$, d = diameter

VOLUME *(V)* of a:

cube	$V = s^3$; where s = side
rectangular container	$V = lwh$; where l = length, w = width, h = height
cylinder	$V = \pi r^2 h$; where $\pi \approx 3.14$, r = radius, h = height

Pythagorean theorem	$c^2 = a^2 + b^2$; where c = hypotenuse, a and b are legs of a right triangle
distance *(d)* between two points in a plane	$d = \sqrt{(x_2 - x_1)^2 + (y_2 - y_1)^2}$; where (x_1, y_1) and (x_2, y_2) are two points in a plane
slope of a line *(m)*	$m = \frac{y_2 - y_1}{x_2 - x_1}$; where (x_1, y_1) and (x_2, y_2) are points in a plane

mean	$mean = \frac{x_1 + x_2 + \ldots + x_n}{n}$; where the x's are the values for which a mean is desired, and n = number of values in the series
median	$median$ = the point in an ordered set of numbers at which half of the numbers are above and half of the numbers are below this value

simple interest *(i)*	$i = prt$; where p = principal, r = rate, t = time
distance *(d)* as function of rate and time	$d = rt$; where r = rate, t = time
total cost *(c)*	$c = nr$; where n = number of units, r = cost per unit

GEOMETRY REVIEW

Directions: For questions 1–13, simply answer each question. You can use the formulas on page 274 for this exercise.

1. A rectangular solid for which every side has the same measurement is called a _____.

2. The side of a square measures 3.2 meters. Find the perimeter of the square.

3. The length of a rectangle is 12 inches. The width is $4\frac{1}{4}$ inches. Find the perimeter of the rectangle.

4. Find the perimeter of the triangle pictured below.

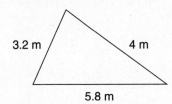

3.2 m   4 m

5.8 m

5. To the nearest foot, what is the circumference of a circle with a diameter of 30 feet?

6. What is the value of 20^3?

7. Simplify the following: $(.03)^2 + (.4)^2$

8. What is the value of $\sqrt{7{,}056}$?

9. Find the area of a square with a side that measures $5\frac{1}{2}$ inches.

10. Find the area of a rectangle with a length of 12.5 cm and a width of 7.4 cm.

11. Find the area of the triangle pictured below.

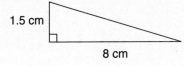

1.5 cm

8 cm

12. What is the area of a circle with a radius of 7 inches? Use $\pi \approx \frac{22}{7}$.

13. Find the volume of a rectangular container with a length of 15 inches, a height of 10 inches, and a width of $3\frac{1}{2}$ inches.

Directions: For questions 14 and 15, choose the best answer to each problem.

14. Sharon wants to put fencing around the rectangular garden in her yard. The garden measures 20 feet by 8 feet. She wants to leave a four-foot opening for a walkway into the garden. Which of the following expressions gives the number of feet of fencing she needs?

  (1) $20 + 8$
  (2) $(2 \times 20) + (2 \times 8)$
  (3) $(2 \times 20) + (2 \times 8) - 4$
  (4) $(20 \times 8) - 4$
  (5) $2(20 - 8)$

15. One side of the square pictured below is 12 inches. The length of the rectangle is 15 inches. Find the rectangle's width in inches if it has the same area as the square.

  (1) 30
  (2) 27
  (3) 19.2
  (4) 9.6
  (5) 6

12 in   15 in

Questions 16–18 refer to the following situation.

The picture below shows the plan of a new pool at the Uptown Community Center. The depth of the pool will be six feet throughout. The edge of the pool will be surrounded by ceramic strips that are six inches long.

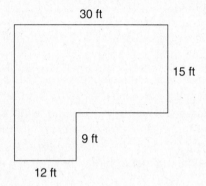

30 ft

15 ft

9 ft

12 ft

16. What is the fewest number of strips needed to completely surround the edge of the pool?
   (1) 96
   (2) 108
   (3) 216
   (4) 432
   (5) Not enough information is given.

17. Find the area in square yards of the bottom of the pool.
   (1) 31
   (2) 62
   (3) 124
   (4) 186
   (5) 532

18. If the pool is filled to its limit, how many cubic feet of water will it hold?
   (1) 3348
   (2) 2232
   (3) 1674
   (4) 1116
   (5) Not enough information is given.

19. In the picture below ∠BOC = 64°. What kind of angle is AOB?
   (1) acute
   (2) right
   (3) obtuse
   (4) straight
   (5) reflex

20. In the picture below, ∠a = 65°. How many degrees are there in ∠d?
   (1) 15°
   (2) 25°
   (3) 35°
   (4) 105°
   (5) 115°

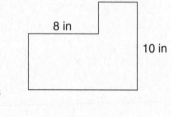

21. Find the area in square inches of the figure shown at the right.
   (1) 130
   (2) 120
   (3) 100
   (4) 98
   (5) Not enough information is given.

5 in

8 in

10 in

22. In triangle XYZ, ∠X = 33° and ∠Y = 57°. What kind of triangle is △XYZ?
   (1) equilateral
   (2) isosceles
   (3) obtuse
   (4) right
   (5) both isosceles and right

23. The sails of the two boats pictured below are similar triangles. Find the height in feet of the small sail.
   (1) 7.2
   (2) 3.6
   (3) 2.5
   (4) 1.8
   (5) 0.9

12 ft

10 ft   3 ft

24. For the triangles below, $\angle G = \angle J$ and $\angle I = \angle L$. Which of the conditions listed below, together with the given information, is enough to guarantee that $\triangle GHI$ is congruent to $\triangle JKL$?

    A. $GI = JL$

    B. $GH = JK$

    C. $\angle H = \angle K$

(1) A only

(2) B only

(3) C only

(4) A or B

(5) B or C

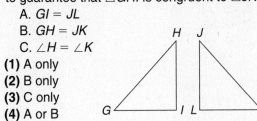

25. In the rectangle below, side BC measures 36 inches and diagonal line AC measures 39 inches. Find the length in inches of side AB.

(1) 15

(2) 18

(3) 30

(4) 33

(5) 42

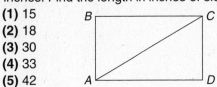

ANSWERS ARE ON PAGES 388–390.

11 Special Topics in Algebra and Geometry

In this chapter you will learn about several different topics in algebra and geometry. Any of the topics below could appear on the GED Math Test.

- The Number Line
- Signed Numbers
- Inequalities
- Monomials
- Factoring
- Using Algebra to Solve Geometry Problems

- Rectangular Coordinates
- Linear Equations
- Slope and Intercepts
- Quadratic Equations
- Simultaneous Equations

THE NUMBER LINE

In algebra you can use a set of numbers you have not used in arithmetic. In this section you will learn about these numbers and how to use them.

The numbers we use in arithmetic can be represented on a line like this:

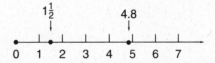

Fractions, decimals, and mixed numbers fit into the spaces between the whole numbers. Notice the points representing $1\frac{1}{2}$ and 4.8. Except for zero, all the numbers on this line are ***positive numbers***, which are numbers greater than zero. The arrow at the right end means that the numbers go on and on.

In algebra we extend this system to include numbers that are less than zero. These are called ***negative numbers***. Temperatures on a thermometer are the most familiar use of positive and negative numbers. When it is 70° outside, we mean that it is 70° above zero. In algebra we call this *positive 70°*. When it is −20° outside, we mean that it is 20° below zero. In algebra we call this *negative 20°*.

We can extend the line shown on page 279 to include both positive and negative numbers:

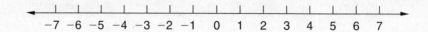

This is called the **number line**. The arrows at both ends mean that both the positive and negative values go on and on.

The positive numbers represent numbers above zero. The negative numbers represent numbers below zero. Zero (0) is neither positive nor negative.

To move to the right along the number line means to find an increasing amount such as a gain in weight or a rise in temperature. To move to the left along the number line means to find a decreasing amount such as a loss of weight or a drop in temperature.

> **TIP:** Positive numbers do not have to be written with a plus sign (+). The number 8 is understood to be +8. Negative numbers, however, must always have a minus (−) sign in front of them.

EXERCISE 1

Directions: Use the number line below to state which letter corresponds to each of the following numbers. Problem 1 is already done as an example. The letter *J* corresponds to +6.

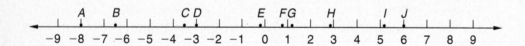

1. + 6

2. − 3

3. − $6\frac{1}{2}$

4. − 8

5. + $\frac{2}{3}$

6. $\frac{5}{4}$

7. + $\frac{16}{3}$

8. 2.75

9. − 3.5

10. − 0.2

11. Mark each of the following numbers on the number line below. The first number, − $1\frac{2}{3}$, has been marked as an example.

$-1\frac{2}{3}$, $3\frac{1}{2}$, +6, −4.25, $\frac{4}{3}$, −5.2, −7.1, +6.4

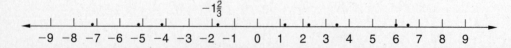

ADDITION OF SIGNED NUMBERS

The entire set of positive and negative numbers is called ***signed numbers***. In the next four sections you will learn to add, subtract, multiply, and divide signed numbers.

> ### RULES FOR ADDING TWO SIGNED NUMBERS
>
> **1.** If the two numbers have the same signs, find the sum of the numbers and give the answer that sign:
>
> - Positive numbers give a positive sum.
> - Negative numbers give a negative sum.
>
> **2.** If the two numbers have different signs, find the difference between the two numbers (subtract the smaller from the larger) and *give the answer the sign of the larger number.*

In the next examples you will see problems involving addition of signed numbers. A negative sign looks very much like a minus sign. To avoid confusion, signed numbers are sometimes written inside parentheses.

EXAMPLE 1 Find $(-16) + (-8)$.

$$\begin{array}{r} -16 \\ + -8 \\ \hline \mathbf{-24} \end{array}$$

STEP 1 Since the numbers have the same signs, find their sum.
STEP 2 Since they are both negative numbers, the answer is negative.

This example could represent a drop in temperature. If the temperature is $-16°$ and then drops another $8°$ $(-8°)$, the temperature will be $-24°$.

EXAMPLE 2 Add $+23$ and -54.

$$\begin{array}{r} -54 \\ +23 \\ \hline \mathbf{-31} \end{array}$$

STEP 1 Since the numbers have different signs, find the difference. Subtract the smaller number (23) from the larger (54).
STEP 2 Give the answer the sign of the larger number, 54. The answer is negative.

This example could represent the following situation: Lois has paid back $23 $(+23)$ of the $54 (-54) she borrowed from her sister. The amount she still owes is $31. Her debt is written as $-$31.

It is also possible to add more than two signed numbers.

> ### STEPS FOR ADDING MORE THAN TWO SIGNED NUMBERS
>
> **1.** Find the sum of the positive numbers and make that sum positive.
>
> **2.** Find the sum of the negative numbers and make that sum negative.
>
> **3.** Find the difference between the two sums and give the answer the sign of the larger sum.

In the next examples, watch for the different ways to write addition of signed numbers.

EXAMPLE 3 $(-9) + (10) + (-8) + (+4) = ?$

$$
\textbf{(1)} \quad
\begin{array}{r} +10 \\ +4 \\ \hline +14 \end{array}
\qquad
\textbf{(2)} \quad
\begin{array}{r} -9 \\ -8 \\ \hline -17 \end{array}
\qquad
\textbf{(3)} \quad
\begin{array}{r} -17 \\ +14 \\ \hline \mathbf{-3} \end{array}
$$

STEP 1 Find the sum of the positive numbers 10 and 4 and make the sum positive.
STEP 2 Find the sum of the negative numbers −9 and −8, and make the sum negative.
STEP 3 Find the difference between 17 and 14 and give the answer a negative sign because 17 is larger.

Notice in the last example that the numbers inside the parentheses are either positive or negative. The plus signs between the parentheses indicate addition.

EXAMPLE 4 Add $-5 + 4 + 7 + (-6)$.

$$
\textbf{(1)} \quad
\begin{array}{r} +4 \\ +7 \\ \hline +11 \end{array}
\qquad
\textbf{(2)} \quad
\begin{array}{r} -5 \\ -6 \\ \hline -11 \end{array}
\qquad
\textbf{(3)} \quad
\begin{array}{r} -11 \\ +11 \\ \hline \mathbf{0} \end{array}
$$

STEP 1 Find the sum of the positive numbers and make the sum positive.
STEP 2 Find the sum of the negative numbers and make the sum negative.
STEP 3 Find the difference between the two sums. Remember that 0 has no sign.

EXERCISE 2

Directions: Solve each problem.

1. $(-9) + (-3)$

2. $6 + (-8) = ?$

3. Find the sum of $+12$ and $-20\frac{1}{2}$.

4. Find the sum of $+12\frac{1}{2}$ and -20.

5. $(+5) + (-8) + (+9) = ?$

6. Find the sum of +8, −6, and −5.

7. −18 + (−2) + 6 = ?

8. Add −6, 8, −4, and +11.

9. 40 + (−7) + (−5) + (−3) + (−10) + (−2) = ?

10. Find the sum of +3, −10, and +7.

11. (−10) + (5) + (−3) + (−9) = ?

12. (−9) + (−4) + (8) + (7) + (−2) = ?

13. At 5:00 A.M. the temperature was −10°. By 8:00 A.M. the temperature had dropped another 4 degrees. What was the 8:00 A.M. temperature?

14. Jack weighed 180 pounds in January. In February he gained 15 more pounds. Then he dieted during March and April and lost 37 pounds. How much did he weigh at the end of April?

15. Mercedes had $235 in her checking account. She deposited $55 and wrote checks for $30, $150, and $120. Did she have enough money in her account to cover the checks?

ANSWERS ARE ON PAGE 390.

SUBTRACTION OF SIGNED NUMBERS

With signed numbers it is possible to do subtraction problems that you could not do before. For example, you can take 9 from 4. Start at +4 on the number line and move 9 spaces to the left.

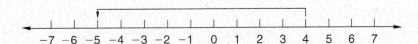

You should be at −5. In algebra this problem is written as (+4) − (+9) = (−5). The minus sign between parentheses indicates subtraction. When you subtract signed numbers, you are finding the distance between them on the number line.

The only difference between adding and subtracting signed numbers is that a subtraction sign changes the sign of the number following it. After you change the sign, follow the rules for adding signed numbers. For example, (+4) − (+9) becomes + 4 − 9. Find the difference between 4 and 9 and give the answer a negative sign because 9 is larger than 4.

STEPS FOR SUBTRACTING SIGNED NUMBERS

1. Change the sign of the number being subtracted and drop the subtraction sign.

2. Follow the rules for adding signed numbers.
   a. If their signs are the same, add the numbers together and give the sum that sign.
   b. If their signs are different, find the difference between them and give the sum the sign of the larger number.

EXAMPLE 1 What is $(-8) - (+3)$?

$(-8) - (+3) = -8 - 3 = -\mathbf{11}$

STEP 1   The minus sign outside the parentheses means that $+3$ is being subtracted. Change $+3$ to -3 and drop the subtraction sign.

STEP 2   Since both signs are now the same, find the sum of the numbers and make the sum negative.

EXAMPLE 2 Find $(-10) - (-2)$.

$(-10) - (-2) = -10 + 2 = -\mathbf{8}$

STEP 1   The minus sign outside the parentheses means that -2 is being subtracted. Change -2 to $+2$ and drop the subtraction sign and the parentheses.

STEP 2   Since the signs are different, find the difference between the two numbers and give the answer the sign of the larger number.

EXAMPLE 3 Simplify $(+6) - (-4) + (-2) - (+5)$.

STEP 1   The two minus signs outside parentheses mean that -4 and $+5$ are being subtracted. Change -4 to $+4$ and $+5$ to -5. Then change the minus signs to plus signs.

$(+6) - (-4) + (-2) - (+5) = +6 + 4 - 2 - 5$

STEP 2   Find the sum of the positive numbers and make the sum positive.

$$\begin{array}{r} +6 \\ +4 \\ \hline +10 \end{array}$$

STEP 3   Find the sum of the negative numbers and make the sum negative.

$$\begin{array}{r} -2 \\ -5 \\ \hline -7 \end{array}$$

STEP 4   Find the difference between 7 and 10 and give the answer the sign of the larger number. The answer is positive 3 $(+3)$.

$$\begin{array}{r} +10 \\ -\ 7 \\ \hline +\ \mathbf{3} \end{array}$$

EXERCISE 3

Directions: Solve each problem.

1. $(+6) - (+4) =$

2. $(-8) - (+3) =$

3. $(-9) - (-8) =$

4. $(+10) - (-9) =$

5. $(+8) - (7) =$

6. $(-9) - (-9) =$

7. $(-10) - 12 =$

8. $(+6) - (-3) + (-2) =$

9. $(-9) - (+4) - (+10) =$

10. $(-15) - (20) + (+6) =$

11. $(-8) + (-13) - (+6) =$

12. $(-3) + (-4) - (-5) - (-6) =$

13. The coastline closest to Rainbow Valley is 22 feet above sea level, and Rainbow Valley is 43 feet below sea level. How many feet lower than the coastline is Rainbow Valley?

14. At dawn it was 7° above zero. By dusk the temperature had dropped to $-17°$. By how much did the temperature drop from dawn to dusk?

ANSWERS ARE ON PAGE 390.

MULTIPLICATION OF SIGNED NUMBERS

The rules for multiplying signed numbers are easy. Before learning the rules, however, study the following applications of multiplying signed numbers.

> **TIP:** Remember to multiply if there is no sign between parentheses.

If you gain two pounds a week for five weeks, you will weigh ten pounds *more* than you weigh now. In algebra this is $(+2)(+5) = +10$.

If you lose two pounds a week for five weeks, you will weigh ten pounds *less* than you weigh now. In algebra this is $(-2)(+5) = -10$.

If you have been gaining two pounds a week for five weeks, you weighed ten pounds less five weeks ago. In algebra this is $(+2)(-5) = -10$.

If you have been losing two pounds a week for five weeks, you weighed ten pounds more five weeks ago. In algebra this is $(-2)(-5) = +10$.

The pattern to these examples is simple: When the signs of two numbers being multiplied are alike, the answer is positive. When the signs of the two numbers being multiplied are not alike, the answer is negative.

RULES FOR MULTIPLYING TWO SIGNED NUMBERS

1. Multiply the two numbers.

2. a. If the signs of the two numbers are alike, make the product positive.
   b. If the signs of the two numbers are different, make the product negative.

EXAMPLE 1   What is the product of (-8) and (-7)?

$(-8)(-7) = +\textbf{56}$

SOLUTION   Since the signs are alike, the answer is positive.

EXAMPLE 2   What is $(12)(-3)$?

$(12)(-3) = -\textbf{36}$

SOLUTION   Since the signs are different, the answer is negative.

EXAMPLE 3   Find $-3 \cdot 10$.

$-3 \cdot 10 = -\textbf{30}$

SOLUTION   Remember that the dot between the numbers is another symbol for multiplication. Since the signs are different, the answer is negative.

EXAMPLE 4   What is $(-6)(+2)(-3)(+4)$?

$$(-6)(+2)(-3)(+4) \qquad \text{or} \qquad (-6)(+2)(-3)(+4)$$

$$(-12) \quad (-12) \qquad\qquad\qquad (-12)(-3)(+4)$$

$$\textbf{144} \qquad\qquad\qquad\qquad\qquad (36)(+4)$$

$$\textbf{144}$$

SOLUTION   Remember that the rules are for multiplying only two numbers at a time. -6 times $+2$ is negative because the signs are different. The product, -12, times -3 is positive because the signs are alike. The product, $+36$, times $+4$ is also positive because the signs are alike.

The following rule is a shortcut for multiplying more than two signed numbers.

RULES FOR MULTIPLYING MORE THAN TWO SIGNED NUMBERS

1. Multiply all the numbers together.

2. a. If the problem has an even number of negative signs, the final product is positive.
   b. If the problem has an odd number of negative signs, the final product is negative.

EXAMPLE 5 Find $(-2)(-1)(+3)(-5)$.

$$(-2)(-1)(+3)(-5) = -30$$

SOLUTION This problem has three negative signs. Since three is an odd number, the answer is negative. The final product is -30.

EXERCISE 4

Directions: Solve each problem.

1. $(-2)(+9) =$

2. $(-6)(-6) =$

3. $(+5)(-9) =$

4. $(+8)(3) =$

5. $(-\frac{3}{4})(12) =$

6. $(+\frac{2}{3})(-\frac{3}{4}) =$

7. $-8 \cdot 6 \cdot -2 =$

8. $-7 \cdot -103 =$

9. $+5 \cdot +4 \cdot -2 =$

10. $-8 \cdot -\frac{5}{8} =$

11. $(4)(-2)(-1)(-6)(4) =$

12. Find the product of -14 and $+2$.

13. What is the product of -2 and 6?

14. The Sunshine Daycare Center has been getting three new children every month. How many fewer children were in the school six months ago?

ANSWERS ARE ON PAGE 391.

DIVISION OF SIGNED NUMBERS

The rules for dividing signed numbers are similar to the rules for multiplying signed numbers.

RULES FOR DIVIDING SIGNED NUMBERS
1. Divide or reduce the numbers.
2. a. If the signs are alike, make the quotient positive.   **b.** If the signs are different, make the quotient negative.

EXAMPLE 1 What is $\frac{+30}{-6}$?

$$\frac{+30}{-6} = -5$$

SOLUTION Since the signs are different, the quotient is negative.

EXAMPLE 2 What is $\frac{-28}{-12}$?

$$\frac{-28}{-12} = \frac{-28 \div 4}{-12 \div 4} = \frac{7}{3} \text{ or } 2\frac{1}{3}$$

SOLUTION Reduce the fraction. Since the signs are alike, the quotient is positive. Answers in the form of improper fractions are common in algebra. Both $2\frac{1}{3}$ and $\frac{7}{3}$ could appear as answer choices on the GED Test, so you will need to check to see which is appropriate.

EXAMPLE 3 Simplify $\frac{+9}{-15}$.

$$\frac{+9}{-15} = -\frac{3}{5}$$

SOLUTION In this example you cannot divide. Simply reduce the fraction. Since the signs are different, the answer is negative.

EXERCISE 5

Directions: Solve each problem.

1. $\frac{-40}{-20} =$

2. $\frac{-12}{+6} =$

3. Simplify $\frac{72}{-9}$

4. $\frac{+16}{-24} =$

5. $\frac{-15}{+5} =$

6. $\frac{30}{-36} =$

7. Find the value of $\frac{-8}{-1}$

8. $\frac{-13}{26} =$

9. $\frac{144}{-24} =$

10. $\frac{-108}{-9} =$

11. $\frac{-48}{-60} =$

12. $\frac{+65}{-5} =$

13. $\frac{-36}{-24} =$

14. $\frac{-63}{+35} =$

15. $\frac{75}{-100} =$

16. $\frac{-15}{-150} =$

ANSWERS ARE ON PAGE 391.

SIGNED NUMBERS REVIEW

In some problems you will have to perform more than one operation. Review the order of operations you learned earlier.

1. Do all work in parentheses.

2. Find powers and roots.

3. Do all multiplication and division.

4. Do all addition and subtraction.

EXAMPLE $(-4)(-2) - (5)(-3) =$

(1) $(-4)(-2) - (5)(-3) =$

$$+8 \quad - (-15) \quad =$$
(2) $\quad +8 \quad + \quad 15 \quad = +23$

STEP 1 First find the two products.
STEP 2 Since the second product, -15, is being subtracted, change -15 to $+15$. Then follow the rules for addition of signed numbers. Since the numbers have the same sign, find the sum and give the answer that sign.

EXERCISE 6

Directions: Solve each problem.

1. $(15) - (-9) =$

2. $(-6)(+20) =$

3. $-4 + 3 - 7 =$

4. $\frac{-96}{-8} =$

5. $(-8) - (12) =$

6. $\frac{1000}{-10} =$

7. $(-29) + (-14) =$

8. $(-20) - (-21) =$

9. $(20) + (-12) - (+15) =$

10. $(-3)(\frac{2}{3})(-10) =$

11. $\frac{-14}{21} =$

12. $(-1)(\frac{7}{8}) =$

13. $(-3)(5) + \frac{6}{-2} =$

14. $(\frac{-8}{4}) + (\frac{15}{-3}) =$

15. $(-6) + (\frac{30}{5}) =$

16. $(15)(\frac{-2}{3}) - 8 =$

17. $-4 + (-8)(-6) =$

18. $\frac{-36}{9} - (-10) =$

19. $(12)(-2) + (-1)(-15) =$

20. $(\frac{10}{-15}) - (\frac{18}{27}) =$

ANSWERS ARE ON PAGE 391.

INEQUALITIES

You learned in the chapter on the basics of algebra that an equation is a statement that two amounts are equal. An ***inequality*** is a statement that two amounts are not equal. Following are four symbols used to write inequalities.

EXAMPLES OF INEQUALITIES

Symbol	Meaning		Example
<	less than	$3 < 4$	"3 is less than 4."
>	more than	$5 > 2$	"5 is more than 2."
≤	less than or equal to	$m \leq 6$	"m is less than or equal to 6." This means that m can be 6 or any number less than 6, including negative numbers.
≥	more than or equal to	$x \geq 8$	"x is more than or equal to 8." This means that x can be 8 or any number larger than 8.

Solving inequalities is like solving equations. You can perform inverse operations on both sides of inequalities to find the value of the unknown.

EXAMPLE 1 Solve for m in $6m \leq 42$.

$$\frac{6m}{6} \leq \frac{42}{6}$$
$$m \leq 7$$

SOLUTION Divide both sides by 6. The solution is $m \leq 7$. This inequality is true for 7 and every number less than 7.

EXAMPLE 2 For the inequality $n + 2 > 5$, could n be 2?

$$n + 2 > 5$$
$$\underline{-2 \quad -2}$$
$$n > 3$$

SOLUTION Subtract 2 from both sides. The solution is $n > 3$. This inequality is true for every number larger than 3. The number 2 is *not* a solution; n could not be 2.

EXERCISE 7

Directions: Solve each inequality.

1. $c - 3 < 21$

2. $p + 1 > 7$

3. $9w \leq 27$

4. $8x \geq 20$

5. $\frac{s}{6} < 4$

6. $2a > -42$

7. For the inequality $m - 6 > 1$, could m be equal to 7?

8. For the inequality $\frac{1}{2}r \leq 4$, could r equal $\frac{1}{2}$?

9. For the inequality $d + 7 \leq 2$, could d be -6?

10. For $2f < 12$, could f be 4?

ANSWERS ARE ON PAGE 391.

SOLVING LONGER INEQUALITIES

You can solve long inequalities just as you solve long equations. Use inverse operations to simplify the inequalities and remember to take care of addition or subtraction first.

EXAMPLE   Solve $9x - 7 > 11$.

$$(1)\ 9x - 7 > 11 \qquad (2)\ \frac{9x}{9} > \frac{18}{9}$$
$$\underline{+7\quad +7}$$
$$9x \quad\ > 18 \qquad\qquad \boldsymbol{x > 2}$$

STEP 1   Add 7 to both sides of the inequality.
STEP 2   Divide both sides by 9. The solution is $\boldsymbol{x > 2}$.

EXERCISE 8

Directions: Solve each inequality.

1. $5m - 4 \leq 26$

2. $3n + 2 > 14$

3. $4p - 3 < 15$

4. $\frac{x}{3} + 5 \geq 7$

5. $7c - 3 \leq 5c + 15$

6. $8y + 1 < y + 22$

7. $3(s - 2) \geq 2s + 10$

8. $5(a + 3) < 2(a - 6)$

ANSWERS ARE ON PAGE 392.

MULTIPLYING AND DIVIDING MONOMIALS

A *monomial* is an algebraic expression with only one term. A term is a letter, a number, or a group of letters and numbers not separated by plus or minus signs. Three examples of monomials are $-5x$, $2a^2$, and $64y$.

So far in this book you have added and subtracted monomials. You already know that $2x + 3x = 5x$ and that $14a - a = 13a$.

When you multiply or divide monomials, the power of the same letters changes. Look at the following rules and examples.

RULE FOR MULTIPLYING MONOMIALS

For the numbers, follow the rules for multiplying signed numbers. For like letters, *add* the exponents.

EXAMPLE 1 Find $5x \cdot 3x$.

$$5x \cdot 3x = 15x^{1+1} = 15x^2$$

SOLUTION Multiply the numbers and add the exponents of the letters.

> **TIP:** Any letter written without an exponent is understood to be to the first power.

EXAMPLE 2 Find $(-3a^2c)(4a^3c^4)$.

$$(-3a^2c)(4a^3c^4) = -12a^{2+3}\,c^{1+4} = -12a^5c^5$$

SOLUTION Multiply -3 and 4. Add the exponents of a ($2 + 3 = 5$). Add the exponents of c ($1 + 4 = 5$).

RULE FOR DIVIDING MONOMIALS

Follow the rules for dividing signed numbers and *subtract* the exponents of like letters.

EXAMPLE 3 Find $\dfrac{27y^4z^2}{3y^2z}$

$$9y^{4-2}z^{2-1} = 9y^2z$$

SOLUTION Divide 27 by 3. Subtract the exponent of the bottom y from the exponent of the top y ($4 - 2 = 2$). Then subtract the exponent of the bottom z from the exponent of the top z ($2 - 1 = 1$).

EXERCISE 9

Directions: Solve each problem.

1. $4x \cdot 3x =$

6. $10x \cdot \frac{1}{2}x =$

2. $(-4a^2)(-6a^3) =$

7. $\frac{4x^2 y}{xy} =$

3. $m^3 \cdot m^4 =$

8. $\frac{6x^4 y^4}{6x^2 y} =$

4. $a^2 \cdot a =$

9. $\frac{18b^3x^2}{2b^2x^2} =$

5. $(5b^2)(b^4) =$

10. $\frac{12t^3v^4}{6t^2v^3} =$

ANSWERS ARE ON PAGE 392.

FACTORING

Factors are numbers or algebraic terms that, when multiplied together, give a product. For example, the numbers 2 and 5 are factors of 10 because $2 \times 5 = 10$.

The fraction $\frac{1}{2}$ is also a factor of 10. However, we usually use only *whole* number factors (other than the number 1) when factoring a number. A **prime number** is a number that can be divided by only itself and the number one. For example, 5 is a prime number because no whole number other than 5 or 1 divides into it evenly. But 6 is not a prime number, because both 2 and 3 divide into it evenly. **Prime factors** are prime numbers that, when multiplied, yield a product.

EXAMPLE 1 Find the prime factors of 8.

$$8 = \quad 4 \times 2$$

$$8 = 2 \times 2 \times 2$$

STEP 1 Find two whole numbers that multiply together to give 8.

$$4 \times 2 = 8$$

STEP 2 Check to see whether there are prime factors of either 4 or 2. $4 = 2 \times 2$. Therefore, the prime factors of 8 are **2 × 2 × 2**.

EXAMPLE 2   Find the prime factors of 12.

12 =   6 × 2

12 = 3 × 2 × 2

STEP 1   Find two whole numbers that multiply together to give 12.
6 × 2 = 12

STEP 2   Check to see whether there are prime factors of either 6 or 2. 6 = 3 × 2.
The prime factors of 12 are **3 × 2 × 2**.

EXERCISE 10

Directions: Write each of the following whole numbers as a product of prime factors.

1. 9   **5.** 24

2. 10   **6.** 30

3. 18   **7.** 40

4. 20   **8.** 50

ANSWERS ARE ON PAGE 392.

FACTORING WITH VARIABLES

The expression $10x + 6$ has two terms. A ***term*** is a letter, a number, or a group of letters and numbers not separated by plus or minus signs. In many expressions with two terms you can factor out a whole number.

To factor out a whole number, find a number that divides evenly into each term of an expression. Write the number that divides evenly into each term on the outside of a set of parentheses. The result of dividing each term by that number goes inside the parentheses.

EXAMPLE   Factor the expression $10x + 6$.

$10x + 6 = 2(5x + 3)$

SOLUTION   Look for a number that divides evenly into both $10x$ and 6. The number 2 divides evenly into both terms. Write 2 outside a set of parentheses. Write the result of dividing both $10x$ and 6 by 2 on the inside of the parentheses: **2(5x + 3)**.

EXERCISE 11

Directions: Factor a whole number out of each of the following expressions. Then write the factored expression.

1. $4n + 4$

5. $6b + 8$

2. $3p - 6$

6. $6f - 30$

3. $15a - 10$

7. $36y - 9$

4. $14c + 35$

8. $16k + 56$

ANSWERS ARE ON PAGE 392.

FACTORING OUT THE VARIABLE

The expression $x^2 - 4x$ has two terms. There is no whole number other than the number 1 that divides evenly into both terms. However, you can divide both terms by x. As you know from your work with monomials, when you divide x^2 by x, you subtract exponents to get x. When you divide x by x, you get 1.

To factor out a letter from an algebraic expression, divide each term in the expression by the letter that can be found in each term.

EXAMPLE 1 Factor the expression $x^2 - 4x$.

$$x^2 - 4x = x(x - 4)$$

SOLUTION Divide each term by the letter that is in each term: x divided into x^2 is x. x divided into $-4x$ is -4.

EXAMPLE 2 Factor the expression $m^2 - m$.

$$m^2 - m = m(m - 1)$$

SOLUTION Divide each term by the letter m: m divided into m^2 is m, and m divided into m is 1.

EXERCISE 12

Directions: Factor out a letter from each of the following expressions.

1. $c^2 + 8c$

5. $d^2 + 4d$

2. $y^2 - 5y$

6. $n^2 - 8n$

3. $m^2 + 3m$

7. $p^2 - 2p$

4. $a^2 - a$

8. $s^2 + 9s$

ANSWERS ARE ON PAGE 392.

SIMPLIFYING SQUARE ROOTS

There is another useful application of factoring that you may use on the GED. Remember that when you learned to find square roots earlier in this book, all the problems had exact solutions. For example, $\sqrt{81} = 9$ and $\sqrt{144} = 12$. Numbers like 81 and 144 are called **_perfect squares_** because their square roots are whole numbers.

Most numbers do not have whole number square roots. For many numbers, however, you can use factoring to simplify the square root.

RULE FOR SIMPLIFYING SQUARE ROOTS

1. Try to find a factor for the number that is a perfect square.

2. Write the square root of the perfect square outside the $\sqrt{}$ sign and leave the other factor inside the $\sqrt{}$ sign.

EXAMPLE 1 Simplify the square root of 200.

$$\sqrt{200} = \sqrt{100 \cdot 2} = \mathbf{10\sqrt{2}}$$

STEP 1 Think about the factors of 200. There are many: 2, 4, 5, 20, and so on. The combination of factors that includes the largest perfect square is 100 and 2. $\sqrt{200}$ is equal to $\sqrt{100}$ multiplied by $\sqrt{2}$.

STEP 2 Put the whole number square root of 100 outside the $\sqrt{}$ sign. Leave 2 inside the $\sqrt{}$ sign, because there is no whole number square root of 2.

Note: The answer $10\sqrt{2}$ may look strange. The square root of 2 is a mixed decimal that is approximately equal to 1.41. This means that the square root of 200 is approximately 10×1.41, or 14.1. If we multiply 14.1 by 14.1 we get:

$$
\begin{array}{r}
14.1 \\
\times\ 14.1 \\
\hline
14\ 1 \\
564 \\
141 \\
\hline
198.81, \quad \text{which is approximately 200.}
\end{array}
$$

EXAMPLE 2 Simplify $\sqrt{24}$.

$$\sqrt{24} = \sqrt{4} \times \sqrt{6} = \mathbf{2\sqrt{6}}$$

STEP 1 Think of the factors of 24. The combination that includes a perfect square is 4 and 6, so $\sqrt{24}$ is equal to $\sqrt{4}$ multiplied by $\sqrt{6}$.

STEP 2 Write the whole number square root of 4 outside the $\sqrt{}$ sign. Leave 6 inside the $\sqrt{}$ sign.

EXERCISE 13

Directions: Simplify each of the following square roots.

1. $\sqrt{27}$ **5.** $\sqrt{48}$

2. $\sqrt{8}$ **6.** $\sqrt{50}$

3. $\sqrt{20}$ **7.** $\sqrt{12}$

4. $\sqrt{150}$ **8.** $\sqrt{32}$

ANSWERS ARE ON PAGES 392–393.

USING ALGEBRA TO SOLVE GEOMETRY PROBLEMS

Now that you know how to multiply monomials and simplify square roots, you are ready to solve some of the more complex geometry problems that may appear on the GED Test. Look at the next examples carefully to see how to substitute algebraic expressions into geometry formulas.

EXAMPLE 1 The area of a rectangle is 162 sq in. The length of the rectangle is twice as long as the width. Find the width of the rectangle.

(1) width $= x$ **(2)** $A = lw$ **(3)** $\frac{162}{2} = \frac{2x^2}{2}$

length $= 2x$ $162 = 2x \cdot x$ $81 = x^2$

$162 = 2x^2$ $\sqrt{81} = x$

$9 = x$

STEP 1 Let x stand for the width and $2x$ stand for the length.
STEP 2 Substitute 162 for A, $2x$ for l, and x for w in the formula for the area of a rectangle.
STEP 3 Then solve the equation. Notice that the value of x is the square root of 81. The solution is $x = $ **9 inches**.

EXAMPLE 2 The perimeter of a rectangle is 74. The length of the rectangle is 5 more than the width. Find the length of the rectangle.

(1) width $= w$ **(2)** $P = 2l + 2w$

length $= w + 5$ $74 = 2(w + 5) + 2w$

(3) $74 = 2w + 10 + 2w$ **(4)** $w + 5 =$
$74 = 4w + 10$ $16 + 5 = 21$
$\frac{-10 \qquad -10}{64 = 4w}$
$\frac{64}{4} = \frac{4w}{4}$
$16 = w$

STEP 1 Let w stand for the width and $w + 5$ for the length.

STEP 2 Substitute 74 for P and $(w + 5)$ for l in the formula for the perimeter of a rectangle.

STEP 3 Solve the equation. The solution for w is 16.

STEP 4 Substitute 16 for w in the expression $w + 5$ to find the length of the rectangle. The length is **21**.

Another way to solve complex geometry problems is to substitute answer choices into formulas.

EXAMPLE 3 The perimeter of a rectangle is 56 feet. The length is three times the width. Find the width of the rectangle in feet.

(1) 5   **(2)** 7   **(3)** 12   **(4)** 14

SOLUTION Substitute each answer choice into the formula $P = 2l + 2w$.

For choice **(1)**, width = 5 and length = $3 \times 5 = 15$.

$$P = 2(15) + 2(5) = 30 + 10 = 40 \text{ ft}$$

For choice **(2)**, width = 7 and length = $3 \times 7 = 21$.

$$P = 2(21) + 2(7) = 42 + 14 = 56 \text{ ft}$$

Choice **(2) 7** is correct.

EXERCISE 14

Directions: Solve each problem.

1. The area of a rectangle is 32 square feet. The width is half of the length. Find the length.

2. The area of a triangle is 16 square inches. The height of the triangle is half of the base. Find the height of the triangle.

3. A rectangle has an area of 96. The width is $\frac{2}{3}$ of the length. Find the length.

4. A rectangle has an area of 98 square meters. The length is twice the width. Find the measurement of the length.

5. A rectangle has a perimeter of 48 feet. The length is twice the width. Find the measurement of the length.

6. A triangle has an area of 24. The base is three times the height. Find the base.

    (1) 4
    (2) 6
    (3) 8
    (4) 12
    (5) 16

7. A rectangle has a perimeter of 60 inches. The ratio of the width to the length is 2:3. Find the length in inches. (*Hint:* Let 2*x* stand for the width.)

   (1) 12
   (2) 18
   (3) 24
   (4) 30
   (5) 36

8. The area of the triangle at the right is 216. The ratio of *AB* to *AC* is 3:4. Find the length of *AB*.

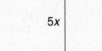

   (1) 36
   (2) 30
   (3) 24
   (4) 18
   (5) 12

9. For the rectangle at the right the ratio of *WX* to *WZ* is 5:6. The perimeter of the rectangle is 110 feet. Find the length in feet of *WZ*.

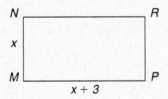

   (1) 20
   (2) 25
   (3) 30
   (4) 40
   (5) 50

10. The perimeter of the rectangle at the right is 34 feet. *MP* is 3 feet longer than *MN*. Find the measurement in feet of *MN*.

   (1) 21
   (2) 14
   (3) 12
   (4) 10
   (5) 7

ANSWERS ARE ON PAGE 393.

RECTANGULAR COORDINATES

A graph called the ***rectangular coordinate system*** is a useful method for showing many algebraic relationships. The rectangular coordinate system is a flat surface or plane. The plane is divided by a horizontal line called the ***x-axis*** and a vertical line called the ***y-axis***. Each of these two lines is simply a number line like the ones you saw earlier. The lines intersect at the number 0, which is called the ***origin***.

A point anywhere on the graph can be identified by a pair of numbers called the ***coordinates*** of the point. The coordinates are written inside parentheses in the order (*x, y*). The *x*-coordinate has a positive value for points to the right of the *y*-axis and a negative value for points to the left of the *y*-axis. The *y*-coordinate has a positive value for points above the *x*-axis and a negative value for points below the *x*-axis.

The illustration at the right shows a rectangular coordinate system with one point labeled (+6, +4). These coordinates mean that the point is 6 units to the right of the *y*-axis and 4 units above the *x*-axis.

Use the figure below for Examples 1 through 4.

EXAMPLE 1 What are the coordinates of point *A?*

SOLUTION First tell how far point *A* is to the right of the *y*-axis. It is 4 units to the right, or +4. This is the *x*-coordinate. Then tell how far point *A* is above the *x*-axis. It is 3 points above, or +3. This is the *y*-coordinate. The coordinates are **(4, 3)**.

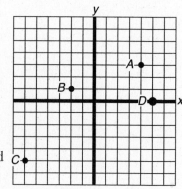

EXAMPLE 2 What are the coordinates of point *B?*

SOLUTION Point *B* is 2 units to the left of the *y*-axis, or −2, and one unit above the *x*-axis, or +1. The coordinates are **(−2, 1)**.

EXAMPLE 3 What are the coordinates of point *C?*

SOLUTION Point *C* is 6 units to the left of the *y*-axis, or −6, and 5 units below the *x*-axis, or −5. The coordinates are **(−6, −5)**.

EXAMPLE 4 What are the coordinates of point *D?*

SOLUTION Point *D* is 5 units to the right of the *y*-axis, or +5. It is neither above nor below the *x*-axis. The coordinates are **(5, 0)**.

EXERCISE 15

Directions: Solve the following problems.

1. Write the coordinates for each point shown on the rectangular coordinate system below.

   Point *A* = (   )

   Point *B* = (   )

   Point *C* = (   )

   Point *D* = (   )

   Point *E* = (   )

   Point *F* = (   )

   Point *G* = (   )

   Point *H* = (   )

   Point *I* = (   )

   Point *J* = (   )

   Point *K* = (   )

   Point *L* = (   )

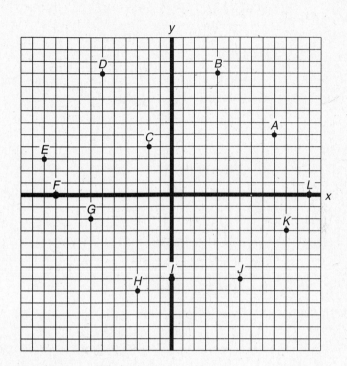

2. Mark the following points on the coordinate system below.

   Point *A* = (+6, +4)

   Point *B* = (−5, +3)

   Point *C* = (−2, −7)

   Point *D* = (+1, −6)

   Point *E* = (−8, 0)

   Point *F* = (+3, 0)

   Point *G* = (0, −4)

   Point *H* = (0, +7)

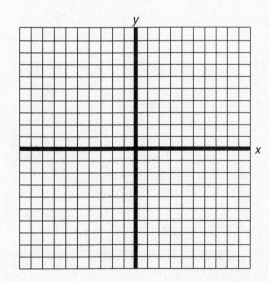

ANSWERS ARE ON PAGES 393–394.

DISTANCES ON THE RECTANGULAR COORDINATE SYSTEM

Distance on the rectangular coordinate system is not measured in inches, feet, and meters as you used in geometry. Instead it is measured in units of whole numbers as you will see in this section. On the GED you may be asked to find the distance between two points on the rectangular coordinate system, or plane as it is sometimes called.

In some cases you can simply count the number of spaces between two points.

EXAMPLE 1 What is the distance from *A* to *B* on the graph at the right?

4 + 1 = **5**

SOLUTION *A* is 4 units above the *x*-axis, and *B* is 1 unit below. The distance between them is the total: 4 + 1 = 5.

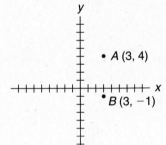

EXAMPLE 2 What is the distance from *C* to *D* on the graph at the right?

2 + 5 = **7**

SOLUTION *C* is 2 units to the left of the *y*-axis, and *D* is 5 units to the right. The distance between them is 2+5 = 7.

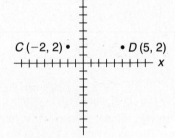

TIP: Distance is *always* positive regardless of the signs of the coordinates.

The distance between *S* and *T* in the figure at the right is more complicated. The distance is the hypotenuse of a right triangle, where the legs are shown by the two dotted lines. There is a special formula for finding the distance between any two points on the rectangular coordinate system. This formula looks complicated, but it is based on the Pythagorean theorem that you learned on page 268.

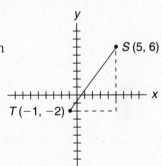

FORMULA FOR DISTANCE BETWEEN TWO POINTS IN A PLANE

$d = \sqrt{(x_2 - x_1)^2 + (y_2 - y_1)^2}$ where (x_1, y_1) and (x_2, y_2) are two points in the plane.

Point T on the last graph has the coordinates $(-1, -2)$. This is (x_1, y_1) in the formula. Point S has the coordinates $(5, 6)$. This is (x_2, y_2) in the formula.

It is important to realize that the small numbers 1 and 2 below a variable are not involved in any of your computations. They are called **subscripts** and are used for labels and identification only.

EXAMPLE 3 Find the distance from S to T in the preceding figure.

$$d = \sqrt{(x_2 - x_1)^2 + (y_2 - y_1)^2}$$

$$d = \sqrt{[5 - (-1)]^2 + [6 - (-2)]^2}$$

$$d = \sqrt{(5 + 1)^2 + (6 + 2)^2}$$

$$d = \sqrt{6^2 + 8^2}$$

$$d = \sqrt{36 + 64}$$

$$d = \sqrt{100}$$

$$d = \mathbf{10}$$

SOLUTION Substitute 5 for x_2, -1 for x_1, 6 for y_2, and -2 for y_1 in the formula for the distance between two points. Notice how the parentheses are used to show that -1 and -2 are being subtracted. The distance between S and T is 10.

EXERCISE 16

Directions: Solve each problem. Use the formula $d = \sqrt{(x_2 - x_1)^2 + (y_2 - y_1)^2}$ for the distance between two points on a plane when necessary. Approximate if your answer is not a perfect square. Use the graph below for questions 1 and 2.

1. What is the distance from point A to point C?

2. What is the distance from B to C?

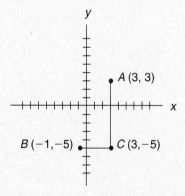

Directions: Use the graph at the right for questions 3 and 4.

3. Find the distance from E to F.

4. What is the distance from D to F?

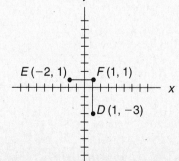

5. What is the distance from point *G* to point *H* in the graph at the right?

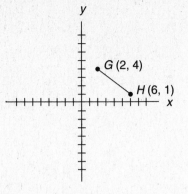

6. Find the distance from *I* to *J* in the graph at the right.

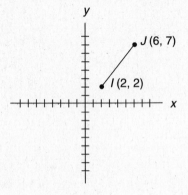

7. What is the distance from point *K* to point *L* on the graph at the right?

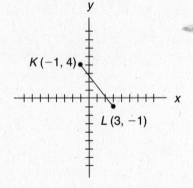

8. What is the distance from *M* to *N* on the graph at the right?

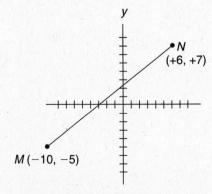

ANSWERS ARE ON PAGE 394.

LINEAR EQUATIONS

The equation $y = x + 2$ has many solutions. If you select values for x, you can find the corresponding values for y by substituting and solving the equation.

Suppose you let $x = 1, 3$, and -2 for the equation $y = x + 2$:

If $x = 1$, then $y = 1 + 2 = 3$.
If $x = 3$, then $y = 3 + 2 = 5$.
If $x = -2$, then $y = -2 + 2 = 0$.

The three values of x and their corresponding values of y are the coordinates for three points on the rectangular coordinate plane: (1, 3) (3, 5), and (−2, 0).

The graph at the right shows these three points. Notice that the points lie in a straight line. The coordinates of any point on the line are solutions to the equation $y = x + 2$. This type of equation is called a ***linear equation*** because its graph forms a straight line.

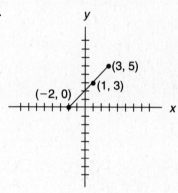

EXAMPLE 1 Make a graph of the equation
$y = 2x - 1$. Let $x = 2, 5$, and -1.
If $x = 2$, then $y = 2(2) - 1$
                       $= 4 - 1$
                       $= 3$
If $x = 5$, then $y = 2(5) - 1$
                       $= 10 - 1$
                       $= 9$
If $x = -1$, then $y = 2(-1) - 1$
                       $= -2 - 1$
                       $= -3$

x	y
2	3
5	9
−1	−3

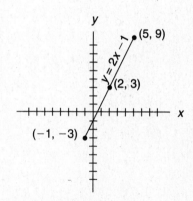

STEP 1 Substitute each value of x into the equation to find the corresponding value of y.
STEP 2 Make a table of the x and y values.
STEP 3 Put these points on the coordinate plane and connect them with a straight line.

On the GED you will not have to make a graph of an equation, but you may need to know whether certain points lie on the line of an equation.

To find out whether a point is on the graph of an equation, substitute the x-coordinate of the point into the equation. If the solution to the equation is the same as the y-coordinate, then the point is on the graph of the equation.

EXAMPLE 2 Is the point (2, 3) on the graph of $y = 2x - 1$?

$y = 2x - 1$

$y = 2(2) - 1 = 4 - 1 = 3$

SOLUTION Substitute 2 for x in $y = 2x - 1$. This gives y the value of 3. Therefore point $(2, 3)$ is on the graph of $y = 2x - 1$.

EXAMPLE 3 Is the point $(-2, -4)$ on the graph of the equation $y = 2x - 1$?

$$y = 2x - 1$$

$$y = 2(-2) - 1 = -4 - 1 = -5$$

SOLUTION Substitute -2 for x in $y = 2x - 1$. This gives y the value of -5. Point $(-2, -4)$ is not on the graph of $y = 2x - 1$.

EXERCISE 17

Directions: For the equations in problems 1–4, fill in the table for each given value of x. Then put the points on the graph and connect them.

1. $y = x + 3$

x	y
1	
4	
−3	

3. $y = \frac{x}{3} + 1$

x	y
6	
3	
−3	

2. $y = 2x - 3$

x	y
5	
3	
0	

4. $y = -x + 5$

x	y
8	
5	
1	

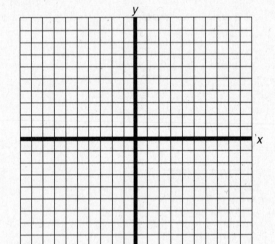

5. Is the point $(2, 5)$ on the graph of the equation $y = 3x - 1$?

6. Is the point $(3, 4)$ on the graph of the equation $y = 4x - 5$?

7. Is the point $(6, 7)$ on the graph of the equation $y = \frac{x}{2} + 4$?

8. Is the point $(3, 2)$ on the graph of the equation $y = \frac{2}{3}x + 1$?

9. Is the point $(8, -5)$ on the graph of the equation $y = -x + 3$?

10. Is the point $(6, -2)$ on the graph of the equation $y = \frac{-x}{2} + 1$?

ANSWERS ARE ON PAGES 394–395.

SLOPE AND INTERCEPTS

Slope is a measure of how "steep" a line is. Slope tells something about what a linear equation looks like.

- A line that goes up from left to right has a positive slope.

- A line that goes down from left to right has a negative slope.

- A horizontal line has a zero slope.

- A vertical line has an undefined slope. It has no meaning.

Look at the graphs of the two linear equations at the right. The line for the equation $y = \frac{3}{2}x + 3$ has a positive slope. It rises from left to right. The line for the equation $y = -x - 1$ has a negative slope. It goes down from left to right.

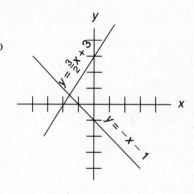

Look at the graphs of the two linear equations at the right. The line for the equation $y = -2$ has a zero slope. The line for the equation $x = 2$ has an undefined slope.

Positive and negative slopes have exact values. A high value for a slope means the line is very steep. To find the exact value of the slope of a line, substitute values into the following formula.

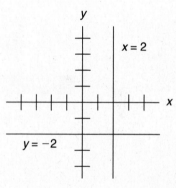

SLOPE OF A LINE

$\text{slope} = \dfrac{y_2 - y_1}{x_2 - x_1}$ where (x_1, y_1) and (x_2, y_2) are the coordinates of two points on the graph of a linear equation.

In words this formula means: Divide the difference between two y-values by the difference between two x-values.

EXAMPLE 1 What is the slope of a line that passes through the points (2, 5) and (6, 13)?

$$\text{slope} = \frac{13 - 5}{6 - 2} = \frac{8}{4} = 2$$

SOLUTION Subtract the y-values, $13 - 5 = 8$, and subtract the x-values, $6 - 2 = 4$. Then divide 8 by 4. The slope is **+2**.

An ***intercept*** tells where a line crosses an axis. On the graph at the right the line labeled *m* crosses the *y*-axis at +3. The coordinates of the *y*-intercept are (0, 3). The line crosses the *x*-axis at −2. The coordinates of the *x*-intercept are (−2, 0).

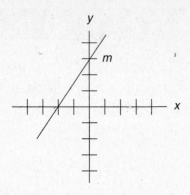

FINDING THE *Y*-INTERCEPT

To find the *y*-intercept of a linear equation, substitute 0 for *x* and solve for *y*.

EXAMPLE 2 What is the *y*-intercept of the equation $y = 4x - 5$?

$$y = 4x - 5$$
$$y = 4(0) - 5$$
$$= 0 - 5$$
$$= -5$$

SOLUTION Replace *x* with 0 and solve for *y* in $y = 4x - 5$. The coordinates of the *y*-intercept are **(0, −5)**.

FINDING THE *X*-INTERCEPT

To find the *x*-intercept of a linear equation, substitute 0 for *y* and solve for *x*.

EXAMPLE 3 What is the *x*-intercept of the equation $y = 3x - 6$?

$$
\begin{aligned}
y &= 3x - 6 \\
0 &= 3x - 6 \\
+6 & +6 \\
\hline
6 &= 3x \\
2 &= x
\end{aligned}
$$

SOLUTION Replace *y* with 0 and solve for *x* in $y = 3x - 6$. The coordinates of the *x*-intercept are **(2, 0)**.

EXERCISE 18

Directions: Solve each problem.

1. Fill in each blank with the letter that corresponds to a line on the graph at the right.

   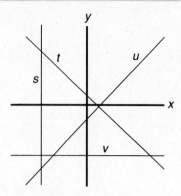

   a. The slope of line _____ is positive.

   b. The slope of line _____ is negative.

   c. The slope of line _____ is zero.

   d. The slope of line _____ is undefined.

2. What is the slope of a line that passes through both of the following points?

   a. (3, 2) and (5, 8)

   b. (2, 5) and (10, 9)

   c. (3, 6) and (5, 2)

   d. (2, 4) and (−7, 10)

   e. (3, −3) and (−1, 5)

3. Write the coordinates for the *x*-intercept and the *y*-intercept for each of the following equations.

	x-intercept	*y*-intercept
a. $y = 3x - 9$		
b. $y = x - 6$		
c. $y = \frac{x}{2} + 5$		
d. $y = \frac{3}{4}x + 12$		
e. $y = 2x - 1$		

ANSWERS ARE ON PAGE 395.

QUADRATIC EQUATIONS

One type of problem that you may see on the GED Mathematics Test is the quadratic equation. A ***quadratic equation*** is an equation where the unknown is raised to the second power.

You have already used equations that are raised to the second power. The Pythagorean theorem and the formula for the distance between two points on the rectangular coordinate plane are examples.

Quadratic equations have two solutions. Think about the example $x^2 = 9$. Both +3 and −3 are solutions to this equation. $(+3)(+3) = +9$ and $(−3)(−3) = 9$. With the Pythagorean theorem and the distance between two points, we were interested in the positive solutions only.

There are different ways to solve a quadratic equation, and there is not space in this book to discuss each one. To succeed on problems using quadratics, you can use the answer solutions given with the problem. Look at the following example to see how this is done.

EXAMPLE Which of the following expresses the solutions to

$x^2 - 8x + 12 = 0$?

(1) $x = 3$ and $x = 4$

(2) $x = 6$ and $x = 2$

(3) $x = -3$ and $x = 4$

(4) $x = 6$ and $x = -2$

(5) $x = -6$ and $x = -2$

STEP 1 Try the solutions in answer choice **(1)**. First substitute 3 into the equation.

$x^2 - 8x + 12 = 0$

$3^2 - 8(3) + 12 = 0$

$9 - 24 + 12 = 0$

$- 24 + 21 = 0$ **Incorrect**

Since $-24 + 21$ does not equal 0, answer choice **(1)** is incorrect.

STEP 2 Try the solutions in answer choice **(2)**. First substitute 6 into the equation.

$x^2 - 8x + 12 = 0$

$6^2 - 8(6) + 12 = 0$

$36 - 48 + 12 = 0$

$- 48 + 48 = 0$ **Correct**

Since $-48 + 48 = 0$, you know that the first solution, $x = 6$, in answer choice **(2)** is correct. Now substitute the other value, $x = 2$, into the equation.

$x^2 - 8x + 12 = 0$

$2^2 - 8(2) + 12 = 0$

$4 - 16 + 12 = 0$

$- 16 + 16 = 0$ **Correct**

Since $-16 + 16 = 0$, you know that $x = 2$ is also a solution to the equation. This means that answer choice **(2)** is correct.

For more practice, try substituting the other answer choices for the example into the equation.

TIP: Remember that you must check *both* values for each solution.

EXERCISE 19

Directions: For these problems, choose the correct solution to each quadratic equation.

1. $x^2 - 14x + 48 = 0$
  (1) $x = 4$ and $x = 12$
  (2) $x = 3$ and $x = -16$
  (3) $x = 6$ and $x = 8$
  (4) $x = 2$ and $x = -24$

2. $x^2 - 3x - 10 = 0$
  (1) $x = 5$ and $x = -2$
  (2) $x = 10$ and $x = 1$
  (3) $x = 2$ and $x = -5$
  (4) $x = -10$ and $x = -1$

3. $x^2 - x - 12 = 0$
  (1) $x = 2$ and $x = 6$
  (2) $x = 12$ and $x = -1$
  (3) $x = -4$ and $x = 3$
  (4) $x = 4$ and $x = -3$

4. $x^2 - 9x + 8 = 0$
  (1) $x = 8$ and $x = 1$
  (2) $x = 4$ and $x = -2$
  (3) $x = -4$ and $x = 2$
  (4) $x = -8$ and $x = 1$

5. $x^2 - 15x + 44 = 0$
  (1) $x = 2$ and $x = 22$
  (2) $x = 4$ and $x = 11$
  (3) $x = -4$ and $x = 11$
  (4) $x = 44$ and $x = -1$

6. $x^2 + 11x + 18 = 0$
  (1) $x = 6$ and $x = -3$
  (2) $x = -1$ and $x = 18$
  (3) $x = -9$ and $x = -2$
  (4) $x = -6$ and $x = 3$

ANSWERS ARE ON PAGE 396.

SCIENTIFIC NOTATION

Scientists and mathematicians often use a shortened method of writing numbers called ***scientific notation***. This method of expressing numbers uses the number 10 and an exponent to simplify large or small numbers.

Before you practice scientific notation, study the following chart. This chart lists some powers of ten with both positive *and* negative exponents. Negative exponents indicate numbers smaller than one, or fractional powers of ten. For instance, $10^{-1} = \frac{1}{10} = .1$. As you can see, the negative sign indicates a reciprocal. (The reciprocal of 10 is $\frac{1}{10}$.)

$$10^0 = 1$$

$$10^1 = 10 \qquad\qquad 10^{-1} = \frac{1}{10} = .1$$

$$10^2 = 100 \qquad\qquad 10^{-2} = \frac{1}{100} = .01$$

$$10^3 = 1000 \qquad\qquad 10^{-3} = \frac{1}{1000} = .001$$

$$10^4 = 10,000 \qquad\qquad 10^{-4} = \frac{1}{10,000} = .0001$$

$$10^5 = 100,000 \qquad\qquad 10^{-5} = \frac{1}{100,000} = .00001$$

RULES FOR WRITING NUMBERS IN SCIENTIFIC NOTATION

1. Ignore the zeros in the number and represent it as a whole number or mixed decimal between 1 and 10.

2. Next to this number, write a multiplication sign and 10 to the correct power, which will be either positive or negative. To find the correct power, count the number of places the decimal point must move to get from the original number to the number between one and ten. If the point must move to the left, use a positive exponent. If the point must move to the right, use a negative exponent.

EXAMPLE 1   Express the number 45,000,000 in scientific notation.

STEP 1   Take off the zeros and represent 45,000,000 as a whole number or mixed decimal between 1 and 10.

A decimal point should be inserted between 4 and 5 to get 4.5.

STEP 2   Find the power of ten that, if multiplied by 4.5, equals 45,000,000.

To find the correct power, count the number of places the decimal point must move to get from 45,000,000 to 4.5. It must move 7 places to the left.

So $45,000,000 = \mathbf{4.5 \times 10^7}$.

7 places left

EXAMPLE 2   Express .0024 in scientific notation.

STEP 1   Represent the number as a number between 1 and 10.

The decimal point should be inserted between 2 and 4 to get 2.4.

STEP 2   Set up a multiplication equation between 2.4 and the correct power of ten.

$.0024 = \mathbf{2.4 \times 10^{-3}}$

3 places right

EXERCISE 20

Directions: For problems 1–9, express each number in scientific notation.

1. 700

2. .0446

3. 95,000,000

4. .00066

5. 17,000

6. 850,000

7. .00009

8. 6,930,000

9. .0000033

Directions: For problems 10–18, the numbers are already written in scientific notation. Find the actual value that each represents.

10. 2.74×10^3

11. 9.1×10^{-2}

12. 4.882×10^4

13. 1.98×10^{-5}

14. 5.2×10^0

15. 4.9×10^6

16. 1.1×10^{-6}

17. 3.25×10^5

18. 8.4×10^{-8}

ANSWERS ARE ON PAGE 396.

GED Practice
EXERCISE 21

Directions: Choose the best answer to each problem.

1. By some estimates the population of the world in the year 2010 will be 7,240,000,000. Which of the following represents this number?

(1) 7.24×10^6
(2) 7.24×10^9
(3) 7.24×10^{10}
(4) 724×10
(5) 724×10^3

2. One minute equals .0000019 year. Which of the following represents this decimal?

(1) 1.9×10^4
(2) 1.9×10^6
(3) 1.9×10^{-4}
(4) 1.9×10^{-6}
(5) 1.9×10^{-8}

ANSWERS ARE ON PAGE 396.

Post-Test

The test that follows will give you a chance to see if you are prepared for the GED Mathematics Test. Like the GED Math Test, this test contains 56 multiple-choice questions.

Answer every question. Use the formulas on page 274 when necessary. When you are finished, check your answers. The evaluation chart at the end of the answers will help you determine which areas to review before you take the GED Math Test.

POST-TEST ANSWER GRID

1 ① ② ③ ④ ⑤	20 ① ② ③ ④ ⑤	39 ① ② ③ ④ ⑤
2 ① ② ③ ④ ⑤	21 ① ② ③ ④ ⑤	40 ① ② ③ ④ ⑤
3 ① ② ③ ④ ⑤	22 ① ② ③ ④ ⑤	41 ① ② ③ ④ ⑤
4 ① ② ③ ④ ⑤	23 ① ② ③ ④ ⑤	42 ① ② ③ ④ ⑤
5 ① ② ③ ④ ⑤	24 ① ② ③ ④ ⑤	43 ① ② ③ ④ ⑤
6 ① ② ③ ④ ⑤	25 ① ② ③ ④ ⑤	44 ① ② ③ ④ ⑤
7 ① ② ③ ④ ⑤	26 ① ② ③ ④ ⑤	45 ① ② ③ ④ ⑤
8 ① ② ③ ④ ⑤	27 ① ② ③ ④ ⑤	46 ① ② ③ ④ ⑤
9 ① ② ③ ④ ⑤	28 ① ② ③ ④ ⑤	47 ③ ④ ⑤
10 ① ② ③ ④ ⑤	29 ① ② ③ ④ ⑤	48 ① ② ③ ④ ⑤
11 ① ② ③ ④ ⑤	30 ① ② ③ ④ ⑤	49 ① ② ③ ④ ⑤
12 ① ② ③ ④ ⑤	31 ① ② ③ ④ ⑤	50 ① ② ③ ④ ⑤
13 ① ② ③ ④ ⑤	32 ① ② ③ ④ ⑤	51 ① ② ③ ④ ⑤
14 ① ② ③ ④ ⑤	33 ① ② ③ ④ ⑤	52 ① ② ③ ④ ⑤
15 ① ② ③ ④ ⑤	34 ① ② ③ ④ ⑤	53 ① ② ③ ④ ⑤
16 ① ② ③ ④ ⑤	35 ① ② ③ ④ ⑤	54 ① ② ③ ④ ⑤
17 ① ② ③ ④ ⑤	36 ① ② ③ ④ ⑤	55 ① ② ③ ④ ⑤
18 ① ② ③ ④ ⑤	37 ① ② ③ ④ ⑤	56 ① ② ③ ④ ⑤
19 ① ② ③ ④ ⑤	38 ① ② ③ ④ ⑤	

Directions: Solve the problems.

1. What is the perimeter in meters of the figure below?

(1) 14
(2) 28
(3) 29
(4) 47.04
(5) 48

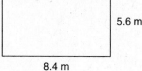

5.6 m

8.4 m

2. In the figure below, ∠AOB is a right angle. Find the measurement of ∠COD.

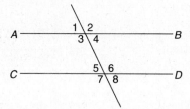

B

C

45°

A

O

D

(1) 25°
(2) 35°
(3) 45°
(4) 55°
(5) Not enough information is given.

3. In the figure below, *AB* is parallel to *CD,* and ∠2 = 119°. Find ∠8.

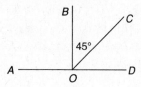

A   1 2   B
                      3 4

C   5 6   D
                      7 8

(1) 71°
(2) 61°
(3) 29°
(4) 19°
(5) 9°

4. In the tool shop at Acme, Inc., 35 employees work 40 hours a week at an average wage of $8 an hour. Which of the following tells the total weekly payroll for the employees in the tool shop at Acme?

(1) $\dfrac{35 \times 40}{8}$
(2) 35 × 40 × 8
(3) 35 + 40 × 8
(4) 35(40 + 8)
(5) 8(35 + 40)

5. In △XYZ ∠X = 65° and ∠Y = 50°. What kind of triangle is XYZ?

(1) right
(2) scalene
(3) isosceles
(4) equilateral
(5) Not enough information is given.

6. Grace has to type a 2500-word report and a 500-word letter. She can type 65 words per minute. Which of the following expresses the number of minutes she will need to type both the report and the letter?

(1) $\dfrac{2500 + 500}{65}$
(2) 65 × 2000 + 65 × 500
(3) 65(2500 + 500)
(4) $\dfrac{2500 + 500}{65}$
(5) $\dfrac{2500}{65} + 500$

7. What is the area of the shaded part of the figure below?

(1) 1000 sq ft
(2) 886 sq ft
(3) 686 sq ft
(4) 569 sq ft
(5) 56.9 sq ft

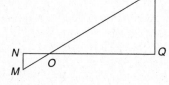

40 ft

20 ft

30 ft

8. For a picnic Anna bought 12 six-packs of soft drinks at $2.40 a six-pack and 8 pounds of beef at $3.50 a pound. Which of the following expresses the total cost of Anna's purchases?

(1) (12 + 8)(2.40 + 3.50)
(2) (12 × 8) + (2.40 × 3.50)
(3) 12(2.40 + 3.50)
(4) 12 + 2.40 × 8 + 2.50
(5) (12 × 2.40) + (8 × 3.50)

9. In the picture below, *MN* = 10, *NO* = 3, and *QO* = 48. Find *PQ*.

(1) 480
(2) 360
(3) 320
(4) 240
(5) 160

P

N   O   Q
M

10. Solve for *r* in the equation $9r - 8 = 6r + 7$.

    (1) $\frac{1}{3}$
    (2) 1
    (3) 3
    (4) 5
    (5) 15

11. Find the volume of a cylindrical tank with a height of 15 feet and a radius of 5 feet. Round off your answer to the nearest cubic foot.

    (1) 1178 cu ft
    (2) 707 cu ft
    (3) 471 cu ft
    (4) 236 cu ft
    (5) Not enough information is given.

12. James, Steve, and Charlie worked together to build a garage. Steve worked twice as many hours as James, and Charlie worked 10 hours more than Steve. Altogether the three of them worked 100 hours. How many hours did Charlie work?

    (1) 26
    (2) 33
    (3) 36
    (4) 46
    (5) 50

13. The ratio of male employees to female employees at a certain factory is 5:3. Altogether there are 96 employees. How many women work at the factory?

    (1) 64
    (2) 60
    (3) 36
    (4) 32
    (5) 28

14. The height of a triangle is three times the base. The area of the triangle is 96. Find the height of the triangle.

    (1) 4
    (2) 8
    (3) 16
    (4) 24
    (5) 48

15. Louie drove for 3 hours at an average speed of 18 mph and for 2 hours at 52 mph. Which of the following expresses the total distance he drove?

    (1) $(3 \times 2) + (18 + 52)$
    (2) $(3 \times 18) + (2 \times 52)$
    (3) $\frac{18}{3} + \frac{52}{2}$
    (4) $(3 + 18) \times (2 + 52)$
    (5) $3(18 + 52) \times 2$

16. Geraldine bought 4 pounds of apples at $.89 a pound. Then she went back to the store to buy 5 more pounds of the apples at the same price. Which of the following expresses the total amount she paid for apples?

    (1) $.89 \times 4 \times 5$
    (2) $.89 + 4 + 5$
    (3) $5 + (.89 \times 4)$
    (4) $(4 + 5) + .89$
    (5) $.89(4 + 5)$

17. To build a cabinet, Paul needs 8 pieces of lumber each $38\frac{1}{2}$ inches long. How many 10-foot boards should he buy?

    (1) 1
    (2) 2
    (3) 3
    (4) 4
    (5) 5

18. For the two triangles pictured below, $DE = GH$ and $EF = HI$. Which of the following, along with the information given, is enough to make the triangles congruent?

    A. $\angle D = \angle H$
    B. $DF = GI$
    C. $\angle E = \angle H$

    (1) A only
    (2) B only
    (3) C only
    (4) A or B
    (5) B or C

Directions: Use the following passage to answer questions 19–21.

Mr. and Mrs. Allen are planning to buy a house that is listed at $46,500. The day they sign papers for the house, they must pay a down payment of 10% of the price. That day they also have to pay $1200 to their lawyer, $2790 as a commission to the real estate agent, and $450 for other expenses involved in the purchase.

19. Find the total amount the Allens must pay the day they sign papers.

(1) $4440
(2) $6300
(3) $7890
(4) $8640
(5) $9090

20. The commission the real estate agent receives is what percent of the total list price of the house?

(1) 3%
(2) 5%
(3) 6%
(4) 10%
(5) Not enough information is given.

21. The real estate agent must pay part of the commission to his employer. What amount does the agent receive for himself?

(1) $3035
(2) $2790
(3) $2092
(4) $1395
(5) Not enough information is given.

22. The two figures below have equal areas. Find the side of the square.

(1) 20
(2) 40
(3) 100
(4) 200
(5) Not enough information is given.

23. Alvaro drove 236 miles on 18 gallons of gasoline and another 135 miles on 10 gallons of gasoline. What was the price Alvaro paid per gallon of gasoline?

(1) $0.95
(2) $1.02
(3) $1.10
(4) $1.15
(5) Not enough information is given.

24. What are the coordinates of the *y*-intercept of the equation $y = \frac{2}{3}x - 5$?

(1) $(0, \frac{2}{3})$
(2) $(\frac{2}{3}, 0)$
(3) $(0, -5)$
(4) $(-5, 0)$
(5) $(\frac{2}{3}, -5)$

25. At the Central County post office the ratio of men to women employees is 4:3. 92 men work there. Which expression gives the total number of *people* who work at the post office?

(1) $(7 \times 92)/4$
(2) $(3 \times 92)/4$
(3) $(4 \times 92)/7$
(4) $(4 \times 7)/92$
(5) $(4 \times 92)/3$

26. Solve for *w* in $3w + 1 \le 7(3 - w)$.

(1) $w \le 2$
(2) $w \le 4$
(3) $w \le 5$
(4) $w \le 10$
(5) $w \le 20$

27. Which of the following is the same as $x^2 - 8x$?

(1) $x \cdot -8$
(2) $(x - 8)(x + 8)$
(3) $x^2 + 8x$
(4) $x(1 - 8)$
(5) $x(x - 8)$

28. Which of the following is the same as $6a + 24b - 18$?

(1) $(6a + 4b)(4a - 3)$
(2) $6a(1 + 4b - 3)$
(3) $6(a + 4b - 3)$
(4) $(a + b)(6 + 4 - 18)$
(5) $6(1 + 4b - 3a)$

29. Marva spends $\frac{1}{3}$ of her income on rent, $\frac{1}{5}$ on food, and $\frac{3}{10}$ on loan payments. What total fraction of her income does she pay for these expenses?

(1) $\frac{8}{30}$

(2) $\frac{11}{20}$

(3) $\frac{19}{30}$

(4) $\frac{5}{6}$

(5) Not enough information is given.

Directions: Use the following passage to answer questions 30–32.

Sam is building a cabinet. The materials he needs will cost $480. To determine the price he will charge his customer, Sam adds in a profit of 20% of the cost of the materials and additional expenses of 10% of the cost of materials. Sam usually charges 40% of the total price at the beginning. The customer must pay the balance when the job is finished.

30. Find the total price of the cabinet.

(1) $780
(2) $672
(3) $624
(4) $504
(5) Not enough information is given.

31. Find the down payment the customer must pay.

(1) $374.40
(2) $249.60
(3) $230.40
(4) $192.00
(5) Not enough information is given.

32. Sam pays an assistant $7.50 an hour. How much profit is left over for Sam after he pays his assistant?

(1) $ 81.00
(2) $ 88.50
(3) $103.50
(4) $117.30
(5) Not enough information is given.

33. If Carmen cuts a 25-inch wire into pieces $\frac{1}{8}$ inch long, how many pieces of wire will she have?

(1) 3

(2) $3\frac{1}{8}$

(3) 20

(4) 200

(5) 250

34. A butcher sliced a roast weighing 4.56 pounds from a leg of lamb that weighs 7 pounds. What is the weight (in pounds) of the remaining leg of lamb?

(1) 1.08
(2) 2.36
(3) 2.44
(4) 3.44
(5) 11.56

35. Arrange the following lengths of 2" × 4" lumber in order from shortest to longest.

A: $2\frac{1}{2}$ feet

B: $33\frac{1}{3}$ inches

C: 3 feet $3\frac{1}{3}$ inches

D: 29 inches

E: 3 feet

(1) A, B, D, E, C
(2) B, D, A, E, C
(3) C, D, A, B, E
(4) D, A, B, E, C
(5) C, B, D, A, E

36. Alfredo drove 20 miles north and then 48 miles east. Find the shortest distance in miles Alfredo is from his starting point.

(1) 68
(2) 52
(3) 46
(4) 34
(5) 24

37. Which of the following expresses 67,500,000 in scientific notation?

(1) 6.75×10^{-7}
(2) 6.75×10^{6}
(3) 6.75×10^{7}
(4) 6.00×10^{-6}
(5) 6.57×10^{-7}

38. Which of the following points lies on the line of the graph of the equation $y = 3x - 2$?

(1) (2, 5)
(2) (1, −4)
(3) (4, 14)
(4) (3, 7)
(5) (0, 2)

Directions: Use the table below to answer questions 39 and 40.

UNEMPLOYMENT RATES			
	1987	**1989**	**1991**
Total	6.2%	5.3%	6.7%
16–19 years	16.9	15.0	18.6
20–24 years	9.7	8.6	10.8
25–44 years	5.4	4.5	6.0
45–64 years	3.8	3.2	4.4
65 years and older	2.5	2.6	3.3

Source: Bureau of Labor Statistics

39. Based on the information in the table, the 1991 unemployment rate for 16- to 19-year-olds was about

(1) twice the rate for 25- to 44-year-olds
(2) half the rate for 25- to 44-year-olds
(3) the same as the rate for 25- to 44-year-olds
(4) three times the rate for 25- to 44-year-olds
(5) one-third the rate for 25- to 44-year-olds

40. For what year shown on the table was the total unemployment rate less than 6%?

(1) 1987
(2) 1989
(3) 1991
(4) both 1987 and 1989
(5) both 1987 and 1991

41. At a sale Ruth bought four cans of pea soup, six cans of tomato soup, and ten cans of chicken soup. There were no labels on the soup cans.

The first can she opened turned out to be tomato soup. The second can she opened was chicken soup. What is the probability that the third can she opens will be pea soup?

(1) $\frac{3}{20}$

(2) $\frac{1}{6}$

(3) $\frac{1}{5}$

(4) $\frac{2}{9}$

(5) $\frac{1}{4}$

42. Jack sells used cars at his garage. The four cars he has for sale now are priced at $2380, $4950, $8265, and $5790, respectively. Find the median price of the cars.

(1) $5320
(2) $5346
(3) $5370
(4) $5400
(5) $5790

43. The area of the triangle pictured below is 192. The ratio of side *AB* to side *AC* is 2:3. Find the length of side *AB*.

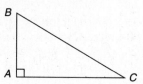

(1) 4
(2) 8
(3) 12
(4) 16
(5) 24

Directions: Use the diagram below to answer questions 44 and 45.

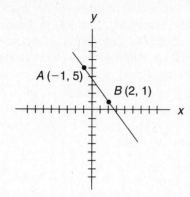

44. What is the slope of the line that passes through points *A* and *B*?

(1) $\frac{5}{2}$

(2) $-\frac{5}{2}$

(3) $-\frac{4}{3}$

(4) $\frac{3}{4}$

(5) $-\frac{2}{5}$

45. What is the distance between points *A* and *B*?

(1) 5

(2) 7

(3) 8

(4) 9

(5) 11

Directions: Use the table below to answer questions 46–48.

CORN PRODUCTION OF FOUR FARMERS				
	Farmer A	Farmer B	Farmer C	Farmer D
Yield (bushels/ acre)	135	167	148	112
Cost ($/bushel)	$3.40	$2.20	$1.90	$1.40
Net ($/acre*)	–$135	$33.40	$74	$112

*Based on a price of $2.40/bushel.

46. Which farmer had the highest yield?

(1) A

(2) B

(3) C

(4) D

(5) Not enough information is given.

47. If farmers C and D each have 200 acres of corn, how much more does farmer D net than farmer C?

(1) $ 4,600

(2) $ 7,600

(3) $ 8,120

(4) $20,320

(5) Not enough information is given.

48. Based on the information in the table, which of the following statements is true?

(1) The lower the cost, the higher the profit.

(2) The higher the yield, the higher the profit.

(3) A higher yield results in lower profits.

(4) Higher profits come from higher costs.

(5) Higher profits come from lower yields.

49. Arrange the weights of the following packages in order from lightest to heaviest:

package A: .5 kilogram
package B: 485 grams
package C: 1.1 kilograms
package D: 0.65 kilogram
package E: 1200 grams

(1) B, A, D, C, E

(2) A, C, E, D, B

(3) A, B, D, C, E

(4) C, D, B, A, E

(5) C, B, A, E, D

50. Eighteen railroad ties, each 3.9 meters long, are laid end to end. How many meters do the ties cover in total?

(1) 21

(2) 21.9

(3) 39

(4) 70.2

(5) 702

Directions: Problems 51–53 refer to the following passage.

A new rock band, the Great Divide, plays twice a week at Jack's Bar. The price of admission to see a show is $7.50, and the band keeps 40% of the total ticket sales.

51. If 100 tickets were sold on Thursday night, how much money did the band keep?

(1) $ 100
(2) $ 300
(3) $ 400
(4) $ 450
(5) $3000

52. Kevin, the lead vocalist, wants to take $240 of one week's earnings to do some local advertising. That week the bar sold 400 tickets. What percentage of the band's profits will Kevin use for advertising?

(1) 10
(2) 15
(3) 20
(4) 25
(5) 30

53. Each week Kevin pays band expenses, then divides up the band's profits evenly among the band members. During an especially successful week in March the band made $2350 after expenses. How much money did each band member earn?

(1) $ 78.33
(2) $195.83
(3) $470.00
(4) $587.50
(5) Not enough information is given.

54. A computer program can figure out how much lumber a manufacturer needs to buy by multiplying its amount of inventory by .75 and subtracting from that product the amount of lumber sold the previous month. If the manufacturer's lumber sales from January came to 22,500 square feet and its amount of inventory is 95,000 square feet, which of the following expressions gives the amount of lumber that the manufacturer needs to order in February?

(1) .75 × 22,500
(2) .75 × 95,000
(3) (.75 × 95,000) − 22,500
(4) (.75 × 22,500) − 95,000
(5) $\dfrac{95,000 - 22,500}{.75}$

55. The two figures below have the same area. What is the length of side *XY*?

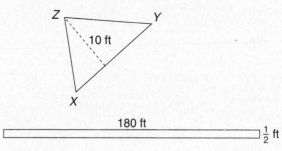

(1) 8 ft
(2) 9 ft
(3) 18 ft
(4) 27 ft
(5) Not enough information is given.

56. Out of a total printing of 10,000 copies 2,600 newsletters were missing pages. Five hundred newsletters had smudged ink. What percent of the newsletters had smudged ink?

(1) 5
(2) 15
(3) 21
(4) 26
(5) 50

ANSWERS START ON THE NEXT PAGE.

Post-Test Answer Key

1. (2) **28 m**
   $P = 2l + 2w$
   $P = 2(8.4) + 2(5.6)$
   $P = 16.8 + 11.2 = 28$

2. (3) **45°**
   $\begin{array}{r} 90° \\ - 45° \\ \hline 45° \end{array}$

3. (2) **61°**
   $\begin{array}{r} 180° \\ - 119° \\ \hline 61° \end{array}$

4. (2) **35 × 40 × 8**

5. (3) **isosceles**
   $\begin{array}{r} 65° \\ + 50° \\ \hline 115° \end{array}$ $\begin{array}{r} 180° \\ - 115° \\ \hline 65° \end{array}$ Since two angles are equal, the triangle is isosceles.

6. (1) $\dfrac{2500 + 500}{65}$

7. (2) **886 sq ft**
   Area of rectangle: $A = lw$
   $A = 40 \times 30$
   $A = 1200$
   Area of circle: $A = \pi r^2$
   $A = 3.14 \times 10^2$
   $A = 3.14 \times 100$
   $A = 314$
   Shaded area: $1200 - 314 = 886$

8. (5) **(12 × 2.40) + (8 × 3.50)**

9. (5) **160**
   $\dfrac{3}{10} = \dfrac{48}{x}$ $\begin{array}{r} 48 \\ \times 10 \\ \hline 480 \end{array}$ $\begin{array}{r} 160 \\ 3\overline{)480} \end{array}$

10. (4) **5**
    $\begin{array}{r} 9r - 8 = \quad 6r + 7 \\ - 6r \quad\quad - 6r \\ \hline 3r - 8 = \quad\quad + 7 \\ + 8 \quad\quad + 8 \\ \hline \dfrac{3r}{3} = \quad\quad \dfrac{15}{3} \\ r = 5 \end{array}$

11. (1) **1178 cu ft**
    $V = \pi r^2 h$
    $V = 3.14 \times 5^2 \times 15$
    $V = 3.14 \times 25 \times 15$
    $V = 1177.5$ to the nearest cu ft $= 1178$

12. (4) **46**
    James's hours $= x$
    Steve's hours $= 2x$
    Charlie's hours $= 2x + 10$
    $\begin{array}{r} x + 2x + 2x + 10 = \quad 100 \\ 5x + 10 = \quad 100 \\ - 10 \quad\quad - 10 \\ \hline \dfrac{5x}{5} = \quad\quad \dfrac{90}{5} \\ x = 18 \end{array}$
    Charlie worked $2(18) + 10 = 46$ hr.

13. (3) **36**
    $\begin{array}{l} \text{male} \quad\quad 5 \\ \text{female} \quad + 3 \\ \hline \quad\quad\quad 8 \end{array}$ $\dfrac{\text{female}}{\text{total}} \quad \dfrac{3}{8} = \dfrac{x}{96}$
    $\begin{array}{r} 96 \\ \times 3 \\ \hline 288 \end{array}$ $\begin{array}{r} 36 \\ 8\overline{)288} \end{array}$

14. (4) **24**
    base $= x$ $A = \dfrac{bh}{2}$
    height $= 3x$ $96 = \dfrac{x \cdot 3x}{2}$
    $\dfrac{2}{3} \cdot \dfrac{96}{1} = \dfrac{3}{2}x^2 \cdot \dfrac{2}{3}$
    $64 = x^2$
    $\sqrt{64} = x$
    $8 = x$
    height $= 3(8) = 24$

15. (2) **(3 × 18) + (2 × 52)**

16. (5) **.89(4 + 5)**

17. (3) **3**
    First find how many inches are needed.
    $38\frac{1}{2} \times 8 = 308$
    Then find how many inches are in the 10-foot boards.
    $10 \text{ ft} \times 12 \text{ in} = 120 \text{ in}$
    Divide.
    $\begin{array}{r} 2.56 \\ 120\overline{)308.00} \\ \underline{240} \\ 68\ 0 \\ \underline{60\ 0} \\ 8\ 00 \\ \underline{7\ 20} \end{array}$
    Paul will need 3 boards.

18. (5) B or C
Condition B fulfills the *side, side, side* requirement.
Condition C fulfills the *side, angle, side* requirement.

19. (5) $9090
down payment:

$$\frac{p}{46,500} = \frac{10}{100} \qquad \begin{array}{r} 46,500 \\ \times\ 10 \\ \hline 465,000 \end{array}$$

$$\begin{array}{r} 4,650 \\ 100\overline{)465,000} \end{array} \qquad \begin{array}{r} \$4650 \\ 1200 \\ 2790 \\ +\ 450 \\ \hline \$9090 \end{array}$$

20. (3) 6%

$$\frac{2,790}{46,500} = \frac{x}{100} \qquad \begin{array}{r} 2,790 \\ \times\ 100 \\ \hline 279,000 \end{array}$$

$$\begin{array}{r} 6\% \\ 46,500\overline{)279,000} \end{array}$$

21. (5) Not enough information is given.

22. (1) 20
Area of rectangle: $A = lw$
$$A = 25 \times 16 = 400$$
Side of square:
$$\begin{aligned} 400 &= s^2 \\ \sqrt{400} &= s \\ 20 &= s \end{aligned}$$

23. (5) Not enough information is given.

24. (3) (0, −5)
$$y = \frac{2}{3}(0) - 5$$
$$y = 0 - 5 = -5$$
Coordinates of the y-intercept are $(0, -5)$.

25. (1) $\dfrac{7 \times 92}{4}$

$$\begin{array}{ll} \text{men} & 4 \\ \text{women} & +\ 3 \\ \hline \text{total} & 7 \end{array} \qquad \frac{\text{men}}{\text{total}} \quad \frac{4}{7} = \frac{92}{x}$$

$$4 \cdot x = 7 \times 92$$
$$x = \frac{7 \times 92}{4} \text{ or } \frac{7 \times 92}{4}$$

26. (1) $w \le 2$
$$\begin{aligned} 3w + 1 &\le 7(3 - w) \\ 3w + 1 &\le 21 - 7w \\ +\ 7w &\qquad +\ 7w \\ \hline 10w + 1 &\le 21 \\ -\ 1 &\quad -\ 1 \\ \hline \frac{10w}{10} &\le \frac{20}{10} \\ w &\le 2 \end{aligned}$$

27. (5) $x(x - 8)$

28. (3) $6(a + 4b - 3)$

29. (4) $\dfrac{5}{6}$
$$\frac{1}{3} + \frac{1}{5} + \frac{3}{10} = \frac{25}{30} = \frac{5}{6}$$

30. (3) $624

$$\begin{array}{r} 20\% \\ +\ 10\% \\ \hline 30\% \end{array} \qquad \frac{p}{480} = \frac{30}{100} \qquad \begin{array}{r} 480 \\ \times\ 30 \\ \hline 14,400 \end{array}$$

$$\begin{array}{r} 144 \\ 100\overline{)14,400} \end{array} \qquad \begin{array}{r} \$480 \\ +\ 144 \\ \hline \$624 \end{array}$$

31. (2) $249.60

$$\frac{p}{624} = \frac{40}{100} \qquad \begin{array}{r} 624 \\ \times\ 40 \\ \hline 24,960 \end{array} \qquad \begin{array}{r} \$249.60 \\ 100\overline{)24,960.00} \end{array}$$

32. (5) Not enough information is given.

33. (4) 200
$$25 \div \frac{1}{8} =$$
$$25 \times 8 = 200$$

34. (3) 2.44
$$\begin{array}{r} 7.00 \\ -\ 4.56 \\ \hline 2.44 \end{array}$$

35. (4) D, A, B, E, C
A: $2\frac{1}{2}$ ft = 30 in
B: $33\frac{1}{3}$ in
C: 3 ft $3\frac{1}{3}$ in = $39\frac{1}{3}$ in
D: 29 in
E: 3 ft = 36 in

36. (2) 52
$$\begin{aligned} c^2 &= a^2 + b^2 \\ c^2 &= 20^2 + 48^2 \\ c^2 &= 400 + 2304 \\ c^2 &= 2704 \\ c &= \sqrt{2704} \\ c &= 52 \end{aligned}$$

37. (3) 6.75×10^7
First remove the zeros and represent 67,500,000 as a number between 1 and 10. → 6.75
Then write a multiplication sign and 10 to the correct power. You are moving the decimal point seven places to the left, so 67,500,000 = 6.75×10^7.

38. (4) (3, 7)
$$\begin{aligned} y &= 3x - 2 \\ 7 &= 3(3) - 2 \\ 7 &= 9 - 2 \\ 7 &= 7 \end{aligned}$$

39. (4) three times the rate for 25- to 44-year-olds
$$\begin{array}{r} 3.1 \\ 6\overline{)18.6} \\ \underline{18} \\ 06 \\ \underline{6} \\ 0 \end{array}$$

40. (2) 1989

41. (4) $\frac{2}{9}$

$$\frac{\text{favorable outcomes}}{\text{total outcomes}} \quad \frac{4}{18} = \frac{2}{9}$$

42. (3) $5370

Find the mean of the two middle prices.

$$\begin{array}{r} \$\ 4{,}950 \\ +\ 5{,}790 \\ \hline \$10{,}740 \end{array} \qquad \begin{array}{r} \$5{,}370 \\ 2\overline{)10{,}740} \end{array}$$

43. (4) 16

height $= 2x$ $\qquad A = \frac{1}{2}bh$

base $= 3x$ $\qquad 192 = \frac{3x \cdot 2x}{2}$

$$192 = \frac{6x^2}{3}$$

$$\frac{192}{3} = \frac{3x^2}{3}$$

$$64 = x^2$$

$$\sqrt{64} = x$$

$$8 = x$$

$$16 = 2x$$

$$AB = 16$$

44. (3) $-\frac{4}{3}$

$$m = \frac{y_2 - y_1}{x_2 - x_1}$$

$$m = \frac{1 - 5}{2 - (-1)} = \frac{-4}{+3} = -\frac{4}{3}$$

45. (1) 5 distance $= \sqrt{(x_2 - x_1)^2 + (y_2 - y_1)^2}$

distance $= \sqrt{[2 - (-1)]^2 + (1 - 5)^2}$

$$= \sqrt{3^2 + (-4)^2}$$

$$= \sqrt{25}$$

$$= 5$$

46. (2) B

47. (2) $7,600

$$\begin{array}{r} \$74 \\ \times\ 200 \\ \hline \$14{,}800 \end{array} \qquad \begin{array}{r} \$112 \\ \times\ 200 \\ \hline \$22{,}400 \end{array} \qquad \begin{array}{r} \$22{,}400 \\ -\ 14{,}800 \\ \hline \$\ 7{,}600 \end{array}$$

48. (1) The lower the cost, the higher the profit.

49. (1) B, A, D, C, E

50. (4) 70.2

$$\begin{array}{r} 1\ 8 \\ \times\ 3.9 \\ \hline 16\ 2 \\ 54 \\ \hline 70.2 \end{array}$$

51. (2) $300

$$100 \times \$7.50 = \$750$$

$$\frac{p}{750} = \frac{40}{100} \qquad \begin{array}{r} 750 \\ \times\ 40 \\ \hline 30{,}000 \end{array} \qquad \begin{array}{r} \$300 \\ 100\overline{)30{,}000} \end{array}$$

52. (3) 20

$$400 \times \$7.50 = \$3000$$

$$\frac{40}{100} \times \frac{\$3000}{1} = \$1200$$

$$\$240 = \frac{x}{100} \times \frac{\$1200}{1}$$

$$\$240 = 12x$$

$$20 = x$$

53. (5) Not enough information is given.

54. (3) $(.75 \times 95{,}000) - 22{,}500$

(inventory $\times$ .75) $-$ sales of previous month

55. (3) 18 ft

area of rectangle: $\frac{1}{2} \times 180 = 90$ sq ft

area of triangle: $\frac{1}{2}bh = \frac{1}{2}b \times 10$

$$90 = \frac{1}{2}b \times 10$$

$$\frac{90}{10} = \frac{\frac{1}{2}b \times 10}{10}$$

$$9 = \frac{1}{2}b$$

$$18 = b$$

56. (1) 5

$$\frac{500}{10{,}000} = \frac{x}{100} \qquad \begin{array}{r} 5 \\ 10{,}000\overline{)50{,}000} \end{array}$$

Post-Test Evaluation Chart

On the following chart, circle the number of any problem you got wrong. After each problem number you will see the name of the section (or sections) where you can find the skills you need to solve the problem. When a problem involves more than one skill, the sections are separated by a slash (/).

This chart should help you decide which areas you need to review before you take the GED Test.

Problem	Section	Starting Page
	Arithmetic	
4, 6, 8, 15, 16, 25, 54	Set-Up Questions	48
13, 41	Ratio, Proportion & Probability	123
17, 35, 49	Measurement	165
19, 20, 21, 30, 31, 32, 51, 52, 56	Proportion & Percent/Item Sets	154
23, 53	Not Enough Information Given	159
24, 44	Graphs	177
29, 33	Fractions	83
34, 50	Decimals	57
37	Scientific Notation	311
39, 40, 46, 47, 48	Tables	188
42	Mean & Median	39
	Geometry	
1, 7, 11	Perimeter, Area, & Volume	226
2, 3, 18	Angles	252
5, 9, 36	Triangles	257
	Algebra	
10, 38	Equations	204
12	Word Problems	21
14, 43, 55	Using Algebra to Solve Geometry Problems	297
22	Square Roots	233
26	Longer Inequalities	291
27, 28	Factoring	293
45	Rectangular Coordinate System	300

Practice Test

The test that follows gives you another chance to see if you are prepared for the GED Mathematics Test. Like the GED Math Test, this test contains 56 multiple-choice questions.

Answer every question. Use the formulas on page 274 when necessary. When you are finished, check your answers. The evaluation chart at the end of the answers will help you determine which areas to review before you take the GED Math Test.

PRACTICE TEST ANSWER GRID

1 ① ② ③ ④ ⑤	20 ① ② ③ ④ ⑤	39 ① ② ③ ④ ⑤
2 ① ② ③ ④ ⑤	21 ① ② ③ ④ ⑤	40 ① ② ③ ④ ⑤
3 ① ② ③ ④ ⑤	22 ① ② ③ ④ ⑤	41 ① ② ③ ④ ⑤
4 ① ② ③ ④ ⑤	23 ① ② ③ ④ ⑤	42 ① ② ③ ④ ⑤
5 ① ② ③ ④ ⑤	24 ① ② ③ ④ ⑤	43 ① ② ③ ④ ⑤
6 ① ② ③ ④ ⑤	25 ① ② ③ ④ ⑤	44 ① ② ③ ④ ⑤
7 ① ② ③ ④ ⑤	26 ① ② ③ ④ ⑤	45 ① ② ③ ④ ⑤
8 ① ② ③ ④ ⑤	27 ① ② ③ ④ ⑤	46 ① ② ③ ④ ⑤
9 ① ② ③ ④ ⑤	28 ① ② ③ ④ ⑤	47 ① ② ③ ④ ⑤
10 ① ② ③ ④ ⑤	29 ① ② ③ ④ ⑤	48 ① ② ③ ④ ⑤
11 ① ② ③ ④ ⑤	30 ① ② ③ ④ ⑤	49 ① ② ③ ④ ⑤
12 ① ② ③ ④ ⑤	31 ① ② ③ ④ ⑤	50 ① ② ③ ④ ⑤
13 ① ② ③ ④ ⑤	32 ① ② ③ ④ ⑤	51 ① ② ③ ④ ⑤
14 ① ② ③ ④ ⑤	33 ① ② ③ ④ ⑤	52 ① ② ③ ④ ⑤
15 ① ② ③ ④ ⑤	34 ① ② ③ ④ ⑤	53 ① ② ③ ④ ⑤
16 ① ② ③ ④ ⑤	35 ① ② ③ ④ ⑤	54 ① ② ③ ④ ⑤
17 ① ② ③ ④ ⑤	36 ① ② ③ ④ ⑤	55 ① ② ③ ④ ⑤
18 ① ② ③ ④ ⑤	37 ① ② ③ ④ ⑤	56 ① ② ③ ④ ⑤
19 ① ② ③ ④ ⑤	38 ① ② ③ ④ ⑤	

1. Amtrak's new high-speed trains can travel as fast as 155 mph. Approximately how many miles can one of these trains go if it maintains its fastest speed for three hours?

    (1) 50
    (2) 200
    (3) 250
    (4) 450
    (5) 600

2. Elena is 1 year more than twice her daughter's age. Let x = the daughter's age. Which expression represents Elena's age?

    (1) $2x$
    (2) $x + 2$
    (3) $2x + 2$
    (4) $2(x + 1)$
    (5) $2x + 1$

Directions: Use the figure below to answer question 3.

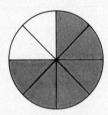

3. Which of the following does *not* represent the part of the figure that is shaded?

    (1) .075
    (2) $\frac{6}{8}$
    (3) 75%
    (4) $\frac{3}{4}$
    (5) 0.75

4. The figure below represents a house and the lot where the house sits. How many feet of fencing are required to completely enclose the lot?

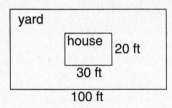

    (1) 200
    (2) 230
    (3) 250
    (4) 300
    (5) Not enough information is given.

5. Which of the following represents the number of degrees in angle x in the picture below?

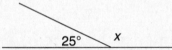

    (1) $2(25°)$
    (2) $90° + 25°$
    (3) $180° - 25°$
    (4) $90° - 25°$
    (5) $180° + 25°$

6. Laura bought 5 raffle tickets to help support her son's school. The school sold a total of 1000 tickets. What is the probability that Laura will win the raffle prize?

    (1) $\frac{1}{5}$
    (2) $\frac{1}{10}$
    (3) $\frac{1}{1000}$
    (4) $\frac{1}{100}$
    (5) $\frac{1}{200}$

7. The list below shows the weight of five friends two months ago.

Carlos	180 lb
Reggie	160 lb
Mike	150 lb
Silvia	140 lb
Anna	130 lb

Each of them went on a diet and managed to lose 10% of his or her weight. Who now weighs 135 lbs?

(1) Carlos
(2) Reggie
(3) Mike
(4) Silvia
(5) Anna

8. Which of the following is *one* solution to the equation $x^2 = 16$?

(1) −8
(2) −4
(3) 2
(4) 8
(5) 32

9. According to a recent census there are 83,186 local governments in the United States. What is the number of local governments rounded off to the nearest 1000?

(1) 90,000
(2) 84,000
(3) 83,200
(4) 83,000
(5) 80,000

Directions: Use the list below to answer questions 10 and 11.

Comparative Prices of Souvenir Sweatshirts		
	Wholesale	Retail
Store A	$10	$20
Store B	$12	$18
Store C	$15	$20
Store D	$16	$28
Store E	$20	$28

10. For which store does the retail price of a sweatshirt show a 50% markup over the wholesale price?

(1) A
(2) B
(3) C
(4) D
(5) E

11. The owner of Store A decided to reduce the retail price of a sweatshirt by 20%. What will be the sale price of the sweatshirt?

(1) $20
(2) $18
(3) $17
(4) $16
(5) $15

12. The picture below shows the dimensions of a typical block in Jose's neighborhood. Which of the following is closest to the distance in feet Jose must walk to go around the block, starting and stopping at the same point?

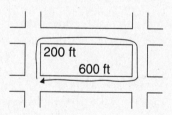

(1) 600×200
(2) $2(600) + 2(200)$
(3) $600 + 200$
(4) 600×400
(5) $\dfrac{600 + 200}{2}$

PRACTICE TEST

13. Which of the following is equal to $10^3 - 10^2$?

 (1) 10
 (2) 20
 (3) 100
 (4) 900
 (5) 1100

14. The steepness of a ramp is measured by the ratio of the rise to the run. What is the steepness of a ramp that rises 4 feet over a run of 36 feet?

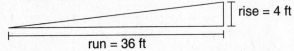

rise = 4 ft

run = 36 ft

 (1) 36
 (2) 6
 (3) 4
 (4) $\frac{1}{6}$
 (5) $\frac{1}{9}$

15. According to the information in the figure below, lines AB and CD must be

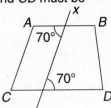

 (1) equal
 (2) parallel
 (3) perpendicular
 (4) intersecting
 (5) corresponding

Directions: The graph below shows the responses to a survey. Parents were asked to name their children's favorite food.

Use the graph to answer questions 16 and 17.

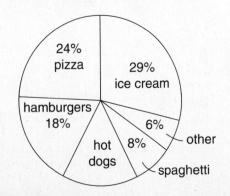

16. What percentage of the parents surveyed named hot dogs as the food their children liked most?

 (1) 5%
 (2) 10%
 (3) 15%
 (4) 75%
 (5) 85%

17. Together, which two categories make up more than half of the responses?

 (1) pizza and ice cream
 (2) ice cream and hamburgers
 (3) hamburgers and hot dogs
 (4) hot dogs and spaghetti
 (5) pizza and other

18. The illustrations below represent the weight of five packages. What are the *three heaviest*?

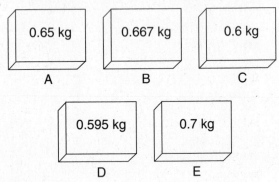

 (1) A, B, C
 (2) A, B, D
 (3) B, C, E
 (4) B, D, E
 (5) A, B, E

Directions: Questions 19 and 20 refer to the figure.

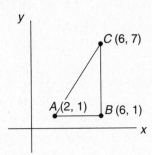

19. What is the distance between points B and C?

 (1) 7
 (2) 6
 (3) 5
 (4) 4
 (5) 1

20. Which of the following represents the distance between points A and C?

(1) 4
(2) 6
(3) 4^2
(4) 6^2
(5) $\sqrt{4^2 + 6^2}$

21. If $2x - 3 = 17$, then $x =$

(1) 5
(2) 10
(3) 15
(4) 20
(5) 25

22. The figure below shows the surface area of a raised platform. Which of the following is closest to the number of square feet of paving stones required to cover the surface of the platform?

(1) 0.314
(2) 3.14
(3) 31.4
(4) 314
(5) 3140

10 ft

Directions: Questions 23–25 refer to the following information.

Steve is a carpenter. He charges his customers "time and materials." This means that he bills his customers for each hour that he and his assistant work, and he also bills his customers for the exact cost of the materials that he uses on a job. Below is a list of the time and materials for the renovation of an enclosed porch.

Time
Steve—40 hours at $30 per hour
Assistant—40 hours at $12 per hour

Materials
10 sheets of gypsum board—$4 *each*
5 boxes of ceramic tiles—$15 *each*
assorted lumber and hardware—$115

23. Which of the following expresses the combined cost in dollars of Steve's and his assistant's time?

(1) 40(30) + 40(12)
(2) 40 × 30 + 12
(3) 40 × 30 × 12
(4) 30(40 + 12)
(5) 12(40 + 30)

24. Steve had to pay 6% sales tax on all materials he used for the job. What was the total sales tax for the materials?

(1) $ 6.90
(2) $12.00
(3) $13.80
(4) $24.38
(5) $27.60

25. Steve deducts 20% of his assistant's wages to pay taxes and social security. What was the assistant's take-home pay for the renovation job?

(1) $384
(2) $396
(3) $408
(4) $440
(5) $460

26. Miguel borrowed $2000 interest free from his brother to buy a used car. So far Miguel has paid back $1200. What percent of the total does he still have to pay?

(1) 12%
(2) 20%
(3) 40%
(4) 60%
(5) Not enough information is given.

27. For which of the following triangles can you use the Pythagorean theorem to find the distance of side x?

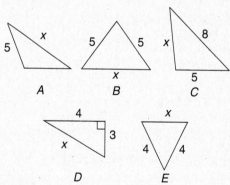

(1) A
(2) B
(3) C
(4) D
(5) E

28. A triangular area in a parking lot has been set aside for landscaping. It measures 25 feet on one side, 35 feet on another, and 40 feet on the third. Which of the following best shows the total feet in concrete curbing required to surround the space?

(1) $2(25) + 2(35)$
(2) $\frac{1}{2} \times 25 \times 40$
(3) $25 + 35 + 40$
(4) $\frac{1}{2} \times 35 \times 40$
(5) $25^2 + 35^2$

29. A baseball batting average equals the number of hits (H) a player gets divided by the number of times at bat (B). Which of the following represents a batting average?

(1) $\frac{H}{B}$

(2) $\frac{H + B}{2}$

(3) $\frac{B}{H}$

(4) $\frac{BH}{2}$

(5) $\frac{H - B}{2}$

30. What is the volume in cubic meters of the rectangular container pictured below?

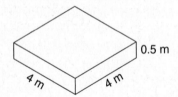

(1) 8
(2) 14
(3) 16
(4) 32
(5) 80

31. If $9m + 5 = 2m + 26$, then $m =$

(1) 2
(2) 3
(3) 5
(4) 7
(5) 14

32. The list below shows the price of navel oranges at five different stores. Which store's price is the lowest?

price of navel oranges

Store A	5 for $.99
Store B	25¢ each
Store C	3 for $1
Store D	$2 a dozen
Store E	2 for 40¢

(1) Store A
(2) Store B
(3) Store C
(4) Store D
(5) Store E

33. The numbers $+6$ and -6 are both solutions to which of the following equations?

(1) $2x = 36$
(2) $x^2 = 36$
(3) $3x = 18$
(4) $2x = 12$
(5) Not enough information is given.

34. What is the measurement of angle B in the figure below?

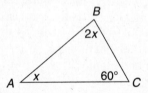

(1 100°
(2) 80°
(3) 60°
(4) 40°
(5) 20°

35. Anna often travels along Route 8, a road that runs east and west. The diagram below shows the distance between Anna's home and the grocery, between the grocery and the post office, and between the post office and the community college.

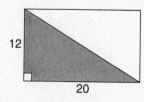

home   grocery   post office   community college

├─0.9 mi─┤├──1.3 mi──┤├────2.1 mi────┤

The dry cleaner Anna uses is exactly three miles from her home in the direction of the community college. Which of the following best describes the location of the cleaner?

(1) between her home and the grocery
(2) between the grocery and the post office
(3) exactly halfway between the grocery and the post office
(4) exactly halfway between her home and the post office
(5) between the post office and the community college

36. If $y = \frac{1}{2}x + 1$, then what is the value of y when $x = 6$?

(1) 2
(2) 3
(3) 4
(4) 6
(5) 7

37. The expression $c^2 + 3c$ is the same as

(1) $c(2 + 3)$
(2) $c(c + 3)$
(3) $2(3 + c)$
(4) $3(2 + c)$
(5) $c(2 + c)$

38. Which of the following represents the area of the shaded part of the figure below?

12

20

(1) $2(20) + 2(12)$
(2) $\frac{20 + 12}{2}$
(3) $20^2 + 12^2$
(4) $\frac{1}{2} \times 20 \times 12$
(5) $\frac{1}{2} + 20 + 12$

39. The Church Street Food Co-op ordered 5 cases of apple juice. Each case contains 8 boxes, and each box contains 12 cans. Which expression shows the total number of cans in the order?

(1) $12 \times 8 \times 5$
(2) $12 + 8 + 5$
(3) $\frac{(12 + 8)}{5}$
(4) $\frac{5}{(12 \times 8)}$
(5) Not enough information is given.

40. For the figure below, $AD = 30$. What is the length of DE?

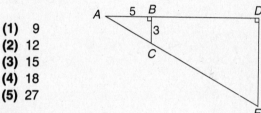

(1) 9
(2) 12
(3) 15
(4) 18
(5) 27

41. If $\frac{2}{3}x \leq 24$, then

(1) $x \leq 8$
(2) $x \leq 12$
(3) $x \leq 16$
(4) $x \leq 20$
(5) $x \leq 36$

42. Which expression represents the number of degrees in vertex angle B in the figure below?

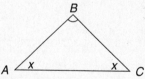

(1) $180° - 2x$
(2) x
(3) $3x$
(4) $180° + x$
(5) $180° - x$

43. The table below shows the coordinates of two points on the graph of a linear function. What is the missing value of y?

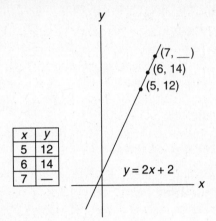

x	y
5	12
6	14
7	—

$y = 2x + 2$

(1) 14
(2) 15
(3) 16
(4) 18
(5) 21

44. According to the information in the figure below, which of the following is true?

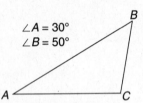

∠A = 30°
∠B = 50°

(1) AB is the longest side.
(2) BC is the longest side.
(3) AC is the longest side.
(4) All three sides are equal.
(5) Sides AB and BC are equal.

45. All five members of the Perez family bought new running shoes. The adult sizes for Mr. and Mrs. Perez cost $49 each. The shoes for their three children were $29 each. Which expression represents the total cost of the shoes?

(1) $\frac{49 + 29}{5}$

(2) $5(49 + 29)$

(3) $5 \times 49 \times 29$

(4) $3(49) + 2(29)$

(5) $2(49) + 3(29)$

46. The illustration below shows the wooden form for pouring a concrete patio. The length will be 12 feet, and the depth will be 4 inches. How many square feet will the surface of the finished patio be?

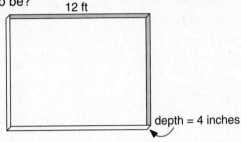

12 ft

depth = 4 inches

(1) 32
(2) 48
(3) 72
(4) 144
(5) Not enough information is given.

47. When $x = 4$, what is the value of $\frac{6}{x^2}$?

(1) $\frac{1}{16}$

(2) $\frac{3}{8}$

(3) $\frac{1}{2}$

(4) $\frac{3}{4}$

(5) 3

Directions: Use the figure below to answer question 48.

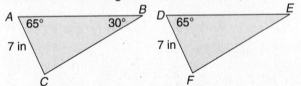

A 65°   B 30°   D 65°   E
7 in   7 in
C   F

48. What must be the measurement of angle F if triangle ABC and triangle DEF are congruent?

(1) 30°
(2) 60°
(3) 65°
(4) 85°
(5) 90°

49. For what values of c is the equation $c^2 + 5c - 24 = 0$ true?

(1) +12 and −2
(2) −12 and +2
(3) +6 and −4
(4) +8 and −3
(5) −8 and +3

50. Juan is now 25 years older than his daughter Sue. In three years the sum of their ages will be 99. If x represents Sue's age now, which equation expresses the sum of their ages in three years?

(1) $2x + 25 = 99$
(2) $2x + 28 = 99$
(3) $x + 25 = 99$
(4) $2x + 31 = 99$
(5) $x + 28 = 99$

51. What is the slope of the line that passes through points P and Q in the figure below?

(1) $\dfrac{6 - 1}{4 - 1}$

(2) $\dfrac{4 - 1}{6 - 1}$

(3) $\dfrac{6}{4 - 1}$

(4) $\dfrac{6 - 1}{4}$

(5) $\dfrac{6}{4}$

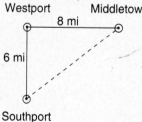

Directions: Use the graph below to answer questions 52 and 53.

VOLUME OF SALES OF 3 COMPANIES

52. For 1985 the volume of sales for Company C was approximately how many times that of Company A?

(1) 4 times
(2) 3 times
(3) twice
(4) one-half
(5) the same

53. For the period shown on the graph, which of the following is true?

(1) Only Company A showed a steady rise in volume of sales.
(2) Only Company B showed a steady rise in volume of sales.
(3) Company A consistently had the lowest volume of sales.
(4) Company C consistently had the lowest volume of sales.
(5) Company A and Company C had nearly the same volume of sales.

54. At the farthest point in its orbit, the moon is 253,000 miles from Earth. Which of the following represents this number of miles in scientific notation?

(1) 253
(2) 2.53×10^3
(3) 2.53×10^5
(4) 2.53×10^6
(5) 253×10

55. Let x represent the total sales in one year of the cars sold at Sal's Used Car Lot. Which expression tells the average monthly sales of cars?

(1) $\dfrac{x}{12}$

(2) $12x$

(3) $12 + x$

(4) $12 - x$

(5) $\dfrac{12}{x}$

56. The map below shows the distances between towns. Westport is directly west of Middletown, and Southport is directly south of Westport. What is the shortest distance in miles between Middletown and Southport?

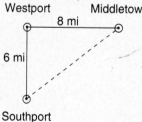

(1) 16
(2) 14
(3) 12
(4) 10
(5) 9

ANSWERS START ON THE NEXT PAGE.

Practice Test Answer Key

1. (4) 450

$d = rt$

$r = 155 \approx 150$

$d = 150 \times 3$

$d = 450$

The closest is 450. (The exact answer is 465.)

2. (5) $2x + 1$

3. (1) .075

$\frac{6}{8}$, 75%, $\frac{3}{4}$, and 0.75 are all equal.

Choice **(1)** is smaller.

4. (5) Not enough information is given.

To find the amount of fencing, you need the perimeter. You do not know the width of the yard.

5. (3) $180° - 25°$

The angles are supplementary. To find x, subtract from 180°.

6. (5) $\frac{1}{200}$

$\frac{\text{tickets bought}}{\text{tickets sold}} = \frac{5}{1000} = \frac{1}{200}$

7. (3) Mike

$\frac{10}{100} = \frac{x}{150}$

$100x = 1500$

$x = 15$

$\begin{array}{r} 150 \\ - 15 \\ \hline 135 \end{array}$

8. (2) −4

$x^2 = 16$

$x = \sqrt{16}$

$x = +4 \text{ or } -4$

9. (4) 83,000

To round to the nearest 1000, look at the hundreds place. 83,<u>1</u>86 rounds down to 83,000.

10. (2) B

11. (4) $16

$\frac{p}{20} = \frac{20}{100}$

$\begin{array}{r} 20 \\ \times\ 20 \\ \hline 400 \end{array}$

$\begin{array}{r} 4 \\ 100\overline{)400} \end{array}$

$\begin{array}{r} \$20 \\ -\ 4 \\ \hline \$16 \end{array}$

12. (2) $2(600) + 2(200)$

$P = 2l + 2w$

$P = 2(600) + 2(200)$

13. (4) 900

$10^3 = 10 \times 10 \times 10 = 1000$

$10^2 = 10 \times 10 = 100$

$1000 - 100 = 900$

14. (5) $\frac{1}{9}$

$\frac{\text{rise}}{\text{run}} = \frac{4}{36} = \frac{1}{9}$

15. (2) parallel

The alternate interior angles are equal. The lines cut by the transversal x must be parallel.

16. (3) 15%

$\begin{array}{ll} 24\% & 100\% \\ 29 & -85 \\ 18 & \overline{15\%} \\ 8 & \\ +\ 6 & \\ \hline 85\% & \end{array}$

17. (1) pizza and ice cream

$\begin{array}{ll} \text{pizza} & 24\% \\ \text{ice cream} & \underline{+29} \\ & 53\% \end{array}$ is more than 50% or $\frac{1}{2}$.

18. (5) A, B, E

A = 0.65 kg = 0.650 kg

B = 0.667 kg = 0.667 kg

C = 0.6 kg = 0.600 kg

D = 0.595 kg = 0.595 kg

E = 0.7 kg = 0.700 kg

The three heaviest are A, B, and E.

19. (2) 6

B is 1 unit above the x-axis.

C is 7 units above the x-axis.

The distance between B and C is $7 - 1 = 6$.

20. (5) $\sqrt{4^2 + 6^2}$

$A = (x_1, y_1) = (2, 1)$

$C = (x_2, y_2) = (6, 7)$

$d = \sqrt{(x_2 - x_1)^2 + (y_2 - y_1)^2}$

$d = \sqrt{(6 - 2)^2 + (7 - 1)^2}$

$d = \sqrt{4^2 + 6^2}$

21. **(2)** **10**

$$2x - 3 = 17$$
$$\underline{+3 \quad +3}$$
$$2x \quad = 20$$
$$\frac{2x}{2} = \frac{20}{2}$$
$$x \quad = 10$$

22. **(4)** **314**

$$A = \pi r^2$$
$$A = 3.14 \times 10^2$$
$$A = 3.14 \times 100$$
$$A = 314$$

23. **(1)** **40(30) + 40(12)**

24. **(3)** **$13.80**

$$10 \times \$4 = \$40 \qquad \frac{p}{230} = \frac{6}{100}$$
$$5 \times \$15 = 75$$
$$\underline{+115}$$
$$\$230 \qquad 100p = 1380$$
$$p = \$13.80$$

25. **(1)** **$384**

$$40 \times \$12 = \$480 \qquad \$480$$
$$\frac{p}{480} = \frac{20}{100} \qquad \underline{-96}$$
$$100p = 9600 \qquad \$384$$
$$p = 96$$

26. **(3)** **40%**

$$\$2000$$
$$\underline{-1200}$$
$$\$800$$

$$\frac{800}{2000} = \frac{x}{100}$$
$$2000x = 80,000$$
$$x = 40\%$$

27. **(4)** ***D***

The Pythagorean relationship applies only to right triangles. Triangle *D* is the only triangle that contains a right angle.

28. **(3)** **25 + 35 + 40**

To surround the space, you need the perimeter.
$$P = a + b + c$$
$$P = 25 + 35 + 40$$

29. **(1)** $\dfrac{H}{B}$

30. **(1)** **8**

$$V = lwh$$
$$V = 4 \times 4 \times 0.5$$
$$V = 8$$

31. **(2)** **3**

$$9m + 5 = 2m + 26$$
$$\underline{-2m \qquad -2m}$$
$$7m + 5 = 26$$
$$\underline{-5 \qquad -5}$$
$$7m \quad = \quad 21$$
$$\frac{7m}{7} = \frac{21}{7}$$
$$m \quad = \quad 3$$

32. **(4)** **Store D**

Store A = $.198 each
$$5\overline{)\$.99}$$

Store B = 25¢ each

Store C = $.333 each
$$3\overline{)\$1.00}$$

Store D = $.166 each
$$12\overline{)\$2.00}$$

Store E = 20¢ each
$$2\overline{)40¢}$$

Store D is least expensive.

33. **(2)** $x^2 = 36$

For $x = 6$, $x^2 = (6)(6) = 36$
For $x = -6$, $x^2 = (-6)(-6) = 36$

34. **(2)** **80°**

$$x + 2x + 60° = 180°$$
$$3x + 60° = 180°$$
$$\underline{ -60° \quad -60°}$$
$$3x \quad = 120°$$
$$\frac{3x}{3} = \frac{120°}{3}$$
$$x \quad = 40°$$

angle $B = 2x = 2(40°) = 80°$

35. **(5)** **between the post office and the community college**

From home to the post office is $0.9 + 1.3 = 2.2$ miles. The dry cleaner is $3.0 - 2.2 = 0.8$ mile beyond the post office. The dry cleaner must be between the post office and the community college.

36. **(3)** **4**

$$y = \frac{1}{2}x + 1$$
$$y = \frac{1}{2}(6) + 1$$
$$y = 3 + 1$$
$$y = 4$$

37. **(2)** ***c*(*c* + 3)**

Factor out *c* from both terms.
$$c^2 + 3c = c(c + 3)$$

38. **(4)** $\frac{1}{2} \times 20 \times 12$

The shaded part is a triangle.
$$A = \frac{1}{2}bh$$
$$A = \frac{1}{2} \times 20 \times 12$$

39. **(1)** **12 × 8 × 5**

40. **(4)** **18**

$$\frac{AB}{BC} = \frac{AD}{DE}$$
$$\frac{5}{3} = \frac{30}{x}$$
$$5x = 90$$
$$x = 18$$

41. (5) $x \leq 36$

$$\frac{2}{3}x \leq 24$$

$$\frac{3}{2} \cdot \frac{2}{3}x \leq 24 \cdot \frac{3}{2}$$

$$x \leq 36$$

42. (1) $180° - 2x$

The three angles total 180°.
angle $B = 180° - 2x$

43. (3) 16

For $x = 5$, $y = 2(5) + 2 = 10 + 2 = 12$
For $x = 6$, $y = 2(6) + 2 = 12 + 2 = 14$
For $x = 7$, $y = 2(7) + 2 = 14 + 2 = 16$

44. (1) *AB* **is the longest side.**

$30° + 50° = 80°$
$\angle C = 180° - 80° = 100°$
Since $\angle C$ is the largest angle, the side across from it, AB, is the longest side.

45. (5) $2(49) + 3(29)$

46. (5) **Not enough information is given.**

To find the square feet on the surface of the patio, you need the area. You know the length of the patio but not the width.

47. (2) $\frac{3}{8}$

$$\frac{6}{x^2} = \frac{6}{4^2} = \frac{6}{16} = \frac{3}{8}$$

48. (4) 85°

If the triangles are congruent, $\angle A = \angle D$, $\angle B = \angle E$, and $\angle F$ must equal $\angle C$. This satisfies the *angle, side, angle* requirement.
$\angle C = 180° - 65° - 30° = 85°$

49. (5) **−8 and +3**

$c^2 + 5c - 24 = 0$
$(c + 8)(c - 3) = 0$

$$\begin{array}{ll} c + 8 = 0 & c - 3 = 0 \\ \quad -8 \;\; -8 & \quad +3 \;\; +3 \\ \hline c \quad\; = -8 & c \quad\; = +3 \end{array}$$

50. (4) $2x + 31 = 99$

	Sue	Juan
age now	x	$x + 25$
age in three years	$x + 3$	$x + 25 + 3$

$x + 3 + x + 25 + 3 = 99$
$2x + 31 \qquad\qquad = 99$

51. (1) $\frac{6 - 1}{4 - 1}$

$$m = \frac{y_2 - y_1}{x_2 - x_1}$$

$$m = \frac{6 - 1}{4 - 1}$$

52. (3) **twice**

In 1985 Company C's sales were about $120,000.
In 1985 Company A's sales were about $60,000.
$120,000 is twice as much as $60,000.

53. (1) **Only Company A showed a steady rise in volume of sales.**

54. (3) 2.53×10^5

55. (1) $\frac{x}{12}$

Divide the total sales x by 12, the number of months in the year.

56. (4) **10**

The Pythagorean theorem applies. The shortest distance from Middletown to Southport is

$$d = \sqrt{8^2 + 6^2}$$
$$d = \sqrt{64 + 36}$$
$$d = \sqrt{100}$$
$$d = 10$$

Practice Test Evaluation Chart

On the following chart, circle the number of any problem you got wrong. After each problem number you will see the name of the section (or sections) where you can find the skills you need to solve the problem. When a problem involves more than one skill, the sections are separated by a slash (/).

This chart should help you decide which areas you need to review before you take the GED Test.

Problem	Section	Starting Page
	Arithmetic	
1	Choosing the Operation/Formulas	26/215
3, 7, 10, 11, 26	Percents	131
6, 14, 29	Probability & Ratio	117/121
9	Rounding and Estimating	30
16, 17, 52, 53	Graphs	177
18, 32	Decimals	53
23, 24, 25	Item Sets	154
39, 45	Set-Up Questions	48
54	Scientific Notation	311
	Geometry	
4, 12, 28	Perimeter & Circumference	226
5, 15, 38	Angles	252
13	Powers	233
22, 30, 46	Area & Volume	238/245
27, 34, 40, 42, 44, 48, 54	Triangles	257
	Algebra	
2, 50, 55	Word Problems	213
8, 33, 49	Quadratic Equations	309
19, 20	Rectangular Coordinate System	300
21, 31, 36	Solving Equations	199
35	The Number Line	279
37	Factoring	293
41	Inequalities	290
43	Linear Equations	305
47	Formulas	215
51	Slope and Intercepts	307

Answer Key

CHAPTER 1

WHOLE NUMBER REVIEW EXERCISE 1
page 12

1. 40   20,000   3
2. 300,000   900   1000
3. 20   60,000,000   400
4. 400,000,000   40,000   600,000
5. 1 × 10,000 = **10,000**
   0 × 1000   = **0** (no thousands)
   4 × 100   = **400**
   9 × 10   = **90**
   6 × 1   = **6**

WHOLE NUMBER REVIEW EXERCISE 2
page 12

	1	3	8	4	6	9	7	10	2	5
8	9	11	16	12	14	17	15	18	10	13
1	2	4	9	5	7	10	8	11	3	6
3	4	6	11	7	9	12	10	13	5	8
6	7	9	14	10	12	15	13	16	8	11
4	5	7	12	8	10	13	11	14	6	9
9	10	12	17	13	15	18	16	19	11	14
5	6	8	13	9	11	14	12	15	7	10
7	8	10	15	11	13	16	14	17	9	12
2	3	5	10	6	8	11	9	12	4	7
10	11	13	18	14	16	19	17	20	12	15

WHOLE NUMBER REVIEW EXERCISE 3
page 13

	12	3	1	4	10	9	7	5	6	8	11	0	2
9	108	27	9	36	90	81	63	45	54	72	99	0	18
7	84	21	7	28	70	63	49	35	42	56	77	0	14
4	48	12	4	16	40	36	28	20	24	32	44	0	8
5	60	15	5	20	50	45	35	25	30	40	55	0	10
2	24	6	2	8	20	18	14	10	12	16	22	0	4
1	12	3	1	4	10	9	7	5	6	8	11	0	2
8	96	24	8	32	80	72	56	40	48	64	88	0	16
10	120	30	10	40	100	90	70	50	60	80	110	0	20
12	144	36	12	48	120	108	84	60	72	96	132	0	24
0	0	0	0	0	0	0	0	0	0	0	0	0	0
11	132	33	11	44	110	99	77	55	66	88	121	0	22
3	36	9	3	12	30	27	21	15	18	24	33	0	6
6	72	18	6	24	60	54	42	30	36	48	66	0	12

WHOLE NUMBER REVIEW EXERCISE 4
page 14

1. 5 × 4 = 20
2. 7 × 8 = 56
3. 3 × 8 = 24
4. 5 × 9 = 45
5. 6 × 5 = 30
6. 7 × 6 = 42
7. 9 × 2 = 18
8. 11 × 11 = 121
9. 12 × 4 = 48
10. 8 × 5 = 40
11. 6 × 3 = 18
12. 9 × 6 = 54
13. 8 × 9 = 72
14. 7 × 4 = 28
15. 9 × 4 = 36
16. 64 ÷ 8 = 8
17. 42 ÷ 6 = 7
18. 25 ÷ 5 = 5
19. 24 ÷ 8 = 3
20. 54 ÷ 9 = 6
21. 36 ÷ 6 = 6
22. 42 ÷ 7 = 6
23. 81 ÷ 9 = 9
24. 56 ÷ 8 = 7
25. 49 ÷ 7 = 7
26. 45 ÷ 5 = 9
27. 32 ÷ 4 = 8
28. 63 ÷ 9 = 7
29. 48 ÷ 6 = 8
30. 21 ÷ 3 = 7

GED PRACTICE:
WHOLE NUMBER REVIEW
page 19

1. **117,807**

$$\begin{array}{r} 25,624 \\ + \ 92,183 \\ \hline 117,807 \end{array}$$

2. **57,919**

$$\begin{array}{r} 60,845 \\ - \ 2,926 \\ \hline 57,919 \end{array}$$

3. **41,231**

$$\begin{array}{r} 48,005 \\ - \ 6,774 \\ \hline 41,231 \end{array}$$

4. **2373**

$$\begin{array}{r} 83 \\ 2096 \\ + \ 194 \\ \hline 2373 \end{array}$$

5. **34,248**

$$\begin{array}{r} 5,708 \\ \times \quad 6 \\ \hline 34,248 \end{array}$$

6. **25,826**

$$\begin{array}{r} 349 \\ \times \quad 74 \\ \hline 1\ 396 \\ 24\ 43 \\ \hline 25,826 \end{array}$$

7. **356,648**

$$\begin{array}{r} 872 \\ \times \quad 409 \\ \hline 7\ 848 \\ 348\ 80 \\ \hline 356,648 \end{array}$$

8. **3,250,000**

$$\begin{array}{r} 65 \\ \times \ 50,000 \\ \hline 3,250,000 \end{array}$$

9. **26 r4**

$$\begin{array}{r} 26\ r4 \\ 17\overline{)446} \\ \underline{34} \\ 106 \\ \underline{102} \\ 4 \end{array}$$

10. **308**

$$8\overline{)2464}$$ = 308

11. **9,006**

$$6\overline{)54,036}$$ = 9,006

12. **14,459**

$$\begin{array}{r} 30,045 \\ - \ 15,586 \\ \hline 14,459 \end{array}$$

13. **3418**

$$\begin{array}{r} 194 \\ 8 \\ 2366 \\ + \ 850 \\ \hline 3418 \end{array}$$

14. **48,000**

$$\begin{array}{r} 96 \\ \times \ 500 \\ \hline 48,000 \end{array}$$

15. **2,184,000**

$$\begin{array}{r} 3,000,000 \\ - \ 816,000 \\ \hline 2,184,000 \end{array}$$

16. **203,406**

$$\begin{array}{r} 29,058 \\ \times \quad 7 \\ \hline 203,406 \end{array}$$

17. **47**

$$\begin{array}{r} 47 \\ 800\overline{)37,600} \\ \underline{32\ 00} \\ 5\ 600 \\ \underline{5\ 600} \\ 0 \end{array}$$

18. **592,000**

$$\begin{array}{r} 74 \\ \times \ 8,000 \\ \hline 592,000 \end{array}$$

19. **4,775,500**

$$\begin{array}{r} 5,040,000 \\ - \ 264,500 \\ \hline 4,775,500 \end{array}$$

20. **306**

$$\begin{array}{r} 306 \\ 35\overline{)10,710} \\ \underline{10\ 5} \\ 21 \\ \underline{0} \\ 210 \\ \underline{210} \\ 0 \end{array}$$

21. **40,720**

$$\begin{array}{r} 5,090 \\ \times \quad 8 \\ \hline 40,720 \end{array}$$

22. **423**

$$\begin{array}{r} 423 \\ 12\overline{)5076} \\ \underline{48} \\ 27 \\ \underline{24} \\ 36 \\ \underline{36} \\ 0 \end{array}$$

23. **6912**

$$\begin{array}{r} 7000 \\ - \ 88 \\ \hline 6912 \end{array}$$

24. **391,084**

$$\begin{array}{r} 400,300 \\ - \ 9,216 \\ \hline 391,084 \end{array}$$

25. **705**

$$4\overline{)2820}$$ = 705

26. **155,700**

$$\begin{array}{r} 346 \\ \times \quad 450 \\ \hline 17\ 300 \\ 138\ 4 \\ \hline 155,700 \end{array}$$

27. **15,792**

$$\begin{array}{r} 2,900 \\ 857 \\ 11,630 \\ + \ 405 \\ \hline 15,792 \end{array}$$

28. 8,060 r3

$$
\begin{array}{r}
8,060\,\text{r}3 \\
7\,\overline{)\,56,423} \\
\underline{56} \\
0\ 42 \\
\underline{42} \\
03
\end{array}
$$

29. 492,869

$$
\begin{array}{r}
1,300,500 \\
-\ 807,631 \\
\hline
492,869
\end{array}
$$

30. 740

$$
\begin{array}{r}
740 \\
19\,\overline{)\,14,060} \\
\underline{13\ 3} \\
76 \\
\underline{76} \\
00
\end{array}
$$

CHAPTER 2

PROBLEM SOLVING EXERCISE 1

pages 22–23

1. **(3)** Find the difference between the number of votes Mr. Sanders received and the number of votes his opponent received.
2. **(3)** How much did the TV cost before it was on sale?
3. **(2)** Find Manny's total car payments for twelve months.
4. **(3)** Find out how far Pancho drove on one gallon of gasoline.
5. **(2)** How much did Gordon weigh at the end of December?
6. **(2)** How much do both Marilyn and Calvin take home in a month?
7. **(3)** Find the distance Carmen can drive with 13 gallons of gas.
8. **(1)** How much more does Gloria need to save for the TV?

PROBLEM SOLVING EXERCISE 2

pages 24–25

1. *Need:* 943 cars sold last month and 387 made in the U.S.
   Do not need: 198 cars made in Japan
2. *Need:* March 1992 unemployment of 10,549 and March 1991 unemployment of 8,248
   Do not need: December 1991 unemployment of 9,307
3. *Need:* 132 miles and 3 hours
   Do not need: 22 miles on one gallon
4. *Need:* 132 miles and 22 miles on one gallon
   Do not need: 3 hours
5. *Need:* $6.50 for a child's ticket and 1230 children
   Do not need: $10.50 for an adult's ticket
6. *Need:* 2500 adults and 1250 high school graduates
   Do not need: 750 college graduates
7. *Need:* California pop. of 30,380,000 and New York pop. of 18,058,000
   Do not need: Texas pop. of 17,349,000
8. *Need:* $134.40 and 64 feet
   Do not need: 4 pounds a foot

9. *Need:* $285 for rent and $400 for food
   Do not need: $1100 income
10. *Need:* $3.69 a pound and 3 pounds of pork chops
    Do not need: $1.99 a pound and 2 pounds of bacon

PROBLEM SOLVING EXERCISE 3

pages 27–28

1. *Question:* How much older is father than son?
   Operation: subtract
2. *Question:* Find hourly wage.
   Operation: divide
3. *Question:* How much were monthly utilities?
   Operation: add
4. *Question:* Find how many dozen eggs are white.
   Operation: subtract
5. *Question:* Find net income.
   Operation: subtract
6. *Question:* Find year when the man was born.
   Operation: subtract
7. *Question:* Find daily pay.
   Operation: multiply
8. *Question:* Find monthly salary.
   Operation: divide
9. *Question:* Find number of minutes needed to type 1700-word letter.
   Operation: divide
10. *Question:* Find total amount in fund.
    Operation: add

PROBLEM SOLVING EXERCISE 4

page 29

problems 1–8, pages 22–23

1. 4,695

$$
\begin{array}{r}
67,576 \\
-\ 62,881 \\
\hline
4,695
\end{array}
$$

2. $258

$$
\begin{array}{r}
\$198 \\
+\ 60 \\
\hline
\$258
\end{array}
$$

3. $2280

$$
\begin{array}{r}
\$190 \\
\times\ 12 \\
\hline
380 \\
190 \\
\hline
\$2280
\end{array}
$$

4. 23 mi

$$
\begin{array}{r}
23 \\
20\,\overline{)\,460} \\
\underline{40} \\
60 \\
\underline{60} \\
0
\end{array}
$$

5. 211 lb

$$
\begin{array}{r}
178 \\
+\ 33 \\
\hline
211
\end{array}
$$

6. **$1,850**

$$
\begin{array}{r}
\$\ 1,850 \\
12\overline{)\$22,200} \\
\underline{12} \\
10\ 2 \\
\underline{9\ 6} \\
60 \\
\underline{60} \\
00
\end{array}
$$

7. **312 mi**

$$
\begin{array}{r}
24 \\
\times\ 13 \\
\hline
72 \\
24 \\
\hline
312
\end{array}
$$

8. **$95**

$$
\begin{array}{r}
\$385 \\
-\ 290 \\
\hline
\$\ 95
\end{array}
$$

problems 1–10, pages 24–25

1. **556 cars**

$$
\begin{array}{r}
943 \\
-\ 387 \\
\hline
556
\end{array}
$$

2. **2,301**

$$
\begin{array}{r}
10,549 \\
-\ 8,248 \\
\hline
2,301
\end{array}
$$

3. **44 mi**

$$
\begin{array}{r}
44 \\
3\overline{)132} \\
\underline{12} \\
12 \\
\underline{12} \\
0
\end{array}
$$

4. **6 gal**

$$
\begin{array}{r}
6 \\
22\overline{)132}
\end{array}
$$

5. **$7995**

$$
\begin{array}{r}
1230 \\
\times\ \$6.50 \\
\hline
615\ 00 \\
7380 \\
\hline
\$7995.00
\end{array}
$$

6. **1250**

$$
\begin{array}{r}
2500 \\
-\ 1250 \\
\hline
1250
\end{array}
$$

7. **12,322,000**

$$
\begin{array}{r}
30,380,000 \\
-\ 18,058,000 \\
\hline
12,322,000
\end{array}
$$

8. **$2.10**

$$
\begin{array}{r}
\$\ 2.10 \\
64\overline{)\$134.40} \\
\underline{128} \\
6\ 4 \\
\underline{6\ 4} \\
00
\end{array}
$$

9. **$115**

$$
\begin{array}{r}
\$400 \\
-\ 285 \\
\hline
\$115
\end{array}
$$

10. **$11.07**

$$
\begin{array}{r}
\$3.69 \\
\times\ 3 \\
\hline
\$11.07
\end{array}
$$

problems 1–10, pages 27–28

1. **29 yr**

$$
\begin{array}{r}
37 \\
-\ 8 \\
\hline
29
\end{array}
$$

2. **$6.50**

$$
\begin{array}{r}
\$\ 6.50 \\
40\overline{)\$260.00} \\
\underline{240} \\
20\ 0 \\
\underline{20\ 0} \\
00
\end{array}
$$

3. **$120**

$$
\begin{array}{r}
\$42 \\
25 \\
+\ 53 \\
\hline
\$120
\end{array}
$$

4. **15 dozen**

$$
\begin{array}{r}
20 \\
-\ 5 \\
\hline
15
\end{array}
$$

5. **$13,616**

$$
\begin{array}{r}
\$18,296 \\
-\ 4,680 \\
\hline
\$13,616
\end{array}
$$

6. **1893**

$$
\begin{array}{r}
1985 \\
-\ 92 \\
\hline
1893
\end{array}
$$

7. **$60**

$$
\begin{array}{r}
\$\ 7.50 \\
\times\ 8 \\
\hline
\$60.00
\end{array}
$$

8. **$1,365**

$$
\begin{array}{r}
\$\ 1,365 \\
12\overline{)\$16,380}
\end{array}
$$

9. **20 min**

$$
\begin{array}{r}
20 \\
85\overline{)1700} \\
\underline{170} \\
00
\end{array}
$$

10. **$112,000**

$$
\begin{array}{r}
\$\ 85,000 \\
+\ 27,000 \\
\hline
\$112,000
\end{array}
$$

PROBLEM SOLVING EXERCISE 5
page 31

1. 60

2. 230

3. 400

4. 6000

5. 8000

6. 7000

7. 25,000

8. 40,000

9. 1060

10. 28,100

11. 16,200

12. 1,480,000

13. 3000

14. 310

15. 8100

PROBLEM SOLVING EXERCISE 6
pages 32–33

1. *Round off wage to nearest dollar:* $8
    Approximate answer: 9 × $8 = **$72**
    Actual answer: **$74.25** $ 8.25
                                    ×   9
                                    ────────
                                    $74.25

2. *Round off speed to nearest ten:* 50 mph
    Approximate answer: 50 × 6 = **300**
    Actual answer: **312 miles**
                                    52
                                  × 6
                                  ────
                                   312

3. *Round off each attendance to nearest 100:* 500, 700, 500
    Approximate answer: 500 + 700 + 500 = **1700**
    Actual answer: **1672 people**   487
                                         662
                                       + 523
                                       ─────
                                        1672

4. *Round off salary to a number easily divided by 12:* $24,000
    Approximate answer: $24,000 ÷ 12 = **$2,000**
    Actual answer: **$2080** $ 2,080
                                   12)$24,960

5. *Round off year of construction to nearest ten:* 1900
    Round off 1988 to nearest ten: 1990
    Approximate answer: 1990 − 1900 = **90**
    Actual answer: **91 years**   1988
                                    − 1897
                                    ──────
                                        91

6. *Round off sale price and savings to nearest ten:* $200 and $60
    Approximate answer: $200 + $60 = **$260**
    Actual answer: **$256** $198
                                  + 58
                                  ─────
                                  $256

7. *Round off price of one carton to nearest dollar:* $2
    Approximate answer: 5 × $2 = **$10**
    Actual answer: **$9.45** $1.89
                                   ×   5
                                   ──────
                                   $9.45

8. *Round off each length to nearest ten:* 100 and 30
    Approximate answer: 100 − 30 = **70**
    Actual answer: **69 inches**   96
                                     − 27
                                     ────
                                       69

PROBLEM SOLVING EXERCISE 7
pages 33–34

1. a. **three**   b. **three**   c. **three**

2. a. **one**   b. **two**   c. **one**

3. a. **four**   b. **one**   c. **two**

4. **(2)** 600

5. **(3)** 10

6. **(1)** 1400

7. **(1)** 30

8. **(3)** 900

9. **(2)** 582

10. **(1)** 721

11. **(2)** 63

12. **(3)** 212

EXERCISE 8
page 36

1. **(4) $2840**

    estimate: $ 3,000
                      12)$36,000

2. **(2) 310**

    estimate: 60
                     × 5
                     ─────────
                     300 miles

3. **(5) $15.95**

    estimate: $3
                     × 5
                     ────
                     $15

4. **(3) 1672**

    estimate: 400
                       700
                     + 500
                     ──────
                      1600

5. **(4) $14.60**

    estimate: $ 15
                     40)$600
                        40
                        ───
                        200
                        200
                        ───
                          0

6. **(2) $1064**

    estimate: 100
                     × $10
                     ──────
                     $1000

7. **(3) $18,960**

    estimate: $20,000
              9)$180,000

8. **(4) $2.89**

    estimate: $3
                     4)$12

PROBLEM SOLVING EXERCISE 9
pages 38–39

1. a. Find cost of educating 30 children in Upperville.
   b. Find cost of educating 30 children in Central City.
   c. Subtract answer to step b from answer to step a.

   Solution: **a.** $7,800   **b.** $2,100
                  $\times$ 30 $\times$ 30
                  $234,000 $63,000

            c. $234,000
                $-$ 63,000
                $171,000

2. a. Find combined income for week.
   b. Find income for year. Multiply weekly income by 52. (1 year = 52 weeks)

   Solution: **a.** $240   **b.** $440
               $+$ 200 $\times$ 52
                $440   880
                        22 00
                    $22,880

3. a. Find total number of cases.
   b. Multiply number of cases by 20.

   Solution: **a.** 4   **b.** 20
                6        $\times$ 20
             $+$ 10   **400 cans**
              20

4. a. Find the distance she drives in 5 hours.
   b. Find the distance she drives in 3 hours.
   c. Add results from steps a and b.

   Solution: **a.** 55   **b.** 35
               $\times$ 5 $\times$ 3
             275   105

           c. 275
              $+$ 105
             380 miles

5. a. Find the amount he makes in 35 hours.
   b. Find the amount he makes in 6 hours.
   c. Add results from steps a and b.

   Solution: **a.** $8.50   **b.** $12.75
               $\times$ 35 $\times$ 6
             42 50 $76.50
            255 0
            $297.50

           c. $297.50
              $+$ 76.50
             $374.00

6. a. Find total monthly payments.
   b. Add total monthly payments to down payment.

   Solution: **a.** $45   **b.** $810
               $\times$ 18 $+$ 150
             360   **$960**
              45
            $810

7. a. Find amount of last year's drive.
   b. Divide result from step a by 5.

   Solution: **a.** $30,400   **b.** $ 6,680
                 $+$ 3,000   5)$33,400
               $33,400

8. a. Find total number of words.
   b. Divide total by 75.

   Solution: **a.** 1000   **b.** 20 min
               $+$ 500   75)1500
             1500   150
                      00

PROBLEM SOLVING EXERCISE 10
page 41

1. a. Mean: **193**
      353   193
       19   3)579
    $+$ 207
      579

   b. Median: **207**
      19   207   353

2. a. Mean: **1995**
     2046   1995
      971   4)7980
     3113
   $+$ 1850
     7980

   b. Median: **1948**
    971 1850 2046 3113
     1850   1948
  $+$ 2046   2)3896
     3896

3. a. Mean: **253**
     240   253
     313   4)1012
     189
  $+$ 270
   1012

   b. Median: **255**
    189   240   270   313
     240   255
  $+$ 270   2)510
    510

4. **173 lb** 187   173
        $+$ 159 2)346
        346

5. **65°** 69   65
      71   5)325
      56
      63
   $+$ 66
    325

6. $24,800

$24,700
23,900
+ 25,800
$74,400

$24,800
3⟌$74,400

7. $26.07

$25.66
33.27
+ 19.28
$78.21

$26.07
3⟌$78.21

8. $240

$240
450⟌$108,000

9. $1,850

3 × $1,650 = $ 4,950
4 × $1,875 = $ 7,500
2 × $2,100 = $ 4,200
$16,650

$ 1,850
9⟌$16,650

10. 47

47
44
+ 50
141

47
3⟌141

PROBLEM SOLVING EXERCISE 11
page 43

1. 96

6 ×2 12 ×2 24 ×2 48 ×2 96

2. 96

81 +3 84 +3 87 +3 90 +3 93 +3 96

3. 20

32 −3 29 −3 26 −3 23 −3 20

4. 37

13 +4 17 +4 21 +4 25 +4 29 +4 33 +4 37

5. 25

10 −5 5 +10 15 −5 10 +10 20 −5 15 +10 25

6. 9

100 −19 81 −17 64 −15 49 −13 36 −11 25 −9 16 −7 9

7. 65

5 +4 9 +8 17 +16 33 +32 65

8. 30

2 +1 3 +2 5 +3 8 +4 12 +5 17 +6 23 +7 30

9. 10

320 ÷2 160 ÷2 80 ÷2 40 ÷2 20 ÷2 10

10. 49

4 ×2 8 −1 7 ×2 14 −1 13 ×2 26 −1 25 ×2 50 −1 49

11. 60

72 −4 68 −4 64 −4 60

12. $0

March	April	May	June	July	August
$30,000	$24,000	$18,000	$12,000	$6,000	0
	−$6,000	−$6,000	−$6,000	−$6,000	−$6,000

13. 48,000

1,500 ×2 3,000 ×2 6,000 ×2 12,000 ×2 24,000 ×2 48,000

PROBLEM SOLVING EXERCISE 12
page 46

1. (4) 30 + 20
2. (2) 5(3 × 4)
3. (2) 9 + (7 + 4)
4. (5) (16 × 14) + (16 × 27)
5. (4) 3(15 − 6)

PROBLEM SOLVING EXERCISE 13
page 47

1. 0
2. 16
3. 4
4. 13
5. 4

PROBLEM SOLVING EXERCISE 14
page 49

1. (3) 5(45 + 30)
2. (2) 4(265 + 304)
3. (1) 200(5 + 10)
4. (3) 9(3 + 4)
5. (4) (4 × 55) + (3 × 40)
6. (1) 12(50 − 10)
7. (2) (3 × 16) + (2 × 24)
8. (1) $\dfrac{\$3.40 + \$8.00 + \$6.50 + \$6.50}{4}$

GED PRACTICE:
PROBLEM SOLVING REVIEW
pages 50–51

1. (4) Find the amount each program gets from the grant.

2. (4) 357

420
− 63
357

3. (3) 138,109

259,056
− 120,947
138,109

4. (3) Divide 81,480 by 84, then add 200.

5. (1) 36,000 6 is in the thousands place. The 4 indicates that you should leave 6 and put zeros to the right of 6.

6. (4) \$25 $10 \times \$1.29 = \$12.90$

$$\begin{array}{r} \$12.90 \\ + \ 12.00 \\ \hline \$24.90 \end{array}$$ to the nearest dollar = \$25

7. (5) \$1040

$$\begin{array}{r} \$56 \\ \times \ 15 \\ \hline 280 \\ 56 \\ \hline \$840 \end{array} \qquad \begin{array}{r} \$ \ 840 \\ + \ 200 \\ \hline \$ \ 1040 \end{array}$$

8. (2) \$14,200 $7 \times \$1100 = \$7700$
$12 - 7 = 5$ months left
$5 \times \$1300 = \$6500$
$\$7700 + \$6500 = \$14,200$

9. (2) 348 $55 \times 6 = 330$
$9 \times 2 = 18$
total $= 348$

10. (4) 34

$$\begin{array}{r} 27 \\ 36 \\ 28 \\ 39 \\ + \ 40 \\ \hline 170 \end{array} \qquad \begin{array}{r} 34 \\ 5\overline{)170} \end{array}$$

11. (2) 1200   1024 1137 1263 1440

$$\begin{array}{r} 1137 \\ + \ 1263 \\ \hline 2400 \end{array} \qquad \begin{array}{r} 1200 \\ 2\overline{)2400} \end{array}$$

12. (2) 9 $30 \div 6 + (3 + 1)$
$5 + 4$
9

13. (1) 63

$$1 \underset{+2}{\diagdown} 3 \underset{+4}{\diagdown} 7 \underset{+8}{\diagdown} 15 \underset{+16}{\diagdown} 31 \underset{+32}{\diagdown} 63$$

14. (2) $4(9 + 15)$

15. (1) $12(9 + 6)$

CHAPTER 3

DECIMALS EXERCISE 1
page 53

1. \$4   20¢   0

2. 5¢   40¢   1¢

DECIMALS EXERCISE 2
page 55

1. a. three   **b.** one   **c.** two
2. a. none   **b.** two   **c.** five

3. a. none   **b.** one   **c.** four
4. a. three   **b.** one   **c.** six
5. a. hundredths or pennies
   b. thousandths
   c. tenths or dimes
6. a. ten-thousandths
   b. hundredths or pennies
   c. hundred-thousandths
7. a. hundredths or pennies
   b. ones
   c. hundreds
8. a. millionths
   b. tenths or dimes
   c. thousandths

DECIMALS EXERCISE 3
page 56

1. .031
2. 2.12
3. .0780
4. 100.03
5. 71.5
6. 4.007
7. 3.0049
8. 13.13
9. 403.1
10. 10.20

DECIMALS EXERCISE 4
page 57

1. a. .067 or **0.067** (The zero in the units' place is often written to show that there is no whole number.)
   b. 3.405 **c.** 8.0906
2. a. 80.025 **b.** 124.009 **c.** 7.5
3. a. 5 (Notice that you do not need to write the decimal point with a whole number.)
   b. .3708 or 0.3708 **c.** 29.3
4. a. 6.3 **b.** .0023 or 0.0023 **c.** 60.0502

DECIMALS EXERCISE 5
page 57

1. .4 or 0.4
2. 6.3
3. .18 or 0.18
4. .009 or 0.009
5. .0002 or 0.0002
6. .013 or 0.013
7. 96.4
8. 5.016
9. 7500.8
10. .125 or 0.125
11. 84.009
12. .0312 or 0.0312
13. 204.03
14. 70.345

DECIMALS EXERCISE 6
page 58

1. a. 0.7   **b.** 0.62   **c.** 0.403
2. a. 0.0029   **b.** 0.101   **c.** 0.9
3. a. 0.8   **b.** 5.23   **c.** 0.4
4. a. 0.31   **b.** 1.68   **c.** 3.04
5. a. 0.062, 0.26, 0.602, 0.62
   b. 0.0034, 0.34, 0.403, 0.43
   c. 0.2, 0.209, 0.21, 0.305
6. a. 0.77, 0.701, 0.7, 0.67
   b. 0.55, 0.511, 0.505, 0.5
   c. 0.12, 0.112, 0.102, 0.011

DECIMALS EXERCISE 7
page 60

1. *Step 1.* Give all lengths the same number of decimal places:
   A—0.800
   B—0.950
   C—0.850
   D—0.090
   E—0.085
   Step 2. Order the lengths from smallest to largest:
   E—0.085
   D—0.090
   A—0.800
   C—0.850
   B—0.950
   Step 3. Find this order in the answer choices:
   (4) E, D, A, C, B

2. *Step 1.* Give all weights the same number of decimal places:
   A—0.600
   B—0.650
   C—0.500
   D—0.550
   E—0.505
   Step 2. Order the weights from lightest to heaviest:
   C—0.500
   E—0.505
   D—0.550
   A—0.600
   B—0.650
   Step 3. Find this order in the answer choices:
   (5) C, E, D, A, B

DECIMALS EXERCISE 8
page 61

1. **1.5**
   .6
   + .9
   ———
   1.5

2. **1.37**
   .57
   + .8
   ———
   1.37

3. **195.909**
   16.
   9.24
   170.3
   + .369
   ————
   195.909

4. **30.446**
   15.23
   4.
   1.816
   + 9.4
   ————
   30.446

5. **233.316**
   12.3
   .016
   5.
   + 216.
   ————
   233.316

6. **29.31**
   4.036
   23.
   2.19
   + .084
   ————
   29.310 = 29.31

7. **119.27**
   83.
   + 36.27
   ————
   119.27

8. **$105.44**
   $84.
   19.65
   .23
   + 1.56
   ————
   $105.44

9. **.05084**
   .0075
   .00128
   .004
   + .03806
   ————
   .05084

DECIMALS EXERCISE 9
page 62

1. **.54**
   .80
   − .26
   ———
   .54

2. **.155**
   .500
   − .345
   ———
   .155

3. **17.68**
   18.00
   − .32
   ———
   17.68

4. **.015**
   .090
   − .075
   ———
   .015

5. **.206**
   .300
   − .094
   ———
   .206

6. **.0055**
   .0080
   − .0025
   ———
   .0055

7. **.275**
   .600
   − .325
   ———
   .275

8. **$16.32**
   $30.00
   − 13.68
   ———
   $16.32

9. **15.37**
   20.00
   − 4.63
   ———
   15.37

DECIMALS EXERCISE 10
pages 62–63

1. **.301**
$$
\begin{array}{r}
.206 \\
+ .095 \\
\hline
.301
\end{array}
$$

2. **$.75 million**

$$
\begin{array}{r}
\$1.35 \\
.85 \\
+ 1.05 \\
\hline
\$3.25 \text{ million}
\end{array}
\qquad
\begin{array}{r}
\$4.00 \text{ million} \\
- 3.25 \\
\hline
\$.75 \text{ million}
\end{array}
$$

3. **(1) 0.65 ft**

$$
\begin{array}{r}
10.65 \text{ feet} \\
+ 0.2 \\
\hline
10.85 \text{ feet}
\end{array}
\qquad
\begin{array}{r}
11.50 \\
- 10.85 \\
\hline
.65 \text{ feet}
\end{array}
$$

4. **(2) 12.3 million**

$$
\begin{array}{r}
248.7 \text{ million} \\
- 226.8 \\
\hline
21.9 \text{ million}
\end{array}
\qquad
\begin{array}{r}
21.9 \text{ million} \\
- 9.6 \\
\hline
12.3 \text{ million}
\end{array}
$$

5. **(3)** 5 − (2.45 + 0.95)

6. **(4)** Multiply 14 by .44, multiply 8 by 1.09, and add the two products.

DECIMALS EXERCISE 11
page 65

1. **.56**

$$
\begin{array}{r}
.8 \text{ one place} \\
\times\ .7 \text{ one place} \\
\hline
.56 \text{ two places}
\end{array}
$$

2. **6.18**

$$
\begin{array}{r}
20.6 \text{ one place} \\
\times\ 0.3 \text{ one place} \\
\hline
6.18 \text{ two places}
\end{array}
$$

3. **.836**

$$
\begin{array}{r}
2.09 \text{ two places} \\
\times\ \ .4 \text{ one place} \\
\hline
.836 \text{ three places}
\end{array}
$$

4. **22.41**

$$
\begin{array}{r}
8.3 \text{ one place} \\
\times\ 2.7 \text{ one place} \\
\hline
5\ 81 \\
16\ 6 \\
\hline
22.41 \text{ two places}
\end{array}
$$

5. **.2268**

$$
\begin{array}{r}
0.378 \text{ three places} \\
\times\ \ 0.6 \text{ one place} \\
\hline
.2268 \text{ four places}
\end{array}
$$

6. **.012**

$$
\begin{array}{r}
.0004 \text{ four places} \\
\times\ \ \ 30 \text{ no places} \\
\hline
.0120 \text{ four places} = .012
\end{array}
$$

7. **.008**

$$
\begin{array}{r}
0.8 \text{ one place} \\
\times\ 0.01 \text{ two places} \\
\hline
.008 \text{ three places}
\end{array}
$$

8. **1.1512**

$$
\begin{array}{r}
1.439 \text{ three places} \\
\times\ \ \ 0.8 \text{ one place} \\
\hline
1.1512 \text{ four places}
\end{array}
$$

9. **.114**

$$
\begin{array}{r}
.076 \text{ three places} \\
\times\ \ 1.5 \text{ one place} \\
\hline
380 \\
76 \\
\hline
.1140 \text{ four places} = .114
\end{array}
$$

10. **$104.16**

$$
\begin{array}{r}
\$24.80 \text{ two places} \\
\times\ \ \ \ \ 4.2 \text{ one place} \\
\hline
4\ 960 \\
99\ 20 \\
\hline
\$104.160 \text{ three places} = \$104.16
\end{array}
$$

11. **$575**

$$
\begin{array}{r}
\$250 \text{ no places} \\
\times\ \ \ \ 2.3 \text{ one place} \\
\hline
75\ 0 \\
500 \\
\hline
\$575.0 \text{ one place} = \$575
\end{array}
$$

12. **$1.45**

$$
\begin{array}{r}
\$1.16 \text{ two places} \\
\times\ \ \ 1.25 \text{ two places} \\
\hline
580 \\
232 \\
1\ 16 \\
\hline
\$1.4500 \text{ four places} = \$1.45
\end{array}
$$

13. 1.432 × 10 =
1.4.32 = **14.32**

14. 0.056 × 100 =
0.05.6 = **5.6**

15. 0.083 × 10 =
0.0.83 = **.83**

16. 19.7 × 1000 =
19.700. = **19,700**

17. **4.5**

$$
\begin{array}{r}
15 \text{ no places} \\
\times\ 0.3 \text{ one place} \\
\hline
4.5 \text{ one place}
\end{array}
$$

18. **357.5**

$$
\begin{array}{r}
143 \text{ no places} \\
\times\ 2.5 \text{ one place} \\
\hline
715 \\
286 \\
\hline
357.5 \text{ one place}
\end{array}
$$

19. **4.2874**

$$
\begin{array}{r}
12.61 \text{ two places} \\
\times\ 0.34 \text{ two places} \\
\hline
5044 \\
3\ 783 \\
\hline
4.2874 \text{ four places}
\end{array}
$$

20. **7950**

7.95 × 1000 =
7.950. = 7950

DECIMALS EXERCISE 12
page 67

1.
```
       6.576
  8)52.608
     48
     ‾‾
     4 6
     4 0
     ‾‾
       60
       56
       ‾‾
       48
       48
       ‾‾
        0
```

2.
```
      84.3
  9)758.7
    72
    ‾‾
    3 8
    3 6
    ‾‾
      27
      27
      ‾‾
       0
```

3.
```
       .75
  14)10.50
     9.8
     ‾‾
      70
      70
      ‾‾
       0
```

4.
```
      .013
  3).039
```

5.
```
       .095
  25)2.375
     2 25
     ‾‾‾
      125
      125
      ‾‾‾
        0
```

6.
```
       .0024
  7).0168
     14
     ‾‾
     28
     28
     ‾‾
      0
```

7.
```
      .4
  24)9.6
     96
     ‾‾
      0
```

8.
```
      .04
  24).96
     96
     ‾‾
      0
```

9.
```
      .15
  18)2.70
     1 8
     ‾‾
      90
      90
      ‾‾
       0
```

10.
```
      3.06
  12)36.72
```

11. $42.3 \div 100 = .42.3 = .423$

12. $.04 \div 10 = .0.04 = .004$

13. $19.5 \div 1000 = .019.5 = .0195$

14. $.65 \div 100 = .00.65 = .0065$

DECIMALS EXERCISE 13
page 68

1.
```
        42
  0.2.)8.4.
```

2.
```
        1 0.5
  .5.)5.2.5
```

3.
```
        2.6
  .13.)33.8
       26
       ‾‾
       7 8
       7 8
       ‾‾
         0
```

4.
```
          15
  .028.).420.
        28
        ‾‾
        1 40
        1 40
        ‾‾‾
           0
```

5.
```
         .27
  1.2.).3.24
        2 4
        ‾‾
         84
         84
         ‾‾
          0
```

6.
```
         20 90
  .04.)83.60.
       8
       ‾
       03
        0
        ‾
        3 6
        3 6
        ‾‾
        00
```

7.
```
          4
  25.3.)101.2.
        101 2
        ‾‾‾‾
            0
```

8.
```
        30 20
  .03.)90.60.
```

9.
```
         50
  .134.)6.700.
        670
        ‾‾‾
        00
```

10.

$$\begin{array}{r} 50 \\ 1.28\overline{\smash{)}64.00.} \\ \underline{64\ 0} \\ 00 \end{array}$$

11.

$$\begin{array}{r} 8\ 00 \\ .12\overline{\smash{)}96.00.} \\ \underline{96} \\ 0\ 00 \end{array}$$

12.

$$\begin{array}{r} 60 \\ 4.35.\overline{\smash{)}261.00.} \\ \underline{261\ 0} \\ 00 \end{array}$$

DECIMALS EXERCISE 14
page 69

1. (4) Add 5.4 and 7.1, then divide by 2.

2. (4) 7($5.20) + 2.5($7.80)

3. (1) 2.5(60) + 1.5(48)

4. (3) 4 − 2(1.45)

DECIMALS EXERCISE 15
page 70

1. $15.58

$$\begin{array}{r} \$1.298 \\ \times\ \ \ 12 \\ \hline 2\ 596 \\ 12\ 98 \\ \hline \$15.576 \end{array}$$

to the nearest penny = $15.58

2. 160 miles

$$\begin{array}{r} 4\ 5 \\ \times\ \ 3.5 \\ \hline 22\ 5 \\ 135 \\ \hline 157.5 \end{array}$$

to the nearest ten miles = 160 miles

3. $294

$$\begin{array}{r} \$7.85 \\ \times\ 37.5 \\ \hline 3\ 925 \\ 54\ 95 \\ 235\ 5 \\ \hline \$294.375 \end{array}$$

to the nearest dollar = $294

4. 30 cm

$$\begin{array}{r} 2.54 \\ \times\ \ 12 \\ \hline 5\ 08 \\ 25\ 4 \\ \hline 30.48 \end{array}$$

to the nearest centimeter = 30

5. $8.38

$$\begin{array}{r} \$3.49 \\ \times\ \ 2.4 \\ \hline 1396 \\ 698 \\ \hline \$8.376 \end{array}$$

to the nearest penny = $8.38

DECIMALS EXERCISE 16
page 71

1. .03

$$\begin{array}{r} .026 \\ 15\overline{\smash{)}.400} \\ \underline{30} \\ 100 \\ \underline{90} \\ 10 \end{array}$$

to the nearest hundredth = .03

2. .01

$$\begin{array}{r} .006 \\ 3\overline{\smash{)}.020} \end{array}$$

to the nearest hundredth = .01

3. .1

$$\begin{array}{r} .08 \\ 6\overline{\smash{)}.50} \end{array}$$

to the nearest tenth = .1

4. .4

$$\begin{array}{r} .37 \\ .8.\overline{\smash{)}.3.00} \end{array}$$

to the nearest tenth = .4

DECIMALS EXERCISE 17
page 73

1. $180.24
Need: Price at store X of $1199.75
   Cash rebate at store X of $100
   Price at store Y of $1279.99
Solution:

$$\begin{array}{r} \$1199.75 \\ -\ \ 100. \\ \hline \$1099.75 \end{array} \qquad \begin{array}{r} \$1279.99 \\ -\ 1099.75 \\ \hline \$\ \ \ 180.24 \end{array}$$

2. $1788
Need: Down payment at store X of $150
   Monthly payments at store X of $45.50
   Number of months in three years, 36
Solution:

$$\begin{array}{r} \$45.50 \\ \times\ \ \ 36 \\ \hline 273\ 00 \\ 1365\ 0 \\ \hline \$1638.00 \end{array} \qquad \begin{array}{r} \$1638.00 \\ +\ 150.00 \\ \hline \$1788.00 \end{array}$$

3. $1510.40
Need: Down payment at store Y of $200
   Monthly payments at store Y of $54.60
   Number of months in two years, 24
Solution:

$$\begin{array}{r} \$54.60 \\ \times\ \ \ 24 \\ \hline 218\ 40 \\ 1092\ 0 \\ \hline \$1310.40 \end{array} \qquad \begin{array}{r} \$1310.40 \\ +\ 200.00 \\ \hline \$1510.40 \end{array}$$

4. $277.60
Need: Total cost at store X from problem 2, $1788.00
   Total cost at store Y from problem 3, $1510.40
Solution:

$$\begin{array}{r} \$1788.00 \\ -\ \$1510.40 \\ \hline \$\ \ \ 277.60 \end{array}$$

5. $688.25

Need: Price of furniture at store X of $1199.75

Cash rebate at store X of $100

Total installment price at store X from problem 2, $1788

Solution:

$$\begin{array}{r} \$1199.75 \\ -\ \ \ 100 \\ \hline \$1099.75 \end{array} \qquad \begin{array}{r} \$1788.00 \\ -\ 1099.75 \\ \hline \$\ \ 688.25 \end{array}$$

6. $340

Need: Assistant's wage of $8.50 and 40 hours

Solution:

$$\begin{array}{r} \$8.50 \\ \times\ \ \ 40 \\ \hline \$340.00 \end{array}$$

7. $4160

Need: Assistant's total wages from problem 6, $340

Materials and expenses of $10,500

Price for job of $15,000

Solution:

$$\begin{array}{r} \$10,500 \\ +\ \ \ \ 340 \\ \hline \$10,840 \end{array} \qquad \begin{array}{r} \$15,000 \\ -\ 10,840 \\ \hline \$\ \ 4,160 \end{array}$$

GED PRACTICE: DECIMALS REVIEW

pages 74–77

1. hundredths

2. 70.016

3. 60.043

4. 408.0015

5. .06, .066, .6, .606

6. 42.995

$$\begin{array}{r} 36 \\ 2.93 \\ .065 \\ +\ \ 4 \\ \hline 42.995 \end{array}$$

7. .0737

$$\begin{array}{r} .0800 \\ -\ .0063 \\ \hline .0737 \end{array}$$

8. .016

$$\begin{array}{r} 3.2 \\ \times\ .005 \\ \hline .0160 \end{array} = .016$$

9. .027

$$\begin{array}{r} .027 \\ 15\overline{)\ .405} \\ \underline{30} \\ 105 \\ \underline{105} \\ 0 \end{array}$$

10. 200

$$\begin{array}{r} 200 \\ .045\overline{)\ 9.000} \end{array}$$

11. (3) 12.94 million

$$\begin{array}{r} 9.75\ \text{million} \\ +\ 3.19 \\ \hline 12.94\ \text{million} \end{array}$$

12. (1) 1.25 yards

$$\begin{array}{r} 3.00 \\ -\ 1.75 \\ \hline 1.25 \end{array}$$

13. (3) 18.6 miles

$$\begin{array}{r} 18.58 \\ 12\overline{)\ 223.00} \\ \underline{12} \\ 103 \\ \underline{96} \\ 7\ 0 \\ \underline{6\ 0} \\ 1\ 00 \\ \underline{96} \\ 4 \end{array}$$

to the nearest tenth = 18.6

14. (1) $1.77

$$\begin{array}{r} \$.034 \\ \times\ \ \ 52 \\ \hline 68 \\ 1\ 70 \\ \hline \$1.768 \end{array}$$

to the nearest penny = $1.77

15. (2) $25.78

$$\begin{array}{r} 100.0 \\ -\ 56.3 \\ \hline 43.7 \end{array} \qquad \begin{array}{r} 43.7 \\ \times\ \$.59 \\ \hline 3\ 933 \\ 21\ 85 \\ \hline \$25.783 \end{array}$$

to the nearest penny = $25.78

16. (5) .293

$$\begin{array}{r} .2933 \\ 75\overline{)\ 22.0000} \\ \underline{15\ 0} \\ 7\ 00 \\ \underline{6\ 75} \\ 250 \\ \underline{225} \\ 250 \\ \underline{225} \end{array}$$

to the nearest thousandth = .293

17. (4) D, B, E, C, A

D = 0.125

B = 0.750

E = 1.125

C = 1.750

A = 1.800

18. (3) $60.00

$$\begin{array}{r} \$7.80 \\ \times\ \ \ 5 \\ \hline \$39.00 \end{array} \qquad \begin{array}{r} \$8.40 \\ \times\ 2.5 \\ \hline 4\ 200 \\ 16\ 80 \\ \hline \$21.000 \end{array} \qquad \begin{array}{r} \$39 \\ +\ 21 \\ \hline \$60 \end{array}$$

19. (3) Multiply 3.6 by 3, then subtract 3.6.

20. (4) 5(125) + 3(190)

21. (5) 32.5

$$\begin{array}{r} 13 \\ 4 \\ +\ 15.5 \\ \hline 32.5\ \text{hours} \end{array}$$

22. (4) $96.60

$$\begin{array}{r} \$1.38 \\ \times\ \ 70 \\ \hline \$96.60 \end{array}$$

23. (4) 1.5

$$\begin{array}{r} 17.0 \\ -\ 15.5 \\ \hline 1.5\ \text{hours} \end{array}$$

24. (2) 48

$$\begin{array}{r} 47.8 \text{ mph to the nearest unit} = 48 \\ 13\overline{)622.0} \\ \underline{52} \\ 102 \\ \underline{91} \\ 11\,0 \\ \underline{10\,4} \\ 6 \end{array}$$

CHAPTER 4

FRACTIONS EXERCISE 1
page 80

1. $\frac{1}{3}$ 4. $\frac{3}{8}$

2. $\frac{5}{6}$ 5. $\frac{2}{5}$

3. $\frac{1}{2}$

FRACTIONS EXERCISE 2
page 81

1. $2\frac{1}{3}$ 4. $1\frac{5}{8}$

2. $1\frac{1}{4}$ 5. $5\frac{1}{6}$

3. $1\frac{1}{4}$ 6. $3\frac{1}{3}$

FRACTIONS EXERCISE 3
page 82

1. $\frac{5}{3}$ 4. $\frac{6}{6}$

2. $\frac{7}{4}$ 5. $\frac{9}{4}$

3. $\frac{3}{2}$ 6. $\frac{9}{6}$

FRACTIONS EXERCISE 4
pages 82–83

1. $\frac{1}{3}$ 5. $\frac{137}{200}$

2. $\frac{5}{12}$ 6. $\frac{11}{24}$

3. $\frac{199}{800}$ 7. $\frac{2}{7}$

4. $\frac{7}{50}$

FRACTIONS EXERCISE 5
page 84

In these answers the number following the phrase *reduce by* tells what number to divide the numerator and denominator by to reduce to lowest terms in one step.

1. $\frac{6}{10} = \frac{3}{5}$ $\frac{4}{6} = \frac{2}{3}$ $\frac{14}{20} = \frac{7}{10}$
reduce by 2   reduce by 2   reduce by 2

$\frac{4}{32} = \frac{1}{8}$ $\frac{18}{36} = \frac{1}{2}$ $\frac{18}{24} = \frac{3}{4}$
reduce by 4   reduce by 18   reduce by 6

2. $\frac{25}{35} = \frac{5}{7}$ $\frac{45}{50} = \frac{9}{10}$ $\frac{15}{40} = \frac{3}{8}$
reduce by 5   reduce by 5   reduce by 5

$\frac{45}{60} = \frac{3}{4}$ $\frac{30}{45} = \frac{2}{3}$ $\frac{10}{25} = \frac{2}{5}$
reduce by 15   reduce by 15   reduce by 5

FRACTIONS EXERCISE 6
page 85

$\frac{70}{100} = \frac{7}{10}$ $\frac{50}{60} = \frac{5}{6}$ $\frac{80}{160} = \frac{1}{2}$
reduce by 10   reduce by 10   reduce by 80

$\frac{40}{200} = \frac{1}{5}$ $\frac{30}{200} = \frac{3}{20}$ $\frac{50}{250} = \frac{1}{5}$
reduce by 40   reduce by 10   reduce by 50

FRACTIONS EXERCISE 7
page 85

$\frac{7}{28} = \frac{1}{4}$ $\frac{9}{30} = \frac{3}{10}$ $\frac{27}{45} = \frac{3}{5}$
reduce by 7   reduce by 3   reduce by 9

$\frac{22}{33} = \frac{2}{3}$ $\frac{17}{34} = \frac{1}{2}$ $\frac{13}{39} = \frac{1}{3}$
reduce by 11   reduce by 17   reduce by 13

FRACTIONS EXERCISE 8
page 87

1. **a.** $\frac{6}{15} = \frac{2}{5}$ **b.** $\frac{9}{15} = \frac{3}{5}$ **c.** $\frac{3}{15} = \frac{1}{5}$

2. **a.** $\frac{18}{24} = \frac{3}{4}$ **b.** $\frac{6}{24} = \frac{1}{4}$

3. **a.** $\$60 + \$30 = \$90$ **b.** $\frac{30}{90} = \frac{1}{3}$

   c. $\frac{60}{90} = \frac{2}{3}$

4. **a.** $175 + 125 = 300$ mi   **b.** $\frac{175}{300} = \frac{7}{12}$

   c. $\frac{125}{300} = \frac{5}{12}$

5. **a.** $\frac{300}{1200} = \frac{1}{4}$ **b.** $\frac{450}{1200} = \frac{3}{8}$

   c. $\frac{150}{1200} = \frac{1}{8}$ **d.** $\frac{120}{1200} = \frac{1}{10}$

FRACTIONS EXERCISE 9
pages 88–89

1. $\frac{10}{4} = 2\frac{2}{4} = 2\frac{1}{2}$
$$4\overline{)10}$$
$$\underline{8}$$
$$2$$

2. $\dfrac{8}{6} = \quad 1\dfrac{2}{6} \quad = 1\dfrac{1}{3}$

$6\overline{)8}$
$\quad \underline{6}$
$\quad 2$

3. $\dfrac{28}{8} = \quad 3\dfrac{4}{8} = 3\dfrac{1}{2}$

$8\overline{)28}$
$\quad \underline{24}$
$\quad 4$

4. $\dfrac{10}{3} = \quad 3\dfrac{1}{3}$

$3\overline{)10}$
$\quad \underline{9}$
$\quad 1$

5.
$1\dfrac{2}{3}$	$4\dfrac{1}{2}$	$2\dfrac{3}{5}$	$5\dfrac{1}{6}$
$1\dfrac{6}{9}=1\dfrac{2}{3}$	$4\dfrac{4}{8}=4\dfrac{1}{2}$	$2\dfrac{3}{5}$	$5\dfrac{1}{6}$
$9\overline{)15}$	$8\overline{)36}$	$5\overline{)13}$	$6\overline{)31}$
$\underline{9}$	$\underline{32}$	$\underline{10}$	$\underline{30}$
6	4	3	1

6.
3	$1\dfrac{3}{4}$	1	$1\dfrac{1}{3}$
3	$1\dfrac{12}{16}=1\dfrac{3}{4}$	1	$1\dfrac{6}{18}=1\dfrac{1}{3}$
$2\overline{)6}$	$16\overline{)28}$	$15\overline{)15}$	$18\overline{)24}$
$\underline{6}$	$\underline{16}$	$\underline{15}$	$\underline{18}$
0	12	0	6

7.
$1\dfrac{3}{4}$	7	$4\dfrac{1}{6}$	$3\dfrac{1}{2}$
$1\dfrac{3}{4}$	7	$4\dfrac{2}{12}=4\dfrac{1}{6}$	$3\dfrac{3}{6}=3\dfrac{1}{2}$
$4\overline{)7}$	$3\overline{)21}$	$12\overline{)50}$	$6\overline{)21}$
$\underline{4}$	$\underline{21}$	$\underline{48}$	$\underline{18}$
3	0	2	3

FRACTIONS EXERCISE 10
page 90

1.
1	$\dfrac{2}{3}$	$1\dfrac{4}{15}$
$\dfrac{2}{5}$	$\dfrac{2}{9}$	$\dfrac{8}{15}$
$+\dfrac{3}{5}$	$+\dfrac{4}{9}$	$+\dfrac{11}{15}$
$\dfrac{5}{5}=1$	$\dfrac{6}{9}=\dfrac{2}{3}$	$\dfrac{19}{15}=1\dfrac{4}{15}$

2.
$1\dfrac{1}{4}$	$13\dfrac{2}{5}$	13
$\dfrac{5}{8}$	$9\dfrac{3}{10}$	$10\dfrac{2}{3}$
$+\dfrac{5}{8}$	$+4\dfrac{1}{10}$	$+2\dfrac{1}{3}$
$\dfrac{10}{8}=1\dfrac{2}{8}=1\dfrac{1}{4}$	$13\dfrac{4}{10}=13\dfrac{2}{5}$	$12\dfrac{3}{3}=13$

3.
$14\dfrac{4}{9}$	$22\dfrac{1}{4}$	$\dfrac{3}{4}$
$6\dfrac{5}{9}$	$1\dfrac{7}{8}$	$\dfrac{5}{16}$
$+7\dfrac{8}{9}$	$+20\dfrac{3}{8}$	$+\dfrac{7}{16}$
$13\dfrac{13}{9}=14\dfrac{4}{9}$	$21\dfrac{10}{8}=22\dfrac{2}{8}=22\dfrac{1}{4}$	$\dfrac{12}{16}=\dfrac{3}{4}$

4.
$1\dfrac{3}{4}$	$16\dfrac{11}{12}$	$13\dfrac{8}{9}$
$\dfrac{3}{4}$	$2\dfrac{7}{12}$	$5\dfrac{4}{9}$
$\dfrac{1}{4}$	$4\dfrac{11}{12}$	$4\dfrac{5}{9}$
$+\dfrac{3}{4}$	$+9\dfrac{5}{12}$	$+3\dfrac{8}{9}$
$\dfrac{7}{4}=1\dfrac{3}{4}$	$15\dfrac{23}{12}=16\dfrac{11}{12}$	$12\dfrac{17}{9}=13\dfrac{8}{9}$

FRACTIONS EXERCISE 11
page 91

1.
$\dfrac{1}{2}$	$6\dfrac{2}{3}$	$2\dfrac{1}{2}$
$\dfrac{5}{8}$	$8\dfrac{5}{6}$	$4\dfrac{7}{8}$
$-\dfrac{1}{8}$	$-2\dfrac{1}{6}$	$-2\dfrac{3}{8}$
$\dfrac{4}{8}=\dfrac{1}{2}$	$6\dfrac{4}{6}=6\dfrac{2}{3}$	$2\dfrac{4}{8}=2\dfrac{1}{2}$

2.
$2\dfrac{3}{5}$	$\dfrac{3}{10}$	$4\dfrac{3}{5}$
$10\dfrac{4}{5}$	$\dfrac{19}{20}$	$6\dfrac{13}{15}$
$-8\dfrac{1}{5}$	$-\dfrac{13}{20}$	$-2\dfrac{4}{15}$
$2\dfrac{3}{5}$	$\dfrac{6}{20}=\dfrac{3}{10}$	$4\dfrac{9}{15}=4\dfrac{3}{5}$

3.
$\dfrac{2}{9}$	$7\dfrac{2}{3}$	$\dfrac{2}{3}$
$\dfrac{25}{36}$	$8\dfrac{5}{6}$	$4\dfrac{17}{18}$
$-\dfrac{17}{36}$	$-1\dfrac{1}{6}$	$-4\dfrac{5}{18}$
$\dfrac{8}{36}=\dfrac{2}{9}$	$7\dfrac{4}{6}=7\dfrac{2}{3}$	$\dfrac{12}{18}=\dfrac{2}{3}$

FRACTIONS EXERCISE 12
page 93

1.
$7\dfrac{1}{3}$	$7\dfrac{3}{8}$	$2\dfrac{5}{12}$
$9 \quad = 8\dfrac{3}{3}$	$11 \quad = 10\dfrac{8}{8}$	$8 \quad = 7\dfrac{12}{12}$
$-1\dfrac{2}{3} = 1\dfrac{2}{3}$	$-3\dfrac{5}{8} = 3\dfrac{5}{8}$	$-5\dfrac{7}{12} = 5\dfrac{7}{12}$
$7\dfrac{1}{3}$	$7\dfrac{3}{8}$	$2\dfrac{5}{12}$

2. $\dfrac{1}{2}$ $\quad\quad\quad 7\dfrac{3}{4}$ $\quad\quad\quad 9\dfrac{11}{16}$ $\quad\quad\quad 12\dfrac{4}{9}$

$$7 = 6\dfrac{2}{2}$$
$$-\ 6\dfrac{1}{2} = 6\dfrac{1}{2}$$
$$\dfrac{1}{2}$$

$$9 = 8\dfrac{4}{4}$$
$$-\ 1\dfrac{1}{4} = 1\dfrac{1}{4}$$
$$7\dfrac{3}{4}$$

$$12 = 11\dfrac{16}{16}$$
$$-\ 2\dfrac{5}{16} = 2\dfrac{5}{16}$$
$$9\dfrac{11}{16}$$

$$20\dfrac{5}{36} = 19\dfrac{36}{36} + \dfrac{5}{36} = 19\dfrac{41}{36}$$
$$-\ 7\dfrac{25}{36} = \qquad\qquad\qquad 7\dfrac{25}{36}$$
$$12\dfrac{16}{36} = 12\dfrac{4}{9}$$

3. $2\dfrac{1}{2}$

$$5\dfrac{1}{8} = 4\dfrac{8}{8} + \dfrac{1}{8} = 4\dfrac{9}{8}$$
$$-\ 2\dfrac{5}{8} \qquad\qquad\qquad 2\dfrac{5}{8}$$
$$2\dfrac{4}{8} = 2\dfrac{1}{2}$$

$6\dfrac{3}{5}$

$$8\dfrac{2}{5} = 7\dfrac{5}{5} + \dfrac{2}{5} = 7\dfrac{7}{5}$$
$$-\ 1\dfrac{4}{5} = \qquad\qquad\quad 1\dfrac{4}{5}$$
$$6\dfrac{3}{5}$$

$\dfrac{1}{2}$

$$3\dfrac{1}{4} = 2\dfrac{4}{4} + \dfrac{1}{4} = 2\dfrac{5}{4}$$
$$-\ 2\dfrac{3}{4} = \qquad\qquad\quad 2\dfrac{3}{4}$$
$$\dfrac{2}{4} = \dfrac{1}{2}$$

4. $7\dfrac{3}{4}$

$$24\dfrac{11}{16} = 23\dfrac{16}{16} + \dfrac{11}{16} = 23\dfrac{27}{16}$$
$$-\ 16\dfrac{15}{16} = \qquad\qquad\qquad\quad 16\dfrac{15}{16}$$
$$7\dfrac{12}{16} = 7\dfrac{3}{4}$$

$1\dfrac{2}{3}$

$$9\dfrac{1}{3} = 8\dfrac{3}{3} + \dfrac{1}{3} = 8\dfrac{4}{3}$$
$$-\ 7\dfrac{2}{3} = \qquad\qquad\quad 7\dfrac{2}{3}$$
$$1\dfrac{2}{3}$$

$7\dfrac{2}{5}$

$$12\dfrac{3}{10} = 11\dfrac{10}{10} + \dfrac{3}{10} = 11\dfrac{13}{10}$$
$$-\ 4\dfrac{9}{10} = \qquad\qquad\qquad\quad 4\dfrac{9}{10}$$
$$7\dfrac{4}{10} = 7\dfrac{2}{5}$$

5. $2\dfrac{2}{3}$

$$11\dfrac{7}{12} = 10\dfrac{12}{12} + \dfrac{7}{12} = 10\dfrac{19}{12}$$
$$-\ 8\dfrac{11}{12} = \qquad\qquad\qquad\quad 8\dfrac{11}{12}$$
$$2\dfrac{8}{12} = 2\dfrac{2}{3}$$

$1\dfrac{1}{2}$

$$15\dfrac{7}{24} = 14\dfrac{24}{24} + \dfrac{7}{24} = 14\dfrac{31}{24}$$
$$-\ 13\dfrac{19}{24} = \qquad\qquad\qquad\quad 13\dfrac{19}{24}$$
$$1\dfrac{12}{24} = 1\dfrac{1}{2}$$

FRACTIONS EXERCISE 13
page 94

1. 10 12 36
2. 6   18 40
3. 18 24 20
4. 20 12 24
5. 18 40 36

FRACTIONS EXERCISE 14
page 96

In these answers the number following the phrase *raise by* tells you what number to multiply both the numerator and the denominator of the original fraction by. The letters *xp* stand for cross product.

1. $\dfrac{3}{5} = \dfrac{12}{20}$ $\quad$ $\dfrac{5}{12} = \dfrac{10}{24}$ $\quad$ $\dfrac{7}{8} = \dfrac{35}{40}$ $\quad$ $\dfrac{3}{4} = \dfrac{12}{16}$
raise by 4 $\quad\quad$ raise by 2 $\quad\quad$ raise by 5 $\quad\quad$ raise by 4
$xp = 60$ $\quad\quad\quad$ $xp = 120$ $\quad\quad$ $xp = 280$ $\quad\quad$ $xp = 48$

2. $\dfrac{5}{11} = \dfrac{20}{44}$ $\quad$ $\dfrac{13}{20} = \dfrac{26}{40}$ $\quad$ $\dfrac{7}{10} = \dfrac{42}{60}$ $\quad$ $\dfrac{13}{20} = \dfrac{65}{100}$
raise by 4 $\quad\quad$ raise by 2 $\quad\quad$ raise by 6 $\quad\quad$ raise by 5
$xp = 220$ $\quad\quad$ $xp = 520$ $\quad\quad$ $xp = 420$ $\quad\quad$ $xp = 1300$

3. $\dfrac{3}{4} = \dfrac{75}{100}$ $\quad$ $\dfrac{5}{9} = \dfrac{20}{36}$ $\quad$ $\dfrac{1}{8} = \dfrac{3}{24}$ $\quad$ $\dfrac{1}{3} = \dfrac{12}{36}$
raise by 25 $\quad\quad$ raise by 4 $\quad\quad$ raise by 3 $\quad\quad$ raise by 12
$xp = 300$ $\quad\quad$ $xp = 180$ $\quad\quad$ $xp = 24$ $\quad\quad$ $xp = 36$

FRACTIONS EXERCISE 15
page 98

1. $1\dfrac{5}{12}$

$$\dfrac{5}{6} = \dfrac{10}{12}$$
$$+\ \dfrac{7}{12} = \dfrac{7}{12}$$
$$\dfrac{17}{12} = 1\dfrac{5}{12}$$

$1\dfrac{5}{12}$

$$\dfrac{2}{3} = \dfrac{8}{12}$$
$$+\ \dfrac{3}{4} = \dfrac{9}{12}$$
$$\dfrac{17}{12} = 1\dfrac{5}{12}$$

$2\dfrac{1}{12}$

$$\dfrac{2}{3} = \dfrac{8}{12}$$
$$\dfrac{7}{12} = \dfrac{7}{12}$$
$$+\ \dfrac{5}{6} = \dfrac{10}{12}$$
$$\dfrac{25}{12} = 2\dfrac{1}{12}$$

2. $14\frac{1}{6}$ $9\frac{2}{3} = 9\frac{4}{6}$
  $+4\frac{1}{2}= 4\frac{3}{6}$
  $13\frac{7}{6} = 14\frac{1}{6}$

$13\frac{11}{24}$ $10\frac{1}{8} = 10\frac{3}{24}$
  $+3\frac{1}{3}= 3\frac{8}{24}$
  $13\frac{11}{24}$

$25\frac{11}{20}$ $9\frac{1}{2} = 9\frac{10}{20}$
  $8\frac{3}{4} = 8\frac{15}{20}$
  $+7\frac{3}{10} = 7\frac{6}{20}$
  $24\frac{31}{20} = 25\frac{11}{20}$

3. $7\frac{1}{3}$ $2\frac{5}{6} = 2\frac{5}{6}$
  $+4\frac{1}{2} = 4\frac{3}{6}$
  $6\frac{8}{6} = 7\frac{2}{6} = 7\frac{1}{3}$

$1\frac{7}{20}$ $\frac{1}{2} = \frac{10}{20}$
  $\frac{1}{4} = \frac{5}{20}$
  $+\frac{3}{5}= \frac{12}{20}$
  $\frac{27}{20} = 1\frac{7}{20}$

$12\frac{19}{24}$ $4\frac{1}{3} = 4\frac{8}{24}$
  $1\frac{5}{6} = 1\frac{20}{24}$
  $+6\frac{5}{8} = 6\frac{15}{24}$
  $11\frac{43}{24} = 12\frac{19}{24}$

4. $\frac{1}{5}$ $\frac{7}{10} = \frac{7}{10}$
  $-\frac{1}{2}= \frac{5}{10}$
  $\frac{2}{10} = \frac{1}{5}$

$\frac{11}{12}$ $2\frac{2}{3} = 1\frac{12}{12} + \frac{8}{12} = 1\frac{20}{12}$
  $-1\frac{3}{4}= 1\frac{9}{12}$
  $\frac{11}{12}$

$\frac{1}{40}$ $\frac{5}{8} = \frac{25}{40}$
  $-\frac{3}{5} = \frac{24}{40}$
  $\frac{1}{40}$

5. $4\frac{9}{20}$ $8\frac{1}{5} = 7\frac{20}{20} + \frac{4}{20} = 7\frac{24}{20}$
  $-3\frac{3}{4}= 3\frac{15}{20}$
  $4\frac{9}{20}$

$2\frac{1}{10}$ $11\frac{3}{5} = 11\frac{6}{10}$
  $-9\frac{1}{2}= 9\frac{5}{10}$
  $2\frac{1}{10}$

$3\frac{5}{6}$ $9\frac{1}{2} = 8\frac{6}{6} + \frac{3}{6} = 8\frac{9}{6}$
  $-5\frac{2}{3}= 5\frac{4}{6}$
  $3\frac{5}{6}$

6. $8\frac{5}{8}$ $16\frac{1}{4} = 15\frac{8}{8} + \frac{2}{8} = 15\frac{10}{8}$
  $-7\frac{5}{8}= 7\frac{5}{8}$
  $8\frac{5}{8}$

$4\frac{7}{24}$ $7\frac{11}{12} = 7\frac{22}{24}$
  $-3\frac{5}{8}= 3\frac{15}{24}$
  $4\frac{7}{24}$

$5\frac{3}{5}$ $8\frac{7}{20} = 7\frac{20}{20} + \frac{7}{20} = 7\frac{27}{20}$
  $-2\frac{3}{4}= 2\frac{15}{20}$
  $5\frac{12}{20} = 5\frac{3}{5}$

FRACTIONS EXERCISE 16
pages 98–99

1. $1\frac{1}{3}$ yards $5 = 4\frac{3}{3}$
  $-3\frac{2}{3} = 3\frac{2}{3}$
  $1\frac{1}{3}$

2. a. $6\frac{7}{8}$ lb $2\frac{1}{2} = 2\frac{4}{8}$
  $2\frac{5}{8} = 2\frac{5}{8}$
  $+1\frac{3}{4} = 1\frac{6}{8}$
  $5\frac{15}{8} = 6\frac{7}{8}$

b. $13\frac{1}{4}$ lb 10
  $+3\frac{1}{4}$
  $13\frac{1}{4}$

c. Yes $6\frac{7}{8} = 6\frac{7}{8}$
  $+13\frac{1}{4} = 13\frac{2}{8}$
  $19\frac{9}{8} = 20\frac{1}{8}$

Yes, the weight is more than 20 pounds.

3. $\frac{13}{16}$ Use 1 as the Robinsons' entire income.

  $1 = \frac{16}{16}$
  $-\frac{3}{16} = \frac{3}{16}$
  $\frac{13}{16}$

4. $6\frac{1}{10}$ **miles**

$$2\frac{9}{10} = 2\frac{9}{10}$$
$$+\,3\frac{1}{2} = 3\frac{5}{10}$$
$$5\frac{14}{10} = 6\frac{4}{10} = 6\frac{2}{5}$$

$$12\frac{1}{2} = 12\frac{5}{10}$$
$$-\,6\frac{2}{5} = 6\frac{4}{10}$$
$$6\frac{1}{10} \text{ miles}$$

5. a. $61\frac{13}{16}$ **lb**

$$16\frac{3}{4} = 16\frac{12}{16}$$
$$20\frac{1}{2} = 20\frac{8}{16}$$
$$+\,24\frac{9}{16} = 24\frac{9}{16}$$
$$60\frac{29}{16} = 61\frac{13}{16}$$

b. $38\frac{3}{16}$ **lb**

$$100 = 99\frac{16}{16}$$
$$-\,61\frac{13}{16} = 61\frac{13}{16}$$
$$38\frac{3}{16}$$

6. (2) $178\frac{1}{2}$

7. (1) $21\frac{1}{8}$ $\quad 19\frac{1}{8} \quad 19\frac{5}{8} \quad 20\frac{1}{8} \quad 20\frac{5}{8}$
$$+\frac{4}{8} \quad +\frac{4}{8} \quad +\frac{4}{8} \quad +\frac{4}{8}$$

$$20\frac{5}{8}$$
$$+\,\frac{4}{8}$$
$$20\frac{9}{8} = 21\frac{1}{8}$$

8. (4) $28\frac{9}{16}$ **in**

$$8\frac{5}{8} = 8\frac{5}{16}$$
$$10\frac{1}{2} = 10\frac{8}{16}$$
$$+\,9\frac{3}{4} = 9\frac{12}{16}$$
$$27\frac{25}{16} = 28\frac{9}{16}$$

FRACTIONS EXERCISE 17
page 100

1. $\frac{3}{4} \times \frac{5}{7} = \frac{15}{28}$
$$\frac{2}{3} \times \frac{1}{2} = \frac{2}{6} = \frac{1}{3}$$
$$\frac{1}{10} \cdot \frac{5}{8} = \frac{5}{80} = \frac{1}{16}$$
$$\frac{7}{8} \times \frac{1}{5} = \frac{7}{40}$$

2. $\frac{1}{4} \times \frac{5}{16} = \frac{5}{64}$
$$\frac{3}{10} \cdot \frac{3}{5} = \frac{9}{50}$$
$$\frac{2}{9} \times \frac{3}{5} = \frac{6}{45} = \frac{2}{15}$$
$$\frac{3}{5} \times \frac{1}{6} = \frac{3}{30} = \frac{1}{10}$$

FRACTIONS EXERCISE 18
page 102

1. $\frac{3}{4} \times \frac{6}{7} = \frac{9}{14}$
$$\frac{14}{15} \times \frac{3}{7} = \frac{2}{5}$$
$$\frac{4}{5} \cdot \frac{5}{6} = \frac{2}{3}$$
$$\frac{4}{9} \times \frac{3}{8} = \frac{1}{6}$$

2. $\frac{5}{8} \times \frac{2}{15} = \frac{1}{12}$
$$\frac{9}{10} \times \frac{2}{3} = \frac{3}{5}$$
$$\frac{3}{20} \times \frac{1}{3} = \frac{1}{20}$$
$$\frac{4}{5} \times \frac{5}{24} = \frac{1}{6}$$

3. $\frac{2}{3} \cdot \frac{9}{20} = \frac{3}{10}$
$$\frac{6}{7} \times \frac{7}{8} \times \frac{4}{5} = \frac{3}{5}$$
$$\frac{9}{10} \times \frac{1}{4} \times \frac{8}{9} = \frac{1}{5}$$
$$\frac{3}{4} \times \frac{2}{9} \times \frac{15}{16} = \frac{5}{32}$$

FRACTIONS EXERCISE 19
page 103

1. $\frac{1}{2} \times \frac{16}{1} = \frac{8}{1} = 8$
$$\frac{10}{1} \times \frac{2}{3} = \frac{20}{3} = 6\frac{2}{3}$$
$$\frac{3}{8} \times \frac{12}{1} = \frac{9}{2} = 4\frac{1}{2}$$
$$\frac{8}{1} \cdot \frac{7}{10} = \frac{28}{5} = 5\frac{3}{5}$$

2. $\frac{2}{5} \times \frac{10}{1} = \frac{4}{1} = 4$
$$\frac{9}{1} \times \frac{11}{20} = \frac{99}{20} = 4\frac{19}{20}$$
$$\frac{5}{6} \times \frac{9}{1} = \frac{15}{2} = 7\frac{1}{2}$$
$$\frac{15}{1} \times \frac{7}{100} = \frac{21}{20} = 1\frac{1}{20}$$

3. $\frac{18}{1} \times \frac{2}{3} = \frac{12}{1} = 12$
$$\frac{20}{1} \cdot \frac{4}{5} = \frac{16}{1} = 16$$
$$\frac{4}{15} \times \frac{36}{1} = \frac{48}{5} = 9\frac{3}{5}$$
$$\frac{24}{1} \times \frac{3}{10} = \frac{36}{5} = 7\frac{1}{5}$$

FRACTIONS EXERCISE 20
page 103

1. $\frac{6}{3} + \frac{2}{3} = \mathbf{\frac{8}{3}}$

$\frac{8}{8} + \frac{5}{8} = \mathbf{\frac{13}{8}}$

$\frac{40}{5} + \frac{2}{5} = \mathbf{\frac{42}{5}}$

$\frac{12}{4} + \frac{1}{4} = \mathbf{\frac{13}{4}}$

$\frac{18}{6} + \frac{5}{6} = \mathbf{\frac{23}{6}}$

2. $\frac{35}{7} + \frac{4}{7} = \mathbf{\frac{39}{7}}$

$\frac{6}{2} + \frac{1}{2} = \mathbf{\frac{7}{2}}$

$\frac{21}{3} + \frac{1}{3} = \mathbf{\frac{22}{3}}$

$\frac{54}{9} + \frac{2}{9} = \mathbf{\frac{56}{9}}$

$\frac{30}{3} + \frac{1}{3} = \mathbf{\frac{31}{3}}$

3. $\frac{60}{5} + \frac{3}{5} = \mathbf{\frac{63}{5}}$

$\frac{36}{4} + \frac{1}{4} = \mathbf{\frac{37}{4}}$

$\frac{39}{3} + \frac{2}{3} = \mathbf{\frac{41}{3}}$

$\frac{45}{3} + \frac{1}{3} = \mathbf{\frac{46}{3}}$

$\frac{32}{8} + \frac{3}{8} = \mathbf{\frac{35}{8}}$

FRACTIONS EXERCISE 21
page 106

1. $\frac{1}{3} \div \frac{1}{6} =$ $5 \div \frac{5}{6} =$

$\frac{1}{3} \times \frac{6}{1} = \frac{2}{1} = \mathbf{2}$ $\frac{5}{1} \times \frac{6}{5} = \frac{6}{1} = \mathbf{6}$

$4\frac{1}{2} \div \frac{3}{4} =$ $2\frac{2}{3} \div \frac{2}{15} =$

$\frac{9}{2} \times \frac{4}{3} = \frac{6}{1} = \mathbf{6}$ $\frac{8}{3} \times \frac{15}{2} = \frac{20}{1} = \mathbf{20}$

2. $\frac{1}{3} \div \frac{2}{3} =$ $\frac{5}{7} \div \frac{5}{14} =$

$\frac{1}{3} \times \frac{3}{2} = \mathbf{\frac{1}{2}}$ $\frac{5}{7} \times \frac{14}{5} = \mathbf{2}$

$4 \div \frac{3}{8} =$ $\frac{5}{9} \div \frac{3}{4} =$

$\frac{4}{1} \times \frac{8}{3} = \frac{32}{3} = \mathbf{10\frac{2}{3}}$ $\frac{5}{9} \times \frac{4}{3} = \mathbf{\frac{20}{27}}$

3. $5\frac{5}{6} \div \frac{7}{8} =$ $\frac{9}{10} \div \frac{3}{5} =$

$\frac{35}{6} \times \frac{8}{7} = \frac{20}{3} = \mathbf{6\frac{2}{3}}$ $\frac{9}{10} \times \frac{5}{3} = \frac{3}{2} = \mathbf{1\frac{1}{2}}$

$10 \div \frac{5}{6} =$ $3\frac{1}{3} \div \frac{1}{3} =$

$\frac{10}{1} \times \frac{6}{5} = \mathbf{12}$ $\frac{10}{3} \times \frac{3}{1} = \mathbf{10}$

FRACTIONS EXERCISE 22
page 107

1. $10 \div 1\frac{1}{2} =$

$\frac{10}{1} \div \frac{3}{2} =$

$\frac{10}{1} \times \frac{2}{3} = \frac{20}{3} = \mathbf{6\frac{2}{3}}$

$1\frac{1}{3} \div 3\frac{1}{5} =$

$\frac{4}{3} \div \frac{16}{5} =$

$\frac{4}{3} \times \frac{5}{16} = \mathbf{\frac{5}{12}}$

$6 \div 1\frac{1}{3} =$

$\frac{6}{1} \div \frac{4}{3} =$

$\frac{6}{1} \times \frac{3}{4} = \frac{9}{2} = \mathbf{4\frac{1}{2}}$

2. $2\frac{1}{2} \div 3\frac{1}{4} =$

$\frac{5}{2} \div \frac{13}{4} =$

$\frac{5}{2} \times \frac{4}{13} = \mathbf{\frac{10}{13}}$

$21 \div 4\frac{1}{5} =$

$\frac{21}{1} \div \frac{21}{5} =$

$\frac{21}{1} \times \frac{5}{21} = \frac{5}{1} = \mathbf{5}$

$2\frac{2}{9} \div 2 =$

$\frac{20}{9} \div \frac{2}{1} =$

$\frac{20}{9} \times \frac{1}{2} = \frac{10}{9} = \mathbf{1\frac{1}{9}}$

3. $\frac{9}{10} \div 3 =$

$\frac{9}{10} \div \frac{3}{1} =$

$\frac{9}{10} \times \frac{1}{3} = \mathbf{\frac{3}{10}}$

$1\frac{3}{4} \div 7 =$

$\frac{7}{4} \div \frac{7}{1} =$

$\frac{7}{4} \times \frac{1}{7} = \mathbf{\frac{1}{4}}$

$5\frac{5}{6} \div 7 =$

$\frac{35}{6} \div \frac{7}{1} =$

$\frac{35}{6} \times \frac{1}{7} = \mathbf{\frac{5}{6}}$

4. $\frac{3}{4} \div 3\frac{1}{5} =$

$\frac{3}{4} \div \frac{16}{5} =$

$\frac{3}{4} \times \frac{5}{16} = \mathbf{\frac{15}{64}}$

$3\frac{3}{4} \div 4 =$

$\frac{15}{4} \div \frac{4}{1} =$

$\frac{15}{4} \times \frac{1}{4} = \mathbf{\frac{15}{16}}$

$10 \div 1\frac{2}{3} =$

$\frac{10}{1} \div \frac{5}{3} =$

$\frac{10}{1} \times \frac{3}{5} = \frac{6}{1} = \mathbf{6}$

5. $12 \div \frac{2}{3} =$

$\frac{12}{1} \div \frac{2}{3} =$

$\frac{12}{1} \times \frac{3}{2} = \mathbf{18}$

$\frac{3}{4} \div \frac{9}{10} =$

$\frac{3}{4} \times \frac{10}{9} = \mathbf{\frac{5}{6}}$

$1\frac{2}{3} \div \frac{5}{6} =$

$\frac{5}{3} \div \frac{5}{6} =$

$\frac{5}{3} \times \frac{6}{5} = \mathbf{2}$

6. $\frac{1}{2} \div \frac{3}{4} =$

$\frac{1}{2} \times \frac{4}{3} = \mathbf{\frac{2}{3}}$

$4\frac{1}{5} \div \frac{7}{10} =$

$\frac{21}{5} \div \frac{7}{10} =$

$\frac{21}{5} \times \frac{10}{7} = \mathbf{6}$

$6 \div \frac{2}{9} =$

$\frac{6}{1} \div \frac{2}{9} =$

$\frac{6}{1} \times \frac{9}{2} = \mathbf{27}$

FRACTIONS EXERCISE 23
pages 109–110

1. Answer should be more than $62\frac{1}{2}$ pounds.
Multiplication

$3 \times 62\frac{1}{2} =$

$\frac{3}{1} \times \frac{125}{2} = \frac{375}{2} = \mathbf{187\frac{1}{2}}$

2. Answer should be less than \$38.
Division
\$38 comes first. It is being divided up.

$38 \div 9\frac{1}{2} =$

$\frac{38}{1} \div \frac{19}{2} =$

$\frac{38}{1} \times \frac{2}{19} = \frac{4}{1} = \mathbf{\$4}$

3. Answer should be less than 17. You are dividing by something larger than one.
Division
$17\frac{1}{2}$ comes first.

$17\frac{1}{2} \div 1\frac{1}{2} =$

$\frac{35}{2} \div \frac{3}{2} =$

$\frac{35}{2} \times \frac{2}{3} = \frac{35}{3} = \mathbf{11\frac{2}{3}}$

4. Answer should be more than \$8.20.
Multiplication.

$8\frac{1}{2} \times \$8.20 =$

$\frac{17}{2} \times \frac{8.20}{1} = \frac{69.70}{1} = \mathbf{\$69.70}$

5. Answer should be less than 90. You are dividing by something larger than one.
Division
90 comes first. It is being divided up.

$90 \div 1\frac{1}{2} =$

$\frac{90}{1} \div \frac{3}{2} =$

$\frac{90}{1} \times \frac{2}{3} = \frac{60}{1} = \mathbf{60}$

6. (1) \$600

$$\begin{array}{r} \$21,500 \\ + \$14,500 \\ \hline \$36,000 \end{array} \text{ yearly income}$$

$$\begin{array}{r} \$\;3,000 \\ \hline 12)\$36,000 \end{array} \text{ monthly income}$$

$\frac{1}{5} \times \frac{3000}{1} = 600$

7. (3) $\frac{29}{40}$

$\frac{1}{5} = \frac{8}{40}$

$\frac{2}{5} = \frac{16}{40}$

$+\frac{1}{8} = \frac{5}{40}$

$\overline{\phantom{+\frac{1}{8} =} \frac{29}{40}}$

8. (2) \$4500 $\frac{1}{8} \times \frac{36,000}{1} = \$4,500$

9. (4) $40 First find $\frac{2}{5}$ of monthly income.

$$\frac{2}{5} \times \frac{3000}{1} = 1200$$

Divide $1200 by 30.

$1200 \div 30 = 40 each day.

10. (4) $3625 $\quad \frac{1}{4} \times \frac{14,500}{1} = $3,625$

FRACTIONS EXERCISE 24
page 111

1. $.6 = \frac{6}{10} = \frac{3}{5}$ $\qquad .5 = \frac{5}{10} = \frac{1}{2}$

   $.45 = \frac{45}{100} = \frac{9}{20}$ $\qquad .80 = \frac{80}{100} = \frac{4}{5}$

2. $.125 = \frac{125}{1000} = \frac{1}{8}$ $\qquad .065 = \frac{65}{1000} = \frac{13}{200}$

   $.15 = \frac{15}{100} = \frac{3}{20}$ $\qquad .96 = \frac{96}{100} = \frac{24}{25}$

3. $.024 = \frac{24}{1000} = \frac{3}{125}$ $\qquad .0002 = \frac{2}{10,000} = \frac{1}{5000}$

   $.010 = \frac{10}{1000} = \frac{1}{100}$ $\qquad .34 = \frac{34}{100} = \frac{17}{50}$

FRACTIONS EXERCISE 25
page 112

1. $\overset{.75}{4)3.00}$ $\quad \overset{.33\frac{1}{3}}{3)1.00}$ $\quad \overset{.7}{10)7.0}$ $\quad \overset{.625}{8)5.000}$ or $.62\frac{1}{2}$

2. $\overset{.5}{2)1.0}$ $\quad \overset{.05}{20)1.00}$ $\quad \overset{.83\frac{1}{3}}{6)5.00}$ $\quad \overset{.44\frac{4}{9}}{9)4.00}$

3. $\overset{.08\frac{1}{3}}{12)1.00}$ $\quad \overset{.66\frac{2}{3}}{3)2.00}$ $\quad \overset{.12}{25)3.00}$ $\quad \overset{.16\frac{2}{3}}{6)1.00}$

FRACTIONS EXERCISE 26
page 113

1. **(1)** $6\frac{1}{3}$

   Step 1: Change decimal to a fraction:

   $9.5 = \frac{95}{10} = 9\frac{1}{2}$

   Step 2: Add three fractions:

   $9\frac{1}{2} = 9\frac{3}{6}$
   $4\frac{1}{3} = 4\frac{2}{6}$
   $5\frac{1}{6} = 5\frac{1}{6}$
   $\overline{\qquad 18\frac{6}{6} = 19}$

   Step 3: Divide by 3 to find average:

   $\overset{6\frac{1}{3}}{3)19}$

2. **(3)** $4\frac{3}{4}$ $\quad 8\frac{1}{2} = 7\frac{4}{4} + \frac{2}{4} = 7\frac{6}{4}$
   $\qquad\qquad\quad -3\frac{3}{4} = \qquad\qquad 3\frac{3}{4}$
   $\qquad\qquad\qquad\qquad\qquad\qquad \overline{4\frac{3}{4}}$ feet

3. (2) $\quad 4.9 \qquad 2\frac{1}{2} = 2.5 \qquad \overset{4.85}{3)14.55}$ to the nearest
$\qquad\qquad\qquad 5\frac{3}{4} = 5.75 \qquad\qquad$ tenth =
$\qquad\qquad\qquad +6.3 = \underline{6.3} \qquad\qquad$ 4.9 pounds
$\qquad\qquad\qquad\qquad\qquad 14.55$

4. (2) $.75(2.50) + 1.5(3.90)$
5. (4) $10 - 3.5 - .75$

FRACTIONS EXERCISE 27
page 114

1. **a.** $\frac{1}{2} = \frac{9}{18}$ and $\frac{4}{9} = \frac{8}{18}$

   $\frac{1}{2}$ **is larger.**

   b. $\frac{2}{3} = \frac{10}{15}$ and $\frac{3}{5} = \frac{9}{15}$

   $\frac{2}{3}$ **is larger.**

   c. $\frac{3}{4} = \frac{9}{12}$ and $\frac{5}{6} = \frac{10}{12}$

   $\frac{5}{6}$ **is larger.**

2. **a.** $\frac{13}{20} = \frac{13}{20}$ and $\frac{7}{10} = \frac{14}{20}$

   $\frac{7}{10}$ **is larger.**

   b. $\frac{5}{8} = \frac{25}{40}$ and $\frac{3}{5} = \frac{24}{40}$

   $\frac{5}{8}$ **is larger.**

   c. $\frac{1}{6} = \frac{3}{18}$ and $\frac{2}{9} = \frac{4}{18}$

   $\frac{2}{9}$ **is larger.**

3. **a.** $\frac{5}{6} = \frac{25}{30}$ and $\frac{7}{10} = \frac{21}{30}$

   $\frac{5}{6}$ **is larger.**

   b. $\frac{5}{12} = \frac{15}{36}$ and $\frac{5}{9} = \frac{20}{36}$

   $\frac{5}{9}$ **is larger.**

   c. $\frac{5}{8} = \frac{25}{40}$ and $\frac{11}{20} = \frac{22}{40}$

   $\frac{5}{8}$ **is larger.**

4. $\frac{5}{8} = \frac{15}{24}, \frac{5}{6} = \frac{20}{24}, \frac{7}{12} = \frac{14}{24}$

   from smallest to largest: $\frac{7}{12}, \frac{5}{8}, \frac{5}{6}$

5. $\frac{7}{10} = \frac{14}{20}, \frac{4}{5} = \frac{16}{20}, \frac{3}{4} = \frac{15}{20}, \frac{13}{20} = \frac{13}{20}$

   from smallest to largest: $\frac{13}{20}, \frac{7}{10}, \frac{3}{4}, \frac{4}{5}$

6. **E, D, A, B, C**

   $A = 5\frac{1}{2} = 5\frac{60}{120}$

   $B = 5.30 = 5\frac{3}{10} = 5\frac{36}{120}$

   $C = 5.2 = 5\frac{2}{10} = 5\frac{24}{120}$

   $D = 5\frac{2}{3} = 5\frac{80}{120}$

   $E = 5\frac{7}{8} = 5\frac{105}{120}$

GED PRACTICE: FRACTIONS REVIEW

pages 114–115

1. $\dfrac{11}{20}$

2. $\dfrac{48}{60} = \dfrac{4}{5}$

3. $\dfrac{52}{8} = 6\dfrac{4}{8} = 6\dfrac{1}{2}$

4. $15\dfrac{7}{8}$

$$7\dfrac{3}{8}$$
$$3\dfrac{5}{8}$$
$$+\ 4\dfrac{7}{8}$$
$$14\dfrac{15}{8} = 15\dfrac{7}{8}$$

5. $3\dfrac{2}{5}$

$$12\dfrac{1}{5} = 11\dfrac{5}{5} + \dfrac{1}{5} = \quad 11\dfrac{6}{5}$$
$$-\ 8\dfrac{4}{5} = \qquad\qquad -\ 8\dfrac{4}{5}$$
$$3\dfrac{2}{5}$$

6. $20\dfrac{19}{20}$

$$5\dfrac{3}{4} = \quad 5\dfrac{15}{20}$$
$$6\dfrac{1}{2} = \quad 6\dfrac{10}{20}$$
$$+\ 8\dfrac{7}{10} = +\ 8\dfrac{14}{20}$$
$$19\dfrac{39}{20} = 20\dfrac{19}{20}$$

7. $4\dfrac{3}{4}$

$$8\dfrac{5}{12} = 7\dfrac{12}{12} + \dfrac{5}{12} = \quad 7\dfrac{17}{12}$$
$$-\ 3\dfrac{2}{3} \qquad\qquad\qquad 3\dfrac{8}{12} =$$
$$4\dfrac{9}{12} = \quad 4\dfrac{3}{4}$$

8. $\dfrac{3}{8} \times \dfrac{1}{6} \times \dfrac{4}{5} = \dfrac{1}{20}$

9. $5 \times \dfrac{3}{10} =$
$$\dfrac{5}{1} \times \dfrac{3}{10} = \dfrac{3}{2} = 1\dfrac{1}{2}$$

10. $\dfrac{21}{3} + \dfrac{2}{3} = \dfrac{23}{3}$

11. $3\dfrac{3}{4} \times 3\dfrac{1}{3} =$
$$\dfrac{15}{4} \times \dfrac{10}{3} = \dfrac{25}{2} = 12\dfrac{1}{2}$$

12. $\dfrac{3}{4} \div \dfrac{1}{8} =$
$$\dfrac{3}{4} \times \dfrac{8}{1} = \dfrac{6}{1} = 6$$

13. $24\dfrac{1}{2} \div 3\dfrac{1}{2} =$
$$\dfrac{49}{2} \div \dfrac{7}{2} = \dfrac{49}{2} \times \dfrac{2}{7} = \dfrac{7}{1} = 7$$

14. $.65 = \dfrac{65}{100} = \dfrac{13}{20}$

15.
$$\begin{array}{r} .24 \\ 25\overline{)6.00} \end{array}$$

16. $\dfrac{5}{9} = \dfrac{5}{9}$ and $\dfrac{2}{3} = \dfrac{6}{9}$

$\dfrac{5}{9}$ **is smaller.**

17. **(4) 371**

$$\begin{array}{r} 524.7 \\ 208.6 \\ +\ 380.9 \\ \hline 1114.2 \end{array}$$

$$\begin{array}{r} 371.4 \quad \text{to the nearest mile} \\ 3\overline{)1114.2} = 371 \end{array}$$

18. **(3)** Multiply $2\dfrac{3}{4}$ by \$7.20, then subtract the product from \$35.00.

19. **(1)** $\dfrac{23}{40}$

$$\begin{array}{lll} \dfrac{1}{5} = & \dfrac{8}{40} & 1 = \dfrac{40}{40} \\ \dfrac{1}{8} = & \dfrac{5}{40} & -\dfrac{17}{40} = \dfrac{17}{40} \\ +\dfrac{1}{10} = & \dfrac{4}{40} & \dfrac{23}{40} \\ & \dfrac{17}{40} \end{array}$$

20. **(5) \$72** $\dfrac{1}{5} \times \dfrac{360}{1} = \dfrac{72}{1} = \$72$

21. **(2) \$69**

Take-home pay $= \dfrac{23}{40} \times \dfrac{360}{1} = \dfrac{207}{1} = 207$

Food $= \dfrac{1}{3} \times \dfrac{207}{1} = \dfrac{69}{1} = \$69$

22. **(4) \$9.20** $41.40 \div 4\dfrac{1}{2} =$
$$41.40 \div 4.5$$

$$\begin{array}{r} \$9.20 \\ 4.5\overline{)41.40} \\ 40\ 5 \\ \hline 90 \\ 90 \\ \hline 0 \end{array}$$

23. **(1)** $21\dfrac{7}{8}$

$$28\dfrac{3}{8} = 27\dfrac{8}{8} + \dfrac{3}{8} = \quad 27\dfrac{11}{8}$$
$$-\ 6\dfrac{1}{2} = \qquad\qquad\qquad 6\dfrac{4}{8}$$
$$21\dfrac{7}{8}$$

24. **(2) 200**
$$\begin{array}{r} 2\ 00 \\ .45\overline{)90.00} \end{array}$$

25. **(1)** $(3 \times 12.50) - 5$

CHAPTER 5

PROBABILITY EXERCISE 1

pages 118–119

1. $\dfrac{1}{6}$

2. $\dfrac{2}{6} = \dfrac{1}{3}$

3. $\dfrac{4}{6} = \dfrac{2}{3}$

4. $\dfrac{1}{6}$

5. $\dfrac{3}{6} = \dfrac{1}{2}$

6. $\dfrac{3}{12} = \dfrac{1}{4}$

PROBABILITY EXERCISE 2
pages 119–120

1. $\dfrac{4}{52} = \dfrac{1}{13}$

2. $\dfrac{16}{20} = \dfrac{4}{5}$

3. $\dfrac{2}{3}$

   $\begin{array}{r} 12 \text{ blue} \\ + \ 6 \text{ white} \\ \hline 18 \text{ total} \end{array}$

   $\dfrac{12}{18} = \dfrac{2}{3}$

4. $\dfrac{2}{1000} = \dfrac{1}{500}$

5. $\dfrac{3}{500}$ $2 + 3 + 1 = 6$ tickets sold to the Robinsons

   $\dfrac{6}{1000} = \dfrac{3}{500}$

6. $\dfrac{15}{200} = \dfrac{3}{40}$

7. $\dfrac{1}{5}$

8. $\dfrac{1}{5}$

9. Together 1 and 5 appear twice. $\dfrac{2}{5}$

10. $\dfrac{3}{5}$

PROBABILITY EXERCISE 3
page 120

1. (4) $\dfrac{1}{8}$ $\begin{array}{r} 1 \text{ white} \\ 3 \text{ gray} \\ + \ 4 \text{ green} \\ \hline 8 \text{ total cans} \end{array}$

   $\dfrac{\text{white}}{\text{total}} = \dfrac{1}{8}$

2. (2) $\dfrac{1}{7}$ Total is down to 7 cans.

   $\dfrac{\text{white}}{\text{total}} = \dfrac{1}{7}$

3. (1) $\dfrac{2}{3}$ Now 1 white can, 1 gray can, and 4 green cans are left.

   $\dfrac{4}{6} = \dfrac{2}{3}$

RATIO AND PROPORTION EXERCISE 4
page 122

1. $\dfrac{12}{15} = \dfrac{4}{5}$ or 4:5

2. a. $\dfrac{\text{women}}{\text{total}}$ $\dfrac{12}{20} = \dfrac{3}{5}$ or 3:5

b. $\dfrac{\text{men}}{\text{total}}$ $\dfrac{20-12}{20}$ $\dfrac{8}{20} = \dfrac{2}{5}$ or 2:5

c. $\dfrac{\text{men}}{\text{women}}$ $\dfrac{8}{12} = \dfrac{2}{3}$ or 2:3

d. $\dfrac{\text{women}}{\text{men}}$ $\dfrac{12}{8} = \dfrac{3}{2}$ or 3:2

3. a. $\dfrac{\text{union}}{\text{total}}$ $\dfrac{105}{105+45}$ $\dfrac{105}{150} = \dfrac{21}{30} = \dfrac{7}{10}$ or 7:10

b. $\dfrac{\text{non union}}{\text{total}}$ $\dfrac{45}{150} = \dfrac{9}{30} = \dfrac{3}{10}$ or 3:10

c. $\dfrac{\text{union}}{\text{non union}}$ $\dfrac{105}{45} = \dfrac{21}{9} = \dfrac{7}{3}$ or 7:3

d. $\dfrac{\text{total}}{\text{union}}$ $\dfrac{150}{105} = \dfrac{30}{21} = \dfrac{10}{7}$ or 10:7

4. $\dfrac{\$ \text{ for education}}{\$ \text{ not for education}}$

   $\dfrac{\$3,000,000}{\$18,000,000 - \$3,000,000}$

   $\dfrac{\$ \ 3,000,000}{\$15,000,000} = \dfrac{1}{5}$ or 1:5

5. $\dfrac{\text{fractions and decimals}}{\text{total number of problems}}$

   $\dfrac{15+5}{50}$ $\dfrac{20}{50} = \dfrac{2}{5}$ or 2:5

RATIO AND PROPORTION EXERCISE 5
page 124

1. 4 $\begin{array}{r} 10 \\ \times \ 6 \\ \hline 60 \end{array}$ $15\overline{)60}\,^{4}$

   $3\tfrac{3}{5}$ $\begin{array}{r} 3 \\ \times \ 6 \\ \hline 18 \end{array}$ $5\overline{)18}\,^{3\frac{3}{5}}$

   $1\tfrac{1}{3}$ $\begin{array}{r} 4 \\ \times \ 3 \\ \hline 12 \end{array}$ $9\overline{)12}\,^{1\frac{3}{9}} = 1\tfrac{1}{3}$

   $3\tfrac{1}{2}$ $\begin{array}{r} 7 \\ \times \ 4 \\ \hline 28 \end{array}$ $8\overline{)28}\,^{3\frac{4}{8}} = 3\tfrac{1}{2}$

2. $1\tfrac{2}{3}$ $\begin{array}{r} 1 \\ \times \ 5 \\ \hline 5 \end{array}$ $3\overline{)5}\,^{1\frac{2}{3}}$

   $2\tfrac{1}{2}$ $\begin{array}{r} 3 \\ \times \ 5 \\ \hline 15 \end{array}$ $6\overline{)15}\,^{2\frac{3}{6}} = 2\tfrac{1}{2}$

   22 $\begin{array}{r} 11 \\ \times \ 4 \\ \hline 44 \end{array}$ $2\overline{)44}\,^{22}$

   36 $\begin{array}{r} 8 \\ \times \ 9 \\ \hline 72 \end{array}$ $2\overline{)72}\,^{36}$

3. $5\frac{1}{3}$ $\dfrac{4}{e} = \dfrac{6}{8}$ $\begin{array}{r} 4 \\ \times\, 8 \\ \hline 32 \end{array}$ $6\overline{)32}\,\dfrac{5\frac{2}{6} = 5\frac{1}{3}}{}$

$9\frac{1}{3}$ $\dfrac{3}{7} = \dfrac{4}{y}$ $\begin{array}{r} 7 \\ \times\, 4 \\ \hline 28 \end{array}$ $3\overline{)28}\,\dfrac{9\frac{1}{3}}{}$

$22\frac{1}{2}$ $\dfrac{15}{40} = \dfrac{x}{60}$ $\begin{array}{r} 15 \\ \times\, 60 \\ \hline 900 \end{array}$ $40\overline{)900}\,\dfrac{22\frac{20}{40} = 22\frac{1}{2}}{}$

40   $\dfrac{30}{a} = \dfrac{12}{16}$ $\begin{array}{r} 16 \\ \times\, 30 \\ \hline 480 \end{array}$ $12\overline{)480}\,\dfrac{40}{}$

RATIO AND PROPORTION EXERCISE 6
page 127

1. **(3) 21**

$\dfrac{\text{acres}}{\text{bushels}}$ $\dfrac{35}{3150} = \dfrac{a}{1890}$ $\begin{array}{r} 1890 \\ \times\, 35 \\ \hline 66{,}150 \end{array}$

$3150\overline{)66{,}150}\,\dfrac{21 \text{ acres}}{}$

2. **(5) $5.10**

$\dfrac{\text{feet}}{\$}$ $\dfrac{6}{3.40} = \dfrac{9}{x}$ $\begin{array}{r} 3.40 \\ \times\, 9 \\ \hline 30.60 \end{array}$ $6\overline{)30.60}\,\dfrac{\$5.10}{}$

3. **(2) $4\frac{1}{3}$**

$\dfrac{\text{inches}}{\text{miles}}$ $\dfrac{2}{150} = \dfrac{x}{325}$ $\begin{array}{r} 325 \\ \times\, 2 \\ \hline 650 \end{array}$

$150\overline{)650}\,\dfrac{4\frac{50}{150}}{} = 4\frac{1}{3} \text{ inches}$

4. **(3) $5\frac{1}{3}$**

$\dfrac{\text{miles}}{\text{hours}}$ $\dfrac{450}{2} = \dfrac{1200}{x}$ $\begin{array}{r} 1200 \\ \times\, 2 \\ \hline 2400 \end{array}$

$450\overline{)2400}\,\dfrac{5\frac{150}{450}}{} = 5\frac{1}{3} \text{ hours}$
$\begin{array}{r} 2250 \\ \hline 150 \end{array}$

5. **(4) 35**

$\dfrac{\text{blue}}{\text{white}}$ $\dfrac{5}{2} = \dfrac{x}{14}$ $\begin{array}{r} 14 \\ \times\, 5 \\ \hline 70 \end{array}$

$2\overline{)70}\,\dfrac{35 \text{ gallons}}{}$

6. **(1) $3\frac{2}{3}$**

$\dfrac{\text{inches}}{\text{degrees}}$ $\dfrac{2\frac{1}{2}}{75} = \dfrac{x}{110}$ $\dfrac{5}{2} \times \dfrac{110}{1} = 275$

$75\overline{)275}\,\dfrac{3\frac{50}{75}}{} = 3\frac{2}{3} \text{ inches}$
$\begin{array}{r} 225 \\ \hline 50 \end{array}$

7. **(3)** $\dfrac{3 \cdot 12}{5}$ $\dfrac{\text{width}}{\text{length}}$ $\dfrac{3}{5} = \dfrac{x}{12}$

8. **(1)** $\dfrac{2 \times 100}{16}$ $\dfrac{\text{parts}}{\text{hours}}$ $\dfrac{16}{2} = \dfrac{100}{x}$

9. **(4)** $\dfrac{2 \times 12}{3}$ $\dfrac{\text{sugar}}{\text{flour}}$ $\dfrac{2}{3} = \dfrac{x}{12}$

10. **(2)** $\dfrac{90 \times 8}{12}$ $\dfrac{\text{cost}}{\text{number}}$ $\dfrac{90}{12} = \dfrac{x}{8}$

RATIO AND PROPORTION REVIEW
PAGE 129

1. **$1500**

$\begin{array}{ll} \text{take-home} & 10 \\ \text{withheld} & +\ 3 \\ \hline \text{total} & 13 \end{array}$

$\dfrac{\text{take-home}}{\text{total}}$ $\dfrac{10}{13} = \dfrac{t}{1950}$

$\begin{array}{r} 1950 \\ \times\, 10 \\ \hline 19{,}500 \end{array}$ $13\overline{)19{,}500}\,\dfrac{\$1{,}500}{}$

2. **20 games**

$\begin{array}{ll} \text{won} & 5 \\ \text{lost} & +\ 3 \\ \hline \text{total} & 8 \end{array}$

$\dfrac{\text{won}}{\text{total}}$ $\dfrac{5}{8} = \dfrac{w}{32}$

$\begin{array}{r} 32 \\ \times\, 5 \\ \hline 160 \end{array}$

$8\overline{)160}\,\dfrac{20 \text{ games won}}{}$

3. **80 women**

$\begin{array}{ll} \text{men} & 7 \\ \text{women} & +\ 2 \\ \hline \text{total} & 9 \end{array}$

$\dfrac{\text{women}}{\text{total}}$ $\dfrac{2}{9} = \dfrac{w}{360}$

$\begin{array}{r} 360 \\ \times\, 2 \\ \hline 720 \end{array}$

$9\overline{)720}\,\dfrac{80 \text{ women}}{}$

4. **500 parts**

$\begin{array}{ll} \text{good} & 20 \\ \text{defective} & +\ 1 \\ \hline \text{total} & 21 \end{array}$

$\dfrac{\text{defective}}{\text{total}}$ $\dfrac{1}{21} = \dfrac{d}{10{,}500}$

$\begin{array}{r} 10{,}500 \\ \times\, 1 \\ \hline 10{,}500 \end{array}$ $21\overline{)10{,}500}\,\dfrac{500 \text{ parts}}{}$

5. 250 people

$$\begin{array}{r} \text{passed} \quad 5 \\ \text{failed} + 1 \\ \hline \text{total} \quad 6 \end{array}$$

$$\frac{\text{passed}}{\text{total}} \quad \frac{5}{6} = \frac{p}{300}$$

$$\begin{array}{r} 300 \\ \times\ 5 \\ \hline 1500 \end{array} \qquad \begin{array}{r} 250 \text{ people passed} \\ 6\overline{)1500} \end{array}$$

6. 216 workers

$$\begin{array}{r} \text{strikers} \quad 3 \\ \text{nonstrikers} + 2 \\ \hline \text{total} \quad 5 \end{array}$$

$$\frac{\text{strikers}}{\text{total}} \quad \frac{3}{5} = \frac{s}{360}$$

$$\begin{array}{r} 360 \\ \times\ 3 \\ \hline 1080 \end{array} \qquad \begin{array}{r} 216 \text{ voted to strike} \\ 5\overline{)1080} \end{array}$$

7. $6\frac{1}{2}$ feet

$$\frac{\text{height}}{\text{distance}} \quad \frac{40}{13} = \frac{20}{x}$$

$$\begin{array}{r} 20 \\ \times\ 13 \\ \hline 60 \\ 20 \\ \hline 260 \end{array} \qquad \begin{array}{r} 6.5 \text{ or } 6\frac{1}{2} \\ 40\overline{)260} \\ 240 \\ \hline 200 \\ 200 \\ \hline 0 \end{array}$$

8. 30 inches

$$\frac{\text{short}}{\text{long}} \quad \frac{4}{6} = \frac{20}{x}$$

$$\begin{array}{r} 20 \\ \times\ 6 \\ \hline 120 \end{array} \qquad \begin{array}{r} 30 \text{ in} \\ 4\overline{)120} \end{array}$$

9. $120

$$\begin{array}{r} \text{makes} \quad \$9 \\ \text{spends} - 7 \\ \hline \$2 \end{array} \qquad \frac{2}{9} = \frac{s}{540}$$

$$\begin{array}{r} 540 \\ \times\ 2 \\ \hline 1080 \end{array} \qquad \begin{array}{r} \$120 \\ 9\overline{)\$1080} \end{array}$$

10. 12 gallons

$$\begin{array}{r} \text{blue} \quad 3 \\ \text{gray} + 2 \\ \hline 5 \end{array} \qquad \frac{\text{gray}}{\text{total}} \quad \frac{2}{5} = \frac{g}{30}$$

$$\begin{array}{r} 30 \\ \times\ 2 \\ \hline 60 \end{array} \qquad \begin{array}{r} 12 \text{ gal} \\ 5\overline{)60} \end{array}$$

CHAPTER 6

PERCENTS EXERCISE 1
page 132

1. 60% 99% 6.5% 2% $83\frac{1}{3}\%$

2. 110% 240% 650%

3. $\frac{1}{4}\%$ 0.9% .65% 0.1%

PERCENTS EXERCISE 2
page 133

1. .09
2. .24
3. 1
4. .003
5. $.87\frac{1}{2}$
6. $.08\frac{1}{3}$
7. .0015
8. 2.75
9. .027
10. .0395
11. .57
12. 10

PERCENTS EXERCISE 3
page 135

1. 81%
2. $37\frac{1}{2}\%$
3. 50%
4. .4%
5. .09%
6. 21.7%
7. 3%
8. $33\frac{1}{3}\%$
9. 210%
10. 485%
11. 392.4%
12. 1.5%

PERCENTS EXERCISE 4
page 136

1. $\frac{1}{5} \times \frac{100\%}{1} = \mathbf{20\%}$

2. $\frac{5}{6} \times \frac{100\%}{1} = \frac{250}{3} = \mathbf{83\frac{1}{3}\%}$

3. $\frac{3}{8} \times \frac{100\%}{1} = \frac{75}{2} = \mathbf{37\frac{1}{2}\%}$

4. $\frac{2}{3} \times \frac{100\%}{1} = \frac{200}{3} = \mathbf{66\frac{2}{3}\%}$

5. $\frac{14}{8} = \frac{7}{4} \qquad \frac{7}{4} \times \frac{100\%}{1} = \mathbf{175\%}$

6. $\frac{9}{10} \times \frac{100\%}{1} = \mathbf{90\%}$

7. $\frac{5}{12} \times \frac{100\%}{1} = \frac{125}{3} = \mathbf{41\frac{2}{3}\%}$

8. $\frac{6}{7} \times \frac{100\%}{1} = \frac{600}{7} = \mathbf{85\frac{5}{7}\%}$

9. $\frac{1}{6} \times \frac{100\%}{1} = \frac{50}{3} = \mathbf{16\frac{2}{3}\%}$

10. $\frac{10}{5} = \frac{2}{1} \qquad \frac{2}{1} \times \frac{100\%}{1} = \mathbf{200\%}$

11. $\frac{1}{12} \times \frac{100\%}{1} = \frac{25}{3} = \mathbf{8\frac{1}{3}\%}$

12. $\frac{2}{11} \times \frac{100\%}{1} = \frac{200}{11} = \mathbf{18\frac{2}{11}\%}$

PERCENTS EXERCISE 5
page 138

1. $\frac{45}{100} = \frac{9}{20}$

2. $37\frac{1}{2} \div 100 = \frac{75}{2} \times \frac{1}{100} = \frac{3}{8}$

3. $6\frac{2}{3} \div 100 = \frac{20}{3} \times \frac{1}{100} = \frac{1}{15}$

4. $\frac{8}{100} = \frac{2}{25}$

5. $\frac{2}{100} = \frac{1}{50}$

6. $83\frac{1}{3} \div 100 = \frac{250}{3} \times \frac{1}{100} = \frac{5}{6}$

7. $\frac{24}{100} = \frac{6}{25}$

8. $33\frac{1}{3} \div 100 = \frac{100}{3} \times \frac{1}{100} = \frac{1}{3}$

9. $28\frac{4}{7} \div 100 = \frac{200}{7} \times \frac{1}{100} = \frac{2}{7}$

10. $\frac{80}{100} = \frac{4}{5}$

11. $\frac{150}{100} = 1\frac{50}{100} = 1\frac{1}{2}$

12. $12\frac{1}{2} \div 100 = \frac{25}{2} \times \frac{1}{100} = \frac{1}{8}$

13. $1.5\% = .015 = \frac{15}{1000} = \frac{3}{200}$

14. $.09\% = .0009 = \frac{9}{10,000}$

15. $.6\% = .006 = \frac{6}{1000} = \frac{3}{500}$

16. $\frac{1}{100}$

PERCENTS EXERCISE 6
page 138

Fraction	Decimal	Percent
$\frac{1}{4}$	.25	25%
$\frac{1}{2}$	.5	50%
$\frac{3}{4}$	.75	75%
$\frac{1}{8}$	.125 or .12$\frac{1}{2}$	12$\frac{1}{2}$% or 12.5%
$\frac{1}{5}$	.2	20%
$\frac{2}{5}$	.4	40%
$\frac{3}{5}$	.6	60%
$\frac{4}{5}$	.8	80%
$\frac{1}{10}$	.1	10%
$\frac{3}{10}$	.3	30%
$\frac{7}{10}$	.7	70%
$\frac{9}{10}$	.9	90%
$\frac{1}{3}$	.33$\frac{1}{3}$	33$\frac{1}{3}$%
$\frac{2}{3}$	.66$\frac{2}{3}$	66$\frac{2}{3}$%

PERCENTS EXERCISE 7
page 140

2. 80% of 25 is 20. $\frac{20}{25} = \frac{80}{100}$

3. 45 is 10% of 450. $\frac{45}{450} = \frac{10}{100}$

4. 16% of 25 equals 4. $\frac{4}{25} = \frac{16}{100}$

5. 30% of 200 is 60. $\frac{60}{200} = \frac{30}{100}$

6. 13 is equal to 20 percent of 65. $\frac{13}{65} = \frac{20}{100}$

7. 107 is 100% of 107. $\frac{107}{107} = \frac{100}{100}$

8. 50 is 50 percent of one hundred. $\frac{50}{100} = \frac{50}{100}$

PERCENTS EXERCISE 8
page 141

1. 25% $\frac{9}{36} = \frac{x}{100}$ $\begin{array}{r}9\\ \times 100\\ \hline 900\end{array}$ $36\overline{)900}$ = 25

2. 40% $\dfrac{14}{35} = \dfrac{x}{100}$ $\begin{array}{r} 14 \\ \times\ 100 \\ \hline 1400 \end{array}$ $\begin{array}{r} 40 \\ 35\overline{)1400} \end{array}$

3. $66\frac{2}{3}$% $\dfrac{50}{75} = \dfrac{x}{100}$ $\begin{array}{r} 50 \\ \times\ 100 \\ \hline 5000 \end{array}$ $\begin{array}{r} 66\frac{2}{3} \\ 75\overline{)5000} \end{array}$

4. 250% $\dfrac{40}{16} = \dfrac{x}{100}$ $\begin{array}{r} 40 \\ \times\ 100 \\ \hline 4000 \end{array}$ $\begin{array}{r} 250 \\ 16\overline{)4000} \end{array}$

5. 75% $\dfrac{120}{160} = \dfrac{x}{100}$ $\begin{array}{r} 120 \\ \times\ 100 \\ \hline 12{,}000 \end{array}$ $\begin{array}{r} 75 \\ 160\overline{)12{,}000} \end{array}$

PERCENTS EXERCISE 9
page 142

1. 27 $\dfrac{p}{90} = \dfrac{30}{100}$ $\begin{array}{r} 90 \\ \times\ 30 \\ \hline 2700 \end{array}$ $\begin{array}{r} 27 \\ 100\overline{)2700} \end{array}$

2. 91 $\dfrac{p}{140} = \dfrac{65}{100}$ $\begin{array}{r} 140 \\ \times\ 65 \\ \hline 9100 \end{array}$ $\begin{array}{r} 91 \\ 100\overline{)9100} \end{array}$

3. 12 $\dfrac{p}{72} = \dfrac{16\frac{2}{3}}{100}$ $72 \times 16\frac{2}{3} = \dfrac{72}{1} \times \dfrac{50}{3}$

$= 1200$

$\begin{array}{r} 12 \\ 100\overline{)1200} \end{array}$

4. 42.5 $\dfrac{p}{500} = \dfrac{8.5}{100}$ $\begin{array}{r} 8.5 \\ \times\ 500 \\ \hline 4250.0 \end{array}$ $\begin{array}{r} 42.5 \\ 100\overline{)4250.0} \end{array}$

5. 180 $\dfrac{p}{60} = \dfrac{300}{100}$ $\begin{array}{r} 60 \\ \times\ 300 \\ \hline 18{,}000 \end{array}$ $\begin{array}{r} 180 \\ 100\overline{)18{,}000} \end{array}$

PERCENTS EXERCISE 10
page 143

1. 36 $\dfrac{18}{w} = \dfrac{50}{100}$ $\begin{array}{r} 18 \\ \times\ 100 \\ \hline 1800 \end{array}$ $\begin{array}{r} 36 \\ 50\overline{)1800} \end{array}$

2. 160 $\dfrac{24}{w} = \dfrac{15}{100}$ $\begin{array}{r} 24 \\ \times\ 100 \\ \hline 2400 \end{array}$ $\begin{array}{r} 160 \\ 15\overline{)2400} \end{array}$

3. 16 $\dfrac{2}{w} = \dfrac{12\frac{1}{2}}{100}$ $\begin{array}{r} 2 \\ \times\ 100 \\ \hline 200 \end{array}$

$200 \div 12\frac{1}{2} = \dfrac{200}{1} \div \dfrac{25}{2} = \dfrac{200}{1} \times \dfrac{2}{25} = 16$

4. 43 $\dfrac{86}{w} = \dfrac{200}{100}$ $\begin{array}{r} 86 \\ \times\ 100 \\ \hline 8600 \end{array}$ $\begin{array}{r} 43 \\ 200\overline{)8600} \end{array}$

PERCENTS EXERCISE 11
page 143

1. percent: 50%

$\dfrac{16}{32} = \dfrac{x}{100}$ $\begin{array}{r} 16 \\ \times\ 100 \\ \hline 1600 \end{array}$ $\begin{array}{r} 50 \\ 32\overline{)1600} \end{array}$

2. part: 72

$\dfrac{p}{90} = \dfrac{80}{100}$ $\begin{array}{r} 80 \\ \times\ 90 \\ \hline 7200 \end{array}$ $\begin{array}{r} 72 \\ 100\overline{)7200} \end{array}$

3. whole: 50

$\dfrac{30}{w} = \dfrac{60}{100}$ $\begin{array}{r} 30 \\ \times\ 100 \\ \hline 3000 \end{array}$ $\begin{array}{r} 50 \\ 60\overline{)3000} \end{array}$

4. part: 36

$\dfrac{p}{800} = \dfrac{4\frac{1}{2}}{100}$

$4\frac{1}{2} \times 800 = \dfrac{9}{2} \times \dfrac{800}{1} = 3600$

$\begin{array}{r} 36 \\ 100\overline{)3600} \end{array}$

5. percent: 28%

$\dfrac{14}{50} = \dfrac{x}{100}$ $\begin{array}{r} 14 \\ \times\ 100 \\ \hline 1{,}400 \end{array}$ $\begin{array}{r} 28 \\ 50\overline{)1400} \end{array}$

6. percent: $33\frac{1}{3}$%

$\dfrac{15}{45} = \dfrac{x}{100}$ $\begin{array}{r} 15 \\ \times\ 100 \\ \hline 1500 \end{array}$ $\begin{array}{r} 33\frac{1}{3} \\ 45\overline{)1500} \end{array}$

7. part: 32.4

$\dfrac{p}{900} = \dfrac{3.6}{100}$ $\begin{array}{r} 3.6 \\ \times\ 900 \\ \hline 3240.0 \end{array}$ $\begin{array}{r} 32.4 \\ 100\overline{)3240.0} \end{array}$

8. percent: 150%

$\dfrac{120}{80} = \dfrac{x}{100}$ $\begin{array}{r} 120 \\ \times\ 100 \\ \hline 12{,}000 \end{array}$ $\begin{array}{r} 150 \\ 80\overline{)12{,}000} \end{array}$

9. whole: 135

$\dfrac{45}{w} = \dfrac{33\frac{1}{3}}{100}$ $\begin{array}{r} 45 \\ \times\ 100 \\ \hline 4500 \end{array}$

$4500 \div 33\frac{1}{3} = \dfrac{4500}{1} \div \dfrac{100}{3} = \dfrac{4500}{1} \times \dfrac{3}{100} = 135$

10. **part: 17.2**

$$\frac{p}{200} = \frac{8.6}{100}$$

$$\begin{array}{r} 8.6 \\ \times\ 200 \\ \hline 1720.0 \end{array}$$

$$100\overline{)1720.0}^{\,17.2}$$

PERCENTS EXERCISE 12
page 145

1. **part: $6**

$$\frac{p}{40} = \frac{15}{100}$$

$$\begin{array}{r} 15 \\ \times\ 40 \\ \hline 600 \end{array}$$

$$100\overline{)600}^{\,\$\,6}$$

2. **percent: 75%**

$$\frac{6{,}000}{8{,}000} = \frac{x}{100}$$

$$\begin{array}{r} 6{,}000 \\ \times\ 100 \\ \hline 600{,}000 \end{array}$$

$$8{,}000\overline{)600{,}000}^{\,75}$$

3. **part: $30**

$$\frac{p}{250} = \frac{12}{100}$$

$$\begin{array}{r} 250 \\ \times\ 12 \\ \hline 500 \\ 250 \\ \hline 3000 \end{array}$$

$$100\overline{)3000}^{\,\$\,30}$$

4. **whole: 215 pounds**

$$\frac{172}{w} = \frac{80}{100}$$

$$\begin{array}{r} 172 \\ \times\ 100 \\ \hline 17{,}200 \end{array}$$

$$80\overline{)17{,}200}^{\,215\ \text{pounds}}$$

5. **percent: 25%**

$$\frac{150}{600} = \frac{x}{100}$$

$$\begin{array}{r} 150 \\ \times\ 100 \\ \hline 15{,}000 \end{array}$$

$$600\overline{)15{,}000}^{\,25}$$

6. **part: $14.40**

$$\frac{p}{240} = \frac{6}{100}$$

$$\begin{array}{r} 240 \\ \times\ 6 \\ \hline 1440 \end{array}$$

$$100\overline{)1440.00}^{\,\$\,14.40}$$

7. **whole: 24 people**

$$\frac{18}{w} = \frac{75}{100}$$

$$\begin{array}{r} 18 \\ \times\ 100 \\ \hline 1800 \end{array}$$

$$75\overline{)1800}^{\,24\ \text{people}}$$

8. **(4) percent: 30%**

$$\frac{6}{20} = \frac{x}{100}$$

$$\begin{array}{r} 100 \\ \times\ 6 \\ \hline 600 \end{array}$$

$$20\overline{)600}^{\,30}$$

9. **(2) part: $345.60**

$$\frac{p}{3840} = \frac{9}{100}$$

$$\begin{array}{r} 3{,}840 \\ \times\ 9 \\ \hline 34{,}560 \end{array}$$

$$100\overline{)34{,}560.00}^{\,\$\,345.60}$$

PERCENTS EXERCISE 13
page 147

1. **$17.40**

First find the markup.

$$\frac{p}{12} = \frac{45}{100}$$

$$\begin{array}{r} 45 \\ \times\ 12 \\ \hline 540 \end{array}$$

$$100\overline{)540.00}^{\,\$\,5.40}$$

Then find the new price

original price	$12.00
markup	+ 5.40
selling price	$17.40

2. **$1440**

First find the assessed value of the farm.

$$\frac{p}{120{,}000} = \frac{60}{100}$$

$$\begin{array}{r} 120{,}000 \\ \times\ 60 \\ \hline 7{,}200{,}000 \end{array}$$

$$100\overline{)7{,}200{,}000}^{\,\$\,72{,}000}$$

Find the taxes on $72,000.

$$\frac{p}{72{,}000} = \frac{2}{100}$$

$$\begin{array}{r} 72{,}000 \\ \times\ 2 \\ \hline 144{,}000 \end{array}$$

$$100\overline{)144{,}000}^{\,\$\,1{,}440}$$

3. **$325**

First find yearly rent.

$$\frac{p}{15{,}600} = \frac{25}{100}$$

$$\begin{array}{r} 15{,}600 \\ \times\ 25 \\ \hline 390{,}000 \end{array}$$

$$100\overline{)390{,}000}^{\,\$\,3{,}900}$$

Find the monthly rent.

$$12\overline{)3900}^{\,\$325}$$

4. **$2070**

First find the down payment.

$$\frac{p}{1800} = \frac{15}{100}$$

$$\begin{array}{r} 1{,}800 \\ \times\ 15 \\ \hline 9\ 000 \\ 18\ 00 \\ \hline 27{,}000 \end{array}$$

$$100\overline{)27{,}000}^{\,\$\,270}$$

Next find the total monthly payments.

$$\begin{array}{r} 36 \\ \times\ \$50 \\ \hline \$1800 \end{array}$$

Finally, find the total.

monthly payments	$1800
down payment	+ 270
total	$2070

5. **(5) $175**

Find 65% of the total.

$$\frac{p}{500} = \frac{65}{100}$$

$$\begin{array}{r} 65 \\ \times\ 500 \\ \hline 32{,}500 \end{array}$$

$$100\overline{)32{,}500}^{\,\$\,325}$$

Then find out what it needs.

want	$500
have	− 325
still need	$175

6. (2) $2400

total deductions = 10% + 5% + 5% = 20%

$$\frac{p}{3000} = \frac{20}{100}$$

$$\begin{array}{r} 3000 \\ \times\ 20 \\ \hline 60,000 \end{array} \qquad \begin{array}{r} \$\ 600 \\ 100\overline{)60,000} \end{array}$$

Subtract deductions from gross salary.

gross salary $3000
deductions   − 600
net salary $2400

7. (5) 4950

First find 125% increase.

$$\frac{p}{2200} = \frac{125}{100}$$

$$\begin{array}{r} 125 \\ \times\ 2200 \\ \hline 25\ 000 \\ 250 \\ \hline 275,000 \end{array} \qquad \begin{array}{r} 2,750 \\ 100\overline{)275,000} \end{array}$$

Then add the increase to the 1983 figure.

1983   2200
increase + 2750
1993   4950

PERCENTS EXERCISE 14
page 149

1. $7\frac{1}{7}\%$

$$\begin{array}{r} 90 \\ -\ 84 \\ \hline 6 \end{array} \quad \frac{6}{84} = \frac{x}{100} \quad \begin{array}{r} 100 \\ \times\ 6 \\ \hline 600 \end{array} \quad \begin{array}{r} 7\frac{12}{84} = 7\frac{1}{7} \\ 84\overline{)600} \\ 588 \\ \hline 12 \end{array}$$

2. 25%

$$\begin{array}{r} 1200 \\ -\ 900 \\ \hline 300 \end{array} \quad \frac{300}{1200} = \frac{x}{100} \quad \begin{array}{r} 300 \\ \times\ 100 \\ \hline 30,000 \end{array}$$

$$\begin{array}{r} 25 \\ 1,200\overline{)30,000} \end{array}$$

3. 20%

$$\begin{array}{r} 12 \\ -\ 10 \\ \hline 2 \end{array} \quad \frac{2}{10} = \frac{x}{100} \quad \begin{array}{r} 100 \\ \times\ 2 \\ \hline 200 \end{array} \quad \begin{array}{r} 20 \\ 10\overline{)200} \end{array}$$

4. $8\frac{1}{3}\%$

$$\begin{array}{r} 300 \\ -\ 275 \\ \hline 25 \end{array} \quad \frac{25}{300} = \frac{x}{100} \quad \begin{array}{r} 25 \\ \times\ 100 \\ \hline 2500 \end{array} \quad \begin{array}{r} 8\frac{1}{3} \\ 300\overline{)2500} \end{array}$$

5. (5) 240%

$$\begin{array}{r} 85,000 \\ -\ 25,000 \\ \hline 60,000 \end{array} \quad \frac{60,000}{25,000} = \frac{x}{100}$$

$$\begin{array}{r} 60,000 \\ \times\ 100 \\ \hline 6,000,000 \end{array}$$

$$\begin{array}{r} 240 \\ 25,000\overline{)6,000,000} \end{array}$$

6. (2) 8%

$$\begin{array}{r} 3600 \\ -\ 3312 \\ \hline 288 \end{array} \quad \frac{288}{3600} = \frac{x}{100} \quad \begin{array}{r} 288 \\ \times\ 100 \\ \hline 28,800 \end{array}$$

$$\begin{array}{r} 8\% \\ 3,600\overline{)28,800} \end{array}$$

PERCENTS EXERCISE 15
page 150

1. $1500

$$\frac{6000}{w} = \frac{80}{100} \quad \begin{array}{r} 6000 \\ \times\ 100 \\ \hline 600,000 \end{array} \quad \begin{array}{r} 7,500 \\ 80\overline{)600,000} \end{array}$$

original price $7500
current price − 6000
depreciation $1500

2. 3200 registered voters

$$\frac{4800}{w} = \frac{60}{100} \quad \begin{array}{r} 4,800 \\ \times\ 100 \\ \hline 480,000 \end{array} \quad \begin{array}{r} 8,000 \\ 60\overline{)480,000} \end{array}$$

registered   8,000
went to polls   − 4,800
did not go to polls 3,200

3. $38

$$\frac{342}{w} = \frac{90}{100} \quad \begin{array}{r} 342 \\ \times\ 100 \\ \hline 34,200 \end{array} \quad \begin{array}{r} 380 \\ 90\overline{)34,200} \end{array}$$

original price $380
sale price   − 342
savings $ 38

4. $2300

$$\frac{6900}{w} = \frac{75}{100} \quad \begin{array}{r} 6,900 \\ \times\ 100 \\ \hline 690,000 \end{array} \quad \begin{array}{r} 9,200 \\ 75\overline{)690,000} \end{array}$$

total $9200
saved − 6900
net $2300

5. 300 people

$$\frac{1800}{w} = \frac{120}{100} \quad \begin{array}{r} 1,800 \\ \times\ 100 \\ \hline 180,000 \end{array} \quad \begin{array}{r} 1,500 \\ 120\overline{)180,000} \end{array}$$

this year   1,800
last year − 1,500
new members 300

PERCENTS EXERCISE 16
page 152

1. **$36.90**
   First find the 18% discount.

   $\frac{x}{50} = \frac{18}{100}$ $\begin{array}{r} 18 \\ \times 50 \\ \hline 900 \end{array}$ $\begin{array}{r} \$9 \\ 100\overline{)900} \end{array}$

   Subtract the discount from the marked price.

   $\begin{array}{r} 50 \\ - 9 \\ \hline 41 \end{array}$

   Then find 10% of the discounted price.

   $\frac{x}{41} = \frac{10}{100}$ $\begin{array}{r} 41 \\ \times 10 \\ \hline 410 \end{array}$ $\begin{array}{r} \$4.10 \\ 100\overline{)410.00} \end{array}$

   Subtract this amount to find the total price.
   $\begin{array}{r} \$41.00 \\ - 4.10 \\ \hline \$36.90 \end{array}$

2. **$12.45**

   $\begin{array}{r} 12\% \\ + 5\% \\ \hline 17\% \end{array}$ $\frac{x}{15} = \frac{17}{100}$ $\begin{array}{r} 17 \\ \times 15 \\ \hline 255 \end{array}$

   $\begin{array}{r} 2.55 \\ 100\overline{)255} \end{array}$ $\begin{array}{r} 15.00 \\ - 2.55 \\ \hline 12.45 \end{array}$

3. **22 students**

   $\begin{array}{r} 30\% \\ + 25\% \\ \hline 55\% \end{array}$ $\frac{x}{40} = \frac{55}{100}$ $\begin{array}{r} 55 \\ \times 40 \\ \hline 2200 \end{array}$ $\begin{array}{r} 22 \\ 100\overline{)2200} \end{array}$

4. **147 people**
   First find the number of no-shows.

   $\frac{x}{1400} = \frac{14}{100}$ $\begin{array}{r} 1400 \\ \times 14 \\ \hline 19,600 \end{array}$ $\begin{array}{r} 196 \\ 100\overline{)19,600} \end{array}$

   Then find the number of no-shows from the Toronto Tour Group.

   $\frac{x}{196} = \frac{75}{100}$

   $\begin{array}{r} 196 \\ \times 75 \\ \hline 14,700 \end{array}$ $\begin{array}{r} 147 \\ 100\overline{)14,700} \end{array}$

5. **21,000 accidents**
   First find the number of accidents caused by carelessness.

   $\frac{x}{240,000} = \frac{25}{100}$ $\begin{array}{r} 240,000 \\ \times 25 \\ \hline 6,000,000 \end{array}$ $\begin{array}{r} 60,000 \\ 100\overline{)6,000,000} \end{array}$

   Then find the number of accidents caused by carelessness *and* involving children.

   $\frac{x}{60,000} = \frac{35}{100}$ $\begin{array}{r} 60,000 \\ \times 35 \\ \hline 2,100,000 \end{array}$ $\begin{array}{r} 21,000 \\ 100\overline{)2,100,000} \end{array}$

PERCENTS EXERCISE 17
page 153

1. $138 \div 2 = $ **69**

2. 10% of 60 = **6**

3. 10% of 360 = 36
   $2 \times 36 = $ **72**

4. 10% of 21.489 = **2.1489**

5. 10% of 360 = 36
   $4 \times 36 = $ **144**

6. 10% of $8.50 = $.85
   $3 \times $.85 = $ **$2.55**

7. 50% of $18,500 = **$9,250**

8. 10% of 700 = 70
   $6 \times 70 = $ **420**

9. 10% of 2.6 = **.26**

10. 50% of 79 = $39\frac{1}{2}$ **or 39.5**

11. **(2) $1368**
    10% of $13,680 = $1,368

12. **(1) 640**
    50% of 1280 = 1280 ÷ 2 = 640

13. **(4) 270**
    10% of 900 = 90
    30% of 900 = 3 × 90 = 270

14. **(3) $34,000**
    50% of $68,000 = $68,000 ÷ 2 = $34,000

PERCENTS EXERCISE 18
page 155

	Lincoln	Milwaukee
cost	$47,700	$58,900
down payment	12%	8%
home improvements	$6200	$2945

1. **(2) $1012**
   12% of $47,700 = $5724
   8% of $58,900 = $4712

   $\begin{array}{r} 5724 \\ - 4712 \\ \hline \$1012 \end{array}$

2. **(3) 5**

   $\frac{\$2,945}{\$58,900} = \frac{x}{100}$ $\begin{array}{r} 2945 \\ \times 100 \\ \hline 294,500 \end{array}$

   $\begin{array}{r} 5\% \\ 58,900\overline{)294,500} \end{array}$

3. **(4) $53,900**
   $\begin{array}{r} \$47,700 \\ + 6,200 \\ \hline \$53,900 \end{array}$

PERCENT3 EXERCISE 19
page 158

1. $375

$$\frac{3000}{1} \times \frac{12.5}{100} = 375$$

2. $842

$$\frac{800}{1} \times \frac{5\overset{1}{4}}{100} = \$42$$

principal	$800
interest	+ 42
total	$842

3. $900

$$\frac{5000}{1} \times \frac{9}{100} \times \frac{2}{1} = 900$$

4. $36

9 months $= \frac{9}{12} = \frac{3}{4}$ year

$$\frac{800}{1} \times \frac{6}{100} \times \frac{3}{4} = 36$$

5. $51.75

6 months $= \frac{6}{12} = \frac{1}{2}$ year

$$\frac{900}{1} \times \frac{11.5}{100} \times \frac{1}{2} = \frac{103.50}{2} = 51.75$$

6. $105

1 year and 6 months $= 1\frac{6}{12} = 1\frac{1}{2}$ years

$$\frac{500}{1} \times \frac{14}{100} \times 1\frac{1}{2} =$$

$$\frac{500}{1} \times \frac{14}{100} \times \frac{3}{2} = 105$$

7. $2300

2 years and 6 months $= 2\frac{6}{12} = 2\frac{1}{2}$ years

$$\frac{6}{100} \times 2\frac{1}{2} \times \frac{2000}{1} =$$

$$\frac{6}{100} \times \frac{5}{2} \times \frac{2000}{1} = 300$$

principal	$2000
interest	+ 300
total	$2300

8. $1095

1 year and 8 months $= 1\frac{8}{12} = 1\frac{2}{3}$ years

$$\frac{900}{1} \times \frac{13}{100} \times 1\frac{2}{3} =$$

$$\frac{900}{1} \times \frac{13}{100} \times \frac{5}{3} = 195$$

principal	$ 900
interest	+ 195
total	$1095

9. $933.33

2 years and 4 months $= 2\frac{4}{12} = 2\frac{1}{3}$ years

$$\frac{4000}{1} \times \frac{10}{100} \times 2\frac{1}{3} =$$

$$\frac{4000}{1} \times \frac{10}{100} \times \frac{7}{3} = \frac{2800}{3}$$

to the nearest penny = $933.33

10. $1332.75

nine months $= \frac{9}{12} = \frac{3}{4}$ year

$$\frac{1200}{1} \times \frac{14.75}{100} \times \frac{3}{4} = 132.75$$

principal	$1200.00
interest	+ 132.75
total	$1332.75

PERCENTS EXERCISE 20
page 160

1. (4) $16,125

Find Fred's raise after 3 months.

$$\frac{p}{1250} = \frac{10}{100}$$

$$\begin{array}{r} 1,250 \\ \times\ 10 \\ \hline 12,500 \end{array} \qquad 100)\overline{12,500}\ \ \overset{125}{}$$

Then find his new monthly salary.

$$\begin{array}{r} \$1250 \\ +\ 125 \\ \hline \$1375 \end{array}$$

Finally, find his yearly salary.

$$\begin{array}{r} \$1250 \\ \times\ \ 3\ \text{months} \\ \hline \$3750 \end{array} \qquad \begin{array}{r} \$1,375 \\ \times\ \ 9\ \text{months} \\ \hline \$12,375 \end{array}$$

$$\begin{array}{r} \$12,375 \\ +\ 3,750 \\ \hline \$16,125 \end{array}$$

2. (3) $187.50

$$\frac{p}{1250} = \frac{15}{100}$$

$$\begin{array}{r} 1250 \\ \times\ 15 \\ \hline 6\ 250 \\ 1\ 250 \\ \hline 18,750 \end{array} \qquad 100)\overline{18,750.00}\ \ \overset{\$\ 187.50}{}$$

3. (5) Not enough information is given. You do not know what percent of gross salary goes for social security.

4. (1) $1485

$$\frac{p}{1375} = \frac{8}{100}$$

$$\begin{array}{r} 1375 \\ \times\ \ 8 \\ \hline 11,000 \end{array} \qquad 100)\overline{11,000}\ \ \overset{110}{} \qquad \begin{array}{r} \$1375 \\ +\ 110 \\ \hline \$1485 \end{array}$$

5. (3) $270

$$\frac{p}{250} = \frac{8}{100}$$

$$\begin{array}{r} 250 \\ \times\ 8 \\ \hline 2000 \end{array} \qquad 100)\overline{2000}\ \ \overset{20}{} \qquad \begin{array}{r} \$250 \\ +\ 20 \\ \hline \$270 \end{array}$$

6. (1) $275

$$\frac{p}{250} = \frac{10}{100}$$

$$\begin{array}{r} 250 \\ \times\ 10 \\ \hline 2500 \end{array} \qquad 100)\overline{2500}\ \ \overset{25}{} \qquad \begin{array}{r} \$250 \\ +\ 25 \\ \hline \$275 \end{array}$$

7. (2) $297

$$\frac{p}{270} = \frac{10}{100}$$

$$\begin{array}{r} 270 \\ \times\ 10 \\ \hline 2700 \end{array} \qquad 100)\overline{2700}\ \ \overset{27}{} \qquad \begin{array}{r} \$270 \\ +\ 27 \\ \hline \$297 \end{array}$$

GED PRACTICE:
PERCENTS REVIEW

pages 161–163

1. $\frac{18}{24} = \frac{3}{4}$ **or 3:4**

2. $\frac{20}{36} = \frac{5}{9}$ **or 5:9**

3. $4\frac{1}{2}$ $\frac{s}{15} = \frac{6}{20}$

$$\begin{array}{c} 15 \\ \times\ 6 \\ \hline 90 \end{array} \qquad 20)\overline{90}\quad \begin{array}{c} 4\frac{10}{20} = 4\frac{1}{2} \end{array}$$

4. 35 $\frac{5}{12} = \frac{x}{84}$

$$\begin{array}{c} 84 \\ \times\ 5 \\ \hline 420 \end{array} \qquad 12)\overline{420}\quad 35$$

5. $.95 = .95. = \mathbf{95\%}$

6. $3.2\% = .03.2 = \mathbf{.032}$

7. $\frac{5}{8} \times \frac{100\%}{1} = \frac{125}{2} = \mathbf{62.5\%}$

8. $\frac{37\frac{1}{2}}{100} = 37\frac{1}{2} \div 100 = \frac{75}{2} \times \frac{1}{100} = \frac{\mathbf{3}}{\mathbf{8}}$

9. 9.72 $\frac{p}{360} = \frac{2.7}{100}$

$$\begin{array}{c} 360 \\ \times\ 2.7 \\ \hline 972.0 \end{array} \qquad 100)\overline{972.00}\quad 9.72$$

10. 60 $\frac{21}{35} = \frac{x}{100}$

$$\begin{array}{c} 21 \\ \times\ 100 \\ \hline 2100 \end{array} \qquad 35)\overline{2100}\quad 60$$

11. 375 $\frac{75}{w} = \frac{20}{100}$

$$\begin{array}{c} 75 \\ \times\ 100 \\ \hline 7500 \end{array} \qquad 20)\overline{7500}\quad 375$$

12. 32 $\frac{48}{w} = \frac{150}{100}$

$$\begin{array}{c} 48 \\ \times\ 100 \\ \hline 4800 \end{array} \qquad 150)\overline{4800}\quad 32$$

13. $27   9 months $= \frac{9}{12} = \frac{3}{4}$ year

$$\frac{450}{1} \times \frac{8}{100} \times \frac{3}{4} = \frac{54}{2} = 27$$

14. (4) $\frac{1}{3}$ $2 + 5 + 4 + 1 = 12$ socks $\frac{4}{12} = \frac{1}{3}$

15. (3) 3:5
won   12 $\frac{12}{20} = \frac{3}{5}$ or 3:5
lost $\underline{+\ 8}$
played   20

16. (3) $64 $\frac{hours}{\$}$ $\frac{6}{38.40} = \frac{10}{x}$

$$\begin{array}{c} 38.40 \\ \times\ 10 \\ \hline 384.00 \end{array} \qquad 6)\overline{384}\quad \$64$$

17. (5) $\frac{\mathbf{(2 \times 215)}}{\mathbf{5}}$ $\frac{total\ \$}{food\ \$}$ $\frac{5}{2} = \frac{215}{x}$

18. (2) 14,250
voted   3
stayed home $\underline{+\ 5}$
total   8

$\frac{voted}{total}$ $\frac{3}{8} = \frac{x}{38,000}$

$$\begin{array}{c} 38,000 \\ \times\ 3 \\ \hline 114,000 \end{array} \qquad 8)\overline{114,000}\quad 14,250$$

19. (5) $2300

$\frac{115}{x} = \frac{5}{100}$

$$\begin{array}{c} 115 \\ \times\ 100 \\ \hline 11,500 \end{array} \qquad 5)\overline{11,500}\quad \$2,300$$

20. (4) $83\frac{1}{3}\%$ $\frac{1000}{1200} = \frac{5}{6} = \frac{x}{100}$

$$\begin{array}{c} 5 \\ \times\ 100 \\ \hline 500 \end{array}$$

$$6)\overline{500}\quad 83\frac{1}{3}\%$$

21. (1) $12\frac{1}{2}\%$

First find the decrease.

$$\begin{array}{c} \$1.20 \\ -\ 1.05 \\ \hline \$\ .15 \end{array}$$

Then find the percent of decrease.

$\frac{.15}{1.20} = \frac{x}{100}$

$$\begin{array}{c} .15 \\ \times\ 100 \\ \hline 15.00 \end{array} \qquad 1.2)\overline{15.0.}\quad 12\frac{1}{2}\%$$

22. (4) **$296.80**

First find the discount.

$\frac{p}{350} = \frac{20}{100}$

$$\begin{array}{c} 350 \\ \times\ 20 \\ \hline 7000 \end{array} \qquad 100)\overline{7000}\quad \$70$$

The selling price is $350 − 70 = $280.
Now find the tax.

$\frac{p}{280} = \frac{6}{100}$

$$\begin{array}{c} 280 \\ \times\ 6 \\ \hline 1680 \end{array} \qquad 100)\overline{1680.00}\quad \$16.80$$

The final price is

$$\begin{array}{c} \$280.00 \\ +\ 16.80 \\ \hline \$296.80 \end{array}$$

23. (2) **$786.70**

$\frac{p}{695} = \frac{6}{100}$

$$\begin{array}{c} 695 \\ \times\ 6 \\ \hline 4150 \end{array} \qquad 100)\overline{4150.00}\quad \$41.50$$

price $695.00
tax   41.50
shipping $\underline{+\ \ 50.00}$
$786.50

24. (5) **Not enough information is given.** You do not know the cost of tolls.

25. (2) $75

$$\frac{p}{749} = \frac{10}{100} = \frac{1}{10}$$

$$\begin{array}{r} 749 \\ \times\ 1 \\ \hline 749 \end{array}$$

$$\underset{10\overline{)749.00}}{\$\ 74.90} \text{ to the nearest dollar} = \$75$$

CHAPTER 7

MEASUREMENT EXERCISE 1
page 168

1. $2\frac{1}{2}$ **lb**

$$\frac{1\,lb}{16\,oz} = \frac{x}{40\,oz} \qquad \begin{array}{r}40\\ \times\ 1\\ \hline 40\end{array} \qquad 16\overline{)40} \quad 2\frac{8}{16} = 2\frac{1}{2}\,lb \\ \underline{32}\\ 8$$

2. 6,000 lb

$$\frac{1\,T}{2000\,lb} = \frac{3\,T}{x} \qquad \begin{array}{r}2000\\ \times\ 3\\ \hline 6000\end{array} \qquad 1\overline{)6000} \quad 6000\,lb$$

3. 2 yd

$$\frac{1\,yd}{3\,ft} = \frac{x}{6\,ft} \qquad \begin{array}{r}6\\ \times\ 1\\ \hline 6\end{array} \qquad 3\overline{)6} \quad 2\,yd$$

4. $3\frac{2}{7}$ **wk**

$$\frac{1\,wk}{7\,days} = \frac{x}{23\,days} \qquad \begin{array}{r}23\\ \times\ 1\\ \hline 23\end{array} \qquad 7\overline{)23} \quad 3\frac{2}{7}$$

5. $\frac{7}{8}$ **lb**

$$\frac{1\,lb}{16\,oz} = \frac{x}{14\,oz} \qquad \begin{array}{r}14\\ \times\ 1\\ \hline 14\end{array} \qquad \frac{14}{16} = \frac{7}{8}\,lb$$

Since 14 is less than 16, you can put the 14 over 16 and reduce.

6. 24 qt

$$\frac{1\,gal}{4\,qt} = \frac{6\,gal}{x} \qquad \begin{array}{r}6\\ \times\ 4\\ \hline 24\end{array} \qquad 1\overline{)24} \quad 24$$

7. $\frac{1}{2}$ **mi**

$$\frac{1\,mi}{5280\,ft} = \frac{x}{2640\,ft} \qquad \begin{array}{r}2640\\ \times\ 1\\ \hline 2640\end{array} \qquad \frac{2640}{5280} = \frac{1}{2}\,mi$$

8. $2\frac{7}{9}$ **yd**

$$\frac{1\,yd}{36\,in} = \frac{x}{100\,in} \qquad \begin{array}{r}100\\ \times\ 1\\ \hline 100\end{array} \qquad 36\overline{)100} \quad 2\frac{28}{36} = 2\frac{7}{9}\,yd \\ \underline{72}\\ 28$$

9. $2\frac{1}{2}$ **cups**

$$\frac{1\,cup}{8\,oz} = \frac{x}{20\,oz} \qquad \begin{array}{r}20\\ \times\ 1\\ \hline 20\end{array} \qquad 8\overline{)20} \quad 2\frac{4}{8} = 2\frac{1}{2}\,cups$$

10. 60 pt

$$\frac{1\,qt}{2\,pt} = \frac{30\,qt}{x} \qquad \begin{array}{r}30\\ \times\ 2\\ \hline 60\end{array} \qquad 1\overline{)60} \quad 60\,pt$$

11. 15,840 ft

$$\frac{1\,mi}{5280\,ft} = \frac{3\,mi}{x} \qquad \begin{array}{r}5280\\ \times\ 3\\ \hline 15,840\end{array} \qquad 1\overline{)15,840} \quad 15,840\,ft$$

12. 6 ft

$$\frac{1\,yd}{3\,ft} = \frac{2\,yd}{x} \qquad \begin{array}{r}3\\ \times\ 2\\ \hline 6\end{array} \qquad 1\overline{)6} \quad 6\,ft$$

13. 33 jars

$$\frac{1\,gal}{4\,qt} = \frac{x}{130\,qt} \qquad \begin{array}{r}130\\ \times\ 1\\ \hline 130\end{array} \qquad 4\overline{)130} \quad 32\frac{2}{4} = 32\frac{1}{2}\,jars$$

14. 72 hr

$$\frac{1\,day}{24\,hr} = \frac{3\,days}{x} \qquad \begin{array}{r}24\\ \times\ 3\\ \hline 72\end{array} \qquad 1\overline{)72} \quad 72\,hr$$

15. $\frac{3}{4}$ **hr**

$$\frac{1\,hr}{60\,min} = \frac{x}{45\,min} \qquad \begin{array}{r}45\\ \times\ 1\\ \hline 45\end{array} \qquad \frac{45}{60} = \frac{3}{4}\,hr$$

16. 2 mi

$$\frac{1\,mi}{5280\,ft} = \frac{x}{10,560\,ft} \qquad \begin{array}{r}10,560\\ \times\ 1\\ \hline 10,560\end{array} \qquad 5280\overline{)10,560} \quad 2\,mi$$

17. $3\frac{1}{3}$ **hr**

$$\frac{60\,min}{1\,hr} = \frac{200\,min}{x} \qquad \begin{array}{r}200\\ \times\ 1\\ \hline 200\end{array} \qquad 60\overline{)200} \quad 3\frac{20}{60} = 3\frac{1}{3}\,hr \\ \underline{180}\\ 20$$

18. 12 trips

$$\frac{1\,T}{2000\,lb} = \frac{3\,T}{6000\,lb} \qquad 500\overline{)6000} \quad 12$$

MEASUREMENT EXERCISE 2
page 170

1.
$$
\begin{array}{r}
1\ \text{ft}\ 7\ \text{in} \\
12\overline{)19} \\
\underline{12} \\
7
\end{array}
$$

2.
$$
\begin{array}{r}
1\ \text{min}\ 15\ \text{sec} \\
60\overline{)75} \\
\underline{60} \\
15
\end{array}
$$

3.
$$
\begin{array}{r}
2\ \text{lb}\ 4\ \text{oz} \\
16\overline{)36} \\
\underline{32} \\
4
\end{array}
$$

4.
$$
\begin{array}{r}
8\frac{1}{3}\ \text{yd} \\
3\overline{)25} \\
\underline{24} \\
1
\end{array}
$$

5.
$$
\begin{array}{r}
3\ \text{hr}\ 20\ \text{min} \\
60\overline{)200} \\
\underline{180} \\
20
\end{array}
$$

6.
$$
\begin{array}{r}
2\ \text{T}\ 500\ \text{lb} \\
2000\overline{)4500} \\
\underline{4000} \\
500
\end{array}
$$

7.
$$
\begin{array}{r}
3\frac{3}{4}\ \text{gal} \\
4\overline{)15} \\
\underline{12} \\
3
\end{array}
$$

8.
$$
\begin{array}{r}
2\ \text{yd}\ 3\ \text{in} \\
36\overline{)75} \\
\underline{72} \\
3
\end{array}
$$

9.
$$
\begin{array}{r}
3\ \text{mi} \\
5280\overline{)15,840} \\
\underline{15,840} \\
0
\end{array}
$$

10.
$$
\begin{array}{r}
6\frac{4}{16} = 6\frac{1}{4}\ \text{lb} \\
16\overline{)100} \\
\underline{96} \\
4
\end{array}
$$

11.
$$
\begin{array}{r}
4\ \text{qt}\ 1\text{pt} \\
2\overline{)9} \\
\underline{8} \\
1
\end{array}
$$

12.
$$
\begin{array}{r}
5\ \text{wk}\ 5\ \text{days} \\
7\overline{)40} \\
\underline{35} \\
5
\end{array}
$$

MEASUREMENT EXERCISE 3
page 171

1. **(4) 3**

$$10 \div 2\frac{2}{3} =$$
$$\frac{10}{1} \div \frac{8}{3} = \frac{10}{1} \times \frac{3}{8} = \frac{15}{4} = 3\frac{3}{4}$$

3 cabinets

2. **(3) 4**

$$8 \div 1\frac{3}{4} =$$
$$\frac{8}{1} \div \frac{7}{4} = \frac{8}{1} \times \frac{4}{7} = \frac{32}{7} = 4\frac{4}{7}$$

4 rakes

MEASUREMENT EXERCISE 4
page 174

1. J $\frac{7}{8}$ in

   K $1\frac{1}{4}$ in

   L $3\frac{1}{2}$ in

   M $4\frac{1}{8}$ in

   N $5\frac{5}{8}$ in

2. P 2.5 cm
   Q 4 cm
   R 6.3 cm
   S 9.2 cm
   T 13.9 cm

3. 36 amperes

4. 14 volts

5. 9 seconds

GED PRACTICE: MEASUREMENT REVIEW
page 175

1. **(2) $10.80**

$$2\ \text{lb}\ 4\ \text{oz} = 2\frac{4}{16} = 2\frac{1}{4}\ \text{lb}$$
$$2\frac{1}{4} \times \$4.80 =$$
$$\frac{9}{4} \times \frac{\$4.80}{1} = \$10.80$$

2. **(4)** $\dfrac{2.5 + 0.96 + 1.2}{3}$

3. **(5) Not enough information is given.**
   You do not know the cost of one can.

4. **(3) 2.85**

$$
\begin{array}{r}
4.00\ \text{m} \\
-1.15 \\
\hline
2.85\ \text{m}
\end{array}
$$

5. **(2) 4**

$$3\ \text{yd}\ 18\ \text{in} = 3\frac{18}{36}\ \text{yd} = 3\frac{1}{2}\ \text{yd}$$
$$15 \div 3\frac{1}{2} =$$
$$\frac{15}{1} \div \frac{7}{2} = \frac{15}{1} \times \frac{2}{7} = \frac{30}{7} = 4\frac{2}{7}$$

4 suits

6. (1) 42.9

$$\begin{array}{r} 36.5 \\ 42.2 \\ +50.1 \\ \hline 128.8 \end{array}$$

$$\begin{array}{r} 42.93 \\ 3\overline{)128.80} \end{array}$$ to the nearest tenth = 42.9

7. (4) $1\frac{3}{4}$

8. (3) $\frac{3}{4}$

$$\begin{array}{l} B = 2\frac{1}{2} = 2\frac{2}{4} = 1\frac{6}{4} \\ A = 1\frac{3}{4} \qquad - 1\frac{3}{4} \\ \hline \qquad\qquad\qquad \frac{3}{4} \text{ inch} \end{array}$$

CHAPTER 8

GRAPHS AND TABLES EXERCISE 1

page 179

1. 12%

2. 59%

3. (2) 30

$$\frac{15}{100} = \frac{p}{200} \qquad \begin{array}{r} 200 \\ \times\ 15 \\ \hline 3000 \end{array} \qquad \begin{array}{r} 30 \\ 100\overline{)3000} \end{array}$$

4. (4) 29%

$$\begin{array}{ll} \$40–\$99,999 & = 14\% \\ \$100,000 \text{ and over} & = 15\% \\ \hline \text{Total} & = 29\% \end{array}$$

5. (1) $\frac{3}{20}$

$$15\% = \frac{15}{100} = \frac{3}{20}$$

GRAPHS AND TABLES EXERCISE 2

page 180

1. 48%

2. $\frac{8}{48} = \frac{1}{6}$

3. $\frac{1}{3}$

You know that $33\frac{1}{3}\% = \frac{1}{3}$.

33% is close to $33\frac{1}{3}\%$.

4. 3 times

$$\begin{array}{r} 3 \\ 11\overline{)33} \end{array}$$

5. $72 billion

$$\frac{p}{900 \text{ billion}} = \frac{8}{100} \qquad \begin{array}{r} 900 \\ \times\ 8 \\ \hline 7200 \end{array} \qquad \begin{array}{r} \$\ 72 \text{ billion} \\ 100\overline{)7200} \end{array}$$

6. (1) Individual income tax and social security tax make up over 80% of the federal budget.

48% + 33% = 81%

GRAPHS AND TABLES EXERCISE 3

page 181

1. (1) $\frac{1}{4}$

Natural gas was 24%.

24% is close to 25% = $\frac{1}{4}$

2. (3) coal and nuclear

3. (3) $10\frac{1}{2}$

$$\begin{array}{r} 10\frac{1}{2} \text{ times} \\ 2\%\overline{)\ 21\%} \end{array}$$

4. (5) $\frac{3}{10}$

21% + 9% = 30%

$$30\% = \frac{30}{100} = \frac{3}{10}$$

GRAPHS AND TABLES EXERCISE 4

page 183

1. the West

The bar ends about halfway between 200 and 250.

2. the Northeast

3. the Midwest and the South

4. (4) 675

$$\begin{array}{r} 3 \\ 100,000\overline{)300,000} \end{array} \qquad \begin{array}{r} 225 \\ \times\ 3 \\ \hline 675 \end{array}$$

5. (5) 540,000

$$\begin{array}{r} 2,500 \\ 100,000\overline{)250,000,000} \end{array}$$ The total country has about 220 physicians per 100,000 people.

2,500 × 220 = 550,000

540,000 is closest.

6. (2) 95

$$\frac{50,000}{100,000} = \frac{1}{2}$$

$$\frac{1}{2} \times 190 = 95$$

The Midwest has about 190 physicians per 100,000 people.

GRAPHS AND TABLES EXERCISE 5

pages 184–185

1. **a.** approximately $255,000
   b. approximately $175,000
   c. approximately $100,000

2. Gas service stations and hardware stores

3. **(4) $10,000**

4. **(2) $\frac{1}{2}$**

   Hardware stores did about $50,000 in business.
   Gas service stations did about $100,000 in business.

5. **(5) $225,000**

car dealers	$175,000
clothing stores	+ 50,000
Total	$225,000

6. **(2) $500,000**

1992 was a little below	$250,000
1993 was a little above	+ 250,000
Total	$500,000

GRAPHS AND TABLES EXERCISE 6

page 187

1. **(4) Percent**

2. **(5) 1989**

3. **(4) 3%**

4. **(2) 1982**

5. **(1) While the unemployment rates for both countries fluctuated, the change was greater in the United States.**

6. **(2) less than in 1990**
   The rate has been dropping for three years.

GRAPHS AND TABLES EXERCISE 7

pages 189–190

1. **77,000**

1989	917,000
1991	−840,000
	77,000

2. **(5) Not enough information is given.**
   1990 memberships are not on the table.

3. **(5)** $\frac{153,000 + 143,000}{2}$

4. **(3) less than the 1991 membership**
   The membership dropped for each year shown on the table.

5. **1980**

6. **(2) $\frac{1}{5}$**

   $20\% = \frac{20}{100} = \frac{1}{5}$

7. **(3) $\frac{1}{2}$**

   $\frac{\text{conservative}}{\text{liberal}} = \frac{17\%}{34\%} = \frac{1}{2}$

8. **(4) more than 20%**

   From 1970 to 1990 the percent who said they were conservative continued to rise.

GED PRACTICE: GRAPHS AND TABLES REVIEW

pages 191–193

1. **$3000**

2. **1989**

3. **rent**

credit card	10%
savings	4
other	16
	30% = rent

4. **(3) $112**

   $\frac{4}{100} = \frac{p}{2800}$

2,800
× 4
11,200

   $100)\overline{11,200}$ $112

5. **(4) $660**

   $\frac{30}{100} = \frac{p}{2200}$

2,200
× 30
66,000

   $100)\overline{66,000}$ $660

6. **(4) about $260**
   credit card expenses for 1993:

   $\frac{10}{100} = \frac{p}{2600}$

2,600
× 10
26,000

   $100)\overline{26,000}$ $260

   The expenditures dropped from 1991 to 1992. If the pattern continues, the expenses for credit card bills should be less than $260 in 1993.

7. **250 million**

8. **2.9%**

9. **(3) 30 million**
   12.1% is about 12%

   $\frac{12}{100} = \frac{p}{250}$

250
× 12
500
250
3000

   $100)\overline{3000}$ $30 million

10. **(2) 25 million**
    From 1970 to 1980 the increase was about 25 million.
    From 1980 to 1990 the increase was also about 25 million.

11. **(4) Asian, Pacific Islander**
    1.8, which is close to 2 times

    $1.6)\overline{2.90}$

12. (1) The population rose steadily, and the racial mix of the country changed.

13. (2) 63%

$19,800 African-American median income
$31,400 non-Hispanic white median income

.63 or 63%

$$31,400 \overline{)19,80000}$$
$$\quad \underline{18\,8400}$$
$$\quad 96000$$
$$\quad \underline{94200}$$
$$\quad 1,800 \text{ R}$$

14. (5) Native Americans

$20,000 1989 median income
−$20,900 1979 median income
−$900

15. (1) 8%

$36,800 1989 median income
−$34,100 1979 median income
$ 2,700

$2,700 income increase = 7.9 or 8%
$34,100 1979 median income

CHAPTER 9

BASICS OF ALGEBRA EXERCISE 1

pages 196–197

1. $x + 9$ or $9 + x$
2. $7x$
3. $5x$
4. $x + 8$ or $8 + x$
5. $x - 10$
6. $x - 1$

7. $\frac{3}{x}$
8. $x - 20$
9. $\frac{x}{15}$
10. $x + \frac{1}{2}$ or $\frac{1}{2} + x$
11. $\frac{x}{2}$
12. $x + 4$ or $4 + x$

BASICS OF ALGEBRA EXERCISE 2

pages 197–198

1. $w + 2$
2. $s - 5$
3. $3c$
4. $\frac{1}{5}i$
5. $\frac{x}{4}$

6. $\frac{5}{6}t$
7. (4) $l - 2$
8. (5) $.06m$
9. (1) $y + 10$
10. (2) $p - 15$

BASICS OF ALGEBRA EXERCISE 3

page 200

1.
$$\begin{array}{rcr} f + 20 &=& 57 \\ -\,20 && -\,20 \\ \hline f &=& 37 \end{array}$$

2.
$$\begin{array}{rcl} b - 19 &=& 28 \\ +19 & +19 & \\ \hline b &=& 47 \end{array}$$

3.
$$\begin{array}{rcl} 33 &=& k - 8 \\ +8 && +8 \\ \hline 41 &=& k \end{array}$$

4.
$$\begin{array}{rcl} 42 &=& t + 7 \\ -7 && -7 \\ \hline 35 &=& t \end{array}$$

5.
$$\begin{array}{rcl} n + 36 &=& 60 \\ -36 & -36 & \\ \hline n &=& 24 \end{array}$$

6.
$$\begin{array}{rcl} 18 &=& d - 6 \\ +6 && +6 \\ \hline 24 &=& d \end{array}$$

7.
$$\begin{array}{rcl} c - 4 &=& 27 \\ +4 & +4 & \\ \hline c &=& 31 \end{array}$$

8.
$$\begin{array}{rcl} 41 &=& e + 18 \\ -18 && -18 \\ \hline 23 &=& e \end{array}$$

9.
$$\begin{array}{rcl} 20 &=& a + 19 \\ -19 && -19 \\ \hline 1 &=& a \end{array}$$

10.
$$\begin{array}{rcl} g - 1 &=& 80 \\ +1 & +1 & \\ \hline g &=& 81 \end{array}$$

11.
$$\begin{array}{rcl} m + 16 &=& 200 \\ -16 && -16 \\ \hline m &=& 184 \end{array}$$

12.
$$\begin{array}{rcl} 43 &=& r - 7 \\ +7 && +7 \\ \hline 50 &=& r \end{array}$$

BASICS OF ALGEBRA EXERCISE 4

page 201

1.
$$8y = 96$$
$$\frac{8y}{8} = \frac{96}{8}$$
$$y = 12$$

2.
$$11 = 2d$$
$$\frac{11}{2} = \frac{2d}{2}$$
$$5\tfrac{1}{2} = d$$

3.
$$15p = 75$$
$$\frac{15p}{15} = \frac{75}{15}$$
$$p = 5$$

4.
$$25z = 100$$
$$\frac{25z}{25} = \frac{100}{25}$$
$$z = 4$$

5.
$$\frac{x}{3} = 9$$
$$3 \cdot \frac{x}{3} = 9 \cdot 3$$
$$x = 27$$

6.
$$9 = \frac{m}{4}$$
$$4 \cdot 9 = \frac{m}{4} \cdot 4$$
$$36 = m$$

7.
$$\frac{a}{5} = 8$$
$$5 \cdot \frac{a}{5} = 8 \cdot 5$$
$$a = 40$$

8.
$$\frac{c}{9} = 2$$
$$9 \cdot \frac{c}{9} = 2 \cdot 9$$
$$c = 18$$

BASICS OF ALGEBRA EXERCISE 5

page 203

1. e
2. f
3. i
4. g
5. b
6. h

7.
$$\begin{array}{rcl} x - 9 &=& 15 \\ +9 && +9 \\ \hline x &=& 24 \end{array}$$

8.
$$6x = 27$$
$$\frac{6x}{6} = \frac{27}{6}$$
$$x = 4\tfrac{3}{6} = 4\tfrac{1}{2}$$

9.
$$\frac{x}{5} = 50$$
$$5 \cdot \frac{x}{5} = 50 \cdot 5$$
$$x = 250$$

10.
$$\begin{array}{rcl} 3 &=& x - 5 \\ +5 && +5 \\ \hline 8 &=& x \end{array}$$

11. $$60 = \tfrac{3}{4}x$$
$$\tfrac{4}{3} \cdot 60 = \tfrac{3}{4}x \cdot \tfrac{4}{3}$$
$$\mathbf{80 = x}$$

12. $7x = 84$
$$\tfrac{7x}{7} = \tfrac{84}{7}$$
$$\mathbf{x = 12}$$

13. **$330**
$$x - 40 = 290$$
$$\underline{+\,40 \qquad +\,40}$$
$$x \qquad = 330$$

14. **$2925**
$$\tfrac{x}{15} = 195$$
$$15 \cdot \tfrac{x}{15} = 195 \cdot 15$$
$$x = 2925$$

15. **$2080**
$$\tfrac{1}{4}x = 520$$
$$4 \cdot \tfrac{1}{4}x = 520 \times 4$$
$$x = \mathbf{\$2080}$$

16. **120 members**
$$.75x = 90$$
$$\tfrac{.75x}{.75} = \tfrac{90}{.75}$$
$$x = 120$$

BASICS OF ALGEBRA EXERCISE 6

page 205

1. e
2. g
3. d
4. f
5. h
6. a
7. c
8. b

9. $2x + 6$

10. $8x - 5$

11. $2x + 4x$ or $4x + 2x$

12. $\tfrac{1}{2}x + 8$ or $8 + \tfrac{1}{2}x$

13. $\tfrac{1}{3}x - 1$

14. $15 - 3x$

15. $\dfrac{x + 7}{4}$ or $(x + 7)/4$

16. $10(x + 12)$ or $10(12 + x)$

17. $9(x - 4)$

BASICS OF ALGEBRA EXERCISE 7

page 207

1. $7m - 2 = 54$
$$\underline{+\,2 \qquad +\,2}$$
$$7m \qquad = 56$$
$$\tfrac{7m}{7} \qquad = \tfrac{56}{7}$$
$$\mathbf{m} \qquad = \mathbf{8}$$

2. $\tfrac{a}{3} + 5 = 9$
$$\underline{\tfrac{a}{3} \quad \dfrac{-\,5}{} \qquad \dfrac{-\,5}{4}}$$
$$3 \cdot \tfrac{a}{3} = 4 \cdot 3$$
$$\mathbf{a} = \mathbf{12}$$

3. $7 = \tfrac{c}{2} + 3$
$$\underline{\dfrac{-\,3}{4} = \dfrac{\ }{\tfrac{c}{2}} \quad \dfrac{-\,3}{}}$$
$$2 \cdot 4 = \tfrac{c}{2} \cdot 2$$
$$\mathbf{8 = c}$$

4. $82 = 9d + 10$
$$\underline{\dfrac{-\,10}{72} = \dfrac{-\,10}{9d}}$$
$$\tfrac{72}{9} = \tfrac{9d}{9}$$
$$\mathbf{8 = d}$$

5. $25c - 17 = 183$
$$\underline{\dfrac{+\,17}{\tfrac{25c}{25}} = \dfrac{+\,17}{\tfrac{200}{25}}}$$
$$\mathbf{c = 8}$$

6. $\tfrac{w}{2} - 7 = 3$
$$\underline{\dfrac{+\,7}{\tfrac{w}{2}} = \dfrac{+\,7}{10}}$$
$$2 \cdot \tfrac{w}{2} = 10 \cdot 2$$
$$\mathbf{w = 20}$$

7. $2 = 6x - 10$
$$\underline{\dfrac{+\,10}{12} = \dfrac{+\,10}{6x}}$$
$$\tfrac{12}{6} = \tfrac{6x}{6}$$
$$\mathbf{2 = x}$$

8. $\tfrac{1}{3}p + 8 = 11$
$$\underline{\dfrac{-\,8}{\tfrac{1}{3}p} = \dfrac{-\,8}{3}}$$
$$3 \cdot \tfrac{1}{3}p = 3 \cdot 3$$
$$\mathbf{p = 9}$$

9. $40 = 13z + 14$
$$\underline{\dfrac{-\,14}{26} = \dfrac{-\,14}{13z}}$$
$$\tfrac{26}{13} = \tfrac{13z}{13}$$
$$\mathbf{2 = z}$$

10. $\tfrac{n}{2} + 3 = 7$
$$\underline{\dfrac{-\,3}{\tfrac{n}{2}} = \dfrac{-\,3}{4}}$$
$$2 \cdot \tfrac{n}{2} = 4 \cdot 2$$
$$\mathbf{n = 8}$$

11. $\frac{3}{4}y - 3 = 12$

$$\underline{\quad + 3 \quad\quad +3\quad}$$

$$\frac{3}{4}y \quad = \quad 15$$

$$\frac{4}{3} \cdot \frac{3}{4}y = 15 \cdot \frac{4}{3}$$

$$\boldsymbol{y = 20}$$

12. $39 = 16k - 9$

$$\underline{+9 \quad\quad\quad +9\quad}$$

$$48 = 16k$$

$$\frac{48}{16} = \frac{16k}{16}$$

$$\boldsymbol{3 = k}$$

13. $10 = 6a + 7$

$$\underline{-7 \quad\quad\quad -7\quad}$$

$$3 = 6a$$

$$\frac{3}{6} = \frac{6a}{6}$$

$$\boldsymbol{\frac{1}{2} = a}$$

14. $9r + 15 = 18$

$$\underline{-15 \quad\quad -15\quad}$$

$$9r \quad = \quad 3$$

$$\frac{9r}{9} \quad = \quad \frac{3}{9}$$

$$\boldsymbol{r = \frac{1}{3}}$$

BASICS OF ALGEBRA EXERCISE 8

page 208

1. $3(x + 4) = 27$

$$3x + 12 = 27$$

$$3x = 27 - 12$$

$$3x = 15$$

$$\boldsymbol{x = 5}$$

2. $10 = 5(a - 3)$

$$10 = 5a - 15$$

$$25 = 5a$$

$$\boldsymbol{5 = a}$$

3. $36 = 4(c + 4)$

$$36 = 4c + 16$$

$$20 = 4c$$

$$\boldsymbol{5 = c}$$

4. $28 = 7m - 32$

$$60 = 7m$$

$$\frac{60}{7} = m$$

$$\boldsymbol{8\frac{4}{7} = m}$$

5. $3(y - 2) = 3$

$$3y - 6 = 3$$

$$3y = 9$$

$$\boldsymbol{y = 3}$$

6. $80 = 8(s + 7)$

$$80 = 8s + 56$$

$$24 = 8s$$

$$\boldsymbol{3 = s}$$

7. $3(t + 10) = 90$

$$3t + 30 = 90$$

$$3t = 60$$

$$\boldsymbol{t = 20}$$

8. $7(m - 2) = 28$

$$7m - 14 = 28$$

$$7m = 42$$

$$\boldsymbol{m = 6}$$

BASICS OF ALGEBRA EXERCISE 9

pages 208–209

1. (3) 8

$$6(8) - 3 = 45$$

$$48 - 3 = 45$$

2. (2) 13

$$2(13) + 1 = 27$$

$$26 + 1 = 27$$

3. (4) 20

$$\frac{20}{5} + 6 = 10$$

$$4 + 6 = 10$$

4. (2) 9

$$25 = 3(9) - 2$$

$$25 = 27 - 2$$

5. (1) 7

$$18 = 7 + 11$$

6. (1) 12

$$50 = 4(12) + 2$$

$$50 = 48 + 2$$

7. (3) 8

$$2(8 - 3) = 10$$

$$2(5) = 10$$

8. (4) 9

$$6(9 + 1) = 60$$

$$6(10) = 60$$

9. (4) 5

$$72 = 8(5 + 4)$$

$$72 = 8(9)$$

10. (2) 12

$$30 = 3(12 - 2)$$

$$30 = 3(10)$$

BASICS OF ALGEBRA EXERCISE 10

page 209

1. e
2. f
3. c
4. b
5. a
6. d
7. $3x - 1 = 5$

$$\underline{+1 = +1}$$

$$3x \quad = \quad 6$$

$$\boldsymbol{x} \quad = \quad \boldsymbol{2}$$

8. $4x - 2 = 18$

$$\underline{+2 = +2}$$

$$4x \quad = \quad 20$$

$$\boldsymbol{x} \quad = \quad \boldsymbol{5}$$

9.
$$
\begin{aligned}
2x + 1 &= 13 \\
-1 &= -1 \\
\hline
2x &= 12 \\
x &= 6
\end{aligned}
$$

10.
$$
\begin{aligned}
6x + 10 &= 34 \\
-10 &= -10 \\
\hline
6x &= 24 \\
x &= 4
\end{aligned}
$$

11.
$$
\begin{aligned}
\tfrac{1}{2}x - 8 &= 12 \\
+8 &= +8 \\
\hline
\tfrac{1}{2}x &= 20 \\
x &= 40
\end{aligned}
$$

12.
$$
\begin{aligned}
\tfrac{x}{8} - 3 &= 6 \\
+3 &= +3 \\
\hline
\tfrac{x}{8} &= 9 \\
x &= 72
\end{aligned}
$$

BASICS OF ALGEBRA EXERCISE 11

page 212

1.
$$
\begin{aligned}
5y - y &= 19 + 9 \\
4y &= 28 \\
\tfrac{4y}{4} &= \tfrac{28}{4} \\
y &= 7
\end{aligned}
$$

2.
$$
\begin{aligned}
6t + 8 + 4t &= 58 \\
8 + 10t &= 58 \\
-8 &\quad -8 \\
\hline
10t &= 50 \\
\tfrac{10t}{10} &= \tfrac{50}{10} \\
t &= 5
\end{aligned}
$$

3.
$$
\begin{aligned}
9c &= 44 - 2c \\
+2c &= \quad +2c \\
\hline
11c &= 44 \\
\tfrac{11c}{11} &= \tfrac{44}{11} \\
c &= 4
\end{aligned}
$$

4.
$$
\begin{aligned}
8m &= 2m + 30 \\
-2m &\quad -2m \\
\hline
6m &= 30 \\
\tfrac{6m}{6} &= \tfrac{30}{6} \\
m &= 5
\end{aligned}
$$

5.
$$
\begin{aligned}
4a + 55 &= 9a \\
-4a &\quad -4a \\
\hline
55 &= 5a \\
\tfrac{55}{5} &= \tfrac{5a}{5} \\
11 &= a
\end{aligned}
$$

6.
$$
\begin{aligned}
4p &= p + 18 \\
-p &\quad -p \\
\hline
3p &= 18 \\
\tfrac{3p}{3} &= \tfrac{18}{3} \\
p &= 6
\end{aligned}
$$

7.
$$
\begin{aligned}
6f &= 14 - f \\
+f &\quad +f \\
\hline
7f &= 14 \\
\tfrac{7f}{7} &= \tfrac{14}{7} \\
f &= 2
\end{aligned}
$$

8.
$$
\begin{aligned}
3 &= y + 8y \\
3 &= 9y \\
\tfrac{3}{9} &= \tfrac{9y}{9} \\
\tfrac{1}{3} &= y
\end{aligned}
$$

9.
$$
\begin{aligned}
8r + 17 &= 5r + 32 \\
-5r &\quad -5r \\
\hline
3r + 17 &= 32 \\
-17 &\quad -17 \\
\hline
\tfrac{3r}{3} &= \tfrac{15}{3} \\
r &= 5
\end{aligned}
$$

10.
$$
\begin{aligned}
7n - 9 &= 3n + 7 \\
-3n &\quad -3n \\
\hline
4n - 9 &= 7 \\
+9 &\quad +9 \\
\hline
\tfrac{4n}{4} &= \tfrac{16}{4} \\
n &= 4
\end{aligned}
$$

11.
$$
\begin{aligned}
6z + 11 &= 5z + 20 \\
-5z &\quad -5z \\
\hline
z + 11 &= 20 \\
-11 &\quad -11 \\
\hline
z &= 9
\end{aligned}
$$

12.
$$
\begin{aligned}
5y - 4 &= 2y + 77 \\
-2y &\quad -2y \\
\hline
3y - 4 &= 77 \\
+4 &\quad +4 \\
\hline
3y &= 81 \\
y &= 27
\end{aligned}
$$

BASICS OF ALGEBRA EXERCISE 12

pages 214–215

1. 13 and 14

First number $= x$

Next number $= x + 1$

(Consecutive means one following another.)

$$
\begin{aligned}
x + x + 1 &= 27 \\
2x + 1 &= 27 \\
-1 &\quad -1 \\
\hline
2x &= 26 \\
\tfrac{2x}{2} &= \tfrac{26}{2} \\
x &= 13 \\
x + 1 &= 14
\end{aligned}
$$

2. **18, 20, and 22**

First number $= x$

Second number $= x + 2$

Third number $= x + 2 + 2 = x + 4$

$$
\begin{aligned}
x + x + 2 + x + 4 &= 60 \\
3x + 6 &= 60 \\
-6 \quad &-6 \\
\hline
3x &= 54 \\
\frac{3x}{3} &= \frac{54}{3} \\
x &= 18 \\
x + 2 &= 20 \\
x + 4 &= 22
\end{aligned}
$$

3. **24 union workers**

Nonunion workers $= x$

Union workers $= 6x$

$$
\begin{aligned}
6x - 8 &= 4x \\
+8 \quad &\quad +8 \\
\hline
6x &= 4x + 8 \\
6x - 4x &= 8 \\
2x &= 8 \\
x &= 4 \\
6x &= 24
\end{aligned}
$$

4. **6 men and 18 women**

Number of men $= x$

Number of women $= 3x$

$$
\begin{aligned}
3x - 2 &= x + 10 \\
-x \quad &\quad -x \\
\hline
2x - 2 &= 10 \\
+2 \quad &\quad +2 \\
\hline
2x &= 12 \\
\frac{2x}{2} &= \frac{12}{2} \\
x &= 6 \\
3x &= 18
\end{aligned}
$$

5. **$270**

Juan's wage $= x$

Felipe's wage $= 3x$

$$
\begin{aligned}
x + 3x &= 360 \\
4x &= 360 \\
\frac{4x}{4} &= \frac{360}{4} \\
x &= 90 \\
3x &= 270
\end{aligned}
$$

6. **(2) $\frac{294}{3}$**

Mrs. Migliaccio's salary $= x$

Mr. Migliaccio's salary $= 2x$

$$
\begin{aligned}
3x &= 294 \\
x &= \frac{294}{3}
\end{aligned}
$$

7. **24 hours**

Jerry's hours $= x$

Jeff's hours $= 2x$

Paul's hours $= 2x + 6$

$$
\begin{aligned}
x + 2x + 2x + 6 &= 51 \\
5x + 6 &= 51 \\
-6 \quad &-6 \\
\hline
5x &= 45 \\
\frac{5x}{5} &= \frac{45}{5} \\
x &= 9 \\
2x + 6 &= 24
\end{aligned}
$$

8. **16,500 people**

Voters who voted $= x$

People who did not vote $= 3x$

$$
\begin{aligned}
x + 3x &= 22{,}000 \\
4x &= 22{,}000 \\
\frac{4x}{4} &= \frac{22{,}000}{4} \\
x &= 5{,}500 \\
3x &= 16{,}500
\end{aligned}
$$

9. **(4) $(4 \times 18) + 2$**

$x =$ Laila's age

$4x =$ David's age

$4x + 2 =$ Nancy's age

$(4 \times 18) + 2$

10. **(1) $(\frac{1}{2} \times 40) + 5$**

$x =$ height of house

$\frac{1}{2}x =$ height of ladder

BASICS OF ALGEBRA EXERCISE 13

page 218

1. **419 mph** $d = r \cdot t$

$$
\begin{aligned}
1{,}676 &= r \cdot 4 \\
\frac{1{,}676}{4} &= \frac{r \cdot 4}{4} \\
419 &= r
\end{aligned}
$$

2. **89 hammers** $c = n \cdot r$

$$
\begin{aligned}
\$111.25 &= n \cdot \$1.25 \\
\frac{111.25}{1.25} &= \frac{n \cdot 1.25}{1.25} \\
89 &= n
\end{aligned}
$$

3. **68 degrees** $F = (\frac{9}{5})C + 32$

$$
\begin{aligned}
F &= (\tfrac{9}{5})20 + 32 \\
F &= 36 + 32 \\
F &= 68
\end{aligned}
$$

4. **$1300** $\qquad i = prt$

$$
\begin{aligned}
\$32.50 &= p \cdot 5\% \, \tfrac{1}{2} \\
\$32.50 &= p \cdot \tfrac{5}{100} \cdot \tfrac{1}{2} \\
\$32.50 &= p \cdot \tfrac{5}{200} \\
\$32.50 &= p \cdot \tfrac{1}{40} \\
\$32.50 \cdot 40 &= p \\
\$1300 &= p
\end{aligned}
$$

GED PRACTICE:
BASICS OF ALGEBRA REVIEW

pages 219–221

1. $x + 11$

Remember, you can use x or any other letter to stand for the unknown.

2. $3a + \frac{1}{3}a$

3. $4c$

4. $\frac{4}{5}s$

5. $9x = 108$
$x = 12$

6. $\frac{c}{4} = 8$
$c = 32$

7.
$$\begin{array}{r} 14 + x = 3x - 8 \\ +8 \qquad +8 \\ \hline 22 + x = 3x \\ -x \quad -x \\ \hline 22 = 2x \\ 11 = x \end{array}$$

8. $\frac{21}{p} + 1 = 8$
$\frac{21}{p} = 7$
$p = 3$

9. $\frac{1}{8}y = 24$
$y = 192$

10. $12.5 = a + 1.5$
$11 = a$

11. $96 + 2x = x + 101$
$2x = x + 5$
$x = 5$

12. $20 - 4z = 5z - 35$
$55 = 9z$
$\frac{55}{9} = z$
$6\frac{1}{9} = z$

13. (4) $x - 18 = 1$

14. (5) $\frac{4}{5}x = 40$

15. (5) $9x - 5 = 6x + 7$

16. (2) **4.25**
$$\begin{array}{r} 7.50 \\ -3.25 \\ \hline 4.25 \end{array}$$

17. (4) **$840** $\quad .10 \times t = 84$
$t = \frac{84}{.10}$
$t = \$840$

18. (3) **70**
Let x = number of men
$x + 25$ = number of women
$x + x + 25 = 115$
$2x + 25 = 115$
$2x = 90$
$x = 45$
$x + 25 = 70$

19. (2) **$4.50**
Let x = Joe's wage
$x - 2$ = Sam's wage
$40(x + x - 2) = \$440$
$40(2x - 2) = 440$
$80x - 80 = 440$
$80x = 520$
$x = \$6.50$
$x - 2 = \$4.50$

20. (4) **26**
Let x = Ed's miles
$x + 6$ = Nina's miles
$x + x + 6 = 46$
$2x + 6 = 46$
$2x = 40$
$x = 20$
$x + 6 = 26$

21. (4) **$46**
$46 \times \$1.00 = \$46$

22. (2) **Ed's rate of walking**

23. (3) **$3(46 \times \$.50)$**

24. (4) **$1020**
Let x = Mel's wages
$x + \$280$ = Kathleen's wages
$x + x + 280 = 1760$
$2x + 280 = 1760$
$2x = 1480$
$x = 740$
$x + 280 = \$1020$

25. (1) **12**
$10n - 7 = 101 + n$
$9n = 108$
$n = 12$

CHAPTER 10

GEOMETRY EXERCISE 1

pages 225–226

1. parallel
2. square
3. perpendicular
4. angle
5. vertical
6. horizontal
7. diameter
8. radius
9. sphere
10. right angle
11. triangle
12. rectangular solid
13. rectangle
14. cube
15. cylinder

GEOMETRY EXERCISE 2

pages 228–229

1. **178 ft**
$P = 2l + 2w$
$P = (2 \times 52) + (2 \times 37)$
$P = 104 + 74 = 178$ ft

2. 57 cm

$P = a + b + c$

$P = 19 + 19 + 19 = 57$ cm

3. 32 yd

$P = 4s$

$P = 4 \times 8 = 32$ yd

4. $8\frac{1}{2}$ in

$P = 2l + 2w$

$P = 2(2\frac{3}{4}) + 2(1\frac{1}{2})$

$P = (\frac{2}{1} \times \frac{11}{4}) + (\frac{2}{1} \times \frac{3}{2})$

$P = \frac{11}{2} + 3$

$P = 5\frac{1}{2} + 3 = 8\frac{1}{2}$ in

5. 2 in

$P = 4s$

$P = \frac{4}{1} \times \frac{1}{2}$

$P = 2$ in

6. $27\frac{1}{2}$ in

$P = a + b + c$

$$7\frac{3}{4} = 7\frac{3}{4}$$
$$9\frac{1}{4} = 9\frac{1}{4}$$
$$+\ 10\frac{1}{2} = 10\frac{2}{4}$$
$$\overline{ 26\frac{6}{4} = 27\frac{1}{2} \text{ in}}$$

7. 23 mi

$P = 2l + 2w$

$P = 2(6.3) + 2(5.2)$

$P = 12.6 + 10.4 = 23$ mi

8. 7 m

$P = 4s$

$P = 4(1.75) = 7.00 = 7$ m

9. 35 ft

$P = a + b + c$

$P = 13 + 13 + 9 = 35$ ft

10. 31.4 yd

$C = \pi d$

$C = 3.14 \times 10 = 31.4$ yd

11. 132 in

$d = 2 \times 21 = 42$ in

$C = \pi d$

$C = \frac{22}{7} \times \frac{42}{1} = 132$ in

12. 4.7 cm

$C = \pi d$

$C = 3.14 \times 1.5 =$

$$\begin{array}{r} 3.14 \\ \times\ 1.5 \\ \hline 1\,570 \\ 3\,14 \\ \hline 4.710 \end{array}$$

to the nearest tenth = 4.7 cm

13. 44 yd

$C = \pi d$

$C = \frac{22}{7} \times \frac{14}{1} = 44$ yd

GEOMETRY EXERCISE 3

page 230

1. (4) 31.4 ft

2. (3) 12.6 yd

3. (2) 6.9 m

4. (3) 37.7 in

5. (2) 157 in

6. (1) 3.1 ft

7. (1) 300 in

GEOMETRY EXERCISE 4

page 232

1. 36 in

$P = 2l + 2w$

$P = (2 \times 8) + (2 \times 10)$

$P = 16 + 20 = 36$ in

2. 78 m

width $= \frac{1}{2} \times 26 = 13$ m

$P = 2l + 2w$

$P = (2 \times 26) + (2 \times 13)$

$P = 52 + 26 = 78$ m

3. 2 ft 1 in

To find the side, divide the perimeter by 4.

$$\begin{array}{c} 25 \text{ in} \\ 4\overline{)100} \end{array} \quad \frac{1 \text{ ft}}{12 \text{ in}} = \frac{x}{25} \quad \begin{array}{r} 25 \\ \times\ 1 \\ \hline 25 \end{array} \quad \begin{array}{c} 2 \text{ ft } 1 \text{ in} \\ 12\overline{)25} \\ 24 \\ \hline 1 \end{array}$$

4. 156 in

$P = 2l + 2w$

$P = (2 \times 36) + (2 \times 42)$

$P = 72 + 84 = 156$ in

5. 78 ft

$$\begin{array}{r} 156 \\ \times\ 6 \\ \hline 936 \end{array}$$ $\dfrac{1\ \text{ft}}{12\ \text{in}} = \dfrac{x}{936}$ $\begin{array}{r} 936 \\ \times\ 1 \\ \hline 936\ \text{in} \end{array}$ $\begin{array}{r} 78\ \text{ft} \\ 12\overline{)936} \end{array}$

6. $46.80

$$\begin{array}{r} 78 \\ \times\ \$.60 \\ \hline \$46.80 \end{array}$$

7. 210 bricks

First find the circumference of the pool in feet.
$C = \pi d$
$C = 3.14 \times 50 = 157$ ft
Change 157 feet to inches.

$$\dfrac{1\ \text{ft}}{12\ \text{ft}} = \dfrac{157}{x}$$ $\begin{array}{r} 157 \\ \times\ 12 \\ \hline 314 \\ 157 \\ \hline 1884 \end{array}$ $\begin{array}{r} 1884\ \text{in} \\ 1\overline{)1884} \end{array}$

Divide the perimeter by the length of one brick.

$$\begin{array}{r} 209\tfrac{1}{3}\ \text{or 210 bricks} \\ 9\overline{)1884} \end{array}$$

8. 7 feet

First change 30 inches to feet.
$\dfrac{1}{12} = \dfrac{x}{30}$ $\begin{array}{r} 2\tfrac{1}{2}\ \text{ft} \\ 12\overline{)30} \end{array}$

Then substitute the information into the perimeter formula.
$P = 2l + 2w$
$19 = 2l + 2(2\tfrac{1}{2})$
$19 = 2l + 5$
Use inverse operations to solve for P.
$19 = 2l + 5$
$19 - 5 = 2l$
$14 = 2l$
$7 = l$

9. (3) $(2 \times 2.3) + (2 \times 1.4)$

10. (1) $2(1.6) + 2.4$

GEOMETRY EXERCISE 5

page 235

1. $6 \times 6 = \mathbf{36}$
2. $1 \times 1 \times 1 = \mathbf{1}$
3. $5 \times 5 \times 5 = \mathbf{125}$
4. $\frac{3}{5} \times \frac{3}{5} = \mathbf{\frac{9}{25}}$
5. $3 \times 3 \times 3 \times 3 \times 3 = \mathbf{243}$
6. $5 \times 5 = 25$
$\quad 3 \times 3 = 9$
$\quad 25 + 9 = \mathbf{34}$
7. $5 \times 5 \times 5 = 125$
$\quad 10 \times 10 = 100$
$\quad 125 - 100 = \mathbf{25}$
8. $.06 \times .06 = \mathbf{.0036}$
9. **1**
Any number to the zero power is 1.
10. $25 \times 25 = \mathbf{625}$

11. $11 \times 11 = 121$
$\quad 4 \times 4 = 16$
$\quad 121 - 16 = \mathbf{105}$
12. $.005 \times .005 = \mathbf{.000025}$
13. $1 + 10 + 100 = \mathbf{111}$
14. $20 \times 20 \times 20 = \mathbf{8000}$
15. **13**
Any number to the first power is that number.
16. $\frac{1}{4} \times \frac{1}{4} \times \frac{1}{4} = \mathbf{\frac{1}{64}}$
17. $10 \times 10 \times 10 \times 10 = \mathbf{10,000}$
18. $8 \times 8 = 64$
$\quad 2 \times 2 \times 2 \times 2 = 16$
$\quad 64 - 16 = \mathbf{48}$
19. $3 \times 3 \times 3 = 27$
$\quad 7 \times 7 = 49$
$\quad 27 + 49 = \mathbf{76}$
20. $0.1 \times 0.1 \times 0.1 = \mathbf{.001}$

GEOMETRY EXERCISE 6

page 237

1. (2) $\sqrt{196} = \mathbf{14}$
Guess 12 because $12 \times 12 = 144$.

$\begin{array}{r} 16 \\ 12\overline{)196} \\ 12 \\ \hline 76 \\ 72 \\ \hline 4 \end{array}$ $\begin{array}{r} 16 \\ +\ 12 \\ \hline 28 \end{array}$ $\begin{array}{r} 14 \\ 2\overline{)28} \end{array}$

2. (1) $\sqrt{441} = \mathbf{21}$
Guess 20 because $20 \times 20 = 400$.

$\begin{array}{r} 22 \\ 20\overline{)441} \\ 40 \\ \hline 41 \\ 40 \\ \hline 1 \end{array}$ $\begin{array}{r} 22 \\ +\ 20 \\ \hline 42 \end{array}$ $\begin{array}{r} 21 \\ 2\overline{)42} \end{array}$

3. (3) $\sqrt{1024} = \mathbf{32}$
Guess 30 because $30 \times 30 = 900$.

$\begin{array}{r} 34 \\ 30\overline{)1024} \\ 90 \\ \hline 124 \\ 120 \\ \hline 4 \end{array}$ $\begin{array}{r} 34 \\ +\ 30 \\ \hline 64 \end{array}$ $\begin{array}{r} 32 \\ 2\overline{)64} \end{array}$

4. (3) $\sqrt{1521} = \mathbf{39}$
Guess 40 because $40 \times 40 = 1600$.

$\begin{array}{r} 38 \\ 40\overline{)1521} \\ 120 \\ \hline 321 \\ 320 \\ \hline 1 \end{array}$ $\begin{array}{r} 38 \\ +\ 40 \\ \hline 78 \end{array}$ $\begin{array}{r} 39 \\ 2\overline{)78} \end{array}$

5. (1) $\sqrt{361} = 19$

Guess 20 because $20 \times 20 = 400$.

$$20\overline{)361} \quad \begin{array}{r} 18 \\ \hline 20 \\ \hline 161 \\ 160 \\ \hline 1 \end{array} \qquad \begin{array}{r} 18 \\ + 20 \\ \hline 38 \end{array} \qquad 2\overline{)38}^{\,19}$$

6. (2) $\sqrt{676} = 26$

Guess 30 because $30 \times 30 = 900$.

$$30\overline{)676}^{\,22} \quad \begin{array}{r} 60 \\ \hline 76 \\ 60 \\ \hline 16 \end{array} \qquad \begin{array}{r} 22 \\ + 30 \\ \hline 52 \end{array} \qquad 2\overline{)52}^{\,26}$$

7. (1) $\sqrt{1849} = 43$

Guess 40 because $40 \times 40 = 1600$.

$$40\overline{)1849}^{\,46} \quad \begin{array}{r} 160 \\ \hline 249 \\ 240 \\ \hline 9 \end{array} \qquad \begin{array}{r} 46 \\ + 40 \\ \hline 86 \end{array} \qquad 2\overline{)86}^{\,43}$$

8. (3) $\sqrt{3364} = 58$

Guess 60 because $60 \times 60 = 3600$.

$$60\overline{)3364}^{\,56} \quad \begin{array}{r} 300 \\ \hline 364 \\ 360 \\ \hline 4 \end{array} \qquad \begin{array}{r} 56 \\ + 60 \\ \hline 116 \end{array} \qquad 2\overline{)116}^{\,58}$$

GEOMETRY EXERCISE 7

pages 240–241

1. a. 180 sq ft $A = lw$
$A = 15 \times 12 = 180$ sq ft

  b. 196 sq ft $A = s^2$
$A = 14^2$
$A = 14 \times 14 = 196$ sq ft

  c. 57 sq in $A = \frac{1}{2}(bh)$
$\frac{19 \times 6}{2} = 57$ sq in

2. 28 sq in $A = lw$
$A = 8 \times 3\frac{1}{2}$
$\frac{8}{1} \times \frac{7}{2} = 28$ sq in

3. 42.25 m² $A = s^2$
$A = 6.5^2$
$A = 6.5 \times 6.5 = 42.25$ m²

4. $25\frac{1}{2}$ sq in $A = \frac{1}{2}bh$
$A = \frac{1}{2} \times 8\frac{1}{2} \times 6$
$A = \frac{1}{2} \times \frac{17}{2} \times 6$
$A = \frac{51}{2} = 25\frac{1}{2}$ sq in

5. 68 cm²
$A = lw$
$A = 12.6 \times 5.4$
$A = 68.04$ to the nearest whole $= 68$ cm²

6. (4) $\frac{1}{2}(12 \times 9)$

$A = \frac{1}{2}(bh)$

$A = \frac{1}{2}(12 \times 9)$

7. (4) $\frac{9}{64}$ sq in

$A = s^2$

$A = \left(\frac{3}{8}\right)^2$

$\frac{3}{8} \times \frac{3}{8} = \frac{9}{64}$ sq in

8. (3) 76.5 cm²

$A = \frac{1}{2}bh$

$A = \frac{17 \times 9}{2} = \frac{153}{2} = 76.5$ cm²

9. (2) 314 sq yd

$A = \pi r^2$

$A = 3.14 \times 10^2$

$A = 3.14 \times 100 = 314$ sq yd

GEOMETRY EXERCISE 8

pages 243–244

1. 108 sq ft
$A = lw$
$A = 12 \times 9 = 108$ sq ft

2. 9 ft
Area of rectangle: $3 \times 27 = 81$ sq ft
Area of square: $A = s^2$
$81 = s^2$
$\sqrt{81} = s$
$9 = s$

3. 80 sq in
$A = lw$
$A = 8 \times 10 = 80$ sq in

4. 45 tiles
Area of room: $A = lw$
$A = 18 \times 10 = 180$ sq ft
Area of one tile: $A = s^2$
$A = 2^2$
$A = 2 \times 2 = 4$ sq ft
$4\overline{)180}^{\,45 \text{ tiles}}$

5. 5 gallons
$A = lw$
$A = 25 \times 40 = 1000$ sq ft
$200\overline{)1000}^{\,5 \text{ gallons}}$

6. 6 sq yd
$A = \frac{bh}{2}$
$\frac{12 \times 9}{2} = 54$ sq ft
$\frac{1 \text{ sq yd}}{9 \text{ sq ft}} = \frac{x}{54} \qquad 9\overline{)54}^{\,6 \text{ sq yd}}$

7. 16 sq yd

$A = lw$

$A = 6 \times 8 = 48$ sq ft

3 windows $= 3 \times 48 = 144$ sq ft

$\dfrac{1 \text{ sq yd}}{9 \text{ sq ft}} = \dfrac{x}{144}$ $\begin{array}{r} 144 \\ \times \ \ 1 \\ \hline 144 \end{array}$ $\begin{array}{r} 16 \text{ sq yd} \\ 9\overline{)144} \end{array}$

8. 1256 sq ft

$A = \pi r^2$

$A = 3.14 \times 20^2$

$A = 3.14 \times 400 = 1256$ sq ft

9. (5) 20 ft

One side is the square root of the area.

$\sqrt{400} = 20$ ft

10. (1) 40 ft

Divide the area by 10 feet.

$\begin{array}{r} 40 \text{ ft} \\ 10\overline{)400} \end{array}$

11. (2) 8 × 12.5

12. (4) $\dfrac{5.8 \times 6}{2}$

GEOMETRY EXERCISE 9

pages 246–247

1. 1620 cu in $V = lwh$

$V = 12 \times 15 \times 9 = 1620$ cu in

2. 512 cu in $V = s^3$

$V = 8^3$

$V = 8 \times 8 \times 8 = 512$ cu in

3. 49 cu in $V = lwh$

$V = 5\frac{1}{4} \times 3\frac{1}{2} \times 2\frac{2}{3} = \frac{21}{4} \times \frac{7}{2} \times \frac{8}{3} = 49$ cu in

4. 1.728 cm³ $V = s^3$

$V = 1.2^3$

$V = 1.2 \times 1.2 \times 1.2 = 1.728$ cm³

5. 75 cu ft $V = lwh$

$V = \frac{30}{1} \times \frac{5}{1} \times \frac{1}{2} = 75$ cu ft

6. 10,990 cu ft $V = \pi r^2 h$

$V = 3.14 \times 10^2 \times 35$

$V = 3.14 \times 100 \times 35 = 10,990$ cu ft

7. (4) 64 cm³

$8 \times 4 \times 2$

8. (3) 1.3

$V = \pi r^2 h$

$V = 3.14 \times 0.4^2 \times 2.5$

$V = 3.14 \times 0.16 \times 2.5$

$V = 1.256$ to the nearest tenth $= 1.3$ m³

9. (4) $1\frac{1}{4} \times 1\frac{1}{4} \times 1\frac{1}{4}$

10. (2) 113 $V = \frac{4}{3}\pi r^3$

$V = \frac{4}{3} \times 3.14 \times 3^3$

$\frac{4}{3} \times \frac{3.14}{1} \times \frac{27}{1} = 113.04$ cu in to the nearest cubic inch $= 113$ cu in

11. (5) 864

First change 2 feet to inches.

2 feet $= 24$ in

$V = lwh$

$V = 24 \times 6 \times 6$

$V = 864$ cu in

12. (2) 12

First find volume of box in inches.

$V = lwh$

$V = 12 \times 6 \times 1$

$V = 72$ cu in

Then divide into volume of carton.

$\begin{array}{r} 12 \\ 72\overline{)864} \end{array}$

GEOMETRY EXERCISE 10

pages 249–251

1. 66 sq in $A = bh$

$A = 11 \times 6 = 66$ sq in

2. 1256 sq in $A = 4\pi r^2$

$A = 4 \times 3.14 \times 10^2$

$A = 4 \times 3.14 \times 100 = 1256$ sq in

3. 136 sq ft

$A = \dfrac{h(b_1 + b_2)}{2}$

$A = \dfrac{8(14 + 20)}{2}$

$A = \dfrac{8 \times 34}{2} = 136$ sq ft

4. 42 in

Find the measurement of the horizontal side at the bottom part of the figure. $10 - 7 = 3$ in

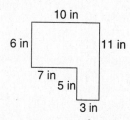

Find the measurement of the vertical side at the right of the figure. $6 + 5 = 11$

Total perimeter:

$P = 10 + 11 + 3 + 5 + 7 + 6 = 42$ in

5. 75 sq in

Area of top: $A = 6 \times 10 = 60$ sq in

Area of bottom: $A = 5 \times 3 = 15$ sq in

Add the areas: $60 + 15 = 75$ sq in

6. 174 sq ft

Find the measurements of the base and height of the triangular part of the figure.

$b = 20 - 13 = 7$ ft and $h = 12 - 8 = 4$ ft

Area of triangle: $A = \frac{1}{2}(bh)$

$$A = \frac{7 \times 4}{2} = 14 \text{ sq ft}$$

Area of rectangle: $A = lw$

$$A = 20 \times 8 = 160 \text{ sq ft}$$

Add the areas: $160 + 14 = 174$ sq ft

7. (5) $12^2 - \pi(4)^2$

8. (2) 32

Area of dining room: $A = lw$

$$A = 9 \times 8 = 72 \text{ sq ft}$$

Area of living room: $A = lw$

$$A = 18 \times 12 = 216 \text{ sq ft}$$

Add the areas: $72 + 216 = 288$ sq ft

Change square feet to square yards:

$$\frac{1 \text{ sq yd}}{9 \text{ sq ft}} = \frac{x}{288} \qquad \begin{array}{r} 288 \\ \times \quad 1 \\ \hline 288 \end{array} \qquad \begin{array}{r} 32 \text{ sq yd} \\ 9\overline{)288} \end{array}$$

9. (4) 888

Total area: $A = lw$

$$A = 50 \times 30 = 1500 \text{ sq ft}$$

Area of pool: $A = bh$

$$A = 34 \times 18 = 612 \text{ sq ft}$$

Subtract: $\begin{array}{r} 1500 \text{ sq ft} \\ -\ 612 \\ \hline 888 \text{ sq ft} \end{array}$

10. (2) The amount of dirt in each truckload

11. (3) 8

Area of rectangle: $A = lw$

$$A = 10 \times 6.4 = 64 \text{ sq in}$$

Find the square root of 64. $\sqrt{64} = 8$ in

12. 15

Area of rectangle at left: $A = lw$

$$A = 12 \times 10 = 120$$

Divide 120 by the height of the rectangle at the right.

$$\begin{array}{r} 15 \\ 8\overline{)120} \end{array}$$

13. (5) Not enough information is given.

Find the measurement of the horizontal side at the bottom of the figure.

$8 + 5 = 13$. Find the measurement of the vertical side at the right of the figure.

$6 + ? = ?$ You do not have enough information to find the area.

14. (3) 140

Area of rectangle: $A = lw$

$$= 12 \times 10$$
$$= 120$$

Area of triangle: $A = \frac{1}{2}bh$

$$= \frac{1}{2} \times 4 \times 10$$
$$= 20$$

Total Area: $120 + 20 = 140$

GEOMETRY EXERCISE 11

page 253

1.	acute	**11.**	right
2.	right	**12.**	acute
3.	obtuse	**13.**	acute
4.	reflex	**14.**	obtuse
5.	right	**15.**	straight
6.	straight	**16.**	reflex
7.	acute	**17.**	right
8.	obtuse	**18.**	acute
9.	reflex	**19.**	obtuse
10.	straight	**20.**	reflex

GEOMETRY EXERCISE 12

pages 256–257

1. $\begin{array}{r} 90° \\ -\ 48° \\ \hline \mathbf{42°} \end{array}$

2. $\begin{array}{r} 180° \\ -\ 48° \\ \hline \mathbf{132°} \end{array}$

3. $\begin{array}{r} 90° \\ -\ 25° \\ \hline \mathbf{65°} \end{array}$

4. $\begin{array}{r} 180° \\ -\ 63° \\ \hline \mathbf{117°} \end{array}$

5. $\angle w$

6. $360°$

7. $\begin{array}{r} 180° \\ -\ 75° \\ \hline \mathbf{105°} \end{array}$

8. $\begin{array}{r} 180° \\ -\ 119° \\ \hline \mathbf{61°} \end{array}$

9. $\begin{array}{r} 180° \\ -\ 80° \\ \hline 100° \end{array} \qquad \begin{array}{r} 50° \\ 2\overline{)100°} \end{array}$

10. obtuse

The supplement of an angle that measures less than 90° must be more than 90°, and the two angles together must total 180°.

11. $\begin{array}{r} 180° \\ -\ 45° \\ \hline \mathbf{135°} \end{array}$

12. 37° Vertical angles are equal.

13. $\begin{array}{r} 180.0° \\ -\ 110.5° \\ \hline \mathbf{69.5°} \end{array}$

14. 30° All the acute angles are equal when parallel lines are crossed by a transversal.

15. 180° The two angles are supplementary.
    − 120°
     60°

GEOMETRY EXERCISE 13
pages 259–260

1. **a.** scalene
   b. right
   c. isosceles
   d. equilateral or equiangular
   e. isosceles
   f. scalene
   g. scalene
   h. equilateral or equiangular
   i. right triangle

2.   65°   180°
    + 25°   − 90°
     90°   **90°**

3. right

4. hypotenuse

5.   65°   180°
    + 50°   − 115°
     115°   **65°** = ∠Y

6. **isosceles**
   There are two 65° angles.

7.   30°   180°
    + 60°   − 90°
     90°   **90°** = ∠C

8. right

9. 180°   **49°**
    − 82°   2)98°
     98°

10. 63°   180°
    × 2   − 126°
     126°   **54°**

11. **isosceles**   5 in   21 in
                    + 8   − 13
                     13 in   8 in
                    Two sides are equal.

12. **scalene**   25°   180°   The three angles
                   + 35°   − 60°   are different.
                    60°   120°

13. **scalene**   4 in   16 in   The three sides
                   + 5   − 9   have different
                    9 in   7 in   measurements.

14. **90°** The right angle measures 90°. The other two
     angles must add up to 90° to make a total of 180°
     for all three angles.

---

15. **110°** The two angles given in the triangle total
     $45° + 65° = 110°$. The third angle in the triangle
     is $180° − 110° = 70°$. ∠X is the supplement of 70:
     $180° − 70° = 110°$.

GEOMETRY EXERCISE 14
pages 263–264

1. **No** For the larger rectangle base:height = 12:6 = 2:1.
    For the smaller rectangle base:height = 3:1. The
    sides are not proportional. $\frac{2}{1}$ does not equal $\frac{3}{1}$.

2. **Yes** For the smaller rectangle base:height = 10:8 =
    5:4. For the larger rectangle base:height = 15:12
    = 5:4. The sides are proportional. $\frac{5}{4} = \frac{5}{4}$

3. **Yes**   45°   180°
            + 85°   − 130°
             130°   50° = ∠O

             50°   180°
            + 45°   − 95°
             95°   85° = ∠B
    Each triangle has angles of 45°, 50°, and 85°.

4. **No**   60°   180°
            + 50°   − 110°
             110°   70° = ∠C

             50°   180°
            + 80°   − 130°
             130°   50° = ∠F
    The angles in these triangles are not the same.

5. **Yes** Find the ratio of one of the equal sides to the
    base for each triangle. For the smaller triangle 6:4
    = 3:2. For the larger triangle 15:10 = 3:2. The
    sides are proportional. $\frac{3}{2} = \frac{3}{2}$.

6. **Yes**   90°   180°
            + 50°   − 140°
             140°   40° = ∠L

             90°   180°
            + 40°   − 130°
             130°   50° = ∠N
    Each triangle has angles of 40°, 50°, and 90°.

7. **21 in**
    $\frac{\text{short leg}}{\text{long leg}}$ $\frac{8}{12} = \frac{14}{x}$ 14   21 in
                                     × 12   8)168
                                      28
                                      14
                                      168

8. **78 ft**
    $\frac{\text{height}}{\text{shadow}}$ $\frac{6}{5} = \frac{x}{65}$ 65   78 ft
                                 × 6   5)390
                                  390

9. **Yes** ∠SUT = ∠VUW because they are vertical. ∠S =
    ∠W because they are both right angles. If we
    subtract the sum of one right angle and one of
    the vertical angles from 180°, we get the same
    third angle for each triangle.

10. 40 ft

$\dfrac{\text{short leg}}{\text{long leg}}\ \dfrac{8}{12}=\dfrac{x}{60}$ $\begin{array}{r}60\\ \times\ 8\\ \hline 480\end{array}$ $\begin{array}{r}40\text{ ft}\\ 12\overline{)480}\end{array}$

11. Yes Each triangle has a right angle. The triangles share $\angle C$. If we subtract the sum of a right angle and $\angle C$ from $180°$, we get the same third angle.

12. 10 in

The length of $AC = 15$ in $+ 10$ in $= 25$ in

$\dfrac{\text{height}}{\text{base}}\ \dfrac{6}{15}=\dfrac{x}{25}$ $\begin{array}{r}25\\ \times\ 6\\ \hline 150\end{array}$ $\begin{array}{r}10\text{ in}\\ 15\overline{)150}\end{array}$

GEOMETRY EXERCISE 15

pages 266–267

1. Yes The missing angle in the left triangle is $60°$. The missing angle at the right is $75°$. The triangles fulfill the *angle, side, angle* requirement.

2. Yes The missing side on the triangle at the right is 5 inches. This fulfills the *side, angle, side* requirement.

3. No The corresponding sides are not equal.

4. Yes The missing side of the triangle on the right is 10 inches. This fulfills the *side, side, side* requirement.

5. No The corresponding angles are not equal.

6. No The three sides are not the same.

7. (1) $AC = DF$ This fulfills the *angle, side, angle* requirement.

8. (2) $\angle X = \angle S$ This fulfills the *side, angle, side* requirement.

9. (1) $GI = JL$ This fulfills the *side, side, side* requirement.

10. (5) **B or C** Condition B fulfills the *side, side, side* requirement. Condition C fulfills the *side, angle, side* requirement.

GEOMETRY EXERCISE 16

page 270

1. $c^2 = a^2 + b^2$
$c^2 = 30^2 + 40^2$
$c^2 = 900 + 1600$
$c^2 = 2500$
$c = \sqrt{2500}$
$c = \textbf{50 ft}$

2. $c^2 = a^2 + b^2$
$c^2 = 10^2 + 24^2$
$c^2 = 100 + 576$
$c^2 = 676$
$c = \sqrt{676}$
$c = \textbf{26 in}$

3. $c^2 = a^2 + b^2$
$c^2 = 12^2 + 5^2$
$c^2 = 144 + 25$
$c^2 = 169$
$c = \sqrt{169}$
$c = \textbf{13 in}$

4. $c^2 = a^2 + b^2$
$c^2 = 12^2 + 16^2$
$c^2 = 144 + 256$
$c^2 = 400$
$c = \sqrt{400}$
$c = \textbf{20 yd}$

5. $c^2 = a^2 + b^2$
$c^2 = 60^2 + 45^2$
$c^2 = 3600 + 2025$
$c^2 = 5625$
$c = \sqrt{5625}$
$c = \textbf{75 mi}$

6. $c^2 = a^2 + b^2$
$30^2 = a^2 + 18^2$
$900 = a^2 + 324$
$576 = a^2$
$\sqrt{576} = a$
$24 = a$

GEOMETRY EXERCISE 17

page 271

1. (3) 30 $c^2 = a^2 + b^2$
$34^2 = a^2 + 16^2$
$1156 = a^2 + 256$
$900 = a^2$
$\sqrt{900} = a$
$30 = a$

2. (2) 15 $c^2 = a^2 + b^2$
$17^2 = a^2 + 8^2$
$289 = a^2 + 64$
$225 = a^2$
$\sqrt{225} = a$
$15 = a$

3. (4) 60 $c^2 = a^2 + b^2$
$c^2 = 48^2 + 36^2$
$c^2 = 2304 + 1296$
$c^2 = 3600$
$c = \sqrt{3600}$
$c = 60$ mi

4. (3) $\sqrt{15^2 + 36^2}$
$c^2 = a^2 + b^2$
$c^2 = 15^2 + 36^2$
$c = \sqrt{15^2 + 36^2}$

GED PRACTICE: GEOMETRY REVIEW

pages 275–277

1. cube

2. 12.8 m
$P = 4s$
$P = 4 \times 3.2 = 12.8$ m

3. $32\frac{1}{2}$ in
$P = 2l + 2w$
$P = (2 \times 12) + (2 \times 4\frac{1}{4})$
$P = 24 + (\frac{2}{1} \times \frac{17}{4})$
$P = 24 + \frac{17}{2}$
$P = 24 + 8\frac{1}{2} = 32\frac{1}{2}$ in

4. 13 m
$P = a + b + c$
$P = 5.8 + 3.2 + 4 = 13$ m

5. 94 ft
$C = \pi d$
$C = 3.14 \times 30$
$C = 94.2$ to the nearest foot $= 94$ ft

6. $20^3 = 20 \times 20 \times 20 = $ **8000**

7. .1609
$(.03)^2 = .03 \times .03 = .0009$
$(.4)^2 = .4 \times .4 = .16$
$\begin{array}{r} .0009 \\ + .16 \\ \hline .1609 \end{array}$

8. 84
Guess 80 because $80 \times 80 = 6400$.

$\begin{array}{r} 88 \\ 80\overline{)7056} \\ 640 \\ \hline 656 \\ 640 \\ \hline 16 \end{array}$
$\begin{array}{r} 88 \\ + 80 \\ \hline 168 \end{array}$
$\begin{array}{r} 84 \\ 168\overline{)} \end{array}$
$\begin{array}{r} 84 \\ \times 84 \\ \hline 7056 \end{array}$

9. $30\frac{1}{4}$ sq in
$A = s^2$
$A = (5\frac{1}{2})^2$
$\frac{11}{2} \times \frac{11}{2} = \frac{121}{4} = 30\frac{1}{4}$ sq in

10. 92.5 cm²
$A = lw$
$A = 12.5 \times 7.4 = 92.5$ cm²

11. 6 cm²
$A = \frac{bb}{2}$
$A = \frac{8 \times 1.5}{2} = 6$ cm²

12. 154 sq in
$A = \pi r^2$
$A = \frac{22}{7} \times 7^2$
$A = 154$ sq in

13. 525 cu in
$V = lwb$
$V = 15 \times 10 \times 3\frac{1}{2}$
$\frac{15}{1} \times \frac{10}{1} \times \frac{7}{2} = 525$ cu in

14. (3) $(2 \times 20) + (2 \times 8) - 4$
First find the perimeter: $P = 2l + 2w$. Then subtract the width of the walkway, which is 4.

15. (4) 9.6
Area of square:
$A = s^2$
$A = 12^2$
$A = 12 \times 12 = 144$ sq in
Divide 144 by the length of the rectangle.
$\begin{array}{r} 9.6 \\ 15\overline{)144.0} \end{array}$

16. (3) 216
Find the missing measurements.

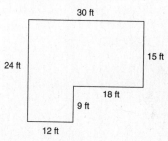

Add the dimensions of each side: $P = 30 + 15 + 18 + 9 + 12 + 24 = 108$ ft. Each ceramic strip is 6 inches or $\frac{1}{2}$ foot. You need at least two strips for every foot: $2 \times 108 = 216$ strips.

17. (2) 62
Area of large rectangle:
$A = lw$
$A = 30 \times 15 = 450$ sq ft
Area of small rectangle:
$A = lw$
$A = 9 \times 12 = 108$ sq ft
Total: $450 + 108 = 558$ sq ft
$\frac{1 \text{ sq yd}}{9 \text{ sq ft}} = \frac{x}{558}$ $\quad \begin{array}{r} 558 \\ \times 1 \\ \hline 558 \end{array}$ $\quad \begin{array}{r} 62 \text{ sq yd} \\ 9\overline{)558} \end{array}$

18. (1) 3348
Volume of large rectangular part:
$V = lwb$
$V = 30 \times 6 \times 15 = 2700$ cu ft
Volume of small rectangular part:
$V = lwb$
$V = 12 \times 6 \times 9 = 648$ cu ft
Total: $2700 + 648 = 3348$ cu ft

19. (3) obtuse

20. (5) 115°
$\begin{array}{r} 180° \\ - 65° \\ \hline 115° \end{array}$

21. (5) Not enough information is given.

22. (4) right
$\begin{array}{r} 33° \\ + 57° \\ \hline 90° \end{array}$ $\quad \begin{array}{r} 180° \\ - 90° \\ \hline 90° \end{array}$ The triangle has one right angle.

23. (2) 3.6

$\dfrac{\text{height}}{\text{base}} \ \dfrac{12}{10} = \dfrac{x}{3}$

$\begin{array}{r} 12 \\ \times\ \ 3 \\ \hline 36 \end{array}$

$\begin{array}{r} 3.6 \text{ ft} \\ 10\overline{)36.0} \end{array}$

24. (4) A or B

Either A or B is enough to guarantee that the triangles are congruent. Either condition fulfills the *angle, side, angle* requirement.

25. (1) 15

$c^2 = a^2 + b^2$
$39^2 = a^2 + 36^2$
$1521 = a^2 + 1296$
$225 = a^2$
$15 = a$

CHAPTER 11

SPECIAL TOPICS EXERCISE 1

page 280

1. J
2. D
3. B
4. A
5. F
6. G
7. I
8. H
9. C
10. E

11.

SPECIAL TOPICS EXERCISE 2

pages 282–283

1.
$\begin{array}{r} -\ 9 \\ -\ 3 \\ \hline -\ 12 \end{array}$

2.
$\begin{array}{r} -\ 8 \\ +\ 6 \\ \hline -\ 2 \end{array}$

3.
$\begin{array}{r} -\ 20\frac{1}{2} \\ +\ 12 \\ \hline -\ 8\frac{1}{2} \end{array}$

4.
$\begin{array}{r} -\ 20 \\ +\ 12\frac{1}{2} \\ \hline -\ 7\frac{1}{2} \end{array}$

5.
$\begin{array}{r} +\ 5 \\ +\ 9 \\ \hline +14 \end{array}$
$\begin{array}{r} +14 \\ -\ 8 \\ \hline +\ 6 \end{array}$

6.
$\begin{array}{r} -\ 6 \\ -\ 5 \\ \hline -\ 11 \end{array}$
$\begin{array}{r} -\ 11 \\ +\ 8 \\ \hline -\ 3 \end{array}$

7.
$\begin{array}{r} -\ 18 \\ -\ 2 \\ \hline -\ 20 \end{array}$
$\begin{array}{r} -\ 20 \\ +\ 6 \\ \hline -\ 14 \end{array}$

8.
$\begin{array}{r} +\ 8 \\ +\ 11 \\ \hline +\ 19 \end{array}$
$\begin{array}{r} -\ 6 \\ -\ 4 \\ \hline -\ 10 \end{array}$
$\begin{array}{r} +\ 19 \\ -\ 10 \\ \hline +\ 9 \end{array}$

9.
$\begin{array}{r} -\ 7 \\ -\ 5 \\ -\ 3 \\ -\ 10 \\ -\ 2 \\ \hline -\ 27 \end{array}$
$\begin{array}{r} +\ 40 \\ -\ 27 \\ \hline +\ 13 \end{array}$

10.
$\begin{array}{r} +\ 3 \\ +\ 7 \\ \hline +\ 10 \end{array}$
$\begin{array}{r} +\ 10 \\ -\ 10 \\ \hline 0 \end{array}$

11.
$\begin{array}{r} -\ 10 \\ -\ 3 \\ -\ 9 \\ \hline -\ 22 \end{array}$
$\begin{array}{r} -\ 22 \\ +\ 5 \\ \hline -\ 17 \end{array}$

12.
$\begin{array}{r} +\ 8 \\ +\ 7 \\ \hline +\ 15 \end{array}$
$\begin{array}{r} -\ 9 \\ -\ 4 \\ -\ 2 \\ \hline -\ 15 \end{array}$
$\begin{array}{r} +\ 15 \\ -\ 15 \\ \hline 0 \end{array}$

13.
$\begin{array}{r} -\ 10° \\ -\ 4° \\ \hline -\ 14° \end{array}$

14.
$\begin{array}{r} +180 \\ +\ 15 \\ \hline +195 \end{array}$
$\begin{array}{r} +195 \\ -\ 37 \\ \hline +158 \end{array}$

15. **No**
$\begin{array}{r} +235 \\ +\ 55 \\ \hline +290 \ \text{in the bank} \end{array}$
$\begin{array}{r} -150 \\ -120 \\ -\ 30 \\ \hline -300 \ \text{in checks} \end{array}$

SPECIAL TOPICS EXERCISE 3

page 285

1. $(+6) - (+4) = +6 - 4 = +2$

2. $(-8) - (+3) = -8 - 3 = -11$

3. $(-9) - (-8) = -9 + 8 = -1$

4. $(+10) - (-9) = +10 + 9 = +19$

5. $(+8) - (7) = +8 - 7 = +1$

6. $(-9) - (-9) = -9 + 9 = 0$

7. $(-10) - 12 = -10 - 12 = -22$

8. $(+6) - (-3) + (-2) = +6 + 3 - 2 = +9 - 2 = +7$

9. $(-9) - (+4) - (+10) = -9 - 4 - 10 = -23$

10. $(-15) - (20) + (+6) = -15 - 20 + 6 = -35 + 6 = -29$

11. $(-8) + (-13) - (+6) =$
$-8 - 13 - 6 = -\mathbf{27}$

12. $(-3) + (-4) - (-5) - (-6) =$
$-3 - 4 + 5 + 6 = -7 + 11 = +\mathbf{4}$

13. $(+22) - (-43) = +22 + 43 = \mathbf{65\ feet\ lower}$

14. $(+7) - (-17) = +7 + 17 = 24.$ The temperature dropped **24 degrees.**

SPECIAL TOPICS EXERCISE 4

Page 287

1. -18
2. $+36$
3. -45
4. $+24$
5. -9
6. $-\frac{1}{2}$
13. -12
7. $+96$
8. $+721$
9. -40
10. $+5$
11. -192
12. -28

14. $(+3)(-6) = -18,$ or 18 fewer children

SPECIAL TOPICS EXERCISE 5

page 288

1. $+2$
2. -2
3. -8
4. $-\frac{2}{3}$
5. -3
6. $-\frac{5}{6}$
7. $+8$
8. $-\frac{1}{2}$
9. -6
10. $+12$
11. $+\frac{4}{5}$
12. -13
13. $+\frac{3}{2}$ or $1\frac{1}{2}$
14. $-\frac{9}{5}$ or $-1\frac{4}{5}$
15. $-\frac{3}{4}$
16. $+\frac{1}{10}$

SPECIAL TOPICS EXERCISE 6

page 289

1. $(15) - (-9) = 15 + 9 = +\mathbf{24}$

2. $(-6)(+20) = -\mathbf{120}$

3. $-4 + 3 - 7 = -11 + 3 = -\mathbf{8}$

4. $\frac{-96}{-8} = +\mathbf{12}$

5. $(-8) - (12) = -8 - 12 = -\mathbf{20}$

6. $\frac{1,000}{-10} = -\mathbf{100}$

7. $(-29) + (-14) = -\mathbf{43}$

8. $(-20) - (-21) = -20 + 21 = +\mathbf{1}$

9. $(20) + (-12) - (+15) = 20 - 12 - 15 = +20 - 27 = -\mathbf{7}$

10. $(-3)(\frac{2}{3})(-10) = -3 \cdot \frac{2}{3} \cdot -10 = +\mathbf{20}$

11. $\frac{-14}{21} = -\frac{\mathbf{2}}{\mathbf{3}}$

12. $(-1)(\frac{7}{8}) = -\frac{\mathbf{7}}{\mathbf{8}}$

13. $(-3)(5) + \frac{6}{-2} = -15 - 3 = -\mathbf{18}$

14. $(\frac{-8}{4}) + (\frac{15}{-3}) = -2 -5 = -\mathbf{7}$

15. $(-6) + (\frac{30}{5}) = -6 + 6 = \mathbf{0}$

16. $(15)(\frac{-2}{3}) - 8 = -10 - 8 = -\mathbf{18}$

17. $-4 + (-8)(-6) = -4 + 48 = +\mathbf{44}$

18. $(\frac{-36}{9}) - (-10) = -4 + 10 = +\mathbf{6}$

19. $(12)(-2) + (-1)(-15) = -24 + 15 = -\mathbf{9}$

20. $(\frac{10}{-15}) - (\frac{18}{27}) = -\frac{2}{3} -\frac{2}{3} = -\frac{\mathbf{4}}{\mathbf{3}}$ or $-1\frac{\mathbf{1}}{\mathbf{3}}$

SPECIAL TOPICS EXERCISE 7

pages 290–291

1.
$$\begin{array}{ccc} c - 3 & < & 21 \\ \underline{+ 3} & & \underline{+\ 3} \\ c & < & \mathbf{24} \end{array}$$

2.
$$\begin{array}{ccc} p + 1 & > & 7 \\ \underline{- 1} & & \underline{-\ 1} \\ p & > & \mathbf{6} \end{array}$$

3. $\frac{9w}{9} \leq \frac{27}{9}$
$w \leq \mathbf{3}$

4. $\frac{8x}{8} \geq \frac{20}{8}$
$x \geq 2\frac{4}{8} = \mathbf{2}\frac{\mathbf{1}}{\mathbf{2}}$

5. $6 \cdot \frac{s}{6} < 4 \cdot 6$
$s < \mathbf{24}$

6. $\frac{2a}{2} > \frac{-42}{2}$
$a > -\mathbf{21}$

7. No $\begin{array}{ccc} m - 6 & > & 1 \\ \underline{+ 6} & & \underline{+ 6} \\ m & > & 7 \end{array}$

Since m is greater than 7, m cannot equal 7.

8. Yes $2 \cdot \frac{1}{2} r \leq 4 \cdot 2$
$r \leq 8$

Since r is less than or equal to 8, r can be $\frac{1}{2}$.

9. Yes $\begin{array}{ccc} d + 7 & \leq & 2 \\ \underline{- 7} & & \underline{-\ 7} \\ d & \leq & - 5 \end{array}$

Since d is less than or equal to -5, d can be -6.

10. Yes $\frac{2f}{2} < \frac{12}{2}$
$f < 6$

Since f is less than 6, f can be 4.

SPECIAL TOPICS EXERCISE 8

page 291

1.
$$5m - 4 \leq 26$$
$$\underline{+ 4 \qquad\quad + 4}$$
$$\frac{5m}{5} \leq \frac{30}{5}$$
$$m \leq 6$$

2.
$$3n + 2 > 14$$
$$\underline{- 2 \qquad\quad - 2}$$
$$\frac{3n}{3} > \frac{12}{3}$$
$$n > 4$$

3.
$$4p - 3 < 15$$
$$\underline{+ 3 \qquad\quad + 3}$$
$$\frac{4p}{4} < \frac{18}{4}$$
$$p < 4\frac{2}{4} = 4\frac{1}{2}$$

4.
$$\frac{x}{3} + 5 \geq 7$$
$$\underline{- 5 \qquad\quad - 5}$$
$$3 \cdot \frac{x}{3} \geq 2 \cdot 3$$
$$x \geq 6$$

5.
$$7c - 3 \leq 5c + 15$$
$$\underline{-5c \qquad\quad - 5c}$$
$$2c - 3 \leq 15$$
$$\underline{+ 3 \qquad\quad + 3}$$
$$\frac{2c}{2} \leq \frac{18}{2}$$
$$c \leq 9$$

6.
$$8y + 1 < y + 22$$
$$\underline{- y \qquad\quad - y}$$
$$7y + 1 < 22$$
$$\underline{- 1 \qquad\quad - 1}$$
$$\frac{7y}{7} < \frac{21}{7}$$
$$y < 3$$

7.
$$3(s - 2) \geq 2s + 10$$
$$3s - 6 \geq 2s + 10$$
$$\underline{-2s \qquad\qquad - 2s}$$
$$s - 6 \geq 10$$
$$\underline{+ 6 \qquad\qquad + 6}$$
$$s \geq 16$$

8.
$$5(a + 3) < 2(a - 6)$$
$$5a + 15 < 2a - 12$$
$$\underline{-2a \qquad\qquad - 2a}$$
$$3a + 15 < -12$$
$$\underline{- 15 \qquad\qquad -15}$$
$$\frac{3a}{3} < \frac{-27}{3}$$
$$a < -9$$

SPECIAL TOPICS EXERCISE 9

page 293

1. $4x \cdot 3x = \mathbf{12x^2}$

2. $(-4a^2)(-6a^3) = \mathbf{24a^5}$

3. $m^3 \cdot m^4 = \mathbf{m^7}$

4. $a^2 \cdot a = \mathbf{a^3}$

5. $(5b^2)(b^4) = \mathbf{5b^6}$

6. $10x \cdot \frac{1}{2}x = \mathbf{5x^2}$

7. $4x^2y \div xy = \mathbf{4x}$

8. $6x^4y^4 \div 6x^2y = \mathbf{x^2y^3}$

9. $18b^3x^2 \div 2b^2x^2 = \mathbf{9b}$

10. $12t^3v^4 \div 6t^2v^3 = \mathbf{2tv}$

SPECIAL TOPICS EXERCISE 10

page 294

1. $9 = 3 \times 3$
2. $10 = 2 \times 5$
3. $18 = 2 \times 3 \times 3$
4. $20 = 2 \times 2 \times 5$
5. $24 = 2 \times 2 \times 2 \times 3$
6. $30 = 2 \times 3 \times 5$
7. $40 = 2 \times 2 \times 2 \times 5$
8. $50 = 2 \times 5 \times 5$

SPECIAL TOPICS EXERCISE 11

page 295

1. $4n + 4 = 4(n + 1)$
2. $3p - 6 = 3(p - 2)$
3. $15a - 10 = 5(3a - 2)$
4. $14c + 35 = 7(2c + 5)$
5. $6b + 8 = 2(3b + 4)$
6. $6f - 30 = 6(f - 5)$
7. $36y - 9 = 9(4y - 1)$
8. $16k + 56 = 8(2k + 7)$

SPECIAL TOPICS EXERCISE 12

page 295

1. $c^2 + 8c = c(c + 8)$
2. $y^2 - 5y = y(y - 5)$
3. $m^2 + 3m = m(m + 3)$
4. $a^2 - a = a(a - 1)$
5. $d^2 + 4d = d(d + 4)$
6. $n^2 - 8n = n(n - 8)$
7. $p^2 - 2p = p(p - 2)$
8. $s^2 + 9s = s(s + 9)$

SPECIAL TOPICS EXERCISE 13

page 297

1. $\sqrt{27} = \sqrt{9 \cdot 3} = 3\sqrt{3}$

2. $\sqrt{8} = \sqrt{4\cdot2} = 2\sqrt{2}$
3. $\sqrt{20} = \sqrt{4\cdot5} = 2\sqrt{5}$
4. $\sqrt{150} = \sqrt{6\cdot25} = 5\sqrt{6}$
5. $\sqrt{48} = \sqrt{16\cdot3} = 4\sqrt{3}$
6. $\sqrt{50} = \sqrt{25\cdot2} = 5\sqrt{2}$
7. $\sqrt{12} = \sqrt{4\cdot3} = 2\sqrt{3}$
8. $\sqrt{32} = \sqrt{16\cdot2} = 4\sqrt{2}$

SPECIAL TOPICS EXERCISE 14

pages 298–299

1. **The length is 8 feet.**
$w = \frac{1}{2}x$
$l = x$

$A = lw$
$32 = x \cdot \frac{1}{2}x$
$32 = \frac{1}{2}x^2$
$2 \cdot 32 = \frac{1}{2}x^2 \cdot 2$
$64 = x^2$
$\sqrt{64} = x$
$8 = x$

2. **The height is 4 inches.**
$h = \frac{x}{2}$
$b = x$

$A = bh/2$
$16 = (x \cdot \frac{x}{2})/2$
$16 = \frac{x^2}{4}$
$4 \cdot 16 = \frac{x^2}{4} \cdot 4$
$64 = x^2$
$\sqrt{64} = x$
$8 = x$
$4 = \frac{1}{2}x$

3. **The length is 12.**
$w = \frac{2}{3}x$
$l = x$

$A = lw$
$96 = x \cdot \frac{2}{3}x$
$\frac{3}{2} \cdot \frac{96}{1} = \frac{3}{2} \cdot \frac{2}{3}x^2$
$144 = x^2$
$\sqrt{144} = x$
$12 = x$

4. **The length is 14 meters.**
$w = x$
$l = 2x$

$A = lw$
$98 = 2x \cdot x$
$98 = 2x^2$
$\frac{98}{2} = \frac{2x^2}{2}$
$49 = x^2$
$\sqrt{49} = x$
$7 = x$
$14 = 2x$

5. **The length is 16 feet.**
$w = x$
$l = 2x$

$P = 2l + 2w$
$48 = 2(2x) + 2x$
$48 = 4x + 2x$
$\frac{48}{6} = \frac{6x}{6}$
$8 = x$
$16 = 2x$

6. **(4) 12**
$h = x$
$b = 3x$

$A = \frac{bh}{2}$
$24 = \frac{3x \cdot x}{2}$
$24 = \frac{3}{2}x^2$
$\frac{2}{3} \cdot 24 = \frac{2}{3} \cdot \frac{3}{2}x^2$
$16 = x^2$
$\sqrt{16} = x$
$4 = x$
$12 = 3x$

7. **(2) 18**
$w = 2x$
$l = 3x$

$P = 2l + 2w$
$60 = 2(3x) + 2(2x)$
$60 = 6x + 4x$
$\frac{60}{10} = \frac{10x}{10}$
$6 = x$
$18 = 3x$

8. **(4) 18**
$h = 3x$
$b = 4x$

$A = \frac{bh}{2}$
$216 = \frac{4x \cdot 3x}{2}$
$216 = \frac{12x^2}{2}$
$\frac{216}{6} = \frac{6x^2}{6}$
$36 = x^2$
$\sqrt{36} = x$
$6 = x$
$18 = 3x$

9. **(3) 30**
$w = 5x$
$l = 6x$

$P = 2l + 2w$
$110 = 2(6x) + 2(5x)$
$110 = 12x + 10x$
$\frac{110}{22} = \frac{22x}{22}$
$5 = x$
$30 = 6x$

10. **(5) 7**
$w = x$
$l = x + 3$

$P = 2l + 2w$
$34 = 2(x + 3) + 2(x)$
$34 = 2x + 6 + 2x$
$34 = 4x + 6$
$\frac{-6}{28} = \frac{-6}{4x}$
$\frac{28}{4} = \frac{4x}{4}$
$7 = x$

SPECIAL TOPICS EXERCISE 15

page 301

1. $A = (+9, +5)$
$B = (+4, +10)$
$C = (-2, +4)$
$D = (-6, +10)$
$E = (-11, +3)$
$F = (-10, 0)$

$G = (-7, -2)$
$H = (-3, -8)$
$I = (0, -7)$
$J = (+6, -7)$
$K = (+10, -3)$
$L = (+12, 0)$

2.

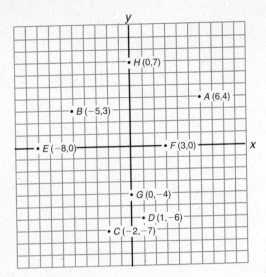

SPECIAL TOPICS EXERCISE 16

pages 303–304

1. A is 3 units above the x-axis.
   C is 5 units below the x-axis.
   The distance from A to C is $3 + 5 = $ **8.**

2. B is 1 unit to the left of the y-axis.
   C is 3 units to the right of the y-axis.
   The distance from B to C is $1 + 3 = $ **4.**

3. E is 2 units to the left of the y-axis.
   F is 1 unit to the right of the y-axis.
   The distance from E to F is $2 + 1 = $ **3.**

4. D is 3 units below the x-axis.
   F is 1 unit above the x-axis.
   The distance from D to F is $1 + 3 = $ **4.**

5. $d = \sqrt{(2-6)^2 + (4-1)^2}$
   $d = \sqrt{(-4)^2 + (3)^2}$
   $d = \sqrt{16 + 9}$
   $d = \sqrt{25}$
   $\boldsymbol{d = 5}$

6. $d = \sqrt{(6-2)^2 + (7-2)^2}$
   $d = \sqrt{4^2 + 5^2}$
   $d = \sqrt{16 + 25}$
   $d = \sqrt{41}$
   $\boldsymbol{d = }$ **approximately 6.4**

7. $d = \sqrt{[3-(-1)]^2 + [(-1)-4]^2}$
   $d = \sqrt{4^2 + (-5)^2}$
   $d = \sqrt{16 + 25}$
   $d = \sqrt{41}$
   $\boldsymbol{d = }$ **approximately 6.4**

8. $d = \sqrt{[+6-(-10)]^2 + [+7-(-5)]^2}$
   $d = \sqrt{(+6+10)^2 + (+7+5)^2}$
   $d = \sqrt{(16)^2 + (12)^2}$
   $d = \sqrt{256 + 144}$
   $d = \sqrt{400}$
   $\boldsymbol{d = 20}$

SPECIAL TOPICS EXERCISE 17

page 306

1. $y = x + 3$

x	y
1	4
4	7
-3	0

$y = 1 + 3 = 4$
$y = 4 + 3 = 7$
$y = -3 + 3 = 0$

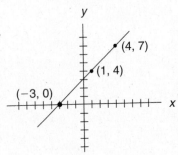

2. $y = 2x - 3$

x	y
5	7
3	3
0	-3

$y = 2(5) - 3 = 10 - 3 = 7$
$y = 2(3) - 3 = 6 - 3 = 3$
$y = 2(0) - 3 = 0 - 3 = -3$

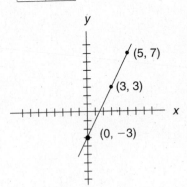

3. $y = \frac{x}{3} + 1$

x	y
6	3
3	2
-3	0

$y = \frac{6}{3} + 1 = 2 + 1 = 3$
$y = \frac{3}{3} + 1 = 1 + 1 = 2$
$y = \frac{-3}{3} + 1 = -1 + 1 = 0$

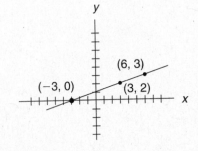

4. $y = -x + 5$

x	y
8	−3
5	0
1	4

$y = -8 + 5 = -3$
$y = -5 + 5 = 0$
$y = -1 + 5 = 4$

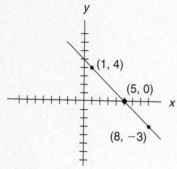

(1, 4)
(5, 0)
(8, −3)

5. Yes $y = 3x - 1$
$y = 3(2) - 1 = 6 - 1 = 5$
(2, 5) is on the graph.

6. No $y = 4x - 5$
$y = 4(3) - 5 = 12 - 5 = 7$
(3, 4) is not on the graph.

7. Yes $y = \frac{x}{2} + 4$
$y = \frac{6}{2} + 4 = 3 + 4 = 7$
(6, 7) is on the graph.

8. No $y = \frac{2}{3}x + 1$
$y = \frac{2}{3}(3) + 1 = 2 + 1 = 3$
(3, 2) is not on the graph.

9. Yes $y = -x + 3$
$y = -8 + 3 = -5$
(8, −5) is on the graph.

10. Yes $y = \frac{-x}{2} + 1$
$y = \frac{-6}{2} + 1 = -3 + 1 = -2$
(6, −2) is on the graph.

SPECIAL TOPICS EXERCISE 18

page 309

1. a. u **b.** t **c.** v **d.** s

2. a. slope $= \frac{8-2}{5-3} = \frac{6}{2} = +3$

b. slope $= \frac{9-5}{10-2} = \frac{4}{8} = +\frac{1}{2}$

c. slope $= \frac{2-6}{5-3} = \frac{-4}{2} = -2$

d. slope $= \frac{10-4}{-7-2} = \frac{6}{-9} = -\frac{2}{3}$

e. slope $= \frac{5-(-3)}{-1-3} = \frac{5+3}{-4} = \frac{-8}{4} = -2$

3. a. x-intercept $= (3, 0)$
$y = 3x - 9$
$0 = 3x - 9$
$\underline{+9 \qquad +9}$
$\frac{9}{3} = \frac{3x}{3}$
$3 = x$
y-intercept $= (0, -9)$
$y = 3x - 9$
$y = 3(0) - 9$
$y = 0 - 9$
$y = -9$

b. x-intercept $= (6, 0)$
$y = x - 6$
$0 = x - 6$
$\underline{+6 \qquad +6}$
$6 = x$
y-intercept $= (0, -6)$
$y = x - 6$
$y = 0 - 6$
$y = -6$

c. x-intercept $= (-10, 0)$
$y = \frac{x}{2} + 5$
$0 = \frac{x}{2} + 5$
$\underline{-5 \qquad -5}$
$2 \cdot -5 = \frac{x}{2} \cdot 2$
$-10 = x$
y-intercept $= (0, 5)$
$y = \frac{x}{2} + 5$
$y = \frac{0}{2} + 5$
$y = 0 + 5$
$y = 5$

d. x-intercept $= (-16, 0)$
$y = \frac{3}{4}x + 12$
$0 = \frac{3}{4}x + 12$
$\underline{-12 \qquad -12}$
$\frac{4}{3} \cdot -12 = \frac{3}{4}x \cdot \frac{4}{3}$
$-16 = x$
y-intercept $= (0, 12)$
$y = \frac{3}{4}x + 12$
$y = \frac{3}{4} \cdot 0 + 12$
$y = 0 + 12$
$y = +12$

e. x-intercept $= (\frac{1}{2}, 0)$

$$y = 2x - 1$$
$$0 = 2x - 1$$
$$\underline{+1 = + 1}$$
$$\frac{1}{2} = \frac{2x}{2}$$
$$\frac{1}{2} = x$$

y-intercept $= (0, -1)$

$$y = 2x - 1$$
$$y = 2(0) - 1$$
$$y = 0 - 1$$
$$\mathbf{y = -1}$$

SPECIAL TOPICS EXERCISE 19

page 311

1. (3) $x = 6$ **and** $x = 8$
$$x^2 - 14x + 48 = 0$$
$$6^2 - 14(6) + 48 = 0$$
$$36 - 84 + 48 = 0$$
$$8^2 - 14(8) + 48 = 0$$
$$64 - 112 + 48 = 0$$

2. (1) $x = 5$ **and** $x = -2$
$$x^2 - 3x - 10 = 0$$
$$5^2 - 3(5) - 10 = 0$$
$$25 - 15 - 10 = 0$$
$$(-2)^2 - 3(-2) - 10 = 0$$
$$4 + 6 - 10 = 0$$

3. (4) $x = 4$ **and** $x = -3$
$$x^2 - x - 12 = 0$$
$$4^2 - 4 - 12 = 0$$
$$16 - 4 - 12 = 0$$
$$(-3)^2 - (-3) - 12 = 0$$
$$9 + 3 - 12 = 0$$

4. (1) $x = 8$ **and** $x = 1$
$$x^2 - 9x + 8 = 0$$
$$8^2 - 9(8) + 8 = 0$$
$$64 - 72 + 8 = 0$$
$$(1)^2 - 9(1) + 8 = 0$$
$$1 - 9 + 8 = 0$$

5. (2) $x = 4$ **and** $x = 11$
$$x^2 - 15x + 44 = 0$$
$$4^2 - 15(4) + 44 = 0$$
$$16 - 60 + 44 = 0$$
$$(11)^2 - 15(11) + 44 = 0$$
$$121 - 165 + 44 = 0$$

6. (3) $x = -9$ **and** $x = -2$
$$x^2 + 11x + 18 = 0$$
$$(-9)^2 + 11(-9) + 18 = 0$$
$$81 - 99 + 18 = 0$$
$$(-2)^2 + 11(-2) + 18 = 0$$
$$4 - 22 + 18 = 0$$

SPECIAL TOPICS EXERCISE 20

pages 312–313

1. 7×10^2
2. 4.46×10^{-2}
3. 9.5×10^7
4. 6.6×10^{-4}
5. 1.7×10^4
6. 8.5×10^5
7. 9×10^{-5}
8. 6.93×10^6
9. 3.3×10^{-6}
10. 2740
11. .091
12. 48,820
13. .0000198
14. 5.2
15. 4,900,000
16. .0000011
17. 325,000
18. .000000084

SPECIAL TOPICS EXERCISE 21

page 313

1. **(2)** 7.24×10^9
2. **(4)** 1.9×10^{-6}

Index